Houghton Mifflin Mathematics

Authors

Lelon R. Capps
William L. Cole

W.G. Quast
Leland Webb

Mary Ann Haubner
Charles E. Allen

Coordinating Author

Ernest R. Duncan

Houghton Mifflin Company BOSTON

Atlanta Dallas Geneva, Ill. Lawrenceville, N.J. Palo Alto Toronto

Authors

Lelon R. Capps
University of Kansas
Lawrence, Kansas

Mary Ann Haubner
Mount Saint Joseph College
Cincinnati, Ohio

Leland Webb
California State College
Bakersfield, California

W. G. Quast
Slippery Rock University
Slippery Rock, Pennsylvania

William L. Cole
Michigan State University
East Lansing, Michigan

Charles E. Allen
Los Angeles Center for Enriched Studies
Los Angeles Unified School District
Los Angeles, California

Coordinating Author

Ernest R. Duncan
Professor Emeritus
Rutgers University
New Brunswick, New Jersey

Consultants

Jane Day
Teacher
Washington Elementary School
San Diego, California

Betty Glenn
Teacher
Homer Adkins Elementary School
Jacksonville, Arkansas

Leroy Dupee
Mathematics Coordinator
Bridgeport Public Schools
Bridgeport, Connecticut

Printed in U.S.A.

ISBN: 0-395-46219-3, cloth edition
ISBN: 0-395-46213-4, paper edition

CDEFGHIJ-KR-9876543210

6 MULTIPLICATION FACTS 157

7 MULTIPLICATION FACTS 183

8 DIVISION FACTS 209

1

Suppose you have 9 red hats and 3 yellow hats. How many red and yellow hats do you have altogether?

ADDITION AND SUBTRACTION FACTS

ADDITION FACTS THROUGH 10

You need to know the addition facts to be good at adding. You can use objects to help you think through the facts.

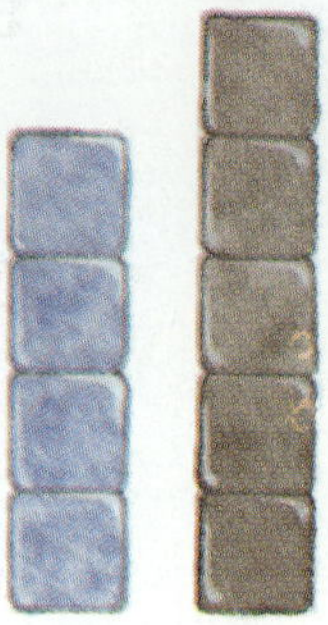

4	plus	5	equals	9
4	+	5	=	9
↑		↑		↑
addend		**addend**		**sum**

$$\begin{array}{r} 4 \\ +\ 5 \\ \hline 9 \end{array}$$

4 **addend**
+ 5 **addend**
9 **sum**

The sum of 4 and 5 is 9.
$4 + 5 = 9$ is a **number sentence.**

M **Zero Property** Some facts are easy to learn if you know that the sum of zero and any other number is that number.

$8 + 0 = 8$
$0 + 8 = 8$

CLASS EXERCISES

Name the addends.

1. $4 + 3 = 7$ **2.** $6 + 2 = 8$ **3.** $3 + 7 = 10$ **4.** $7 + 1 = 8$

Name the sum.

5. 

$6 + 4 =$?

6. 

$7 + 2 =$?

7. 

$8 + 2 =$?

6 MULTIPLICATION FACTS 157

7 MULTIPLICATION FACTS 183

8 DIVISION FACTS 209

1

Suppose you have 9 red hats and 3 yellow hats. How many red and yellow hats do you have altogether?

ADDITION AND SUBTRACTION FACTS

ADDITION FACTS THROUGH 10

You need to know the addition facts to be good at adding. You can use objects to help you think through the facts.

4	plus	5	equals	9
4	+	5	=	9
↑		↑		↑
addend		**addend**		**sum**

$$\begin{array}{r} 4 \\ +\,5 \\ \hline 9 \end{array}\quad \begin{array}{l} \textbf{addend} \\ \textbf{addend} \\ \textbf{sum} \end{array}$$

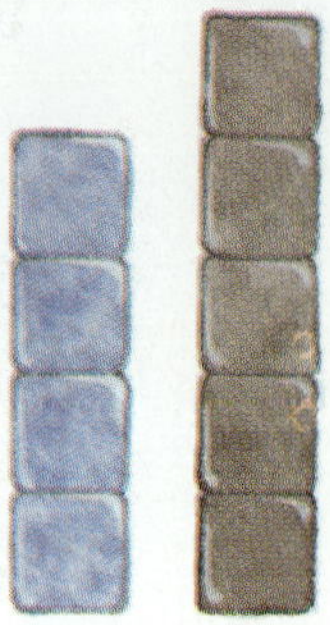

The sum of 4 and 5 is 9.
$4 + 5 = 9$ is a **number sentence.**

M **Zero Property** Some facts are easy to learn if you know that the sum of zero and any other number is that number.

$8 + 0 = 8$
$0 + 8 = 8$

CLASS EXERCISES

Name the addends.

1. $4 + 3 = 7$ **2.** $6 + 2 = 8$ **3.** $3 + 7 = 10$ **4.** $7 + 1 = 8$

Name the sum.

5. 

$6 + 4 = \underline{\ ?\ }$

6. 

$7 + 2 = \underline{\ ?\ }$

7. 

$8 + 2 = \underline{\ ?\ }$

PRACTICE

Add.

8. $1 + 8$	**9.** $5 + 3$	**10.** $2 + 5$	**11.** $5 + 5$	**12.** $1 + 9$	**13.** $1 + 0$
14. $2 + 6$	**15.** $4 + 5$	**16.** $2 + 8$	**17.** $4 + 0$	**18.** $2 + 7$	**19.** $3 + 5$
20. $1 + 7$	**21.** $5 + 0$	**22.** $4 + 2$	**23.** $7 + 3$	**24.** $3 + 2$	**25.** $6 + 1$

Write the answers to all additions as fast as you can. Time yourself.

MENTAL MATH

26. $7 + 0$	**27.** $2 + 3$	**28.** $8 + 1$	**29.** $1 + 6$	**30.** $4 + 6$

31. Think: Yoko found that it took longer to do exercises 26 through 30 on a calculator. Why do you think it took longer on a calculator?

PROBLEM SOLVING APPLICATIONS
Using What You Know

Solve.

32. 3 geese land and then 4 more. How many land in all?

33. 7 geese land and 4 ducks land. Do more geese or ducks land?

34. 5 geese land and then 2 more land. How many land in all?

★ **35.** 3 ducks land. 6 more geese than ducks land. How many geese land?

ADDITION FACTS THROUGH 14

Here are two ideas that can help you remember your addition facts.

Order Property Changing the order of the addends does not change the sum.

$5 + 6 = 11$
$6 + 5 = 11$

Using doubles can help you build facts. $5 + 5 = 10$ is a double. The addends are the same.

Think: $5 + 5 = 10$
$5 + 6$ is one more.
So $5 + 6 = 11$.

CLASS EXERCISES

What is the sum?

1. $7 + 6 =$?
$6 + 7 =$?

2. $8 + 5 =$?
$5 + 8 =$?

3. $8 + 4 =$?
$4 + 8 =$?

4. $9 + 3 =$?
$3 + 9 =$?

5. $4 + 7 =$?
$7 + 4 =$?

6. $6 + 6 =$?

7. $\begin{array}{r} 2 \\ +\ 9 \\ \hline \end{array}$ $\begin{array}{r} 9 \\ +\ 2 \\ \hline \end{array}$

8. $\begin{array}{r} 9 \\ +\ 4 \\ \hline \end{array}$ $\begin{array}{r} 4 \\ +\ 9 \\ \hline \end{array}$

9. $\begin{array}{r} 6 \\ +\ 5 \\ \hline \end{array}$ $\begin{array}{r} 5 \\ +\ 6 \\ \hline \end{array}$

PRACTICE

Add.

10. $\begin{array}{r} 6 \\ +\ 0 \\ \hline \end{array}$	**11.** $\begin{array}{r} 3 \\ +\ 9 \\ \hline \end{array}$	**12.** $\begin{array}{r} 4 \\ +\ 4 \\ \hline \end{array}$	**13.** $\begin{array}{r} 9 \\ +\ 2 \\ \hline \end{array}$	**14.** $\begin{array}{r} 7 \\ +\ 5 \\ \hline \end{array}$	**15.** $\begin{array}{r} 0 \\ +\ 9 \\ \hline \end{array}$
16. $\begin{array}{r} 7 \\ +\ 7 \\ \hline \end{array}$	**17.** $\begin{array}{r} 4 \\ +\ 7 \\ \hline \end{array}$	**18.** $\begin{array}{r} 8 \\ +\ 0 \\ \hline \end{array}$	**19.** $\begin{array}{r} 6 \\ +\ 7 \\ \hline \end{array}$	**20.** $\begin{array}{r} 5 \\ +\ 7 \\ \hline \end{array}$	**21.** $\begin{array}{r} 8 \\ +\ 5 \\ \hline \end{array}$
22. $\begin{array}{r} 7 \\ +\ 1 \\ \hline \end{array}$	**23.** $\begin{array}{r} 3 \\ +\ 8 \\ \hline \end{array}$	**24.** $\begin{array}{r} 9 \\ +\ 4 \\ \hline \end{array}$	**25.** $\begin{array}{r} 7 \\ +\ 6 \\ \hline \end{array}$	**26.** $\begin{array}{r} 9 \\ +\ 5 \\ \hline \end{array}$	**27.** $\begin{array}{r} 8 \\ +\ 3 \\ \hline \end{array}$
28. $\begin{array}{r} 2 \\ +\ 9 \\ \hline \end{array}$	**29.** $\begin{array}{r} 8 \\ +\ 6 \\ \hline \end{array}$	**30.** $\begin{array}{r} 5 \\ +\ 9 \\ \hline \end{array}$	**31.** $\begin{array}{r} 9 \\ +\ 3 \\ \hline \end{array}$	**32.** $\begin{array}{r} 4 \\ +\ 9 \\ \hline \end{array}$	**33.** $\begin{array}{r} 6 \\ +\ 8 \\ \hline \end{array}$

Complete.

MENTAL MATH

34. $6 + 7$ is one more than $6 + 6$, so $6 + 7 =$ _?_

35. $4 + 5$ is one more than $4 + 4$, so $4 + 5 =$ _?_

Write the double that helps you remember this fact.

★ **36.** $2 + 3$ ★ **37.** $3 + 4$ ★ **38.** $5 + 6$ ★ **39.** $4 + 5$

PROBLEM SOLVING APPLICATIONS

Solve.

40. You see 8 seals swimming and 4 seals playing. How many seals do you see in all?

41. You see 5 lions stretching and 3 lions running. Are more lions stretching or running?

★ **42.** The number of bears sleeping plus 6 bears eating is 1 more than 12. How many bears are sleeping?

ADDITION FACTS THROUGH 18

You and a friend need to catch 10 tadpoles for a school project. You catch 7 and your friend catches 8. Do you have enough tadpoles?

Think: You know that 7 + 3 = 10.
So 7 + 8 must be greater than 10.

Yes, you caught enough tadpoles. You can also find the exact number of tadpoles.
Add 7 and 8. 7 + 8 = 15
You have 15 tadpoles.

CLASS EXERCISES

What is the sum?

1. 7 + 7 = ?
7 + 8 = ?
7 + 9 = ?

2. 8 + 7 = ?
8 + 8 = ?
8 + 9 = ?

3. 9 + 7 = ?
9 + 8 = ?
9 + 9 = ?

PRACTICE

Add.

4. $\begin{array}{r} 8 \\ +\,8 \\ \hline \end{array}$ **5.** $\begin{array}{r} 9 \\ +\,6 \\ \hline \end{array}$ **6.** $\begin{array}{r} 8 \\ +\,9 \\ \hline \end{array}$ **7.** $\begin{array}{r} 7 \\ +\,8 \\ \hline \end{array}$ **8.** $\begin{array}{r} 9 \\ +\,9 \\ \hline \end{array}$ **9.** $\begin{array}{r} 6 \\ +\,8 \\ \hline \end{array}$

10. $9 + 7$	**11.** $9 + 0$	**12.** $0 + 8$	**13.** $6 + 9$	**14.** $8 + 0$	**15.** $8 + 6$
16. $0 + 7$	**17.** $9 + 4$	**18.** $8 + 7$	**19.** $6 + 9$	**20.** $7 + 0$	**21.** $9 + 5$
22. $7 + 7$	**23.** $9 + 8$	**24.** $0 + 9$	**25.** $8 + 4$	**26.** $2 + 9$	**27.** $8 + 5$
28. $5 + 8$	**29.** $7 + 9$	**30.** $4 + 8$	**31.** $9 + 3$	**32.** $7 + 5$	**33.** $6 + 7$

Complete.

34. $4 + 9 = 9 + \square$ **35.** $8 + 5 = \square + 8$ ★ **36.** $8 + 7 = \square + 9$

Decide whether the sum is more than 10.
Write *yes* or *no*.

ESTIMATE

37. $9 + 9$ **38.** $6 + 9$ **39.** $8 + 7$ **40.** $8 + 8$

41. $3 + 3$ **42.** $4 + 7$ **43.** $5 + 5$ **44.** $1 + 7$

PROBLEM SOLVING APPLICATIONS
Using Estimation

There are 10 desks in a class. Decide whether there are enough desks for all the children. Write *yes* or *no*.

45. There are 5 children sitting. Then 2 more children come. Are there enough desks?

46. There are 8 children sitting. Then 7 more children come. Are there enough desks?

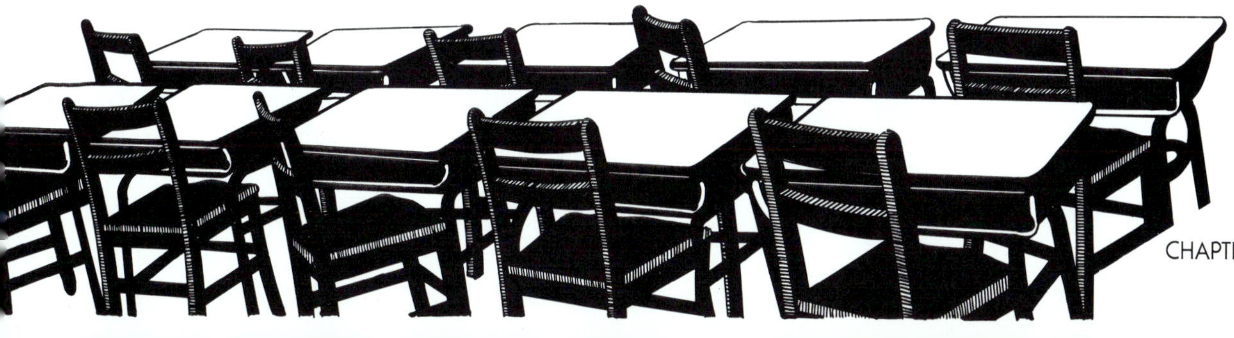

ADDITION OF THREE NUMBERS

Kate hung 4 pictures in the den, 3 pictures in the kitchen, and 5 pictures in the hall. How many pictures did Kate hang in all?

To find out how many in all, she can add the three numbers.

Add two numbers at a time.

$$\begin{array}{r} 4 \\ 3 \\ +\ 5 \\ \hline \end{array} \qquad \begin{array}{r} \boxed{\begin{array}{r}4\\3\end{array}} \\ +\ 5 \\ \hline \end{array} \Rightarrow \begin{array}{r} 7 \\ +\ 5 \\ \hline 12 \end{array}$$

Kate hung 12 pictures in all.

CLASS EXERCISES

What is the sum?

1. $\begin{array}{r} \boxed{\begin{array}{r}3\\2\end{array}} \\ +\ 1 \\ \hline \end{array} \Rightarrow \begin{array}{r} 5 \\ +\ 1 \\ \hline \blacksquare \end{array}$ **2.** $\begin{array}{r} \boxed{\begin{array}{r}2\\3\end{array}} \\ +\ 4 \\ \hline \end{array} \Rightarrow \begin{array}{r} 5 \\ +\ 4 \\ \hline \blacksquare \end{array}$ **3.** $\begin{array}{r} \boxed{\begin{array}{r}4\\1\end{array}} \\ +\ 0 \\ \hline \end{array} \Rightarrow \begin{array}{r} 5 \\ +\ 0 \\ \hline \blacksquare \end{array}$

4. $\begin{array}{r} \boxed{\begin{array}{r}5\\3\end{array}} \\ +\ 3 \\ \hline \end{array} \Rightarrow \begin{array}{r} 8 \\ +\ 3 \\ \hline \blacksquare \end{array}$ **5.** $\begin{array}{r} \boxed{\begin{array}{r}4\\4\end{array}} \\ +\ 7 \\ \hline \end{array} \Rightarrow \begin{array}{r} \blacksquare \\ +\ 7 \\ \hline \blacksquare \end{array}$ **6.** $\begin{array}{r} \boxed{\begin{array}{r}2\\6\end{array}} \\ +\ 9 \\ \hline \end{array} \Rightarrow \begin{array}{r} \blacksquare \\ +\ 9 \\ \hline \blacksquare \end{array}$

PRACTICE

Add.

7. $\begin{array}{r} 5 \\ 2 \\ +\ 7 \\ \hline \end{array}$ **8.** $\begin{array}{r} 7 \\ 1 \\ +\ 6 \\ \hline \end{array}$ **9.** $\begin{array}{r} 6 \\ 3 \\ +\ 4 \\ \hline \end{array}$ **10.** $\begin{array}{r} 4 \\ 5 \\ +\ 2 \\ \hline \end{array}$ **11.** $\begin{array}{r} 3 \\ 3 \\ +\ 6 \\ \hline \end{array}$ **12.** $\begin{array}{r} 8 \\ 1 \\ +\ 4 \\ \hline \end{array}$

13. $\begin{array}{r} 4 \\ 2 \\ +\ 4 \\ \hline \end{array}$ 14. $\begin{array}{r} 5 \\ 4 \\ +\ 7 \\ \hline \end{array}$ 15. $\begin{array}{r} 6 \\ 3 \\ +\ 9 \\ \hline \end{array}$ 16. $\begin{array}{r} 5 \\ 1 \\ +\ 7 \\ \hline \end{array}$ 17. $\begin{array}{r} 7 \\ 0 \\ +\ 4 \\ \hline \end{array}$ 18. $\begin{array}{r} 3 \\ 4 \\ +\ 8 \\ \hline \end{array}$

19. 3 + 5 + 2 = ? **20.** 2 + 2 + 1 = ? **21.** 4 + 3 + 5 = ?

★ **22.** 2 + 6 + 1 + 5 = ? ★ **23.** 5 + 2 + 1 + 9 = ?

MIXED REVIEW

Add.

24. $\begin{array}{r} 3 \\ +\ 4 \\ \hline \end{array}$ **25.** $\begin{array}{r} 6 \\ +\ 6 \\ \hline \end{array}$ **26.** $\begin{array}{r} 0 \\ +\ 5 \\ \hline \end{array}$ **27.** $\begin{array}{r} 7 \\ +\ 5 \\ \hline \end{array}$ **28.** $\begin{array}{r} 9 \\ +\ 3 \\ \hline \end{array}$

29. $\begin{array}{r} 2 \\ +\ 6 \\ \hline \end{array}$ **30.** $\begin{array}{r} 9 \\ +\ 8 \\ \hline \end{array}$ **31.** $\begin{array}{r} 5 \\ +\ 3 \\ \hline \end{array}$ **32.** $\begin{array}{r} 6 \\ +\ 9 \\ \hline \end{array}$ **33.** $\begin{array}{r} 3 \\ +\ 7 \\ \hline \end{array}$

PROBLEM SOLVING APPLICATIONS
Choosing the Operation

Solve.

34. Jim drew 3 bird pictures, 4 tree pictures, and 6 deer pictures. How many pictures did Jim draw altogether?

35. Pedro drew a Moon man. He drew 5 ears on his head, 4 ears on his arm, and 3 ears on his leg. How many ears did Pedro draw in all?

36. Jeff painted a picture of 8 pigs in a field. Then he painted 5 pictures of cows. Did Jeff paint more cows or more pigs?

★ **37.** In an art show, there were 3 fruit pictures, 2 tree pictures, 2 jet pictures, and 5 pet pictures. How many pictures were there in all?

PROBLEM SOLVING
Strategy: Too Much Information

Tom's dog has 4 pups. Sumi's cat has 3 kittens. Bob's dog has 5 pups. How many pups are there in all?

You can use these steps to solve the problem.

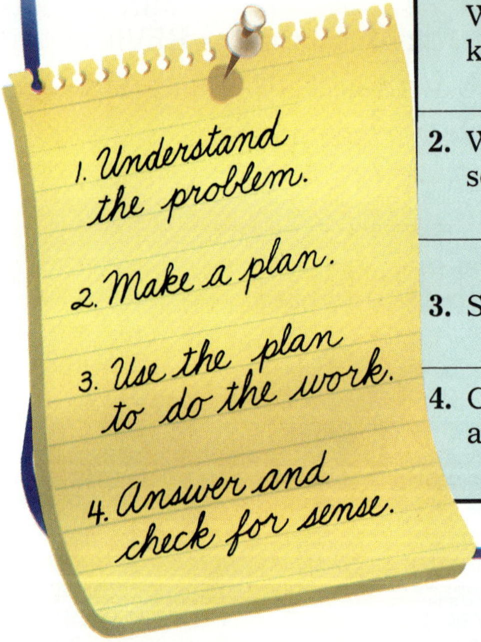

1. What do you know? What do you want to know?	There are 4 pups, 3 kittens, and 5 more pups. You want to know the number of pups in all.
2. What do you do to solve the problem?	You add the number of pups.
3. Show your work.	$4 + 5 = 9$
4. Check to see if your answer makes sense.	9 pups in all. The answer makes sense because you should add just the pups.

CLASS EXERCISES

What are the letters of the facts you need to answer the question?

1. **a.** 9 pups go for a swim.
b. 6 kittens sleep in the shade.
c. The pups wake up 2 kittens.
How many kittens are still sleeping?

2. **a.** Jane brushes 7 white pups.
b. Jim feeds 5 white pups.
c. Jim feeds 4 black pups.
How many pups does Jim feed?

PRACTICE

Write the letters you need. Solve.

3. **a.** 5 kittens play with a ball.
b. 4 dogs chew on bones.
c. 3 kittens play with a string.
How many kittens play in all?

4. **a.** 3 cats watch a fish bowl.
b. 8 fish swim in the bowl.
c. 2 more cats come to watch.
How many cats are there altogether?

5. **a.** 6 dogs dig a hole.
b. 5 bones drop in the hole.
c. 4 more dogs cover the hole.
How many dogs are there in all?

6. **a.** 12 carrots grow.
b. 7 bunnies sniff carrots.
c. 9 bugs watch from leaves.
Are there more bunnies or bugs?

Solve.

7. 3 dogs roll over. 6 seals balance balls. 2 dogs ride bikes. How many dogs do tricks?

★ **8.** 2 cats each have 3 bells. A dog has 2 bells. 3 pups each have 2 bells. How many bells do the cats have?

CHECKPOINT 1

Add. *(pages 2–9)*

1. $\begin{array}{r} 3 \\ +\ 6 \\ \hline \end{array}$ **2.** $\begin{array}{r} 7 \\ +\ 4 \\ \hline \end{array}$ **3.** $\begin{array}{r} 6 \\ 1 \\ +\ 8 \\ \hline \end{array}$

Solve. *(pages 10–11)*

4. 9 birds sing in 7 trees. 8 more birds join them. How many birds in all are there?

Extra practice on page 400

SUBTRACTION FACTS THROUGH 10

If the ants take 4 cubes, how many cubes are left?

To find out how many are left, subtract.

9 minus 4 equals 5

$9 - 4 = 5$

$$\begin{array}{r} 9 \\ -\ 4 \\ \hline 5 \end{array}$$

difference

The difference between 9 and 4 is 5. The difference when 4 is subtracted from 9 is 5.

M This property can help you remember some facts.

Zero Property

If you subtract zero from any number, the difference is that number.	If you subtract a number from itself, the difference is zero.
$9 - 0 = 9$	$9 - 9 = 0$

CLASS EXERCISES

Which is the difference?

1. $6 - 1 = 5$ **2.** $7 - 0 = 7$ **3.** $8 - 4 = 4$ **4.** $10 - 4 = 6$

What is the letter of the example that matches the number sentence?

5. $9 - 4 = \underline{?}$ **6.** $6 - 5 = \underline{?}$

7. $7 - 3 = \underline{?}$ **8.** $8 - 0 = \underline{?}$

A. $\begin{array}{r} 6 \\ -\ 5 \\ \hline \end{array}$ **B.** $\begin{array}{r} 7 \\ -\ 3 \\ \hline \end{array}$ **C.** $\begin{array}{r} 8 \\ -\ 0 \\ \hline \end{array}$ **D.** $\begin{array}{r} 9 \\ -\ 4 \\ \hline \end{array}$

PRACTICE

Subtract.

9. $\begin{array}{r} 5 \\ -\ 3 \\ \hline \end{array}$ **10.** $\begin{array}{r} 5 \\ -\ 5 \\ \hline \end{array}$ **11.** $\begin{array}{r} 6 \\ -\ 0 \\ \hline \end{array}$ **12.** $\begin{array}{r} 9 \\ -\ 9 \\ \hline \end{array}$ **13.** $\begin{array}{r} 8 \\ -\ 6 \\ \hline \end{array}$ **14.** $\begin{array}{r} 9 \\ -\ 7 \\ \hline \end{array}$

15. $\begin{array}{r} 9 \\ -\ 0 \\ \hline \end{array}$ **16.** $\begin{array}{r} 9 \\ -\ 5 \\ \hline \end{array}$ **17.** $\begin{array}{r} 7 \\ -\ 0 \\ \hline \end{array}$ **18.** $\begin{array}{r} 7 \\ -\ 4 \\ \hline \end{array}$ **19.** $\begin{array}{r} 10 \\ -\ 9 \\ \hline \end{array}$ **20.** $\begin{array}{r} 8 \\ -\ 5 \\ \hline \end{array}$

Think: What is the missing number?

MENTAL MATH

21. $\begin{array}{r} 4 \\ +\ \square \\ \hline 4 \end{array}$ **22.** $\begin{array}{r} 4 \\ -\ \square \\ \hline 4 \end{array}$ **23.** $\begin{array}{r} 6 \\ +\ \square \\ \hline 6 \end{array}$ **24.** $\begin{array}{r} 9 \\ -\ \square \\ \hline 0 \end{array}$ **25.** $\begin{array}{r} 5 \\ +\ \square \\ \hline 5 \end{array}$

PROBLEM SOLVING APPLICATIONS
Choosing the Operation

Solve.

26. A waiter has 8 bibs. He gives 5 bibs to the anteaters. How many bibs does the waiter have left?

27. 10 anteaters sit at a picnic table. 6 leave to find ants. How many anteaters are left?

28. An anteater puts 4 peas in a salad and 3 peas on a bun. How many peas does the anteater use?

★ **29.** An anteater has enough bread for 4 sandwiches with 2 slices of bread for each sandwich. If it eats one sandwich, how many slices does it have left?

SUBTRACTION FACTS THROUGH 14

If you know that some facts can be paired, you can memorize your facts more easily.

$$11 - 5 = 6$$
$$11 - 6 = 5$$

If you pick 5 flowers, 6 flowers are left. If you pick 6 flowers, 5 flowers are left.

CLASS EXERCISES

What is the difference?

1. 11 − 2 = ?
11 − 9 = ?

2. 11 − 3 = ?
11 − 8 = ?

3. 11 − 4 = ?
11 − 7 = ?

4. 12 − 3 = ?
12 − 9 = ?

5. 12 − 4 = ?
12 − 8 = ?

6. 12 − 5 = ?
12 − 7 = ?

7. 13 − 4 = ?
13 − 9 = ?

8. 13 − 5 = ?
13 − 8 = ?

9. 13 − 6 = ?
13 − 7 = ?

10. 14 − 5 = ?
14 − 9 = ?

11. 14 − 6 = ?
14 − 8 = ?

12. 14 − 7 = ?

PRACTICE

Subtract.

13.	**14.**	**15.**	**16.**	**17.**	**18.**
11	12	12	13	14	14
− 3	− 6	− 4	− 9	− 7	− 6

19. 13 − 7	**20.** 14 − 9	**21.** 13 − 6	**22.** 12 − 5	**23.** 11 − 7	**24.** 12 − 8
25. 11 − 5	**26.** 14 − 8	**27.** 12 − 9	**28.** 11 − 6	**29.** 13 − 5	**30.** 11 − 9

MIXED REVIEW

Add or subtract.

31. 7 + 4	**32.** 12 − 9	**33.** 5 + 8	**34.** 9 − 9	**35.** 3 + 5
36. 3 + 4	**37.** 11 − 6	**38.** 7 − 2	**39.** 5 + 1	**40.** 3 + 6

PROBLEM SOLVING APPLICATIONS
Choosing the Operation

Solve.

41. Fran picks 12 flowers. She puts 7 in a glass. How many flowers are not in the glass?

42. Lee gives 5 of her 12 flowers to her father. How many flowers does Lee have left?

43. Bruce trims 9 flowers. Lee trims 5 flowers. Who trims more flowers, Bruce or Lee?

★ **44.** Fran puts 4 flowers in a vase. Bruce puts 5 more flowers in the vase. If they want to have 12 flowers in the vase, how many more must they put in the vase?

SUBTRACTION FACTS THROUGH 18

Amy has 16 stickers and May has 9. How many more stickers does Amy have?

To compare, you can match Amy's and May's stickers and count the ones not matched.

You can also subtract to find how many more. $16 - 9 = 7$
Amy has 7 more stickers than May.

CLASS EXERCISES

How many more smiles than stars are there?

1. 16 smile stickers, 7 star stickers
   $16 - 7 = \underline{?}$
2. 17 smile stickers, 8 star stickers
   $17 - 8 = \underline{?}$
3. 9 star stickers, 17 smile stickers
   $17 - 9 = \underline{?}$
4. 9 star stickers, 18 smile stickers
   $18 - 9 = \underline{?}$
5. 15 smile stickers, 8 star stickers
   $15 - 8 = \underline{?}$
6. 16 smile stickers, 9 star stickers
   $16 - 9 = \underline{?}$

PRACTICE

Subtract.

7. $15 - 9$
8. $17 - 8$
9. $18 - 9$
10. $15 - 7$
11. $17 - 9$
12. $16 - 9$

13. $13 - 9$
14. $11 - 6$
15. $16 - 7$
16. $15 - 6$
17. $14 - 9$
18. $12 - 8$

19. $13 - 5$
20. $14 - 8$
21. $12 - 6$
22. $12 - 5$
23. $15 - 8$
24. $12 - 9$

25. $16 - 8$
26. $13 - 6$
27. $13 - 7$
28. $12 - 4$
29. $14 - 7$
30. $11 - 7$

31. $10 - 8$
32. $14 - 5$
33. $13 - 8$
34. $13 - 4$
35. $14 - 6$
36. $11 - 9$

37. Add or subtract in order from left to right.

5	+9	−3	+4	−8	−2	+7

This time do the additions first, then the subtractions. Are the answers the same?

PROBLEM SOLVING APPLICATIONS
Too Much Information

Solve.

38. Clara's sticker book has 10 pages. Each page holds 15 stickers. Clara puts 9 stickers on a blank page. How many more stickers can fit on the page?

39. Danny went to 4 stores before he found pig stickers. He bought 13 stickers. He gave a friend 5. How many stickers did Danny have left?

★ **40.** In 3 weeks Clara got 3 sports stickers and 6 dance stickers. She gave away 4 dance stickers. How many stickers does she have now?

FACT FAMILIES

Subtracting 7 is the opposite of adding 7.

8 + 7 = 15
15 − 7 = 8

Subtracting 8 is the opposite of adding 8.

7 + 8 = 15
15 − 8 = 7

These four facts are related. They use the same numbers. Related facts are called a **fact family.**

To add 8 + 7 on a calculator, you push these keys: [8] [+] [7] [=] 15. What number would the display show if you pushed these keys next?
[−] [7] [=]

CLASS EXERCISES

Complete.

1. 9 + 7 = ?
   16 − 7 = ?
   7 + 9 = ?
   16 − 9 = ?

2. 8 + 5 = ?
   13 − 5 = ?
   5 + 8 = ?
   13 − 8 = ?

3. 6 + 9 = ?
   15 − 9 = ?
   9 + 6 = ?
   15 − 6 = ?

4. 6 + 7 = ?
   13 − 7 = ?
   7 + 6 = ?
   13 − 6 = ?

5. 9 + 8 = ?
   17 − 8 = ?
   8 + 9 = ?
   17 − 9 = ?

PRACTICE

Add or subtract.

6.	7.	8.	9.	10.	11.	12.
8	6	14	14	8	4	12
+ 6	+ 8	− 6	− 8	+ 4	+ 8	− 4

13. $\begin{array}{r} 6 \\ +\ 7 \\ \hline \end{array}$	14. $\begin{array}{r} 10 \\ -\ \ 6 \\ \hline \end{array}$	15. $\begin{array}{r} 11 \\ -\ \ 8 \\ \hline \end{array}$	16. $\begin{array}{r} 9 \\ +\ 4 \\ \hline \end{array}$	17. $\begin{array}{r} 7 \\ +\ 0 \\ \hline \end{array}$	18. $\begin{array}{r} 12 \\ -\ \ 8 \\ \hline \end{array}$
19. $\begin{array}{r} 9 \\ -\ 0 \\ \hline \end{array}$	20. $\begin{array}{r} 8 \\ -\ 8 \\ \hline \end{array}$	21. $\begin{array}{r} 4 \\ +\ 5 \\ \hline \end{array}$	22. $\begin{array}{r} 13 \\ -\ \ 7 \\ \hline \end{array}$	23. $\begin{array}{r} 18 \\ -\ \ 9 \\ \hline \end{array}$	24. $\begin{array}{r} 7 \\ +\ 4 \\ \hline \end{array}$
25. $\begin{array}{r} 7 \\ +\ 8 \\ \hline \end{array}$	26. $\begin{array}{r} 3 \\ +\ 8 \\ \hline \end{array}$	27. $\begin{array}{r} 9 \\ -\ 5 \\ \hline \end{array}$	28. $\begin{array}{r} 8 \\ -\ 0 \\ \hline \end{array}$	29. $\begin{array}{r} 13 \\ -\ \ 5 \\ \hline \end{array}$	30. $\begin{array}{r} 11 \\ -\ \ 4 \\ \hline \end{array}$

Complete. Write the number.

★ **31.** 5 + ▢ = 6 + 3 ★ **32.** 11 − 3 = ▢ + 5 ★ **33.** 6 + ▢ = 13 − 4

CALCULATOR

Which calculator keys would you push to find the missing number? Write the letter.

34. 3 + ▢ = 8 **A.** [5] [−] [3] [=]

35. 3 + ▢ = 5 **B.** [8] [−] [5] [=]

36. 5 + ▢ = 8 **C.** [8] [−] [3] [=]

PROBLEM SOLVING APPLICATIONS
Using Number Sentences

Complete the number sentence.

37. Joe puts 9 apples on one plate and 6 on the other. How many apples does he put on plates?
9 + _?_ = _?_

★ **38.** Ramon puts 9 apples on a blue plate. He puts 5 apples on a red plate. He eats 2 of the apples on the blue plate. How many apples are on the blue plate?
_?_ − _?_ = _?_

PROBLEM SOLVING
Strategy: Choosing the Operation

The clowns need 7 bikes for the first act. The clowns can find only 5 bikes. How many more bikes do they need?

To solve the problem, you can use these four steps.

1. What do you know? What do you want to know?	They have 5 bikes, need 7. How many more bikes are needed?
2. What do you do to solve the problem?	Since you want to know how many *more* bikes are needed, subtract.
3. Show your work.	$7 - 5 = 2$
4. Check to see if your answer makes sense.	They need 2 more bikes. Adding 2 bikes to the 5 makes the 7 they need.

CLASS EXERCISES

Which letter shows the correct plan?

1. There are 9 big clowns and 7 little clowns. How many clowns are there in all?
a. $9 + 7$ **b.** $9 - 7$

2. There are 9 big clowns and 7 little clowns. How many more big clowns are there?
a. $9 + 7$ **b.** $9 - 7$

PRACTICE

Write *add* or *subtract*. Then solve.

3. Big Trunk drank 8 pails of water. Little Trunk drank 3 pails of water. How many more pails of water did Big Trunk drink?

4. The children see 9 monkeys playing at the zoo. They watch 6 monkeys run and hide. How many monkeys did not hide?

5. There are 9 clowns in cars. One clown jumps out. How many clowns are left?

6. Jolly has 9 balls and Happy has 6 balls. How many balls do they have altogether?

7. There were 8 seals in the show. 5 of the seals held balls on their noses. The rest of the seals watched. How many seals watched?

★ **8.** Happy has 3 red balloons, 3 blue balloons, and 3 green balloons. Two of the balloons break. How many balloons are left?

CHECKPOINT 2

Add or subtract. *(pages 12–19)*

1. $16 - 7$ **2.** $14 - 8$ **3.** $11 - 6$

4. $8 + 9$ **5.** $17 - 9$ **6.** $9 + 8$

Write *add* or *subtract*. Then solve. *(pages 20–21)*

7. Happy has 6 balls. He drops 4 of them. How many balls are not dropped?

8. Yoko sees 4 lions and 5 tigers. How many animals does she see?

Extra practice on page 400

CHAPTER 1 TEST

Write the answer. *(pages 2–7)*

1. $\begin{array}{r} 6 \\ +\ 3 \\ \hline \end{array}$	**2.** $\begin{array}{r} 7 \\ +\ 0 \\ \hline \end{array}$	**3.** $\begin{array}{r} 8 \\ +\ 5 \\ \hline \end{array}$	**4.** $\begin{array}{r} 9 \\ +\ 6 \\ \hline \end{array}$	**5.** $\begin{array}{r} 4 \\ +\ 8 \\ \hline \end{array}$

Write the answer. *(pages 8–9)*

6. $\begin{array}{r} 6 \\ 2 \\ +\ 5 \\ \hline \end{array}$	**7.** $\begin{array}{r} 4 \\ 4 \\ +\ 7 \\ \hline \end{array}$	**8.** $\begin{array}{r} 8 \\ 0 \\ +\ 3 \\ \hline \end{array}$	**9.** $\begin{array}{r} 2 \\ 7 \\ +\ 5 \\ \hline \end{array}$	**10.** $\begin{array}{r} 3 \\ 2 \\ +\ 6 \\ \hline \end{array}$

Solve. *(pages 10–11)*

6 girls play softball. 3 boys run races. 4 girls play soccer.

11. How many girls are playing?

12. How many children are playing in all?

Write the answer. *(pages 12–19)*

13. $\begin{array}{r} 9 \\ -\ 0 \\ \hline \end{array}$	**14.** $\begin{array}{r} 7 \\ -\ 7 \\ \hline \end{array}$	**15.** $\begin{array}{r} 12 \\ -\ 9 \\ \hline \end{array}$	**16.** $\begin{array}{r} 14 \\ -\ 5 \\ \hline \end{array}$	**17.** $\begin{array}{r} 17 \\ -\ 8 \\ \hline \end{array}$
18. $\begin{array}{r} 8 \\ -\ 5 \\ \hline \end{array}$	**19.** $\begin{array}{r} 13 \\ -\ 7 \\ \hline \end{array}$	**20.** $\begin{array}{r} 15 \\ -\ 6 \\ \hline \end{array}$	**21.** $\begin{array}{r} 18 \\ -\ 9 \\ \hline \end{array}$	**22.** $\begin{array}{r} 12 \\ -\ 5 \\ \hline \end{array}$

Write *add* or *subtract*. Then solve. *(pages 20–21)*

23. There are 9 girls on the team. Two girls did not play in the game. How many girls played in the game?

24. The Red Team made 7 points. Then they made 5 more points. How many points did the Red Team make in all?

Extra practice on page 401

MATHEMATICS and PHYSICAL EDUCATION

Students made a list of sports they wanted for Sports Day. They listed the number of students needed for each team.

HOW MANY PLAYERS?

PLAYERS ON A TEAM

Sport	Number
Baseball	9
Volleyball	6
Soccer	11
Relay Race	4

Use the table to solve.

1. How many students are needed for 2 teams of baseball?
2. How many students are needed for 2 teams of volleyball?
3. How many more students are needed for 1 team of soccer than 1 team of volleyball?
4. 9 students signed up to play volleyball. How many more students are needed for 2 teams?
5. How many students are needed for 4 relay race teams?

Enrichment

All of the clowns have costumes.

Some of the clowns have hats.

None of the clowns is lying down.

LOGICAL THINKING

Write *all*, *some*, or *none*.

1. ___?___ of the dogs are jumping.
2. ___?___ of the dogs are inside the ring.
3. ___?___ of the dogs are sitting.
4. ___?___ of the dogs are wearing bow ties.
5. ___?___ of the dogs are on leashes.

Write *yes* or *no* to answer the question.

6. If all pears are fruit, can there be some pears that are not fruit?
7. If some plants have flowers, can there be some plants that do not have flowers?
8. If no rabbits fly, can there be some rabbits that do fly?

9. If some numbers are less than 10, can there be some numbers greater than 10?
10. If some numbers are less than 10, are all numbers less than 10?
11. If all children have names, can there be some children without names?
12. If some children walk to school, are there some children who do not walk to school?

★ **13.** Make up an all, some, or none problem for your friends.

CUMULATIVE REVIEW

Choose the best answer. Choose *a*, *b*, *c*, or *d*.

Find the answer.

1. $\begin{array}{r} 5 \\ +\ 3 \\ \hline \end{array}$
a. 8
b. 9
c. 7
d. none of these

2. $\begin{array}{r} 4 \\ +\ 0 \\ \hline \end{array}$
a. 0
b. 40
c. 4
d. none of these

3. $\begin{array}{r} 7 \\ +\ 7 \\ \hline \end{array}$
a. 7
b. 14
c. 0
d. none of these

4. $\begin{array}{r} 7 \\ +\ 6 \\ \hline \end{array}$
a. 12
b. 14
c. 13
d. none of these

5. $\begin{array}{r} 9 \\ +\ 7 \\ \hline \end{array}$
a. 18
b. 16
c. 15
d. none of these

6. $\begin{array}{r} 8 \\ +\ 6 \\ \hline \end{array}$
a. 13
b. 16
c. 15
d. none of these

Find the answer.

7. $\begin{array}{r} 5 \\ 3 \\ +\ 4 \\ \hline \end{array}$
a. 13
b. 12
c. 11
d. none of these

8. $\begin{array}{r} 6 \\ 2 \\ +\ 7 \\ \hline \end{array}$
a. 14
b. 16
c. 15
d. none of these

9. $\begin{array}{r} 4 \\ 0 \\ +\ 9 \\ \hline \end{array}$
a. 14
b. 13
c. 49
d. none of these

Find the answer.

10. $\begin{array}{r} 8 \\ -\ 5 \\ \hline \end{array}$
a. 4
b. 2
c. 3
d. none of these

11. $\begin{array}{r} 9 \\ -\ 0 \\ \hline \end{array}$
a. 9
b. 0
c. 8
d. none of these

12. $\begin{array}{r} 11 \\ -\ 9 \\ \hline \end{array}$
a. 3
b. 1
c. 2
d. none of these

13. $\begin{array}{r} 13 \\ -\ 4 \\ \hline \end{array}$
a. 7
b. 9
c. 8
d. none of these

14. $\begin{array}{r} 16 \\ -\ 9 \\ \hline \end{array}$
a. 10
b. 8
c. 11
d. none of these

15. $\begin{array}{r} 15 \\ -\ 9 \\ \hline \end{array}$
a. 9
b. 8
c. 6
d. none of these

Choose the correct plan and answer.

16. There are 9 goldfish in the tank. There are also 4 guppies. How many more goldfish are there?

a. $9 + 4 = 13$
b. $9 - 4 = 13$
c. $9 - 4 = 5$
d. none of these

17. There are 8 boys and 5 girls at the party. How many children are at the party?

a. $8 + 5 = 12$
b. $8 - 5 = 3$
c. $8 + 5 = 13$
d. none of these

18. Kim has 6 pennies. She gets 5 more. How many pennies does Kim have?

a. $6 + 5 = 11$
b. $6 + 5 = 10$
c. $6 - 5 = 1$
d. none of these

19. There are 12 birds on the fence. 5 birds fly away. How many are left?

a. $12 + 5 = 17$
b. $12 - 5 = 7$
c. $12 - 5 = 6$
d. none of these

LANGUAGE and VOCABULARY REVIEW

Match the word or words to the meaning.

1. addend	**a.** Adding numbers in a different order does not change the sum.
2. Zero Property	**b.** A number added to another number
3. difference	**c.** An example written with an equals sign, such as $3 + 4 = 7$
4. Order Property	**d.** Answer in subtraction
5. number sentence	**e.** Zero plus any number equals that number.

COMPUTER LITERACY

USES OF COMPUTERS

A tool is something that you use to help you do a job.

The **computer** is a tool that works very, very fast. It must always be told what to do.

You can use a computer to make drawings, do arithmetic, or play games.

You can even use it to keep a list of your favorite things!

Can a computer feel happy or cry?

List the tools in the picture.

1. 

2. 

Can the computer do this? Write *yes* or *no*.

3. Eat an apple
4. Add numbers
5. Enjoy a joke
6. Feel tired
7. Subtract numbers
8. Draw a square
9. Play a number game
10. Print a name

2

Suppose you grow sunflowers in rows of 10. How many sunflowers would you have in 8 rows?

PLACE VALUE

TENS AND ONES

We use the **digits** 0, 1, 2, 3, 4, 5, 6, 7, 8, 9 to write all our numbers. To write ten, we use two digits, 1 and 0.

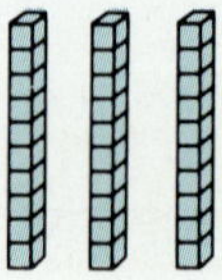

3 tens 0 ones

tens	ones
3	0

→ 30

For 3 tens, say *thirty*. Write the **standard form** as 30.
3 tens 0 ones = 30

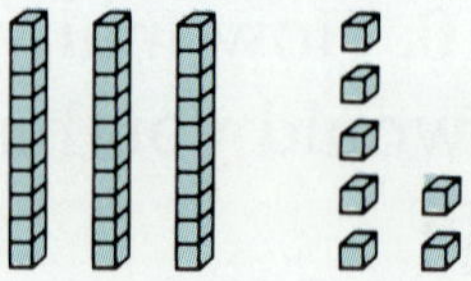

3 tens 7 ones

tens	ones
3	7

→ 37

For 3 tens and 7 ones, say *thirty-seven*. Write the standard form as 37.
3 tens 7 ones = 37

CLASS EXERCISES

Say the number. Write the standard form.

1. 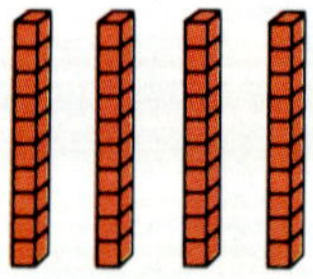

2. 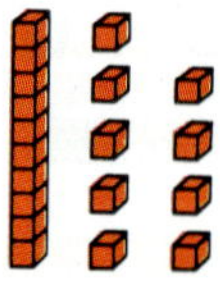

3. 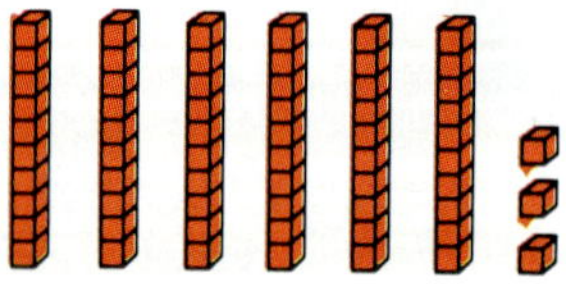

4.

tens	ones
8	0

5.

tens	ones
9	3

6.

tens	ones
7	4

PRACTICE

Write the standard form.

7. 3 tens **8.** 8 tens **9.** 7 tens 8 ones

10. 5 tens 9 ones **11.** 8 tens 2 ones **12.** 4 tens 5 ones

13. 7 tens 7 ones
14. 3 tens 0 ones
15. 6 tens 7 ones
16. 9 tens 8 ones
17. 5 tens 4 ones
18. 8 tens 8 ones
19. sixty-seven
20. twenty-three
21. forty-two
22. ninety-three
23. seventy-nine
24. eighty-six

Write in words.

25. 61 **26.** 42 **27.** 99 **28.** 50

29. Write the one-digit numbers whose names have only 3 letters.

★ **30.** **Think:** Which digit is never used in the tens' place of a two-digit number?

Write the answer.

MIXED REVIEW

31.	**32.**	**33.**	**34.**	**35.**
$7 + 9$	$7 + 7$	$8 + 5$	$9 + 4$	$8 + 7$

36.	**37.**	**38.**	**39.**	**40.**
$13 - 5$	$18 - 9$	$10 - 7$	$16 - 8$	$14 - 9$

PROBLEM SOLVING APPLICATIONS
Choosing the Operation

Solve.

41. Lisa scores 8 points in a game. Then she scores 6 more points. How many points does she score altogether?

42. Julio counts the points for his team. He counts 1 ten and 9 ones. Write the number of points scored.

43. Read Exercises 41 and 42. Does Lisa's team or Julio's team have more points?

COMPARING AND ORDERING NUMBERS THROUGH TENS

This **number line** shows numbers in order from left to right. You can compare numbers on a number line.

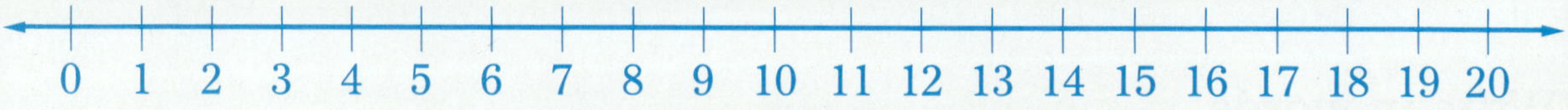

Compare 15 and 18

15 is to the left of 18.
15 comes before 18.
15 is less than 18.
Write *is less than* as $<$.
$15 < 18$

18 is to the right of 15.
18 is after 15.
18 is greater than 15.
Write *is greater than* as $>$.
$18 > 15$

Here is another way to compare numbers.

Compare 24 and 31. Compare the tens.

tens	ones
2	4
3	1

31 has more tens than 24.

$31 > 24$

$24 < 31$

Compare 24 and 27. The tens are the same. Compare the ones.

tens	ones
2	4
2	7

27 has more ones than 24.

$27 > 24$

$24 < 27$

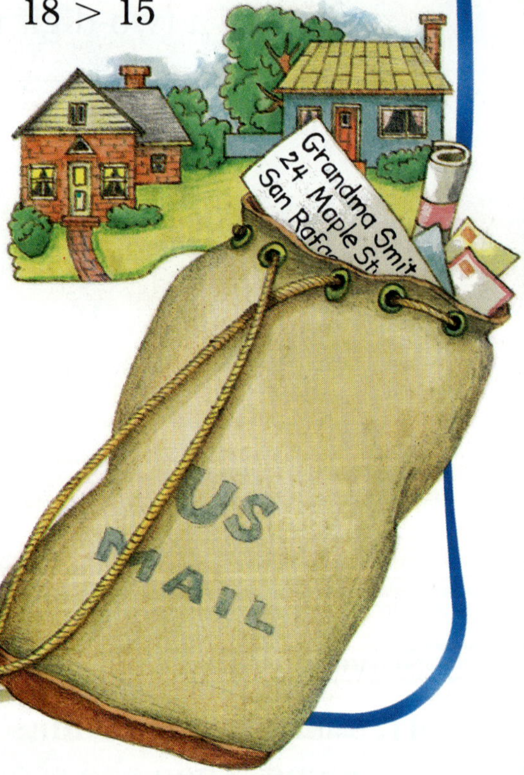

CLASS EXERCISES

Compare the numbers. Write $<$ or $>$.

1. 23 ▒ 27 **2.** 25 ▒ 26 **3.** 28 ▒ 24 **4.** 24 ▒ 21

Compare the numbers. Write < or >.

5.

t	o
3	6
3	9

36 ▢ 39

6.

t	o
5	6
5	5

56 ▢ 55

7.

t	o
9	6
6	4

96 ▢ 64

8.

t	o
7	2
8	1

72 ▢ 81

PRACTICE

Compare the numbers. Write < or >.

9. 21 ▢ 19 **10.** 35 ▢ 32 **11.** 46 ▢ 37 **12.** 41 ▢ 29

13. 27 ▢ 43 **14.** 22 ▢ 19 **15.** 40 ▢ 41 **16.** 24 ▢ 38

17. 17 ▢ 31 **18.** 32 ▢ 40 **19.** 17 ▢ 14 **20.** 20 ▢ 22

21. 29 ▢ 30 **22.** 38 ▢ 41 **23.** 69 ▢ 70 **24.** 50 ▢ 28

25. 24 ▢ 65 **26.** 74 ▢ 68 **27.** 79 ▢ 88 **28.** 66 ▢ 51

Write the numbers that come just before and just after.

29. 22 **30.** 59 **31.** 76 **32.** 30 **33.** 46

Complete. Write <, >, or =.

★ **34.** 4 + 1 ▢ 6 ★ **35.** 6 + 7 ▢ 13 ★ **36.** 5 + 6 ▢ 9

PROBLEM SOLVING APPLICATIONS
Using Between

Solve.

37. What letter comes betweeen C and E in the alphabet? between R and T?

★ **38.** The Greens live at house number 35. The Jones live at house number 39. There is one house between these two houses. What is the number of the house between them?

HUNDREDS, TENS, ONES

You can rename 10 tens as 1 hundred.
The standard form for 1 hundred is 100.

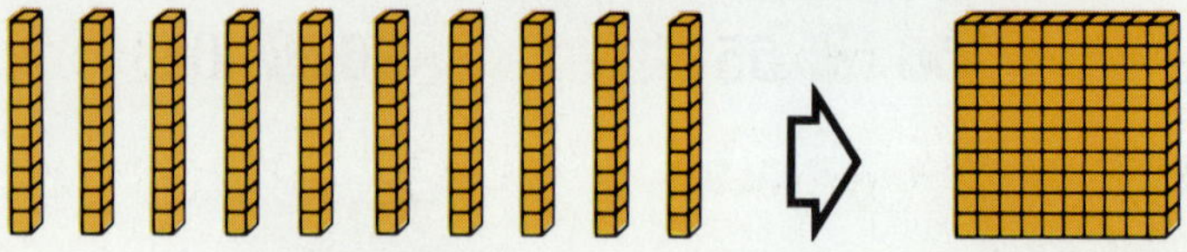

10 tens → 1 hundred

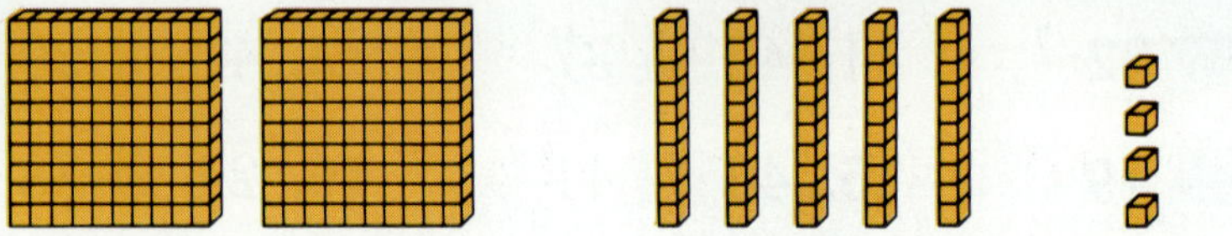

2 hundreds 5 tens 4 ones

hundreds	tens	ones
2	5	4

The standard form is 254. Read 254 as *two hundred fifty-four*. The **value** of the digit 2 in 254 is 200. The value of the 5 is 50. The value of the 4 is 4.

$$200 + 50 + 4 = 254$$

To show 254 on a calculator you press 2, then 5, then 4. This is how 254 may look on a calculator. 254

Think: How can you change 254 to show 257?

CLASS EXERCISES

Say the number. What is the standard form?

1. 

2. 

3.

h	t	o
4	3	6

4.

h	t	o
7	2	4

5.

h	t	o
5	8	0

PRACTICE

Write the standard form.

6. 4 hundred **7.** 9 hundred **8.** 6 hundred

9. 4 hundreds 9 tens 6 ones **10.** 7 hundreds 3 tens 8 ones

11. 8 hundreds 9 tens 4 ones **12.** 6 hundreds 3 tens 0 ones

13. 5 hundreds 9 tens **14.** 4 hundreds 0 tens 6 ones

15. four hundred sixty-eight **16.** seven hundred three

17. 700 + 50 + 3 **18.** 600 + 90 **19.** 700 + 4

Write the value of the digit 4 in the number.

20. 364 **21.** 495 **22.** 342 **23.** 406 **24.** 974

Which symbol and number would you press on a calculator to make this change?

CALCULATOR

25. Change 860 to 864. **26.** Change 105 to 165.

27. Change 47 to 347. **★28.** Change 175 to 275.

PROBLEM SOLVING APPLICATIONS
Reading a Code

S	B	N	O	M	R	I
70	123	52	7	365	105	150

To answer the question, write the code letter for each number.

29. There are *three hundred sixty-five* days in a year. There are *seven* days in a week. *Seven* months have 31 days. There are *fifty-two* weeks in a year. What's new every month?

?
?
?
?

DOLLARS, DIMES, PENNIES

1 dollar 100¢ | **10 dimes** 100¢ | **100 pennies** 100¢

You may write 100¢ as $1.00. Dollars, dimes, and pennies are hundreds, tens, and ones in cents.

dollars	dimes	pennies
4	7	1

⇨ 471¢ ⇨ $4.71

You read $4.71 as *four dollars and seventy-one cents.*

If you have $4.71, do you have more or less than $5.00?

To answer the question, you can think this way.

Think: You know that 4 is less than 5. So $4.71 must be less than $5.00.

CLASS EXERCISES

What is the value? Use $ and . to write the value.

1. 

2.

dollars	dimes	pennies
2	0	0

3.

dollars	dimes	pennies
7	2	9

PRACTICE

Use $ and . to write the value.

4. 400¢ **5.** 320¢ **6.** 829¢ **7.** 605¢

8. 817¢ **9.** 555¢ **10.** 908¢ **11.** 120¢

12. 6 dollars 3 dimes 2 pennies

13. 8 dollars 4 dimes 9 pennies

14. 7 dollars 4 dimes 0 pennies

15. 9 dollars 0 dimes 8 pennies

16. two dollars and fifty-five cents

17. three dollars and eighty-two cents

18. seven dollars and ninety cents

Is the value more or less than $5.00?

ESTIMATE

19. 60¢ **20.** $9.00 **21.** $2.99 **22.** $4.30

23. $3.00 **24.** $9.68 **25.** $6.41 **26.** $1.98

PROBLEM SOLVING APPLICATIONS

Using Money

Solve. (Count dollars, dimes, and pennies.)

27. How much money does Brian have?

28. How much money does Tina have?

29. How much money does Gene have?

30. Who has the most money?

★ **31.** If Brian loses 10¢, how much money will he have?

★ **32.** If Gene spends 50¢, how much money will he have?

COMPARING AND ORDERING NUMBERS THROUGH HUNDREDS

Students in the Stamp Club want to find who has the greater number of stamps.

Compare 352 and 529.
Compare the hundreds.

h	t	o
3	5	2
5	2	9

3 hundreds $<$ 5 hundreds

$300 < 500$

$352 < 529$

Compare 771 and 758.
The hundreds are the same.
Compare the tens.

h	t	o
7	7	1
7	5	8

7 tens $>$ 5 tens

$70 > 50$

$771 > 758$

M You can put numbers in order by comparing them mentally. Order 767, 693, and 845 from greatest to least.

Think: 700 is greater than 600.
800 is greater than 700.
The order is 845, 767, 693.

CLASS EXERCISES

Compare the numbers. Write $<$ or $>$. Then read your answer.

1.

h	t	o
1	0	0
3	0	0

100 ▒ 300

2.

h	t	o
3	2	4
3	5	4

324 ▒ 354

3.

h	t	o
2	3	7
1	4	6

237 ▒ 146

4.

h	t	o
2	4	7
2	4	9

247 ▒ 249

PRACTICE

Compare the numbers. Write $<$ or $>$.

5. 200 ■ 300	**6.** 280 ■ 370	**7.** 290 ■ 350
8. 260 ■ 270	**9.** 261 ■ 274	**10.** 268 ■ 274
11. 280 ■ 481	**12.** 484 ■ 483	**13.** 485 ■ 466
14. 478 ■ 324	**15.** 623 ■ 775	**16.** 960 ■ 750
17. 900 ■ 500	**18.** 831 ■ 931	**19.** 820 ■ 440
20. 472 ■ 485	**21.** 397 ■ 386	**22.** 752 ■ 734

Compare the numbers mentally. Then list them in order from greatest to least.

MENTAL MATH

23. 250, 230, 240, 270

24. 790, 760, 770, 780

25. 920, 720, 870, 620

26. 673, 679, 676, 670

★ **27.** Write the greatest three-digit number that has the digits 6, 8, and 4.

★ **28.** Write the least three-digit number that has the digits 5, 2, and 9.

PROBLEM SOLVING APPLICATIONS
Choosing the Operation

Solve.

29. You have 17 sports stamps. You use 8 of them on letters. How many stamps do you have left?

30. Your red stamp book has 316 stamps. Your green stamp book has 298. Which has more?

31. Your red stamp book can hold 352 stamps. You have 417 stamps. Can you put all your stamps in your red stamp book?

★ **32.** In 1984 Mike collected 609 stamps. In 1985 he collected 584 stamps. In which year did he collect more?

ROUNDING NUMBERS

Emma has exactly 32 stuffed animals. If Emma wants to tell *about* how many animals she has, she can **round** the number.

This is how you can round 32 to the nearest ten.

30 31 32 33 34 35 36 37 38 39 40

32 is nearer to 30 than 40. Round *down* to 30.
38 is nearer to 40 than 30. Round *up* to 40.
35 is halfway between 30 and 40. People agree to round it *up* to 40.

This is how you can round 170 to the nearest hundred.

100 110 120 130 140 150 160 170 180 190 200

170 is nearer to 200 than 100. Round up to 200. Round 140 down to 100. Round 150 up to 200.

You can round numbers between 10 and 100 to the nearest ten and numbers between 100 and 1000 to the nearest hundred.

CLASS EXERCISES

Round to the nearest ten.

1. 42 **2.** 47 **3.** 49

40 41 42 43 44 45 46 47 48 49 50

4. 88 **5.** 82 **6.** 85

80 81 82 83 84 85 86 87 88 89 90

Round to the nearest hundred.

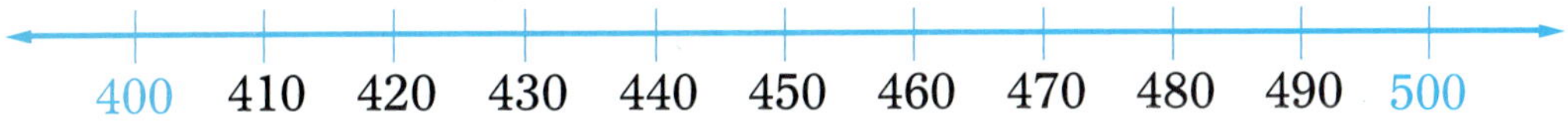

7. 430 **8.** 410 **9.** 450 **10.** 460 **11.** 470

12. 780 **13.** 730 **14.** 710 **15.** 740 **16.** 760

PRACTICE

Round to the nearest ten.

17. 43 **18.** 72 **19.** 88 **20.** 45 **21.** 66

22. 31 **23.** 89 **24.** 55 **25.** 69 **26.** 77

Round to the nearest hundred.

27. 780 **28.** 340 **29.** 510 **30.** 150 **31.** 190

32. 460 **33.** 833 **34.** 258 **35.** 748 **36.** 199

Round to the nearest ten or hundred.

37. 43 **38.** 919 **39.** 775 **40.** 92 **41.** 75

42. 542 **43.** 56 **44.** 652 **45.** 84 **46.** 381

PROBLEM SOLVING APPLICATIONS

Solve.

47. Marie works in a toy store. She counts 872 toys in the back room. To the nearest hundred, about how many toys is that?

★ **48.** There are 34 dump trucks and 38 fire trucks. To the nearest ten, about how many of each kind are there? about how many in all?

PROBLEM SOLVING

Strategy: Using Estimation

For a social studies project, one class asked 120 children to tell their favorite color, kind of television show, and school subject.

You can round 120 and say that *about* 100 children answered questions. Rounded numbers are easier to remember. When you answer the question "*About* how many?" you give an **estimate** of the exact number.

CLASS EXERCISES

Which is the better estimate? Choose *a* or *b*.

1. 42 children like red best. About how many like red best?
- **a.** about 40 children
- **b.** about 50 children

2. 17 children prefer yellow. About how many prefer yellow?
- **a.** about 10 children
- **b.** about 20 children

3. 33 children prefer blue. About how many prefer blue?
- **a.** about 30 children
- **b.** about 40 children

4. 28 children prefer orange. About how many prefer orange?
- **a.** about 20 children
- **b.** about 30 children

PRACTICE

Estimate to solve.

5. 56 children said they liked comedy television shows best. About how many children liked comedy best?

6. 22 children said they liked to watch sports shows the best. About how many children liked sports shows the best?

7. 35 children said they liked family shows the best. About how many children liked family shows the best?

8. 47 children said they liked social studies the best. About how many students liked social studies the best?

9. About 10 children liked nature shows the best. Could 17 children have liked nature shows the best?

10. 52 children said their favorite subject was math. About how many children liked math best?

★ 11. About 20 children liked reading the best. What is the greatest number of children who could have liked reading the best?

★ 12. Use the information from this lesson to do a project like this in your own class.

CHECKPOINT 1

Write the standard form. *(pages 30–31, 34–35)*

1. 4 tens **2.** sixty-five

3. 2 hundreds 7 tens

Write $<$ or $>$. *(pages 32–33, 38–39)*

4. 51 ▢ 49

5. 235 ▢ 352

Round to the nearest ten or hundred. *(pages 40–41)*

6. 37 **7.** 177

Estimate to solve. *(pages 42–43)*

8. 36 children went to the movies. About how many children went to the movies?

Extra practice on page 402

THOUSANDS, HUNDREDS, TENS, ONES

You can rename 10 hundreds as 1 thousand. The standard form is 1000.

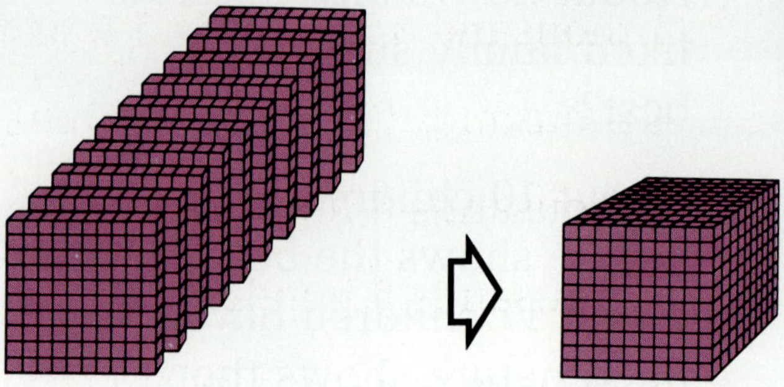

10 hundreds 1 thousand

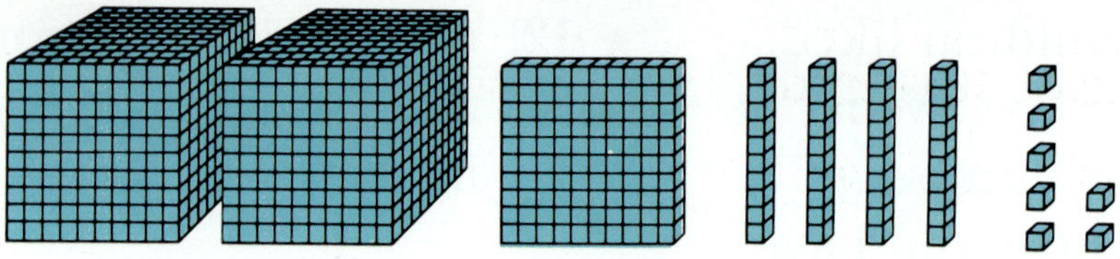

2 thousands 1 hundred 4 tens 7 ones

thousands	hundreds	tens	ones
2	1	4	7

The standard form is 2147. Read 2147 as *two thousand, one hundred forty-seven.* In 2147, the value of the digit 2 is 2000, 1 is 100, 4 is 40, and 7 is 7.

$$2000 + 100 + 40 + 7 = 2147$$

CLASS EXERCISES

Say the number. Write the standard form.

1.

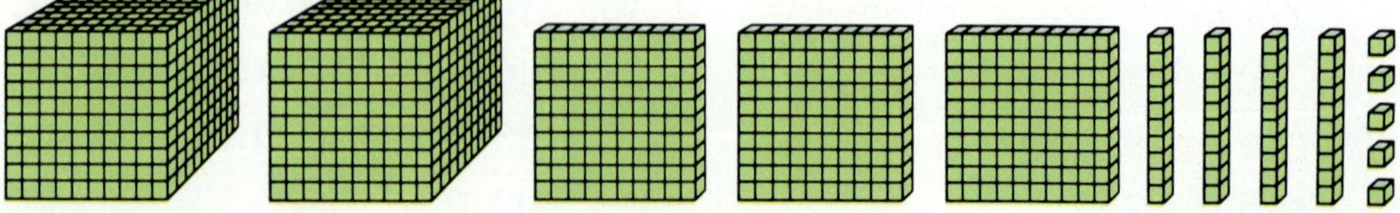

2.

th	h	t	o
3	0	0	1

3.

th	h	t	o
4	8	3	2

4.

th	h	t	o
7	7	3	5

PRACTICE

Write the standard form.

5. 1 thousand 3 hundreds 5 tens 6 ones
6. 4 thousands 2 hundreds 3 tens 7 ones
7. 7 thousands 8 hundreds 2 tens 5 ones
8. 3 thousands 5 hundreds 7 tens 1 one
9. 8 thousands 5 hundreds 6 tens 3 ones
10. 2 thousands 0 hundreds 6 tens 4 ones
11. 5 thousands 6 hundreds 0 tens 0 ones

12. 4000 + 600 + 20 + 8 **13.** 7000 + 900 + 40 + 6

14. 5000 + 900 + 70 **15.** 4000 + 900 + 7

Write the value of the digit 6 in the number.

16. 5643 **17.** 6709 **18.** 8506 **19.** 5162 **20.** 6320

Write the answer.

21. $16 - 9$ **22.** $7 + 5$ **23.** $14 - 8$ **24.** $3 + 9$ **25.** $5 + 6$

MIXED REVIEW

PROBLEM SOLVING APPLICATIONS

Write the standard form for the underlined number.

26. There were one thousand five hundred seventy-one people at one of the Olympic events.

★ **27.** On the first day of the 1984 Los Angeles Olympics, seven thousand two hundred forty-nine people went to see the gymnasts in the morning.

COMPARING AND ORDERING THROUGH THOUSANDS

You compare numbers to find which is greater and which is less.

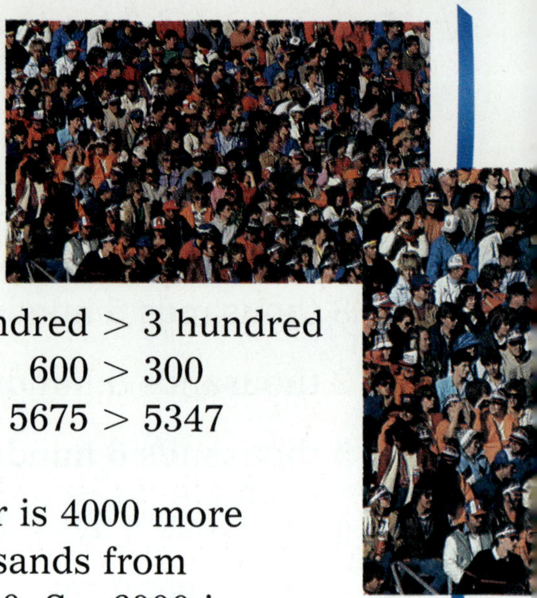

Compare 5675 and 5347.
The thousands are the same.
Compare the hundreds.

thousands	hundreds	tens	ones
5	6	7	5
5	3	4	7

6 hundred $>$ 3 hundred
$600 > 300$
so $5675 > 5347$

M If you want to know what number is 4000 more than 2000, you can count by thousands from 2000. Count: 3000, 4000, 5000, 6000. So, 6000 is 4000 more than 2000.

CLASS EXERCISES

Compare the numbers. Write $<$ or $>$. Read your answer.

1.

th	h	t	o
4	7	3	5
3	5	4	2

4735 ____ 3542

2.

th	h	t	o
9	6	2	0
9	4	3	2

9620 ____ 9432

3.

th	h	t	o
7	5	9	3
7	5	7	3

7593 ____ 7573

PRACTICE

Compare the numbers. Write $<$ or $>$.

4. 4000 ____ 7000 **5.** 4300 ____ 7100 **6.** 6470 ____ 5470

7. 5653 ____ 3748 **8.** 2184 ____ 2547 **9.** 8679 ____ 8574

10. 7999 ____ 8000 **11.** 6666 ____ 6333 **12.** 3883 ____ 3926

13. 2022 ____ 2222 **14.** 1897 ____ 2756 **15.** 1000 ____ 1100

16. 8866 ■ 8997 **17.** 5106 ■ 5114 **18.** 6278 ■ 6279

19. 3000 ■ 2999 **20.** 7631 ■ 7652 **21.** 4999 ■ 5001

Write the numbers in order from least to greatest.

22. 8569, 8525, 8590, 8572 **23.** 6459, 6453, 6450, 6455

24. 9781, 9698, 8543, 9476 **25.** 5684, 4978, 6354, 3698

Write the numbers in order from greatest to least.

26. 5786, 9642, 7436, 8768 **27.** 4653, 4243, 4865, 4489

28. 3533, 3597, 3556, 3578 **29.** 2222, 2229, 2224, 2227

Count mentally to find the number.

MENTAL MATH

30. 2000 more than 5000 **31.** 4000 more than 4000

32. 3000 more than 6000 ★ **33.** 2000 less than 9000

PROBLEM SOLVING APPLICATIONS
Reasonable Answers

Solve and check. The answer may not be a number.

34. There were 1251 hats sold on Saturday. There were 2005 sold on Sunday. On which day were fewer hats sold?

35. There were 5698 people at the game on Saturday and 4957 on Sunday. On which day were there more people?

36. There were 3076 red team fans. There were 2999 blue team fans. Which team had more fans?

★ **37.** If one more fan comes, we'll have 2000 more than 3000 fans. How many fans do we have now?

TEN THOUSANDS AND HUNDRED THOUSANDS

thousands			ones		
hundreds	tens	ones	hundreds	tens	ones
5	9	9	1	3	8

We read 599,138 as *five hundred ninety-nine thousand, one hundred thirty-eight*. Use a comma to set off the thousands.

On a calculator the number may look like this.

599138

You don't see commas on a calculator.

CLASS EXERCISES

Say the number. Write the standard form.

	thousands			ones		
	hundreds	tens	ones	hundreds	tens	ones
1.	6	3	1	0	6	3
2.		4	9	2	7	9
3.	1	9	0	4	3	7
4.		5	5	3	0	4
5.	8	0	9	6	3	0

PRACTICE

Match. Write the letter.

6. 457,369

7. 278,153

8. 135,246

9. 989,674

A. 989 thousand, 674

B. 457 thousand, 369

C. 135 thousand, 246

D. 278 thousand, 153

Write the standard form. Don't forget the comma.

10. 264 thousand

11. 700 thousand

12. 112 thousand, 608

13. 627 thousand, 215

14. 264 thousand, 437

15. 700 thousand, 406

16. 345 thousand, 203

17. 555 thousand, 399

18. one hundred fifteen thousand, seven hundred

19. eight hundred twelve thousand, six hundred five

20. seven hundred ten thousand, two hundred eleven

21. six hundred thousand

22. five hundred six thousand

23. three hundred forty thousand

24. two hundred fifty-one thousand

Match. Write the letter.

CALCULATOR

25. 138 thousand, 742 — **A.** 500005

26. 5 thousand, 905 — **B.** 111000

27. five hundred thousand, five — **C.** 138742

28. one hundred eleven thousand — **D.** 5905

PROBLEM SOLVING APPLICATIONS
Words and Numbers

Shorten the sentence by writing the standard form.

29. Today in Millville two hundred fifty-four thousand, two hundred twenty-seven people watched the parade.

30. One hundred fifteen thousand, nine hundred twenty-three cars parked in the town's parking lots.

31. We estimate that eighty thousand dollars were spent on flags and banners.

32. A hundred thousand more people may come to the parade next year.

Find the information from above. Solve.

★ **33.** How many people may come to the parade next year?

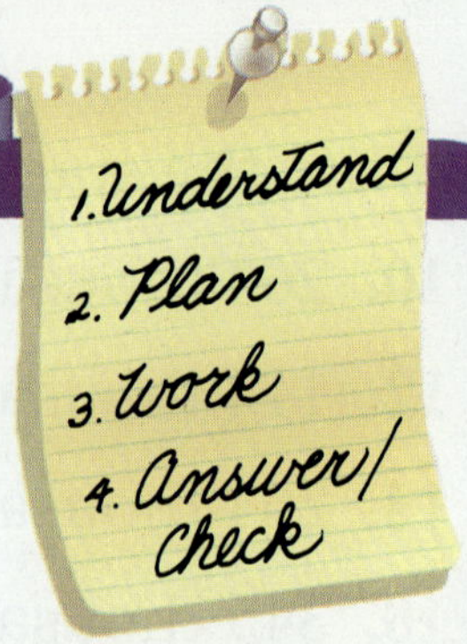

PROBLEM SOLVING

Strategy: Using A Table

The table shows the number of each food item sold each day in one week. How many apples were sold on Wednesday?

To find out, look down from the apple. Look across from Wednesday. There were 8 apples sold on Wednesday.

FOODS SOLD

DAY	SANDWICH	MILK	SOUP	APPLE
Monday	9	9	7	5
Tuesday	6	8	4	3
Wednesday	7	5	9	8
Thursday	5	7	8	6
Friday	8	6	5	4

CLASS EXERCISES

Use the table. Write the total number sold.

1.  Tuesday
2.  Monday
3.  Tuesday and Wednesday
4.  Thursday and Friday

PRACTICE

Use the table. Solve.

5. How many apples were sold on Monday, Tuesday, and Friday?
6. How many more sandwiches were sold on Monday than on Friday?

Use the table. Solve.

STUDENT	SPENT
Anna	65¢
Abe	43¢
Gail	79¢
Juan	85¢
Pat	59¢

7. Who spent less than 65¢?

8. Who spent more than 80¢?

9. Who spent less than 75¢ but more than 50¢?

10. Who spent more than 60¢ but less than 70¢?

11. Who spent more than Abe but less than Anna?

★ **12.** Anna used dimes and pennies to pay for lunch. How many coins did she use if only 5 of them were pennies?

★ **13.** Abe used dimes and pennies to pay for lunch. How many coins did he use if only 3 of them were pennies?

★ **14.** Both Juan and Gail used dimes and pennies to pay for lunch. 8 of Juan's coins were dimes. 7 of Gail's coins were dimes. Who used the greater number of coins, Juan or Gail?

CHECKPOINT 2

Write the standard form.
(pages 44–45, 48–49)

1. 6 thousands 4 hundreds 1 ten

2. 348 thousand 124

3. six hundred thousand

Write $<$ or $>$. *(pages 46–47)*

4. 2743 ____ 3643 **5.** 5241 ____ 5421

Use the table. Solve.
(pages 50–51)

6. Which student spent more than 50¢?

Student	Spent
Pam	45¢
Ted	63¢

Extra practice on page 402

CHAPTER 2 TEST

Write the standard form. *(pages 30–31, 34–37)*

1. sixty-four **2.** 3 hundreds 7 tens 0 ones **3.** 200 + 5

List the numbers in order from greatest to least. *(pages 32–33, 38–39)*

4. 395 375 385 365 **5.** 510 410 610 310

Round to the nearest ten or hundred. *(pages 40–41)*

6. 51 **7.** 673 **8.** 19 **9.** 499 **10.** 85

Estimate to solve. *(pages 42–43)*

11. 26 children swam in the pool. About how many children swam in the pool?

12. 32 children watched a movie. About how many children watched a movie?

Write the standard form. *(pages 44–45, 48–49)*

13. 6 thousands 9 hundreds 2 tens 4 ones **14.** 645 thousand, 700

Compare the numbers. Write < or >. *(pages 46–47)*

15. 3189 ▢ 3520 **16.** 7362 ▢ 7317 **17.** 4999 ▢ 5000

Use facts from the table. Solve. *(pages 50–51)*

18. Which sandwiches cost less than 75¢?

19. Which sandwich costs about 40¢?

20. Which sandwich costs more than 80¢?

21. Which sandwich costs the most?

SANDWICHES	
Egg	42¢
Tuna	85¢
Cheese	65¢

Extra practice on page 403

MATHEMATICS and HISTORY

The President of the United States lives in The White House. The White House is in Washington, D.C.

In 1792, building began on The White House. Since that time many changes have been made to make The White House more comfortable.

PRESIDENT	LIVED IN THE WHITE HOUSE
John Adams	1797–1801
Andrew Jackson	1829–1837
James Polk	1845–1849
Franklin Pierce	1853–1857
Benjamin Harrison	1889–1893
Theodore Roosevelt	1901–1909
Franklin Roosevelt	1933–1945
Harry Truman	1945–1953

FINDING OUT ABOUT HISTORY

Who was President when The White House change took place? Match. Write the letter.

1. Central heating, 1853
2. White House ready for President to move in, 1800
3. Gaslights instead of candles, 1848
4. Electricity, 1890
5. Air conditioning, 1952
6. Running water, 1833
7. Swimming pool, 1942

A. Theodore Roosevelt
B. James Polk
C. Harry Truman
D. Franklin Pierce
E. Andrew Jackson
F. Franklin Roosevelt
G. John Adams
H. Benjamin Harrison

Enrichment

Imagine what writing numbers must have been like before people invented numerals. To write the number 14, people drew 14 marks. Can you imagine writing 500 using marks?

The early Egyptians used a system of numerals that grouped numbers by tens and hundreds. Here is a chart to show the meanings of the Egyptian symbols.

Our numerals	1	10	100
Egyptian numerals	/	∩	𓍢

Here are some Egyptian numerals for numbers.

∩ / means 10 + 1, or 11

𓍢𓍢 ∩ //// means 200 + 10 + 4, or 214

Now read some Egyptian numerals on your own.

EGYPTIAN AND ROMAN NUMERALS

Complete.

1. ∩∩∩∩∩ ///
50 + __?__ = __?__

2. ∩∩∩ /////
__?__ + __?__ = __?__

3. 𓍢𓍢 ∩∩∩∩ //// ////
__?__ + __?__ + __?__ = __?__

Write an Egyptian numeral for the number.

4. 25 **5.** 57 **6.** 112 **7.** 431 **8.** 503

Look at this clock face. Have you seen one like it? The symbols you see are called **Roman numerals.** The symbols I, V, X, and L are used to write numerals through 89.

Our numerals	1	5	10	50
Roman numerals	I	V	X	L

When you use Roman numerals, you do not use the same symbols more than three times in a row. The way you arrange the symbols really matters. Sometimes you add the values of the symbols. Sometimes you subtract.

III means 1 + 1 + 1, or 3
VI means 5 + 1, or 6
XXII means 10 + 10 + 1 + 1, or 22

IV means 5 − 1, or 4
IX means 10 − 1, or 9
XL means 50 − 10, or 40

Count using Roman numerals. Complete.

9. I, II, _?_, _?_, V

10. VI, VII, __?__, IX, __?__

11. __?__, X, XI, __?__, XIII

12. __?__, __?__, XVI, XVII

13. LXI, LXII, LXIII, __?__, __?__

14. __?__, __?__, LVI, LVII, LVIII

Write a Roman numeral for the number.

15. 68 **16.** 49 **17.** 44 **18.** 56 **19.** 89

CUMULATIVE REVIEW

Choose the correct answer. Choose *a*, *b*, *c*, or *d*.
Find the answer.

1. $\begin{array}{r} 5 \\ 2 \\ +\ 5 \\ \hline \end{array}$
a. 11
b. 12
c. 10
d. none of these

2. $\begin{array}{r} 7 \\ 2 \\ +\ 9 \\ \hline \end{array}$
a. 16
b. 11
c. 17
d. none of these

3. $\begin{array}{r} 3 \\ 5 \\ +\ 6 \\ \hline \end{array}$
a. 13
b. 14
c. 11
d. none of these

Choose the correct number sentence.

4. The campers hike 4 miles. Then they hike 3 miles. How many miles do they hike in all?
a. $4 + 3 = 1$
b. $4 - 3 = 1$
c. $4 + 3 = 7$
d. none of these

5. The campers make 9 sandwiches. They eat 7. How many sandwiches are left?
a. $9 - 7 = 2$
b. $9 - 7 = 16$
c. $9 + 7 = 16$
d. none of these

Round to the nearest ten or hundred.

6. 89
a. 80
b. 90
c. 85
d. 70

7. 54
a. 40
b. 50
c. 60
d. 30

8. 110
a. 10
b. 100
c. 200
d. 210

Estimate to solve.

9. Linda saw 43 cows at the fair. About how many cows did she see?
a. about 30 cows
b. about 40 cows
c. about 50 cows
d. about 60 cows

10. Roberto brought 18 rabbits to the fair. About how many rabbits did he bring?
a. about 10 rabbits
b. about 20 rabbits
c. about 30 rabbits
d. about 40 rabbits

Choose the standard form.

11. 6 thousands 3 tens 1 one

a. 631
b. 60031
c. 6031
d. none of these

12. 260 thousand, 403

a. 26,000,403
b. 260,403
c. 26,403
d. none of these

Order the numbers from greatest to least.

13. 454 458 485 468

a. 454 458 468 485
b. 485 458 468 454
c. 485 468 458 454
d. none of these

14. 3791 3632 3872 3581

a. 3872 3791 3632 3581
b. 3632 3581 3791 3872
c. 3872 3791 3581 3632
d. none of these

LANGUAGE and VOCABULARY REVIEW

Use the words below to complete the sentences.

fact family   value   digits   standard form   sum

1. We use __?__ to write all of our numbers.

2. The answer in addition is a __?__.

3. The ______?______ for forty is 40.

4. Four facts that share the same numbers are a ____?____.

5. The __?__ of 5 in 523 is 500.

COMPUTER PARTS

You need to know how to use tools to make them work.

A computer is a tool that works with numbers, letters, and symbols.

The numbers, letters, and symbols you put into a computer are called **input.**

You can use a keyboard, cassette recorder, or disk drive to enter input.

The numbers, letters, and symbols you get out of a computer are called **output.** You may see the output on a screen or on paper from a printer.

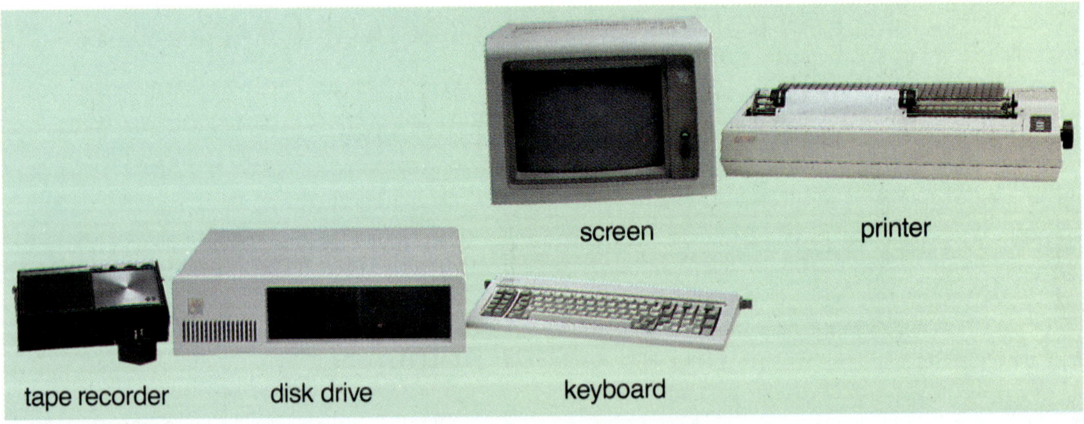

Write *I* if it is input, *O* if it is output.

1. A cassette recorder gives information to a computer.

2. Al presses the A key on the keyboard.

3. Carlos sees `HAVE FUN` on the screen.

4. Marvin sees `7 + 6 = 13` on the screen.

5. Amira presses the 8 on the keyboard.

6. Fay sees `HELLO, FAY` on the screen.

3

The man is putting luggage on two carts. One cart has 30 pieces. The other has 7. How many pieces are on the carts?

ADDITION
GREATER NUMBERS

TWO-DIGIT ADDITION

When you have more than 9 ones, you can rename the ones. You can rename 10 ones as 1 ten.

10 ones 1 ten

Sometimes when you add, you have to rename.

To add 24 and 6, line up the ones and line up the tens.

First add the ones.
Rename 10 ones as 1 ten.

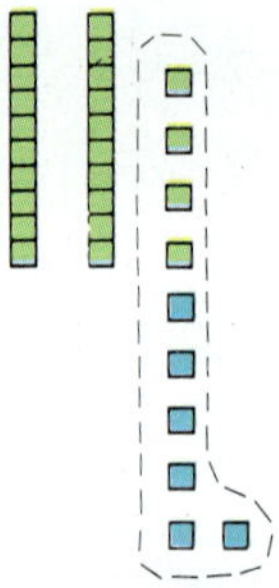

	t	o
	1	
	2	4
+		6
		0

Then add the tens.

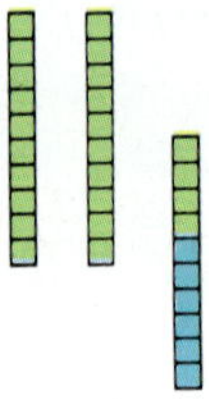

	t	o
	1	
	2	4
+		6
	3	0

Sometimes you may not have to rename. You still add the ones first, then the tens.

$$\begin{array}{r} 23 \\ +\ \ 5 \\ \hline 28 \end{array}$$

CLASS EXERCISES

Can you rename? Tell why or why not.

1. 8 ones **2.** 10 ones **3.** 9 ones **4.** 0 ones

Look at the ones. Do you need to rename?

5.

	t	o
	3	4
+		6

6.

	t	o
	4	2
+		5

7.

	t	o
	3	8
+		2

8.

	t	o
	2	9
+		1

PRACTICE

Add.

9. $16 + 4$ **10.** $32 + 8$ **11.** $24 + 2$ **12.** $43 + 7$ **13.** $54 + 3$

14. $52 + 6$ **15.** $25 + 5$ **16.** $37 + 3$ **17.** $46 + 2$ **18.** $61 + 9$

19. $54 + 6$ **20.** $28 + 2$ **21.** $67 + 2$ **22.** $89 + 1$ **23.** $75 + 4$

24. $45 + 5$ **25.** $53 + 6$ **26.** $41 + 9$ **27.** $23 + 6$

28. $72 + 7$ **29.** $68 + 2$ **30.** $79 + 1$ ★ **31.** $84 + 3 + 3$

MIXED REVIEW

Compare the numbers. Write < or >.

32. 25 □ 37 **33.** 456 □ 376 **34.** 5236 □ 6236

35. 262 □ 267 **36.** 564 □ 578 **37.** 7458 □ 7685

PROBLEM SOLVING APPLICATIONS

The table shows the life spans of some animals. Use the table to solve.

LIFE SPANS

ANIMAL	YEARS
Guinea pig	4
Moose	12
Lion	13
Tiger	16

38. A gorilla lives 4 years longer than a tiger. How long does a gorilla live?

39. How much longer does a lion live than a guinea pig?

40. A cow lives 3 years longer than a moose. How long does a cow live?

41. The life spans of a guinea pig and a tiger together equal that of a horse. How long does a horse live?

TWO-DIGIT ADDITION

The store has 27 pigs and 33 cows. How many toy animals are there altogether?

To find out, you add 27 and 33. Line up the ones and line up the tens.

Add the ones. Rename 10 ones as 1 ten.

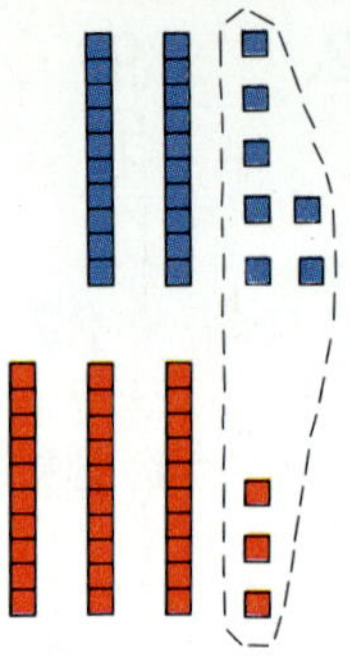

	t	o
	1 2	7
+	3	3
		0

Add the tens.

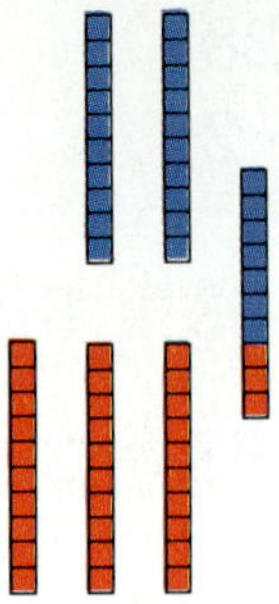

	t	o
	1 2	7
+	3	3
	6	0

There are 60 toys in all.

M Sometimes you can use mental math to add.

To add 23 and 25, think:

$23 + 5 = 28,$

$28 + 20 = 48.$

CLASS EXERCISES

What is the sum?

1.

	t	o
		8
+		2

	t	o
	1	8
+	4	2

2.

	t	o
		7
+		3

	t	o
	4	7
+	1	3

Do you need to rename? Tell why or why not. Name the sum.

3. 26 + 13

4. 16 + 24

5. 35 + 25

6. 64 + 33

7. 19 + 41

PRACTICE

Add.

8. 34 + 26
9. 23 + 47
10. 62 + 23
11. 72 + 18
12. 66 + 24
13. 45 + 15
14. 63 + 25
15. 17 + 33
16. 41 + 48
17. 63 + 17
18. 34¢ + 13¢
19. 42¢ + 38¢
20. 51¢ + 17¢
21. 55¢ + 25¢
22. 71¢ + 19¢
23. 43 + 15
24. 58 + 32
25. 27 + 42
26. 76 + 14
27. 25 + 45
28. 38 + 11
29. 61 + 29
30. 54 + 16

Use mental math. Write just the sum.

MENTAL MATH

31. 61 + 7
32. 63 + 2
33. 32 + 4
34. 43 + 3
35. 14 + 5
36. 18 + 31
37. 26 + 31
38. 53 + 42
39. 24 + 35

PROBLEM SOLVING APPLICATIONS

What's the cost?

40. two pigs
41. two cows
42. a bear and a cow
43. a bear and a pig
44. a pig and a cow

Which costs more?

★ 45. two pigs or one bear

★ 46. two cows or a bear and a pig

TWO-DIGIT ADDITION

Sometimes when you add, you may have more than 10 ones. You can think of 13 as 13 ones or 1 ten 3 ones.

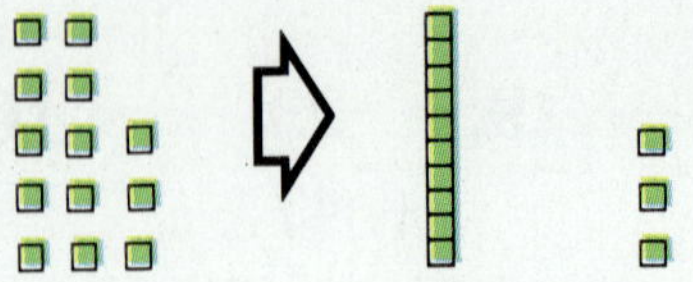

13 ones → 1 ten 3 ones

Now add 14 and 29.

Add the ones. Rename 13 ones as 1 ten 3 ones.

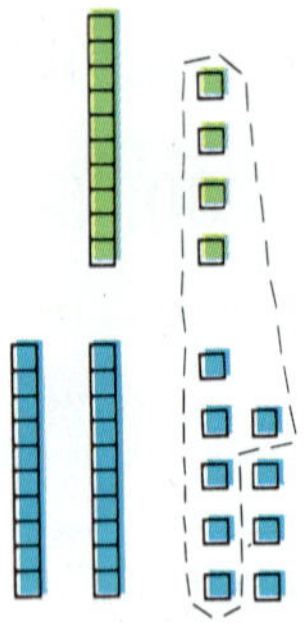

	t	o
	1	
	1	4
+	2	9
		3

Add the tens.

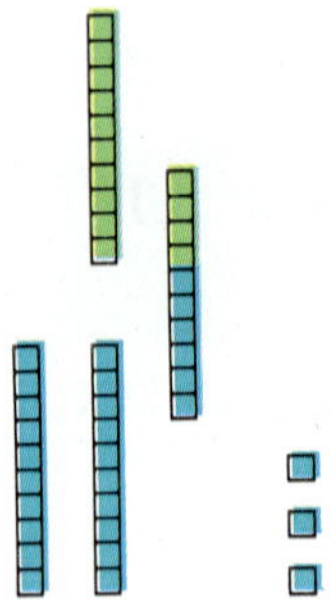

	t	o
	1	
	1	4
+	2	9
	4	3

M You can add 29 + 14 mentally.
Think: 30 is one more than 29.
30 + 14 = 44,
so 29 + 14 = 43.

CLASS EXERCISES

Complete.

1. 14 ones = _?_ ten _?_ ones
2. 17 ones = _?_ ten _?_ ones
3. 15 ones = _?_ ten _?_ ones
4. 11 ones = _?_ ten _?_ one

Add.

5.

	t	o
	4	5
+	1	7

6.

	t	o
	4	5
+	2	7

7.

	t	o
	6	2
+	2	9

8.

	t	o
	4	2
+	1	9

PRACTICE

Add.

9. $\begin{array}{r} 26 \\ +\ 26 \\ \hline \end{array}$	**10.** $\begin{array}{r} 49 \\ +\ 15 \\ \hline \end{array}$	**11.** $\begin{array}{r} 75 \\ +\ 16 \\ \hline \end{array}$	**12.** $\begin{array}{r} 66 \\ +\ 29 \\ \hline \end{array}$	**13.** $\begin{array}{r} 77 \\ +\ 15 \\ \hline \end{array}$
14. $\begin{array}{r} 23 \\ +\ 48 \\ \hline \end{array}$	**15.** $\begin{array}{r} 54 \\ +\ 39 \\ \hline \end{array}$	**16.** $\begin{array}{r} 26 \\ +\ 55 \\ \hline \end{array}$	**17.** $\begin{array}{r} 36 \\ +\ 36 \\ \hline \end{array}$	**18.** $\begin{array}{r} 27 \\ +\ 18 \\ \hline \end{array}$
19. $\begin{array}{r} 45 \\ +\ 32 \\ \hline \end{array}$	**20.** $\begin{array}{r} 17 \\ +\ 47 \\ \hline \end{array}$	**21.** $\begin{array}{r} 45 \\ +\ 34 \\ \hline \end{array}$	**22.** $\begin{array}{r} 72 \\ +\ 18 \\ \hline \end{array}$	**23.** $\begin{array}{r} 63 \\ +\ 27 \\ \hline \end{array}$
24. $\begin{array}{r} 49 \\ +\ 27 \\ \hline \end{array}$	**25.** $\begin{array}{r} 54 \\ +\ 33 \\ \hline \end{array}$	**26.** $\begin{array}{r} 25 \\ +\ 46 \\ \hline \end{array}$	**27.** $\begin{array}{r} 52 \\ +\ 27 \\ \hline \end{array}$	**28.** $\begin{array}{r} 74 \\ +\ 19 \\ \hline \end{array}$

Add in your head. Write just the sum.

MENTAL MATH

29. 64 + 19 **30.** 27 + 59 **31.** 76 + 19

32. 28 + 29 **33.** 39 + 56 **34.** 54 + 29

PROBLEM SOLVING APPLICATIONS

Phil found 28 pine cones. His sister found 39 pine cones. His brother found 26 pine cones.

How many pine cones did they find together?

35. Phil and his sister

36. Phil and his brother

37. Phil's sister and brother

Solve.

38. Who had more than Phil?

ESTIMATING SUMS

About how many oranges are there in a bag of 26 and a bag of 33?

You do not always need an exact answer. To estimate the sum of 26 and 33, round each addend to the nearest ten and add.

```
  26 →    30
+ 33 →  + 30
          60
          ↑ estimated sum
```

There are about 60 oranges in the two bags.

CLASS EXERCISES

Estimate the sum.

```
1.   14 →    10        2.   46 →    50        3.   41 →    40
   + 23 →  + 20           + 32 →  + 30           + 25 →  + 30
             ▒                      ▒                      ▒

4.   42 →    40        5.   73 →    ▒         6.   58 →    ▒
   + 36 →  + 40           + 17 →  + ▒            + 21 →  + ▒
             ▒                      ▒                      ▒
```

PRACTICE

Round to the nearest ten. Estimate the sum.

```
7.   28     8.   23     9.   42     10.   33     11.   41
   + 31        + 52        + 47         + 36         + 23

12.  23     13.  18     14.  22     15.   15     16.   57
   + 56        + 41        + 67         + 34         + 21
```

17. 28 + 61	**18.** 53 + 35	**19.** 65 + 24	**20.** 32 + 46	**21.** 83 + 12
22. 57 + 31	**23.** 44 + 25	**24.** 45 + 34	**25.** 23 + 62	**26.** 53 + 15
27. 35 + 21	**28.** 31 + 25	**29.** 52 + 37	**30.** 70 + 15	**31.** 45 + 23

32. 26 + 23 **33.** 52 + 36 **34.** 60 + 28 **35.** 53 + 25

36. 72 + 21 **37.** 43 + 25 **38.** 15 + 34 **39.** 40 + 38

PROBLEM SOLVING APPLICATIONS

Solve. The problem may ask for an estimate.

40. Pete set out 46 red apples on his fruit stand. Then he set out 32 green apples. About how many apples did Pete set out in all?

41. Jill bought 2 bunches of grapes. One bunch had 25 grapes. The other bunch had 13 grapes. How many grapes did Jill buy in all?

★ **42.** Mimi bought 15 apples. She gave her brother 7. She ate 2. How many apples did she have left?

★ **43.** Pete sold 23 red apples and 16 green apples. He sold 18 purple plums and 31 red plums. Did Pete sell more apples or plums?

TWO-DIGIT ADDITION

Sometimes when you add, you have to rename the tens.

You can rename 12 tens as 1 hundred and 2 tens.

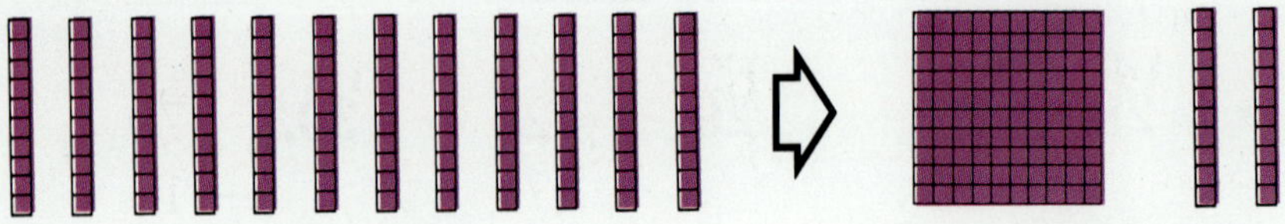

12 tens   1 hundred 2 tens

Now add 73 and 49.

Add the ones. Rename 12 ones as 1 ten 2 ones.

	h	t	o
		1	
		7	3
+		4	9
			2

Add the tens. Rename 12 tens as 1 hundred 2 tens.

	h	t	o
		1	
		7	3
+		4	9
	1	2	2

E To estimate the sum of 73 and 49, round each addend to the nearest ten. Then add. The estimate is 120.

$$\begin{array}{rcr} 73 & \longrightarrow & 70 \\ +\ 49 & \longrightarrow & +\ 50 \\ \hline & & 120 \end{array}$$

CLASS EXERCISES

Complete.

1. 13 tens = _?_ hundred 3 tens
2. 14 tens = _?_ hundred _?_ tens
3. 19 tens = _?_ hundred _?_ tens
4. 18 tens = _?_ hundred _?_ tens

Add. Rename when needed.

5.

	h	t	o
		7	4
+		6	8

6.

	h	t	o
		3	6
+		8	7

7.

	h	t	o
		9	3
+		5	6

PRACTICE

Add.

8. $\begin{array}{r} 94 \\ +\ 23 \\ \hline \end{array}$	**9.** $\begin{array}{r} 52 \\ +\ 49 \\ \hline \end{array}$	**10.** $\begin{array}{r} 40 \\ +\ 75 \\ \hline \end{array}$	**11.** $\begin{array}{r} 63 \\ +\ 59 \\ \hline \end{array}$	**12.** $\begin{array}{r} 75 \\ +\ 86 \\ \hline \end{array}$
13. $\begin{array}{r} 88 \\ +\ 62 \\ \hline \end{array}$	**14.** $\begin{array}{r} 57 \\ +\ 57 \\ \hline \end{array}$	**15.** $\begin{array}{r} 43 \\ +\ 97 \\ \hline \end{array}$	**16.** $\begin{array}{r} 28 \\ +\ 86 \\ \hline \end{array}$	**17.** $\begin{array}{r} 64 \\ +\ 57 \\ \hline \end{array}$
18. $\begin{array}{r} 48 \\ +\ 29 \\ \hline \end{array}$	**19.** $\begin{array}{r} 76 \\ +\ 87 \\ \hline \end{array}$	**20.** $\begin{array}{r} 99 \\ +\ 43 \\ \hline \end{array}$	**21.** $\begin{array}{r} 88 \\ +\ 98 \\ \hline \end{array}$	**22.** $\begin{array}{r} 78 \\ +\ 21 \\ \hline \end{array}$

23. 46 + 75 **24.** 88 + 57 **25.** 24 + 68 **26.** 87 + 36

Round both addends. Estimate the sum.

ESTIMATE

27. 43 + 62 **28.** 71 + 34 **29.** 23 + 54

30. 36 + 48 **31.** 75 + 19 **32.** 29 + 57

Write *true* or *false*.

33. When you round both addends down, the estimate will never be greater than the sum.

34. When you round both addends up, the estimate will never be less than the sum.

PROBLEM SOLVING APPLICATIONS

Solve.

35. Rick has 78 American post cards. His aunt gave him 45 post cards from other lands. How many post cards does Rick have in all?

★ **36.** Linda has more cards than Pam and fewer than Rick. If Pam has 54 cards and Rick has 60, how many cards might Linda have?

MENTAL MATH, ONE ADDEND LESS THAN TEN

Burt and Sue want to add 28 and 5. Burt writes all the numbers. Sue adds mentally.

Sue thinks: 8 + 5 = 13, so 28 + 5 = 33. Sue says adding mentally saves her time.

CLASS EXERCISES

Add. Look for a pattern.

1. 7 + 2 17 + 2 27 + 2 37 + 2	**2.** 6 + 2 16 + 2 26 + 2 36 + 2	**3.** 7 + 3 17 + 3 27 + 3 37 + 3	**4.** 8 + 2 18 + 2 28 + 2 38 + 2
5. 9 + 4 19 + 4 49 + 4 69 + 4	**6.** 8 + 8 28 + 8 58 + 8 68 + 8	**7.** 7 + 6 37 + 6 47 + 6 57 + 6	**8.** 9 + 9 39 + 9 49 + 9 69 + 9

PRACTICE

Add mentally. Write just the answer.

9. 4 + 8	**10.** 14 + 8	**11.** 24 + 8	**12.** 34 + 8	**13.** 54 + 8
14. 3 + 7	**15.** 23 + 7	**16.** 33 + 7	**17.** 43 + 7	**18.** 63 + 7

19. $\begin{array}{r} 14 \\ +\ 8 \\ \hline \end{array}$	**20.** $\begin{array}{r} 23 \\ +\ 7 \\ \hline \end{array}$	**21.** $\begin{array}{r} 18 \\ +\ 9 \\ \hline \end{array}$	**22.** $\begin{array}{r} 28 \\ +\ 3 \\ \hline \end{array}$	**23.** $\begin{array}{r} 36 \\ +\ 9 \\ \hline \end{array}$
24. $\begin{array}{r} 26 \\ +\ 5 \\ \hline \end{array}$	**25.** $\begin{array}{r} 38 \\ +\ 4 \\ \hline \end{array}$	**26.** $\begin{array}{r} 52 \\ +\ 9 \\ \hline \end{array}$	**27.** $\begin{array}{r} 44 \\ +\ 8 \\ \hline \end{array}$	**28.** $\begin{array}{r} 56 \\ +\ 9 \\ \hline \end{array}$
29. $\begin{array}{r} 87 \\ +\ 6 \\ \hline \end{array}$	**30.** $\begin{array}{r} 68 \\ +\ 8 \\ \hline \end{array}$	**31.** $\begin{array}{r} 78 \\ +\ 9 \\ \hline \end{array}$	**32.** $\begin{array}{r} 66 \\ +\ 7 \\ \hline \end{array}$	**33.** $\begin{array}{r} 56 \\ +\ 6 \\ \hline \end{array}$

34. 27 + 4 **35.** 16 + 6 **36.** 28 + 1 **37.** 36 + 9

38. 34 + 9 **39.** 48 + 6 **40.** 67 + 9 **41.** 29 + 8

MIXED REVIEW

List the numbers in order from least to greatest.

42. 35, 26, 42, 34 **43.** 53¢, 56¢, 51¢, 49¢

44. 764, 734, 784, 754 **45.** 536, 495, 659, 327

46. 5467, 3674, 3486, 5429 **47.** 3756, 3879, 3597, 5897

PROBLEM SOLVING APPLICATIONS
Mental Math or Pencil

Use mental math or paper and pencil to solve. Write *m* or *p* to tell which you use.

48. Garth found 34 smooth shells in the lake. He found 8 shells in the sand. How many shells did he find in all?

49. Garth had 27 shells, then got 4 more. Belle had 25 shells, then got 8 more. Who had more shells, Garth or Belle?

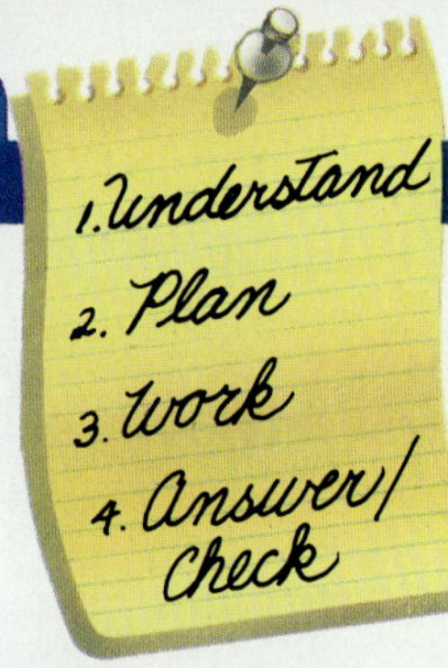

PROBLEM SOLVING

Strategy: Using Pictures

On a hike through Cooper Park, children drew pictures of the birds they saw. You can find out more about the hike by looking at their drawings.

CLASS EXERCISES

Use the pictures on this page to solve.

1. Who drew birds in a tree?
2. Who drew a flock of birds flying?
3. How many baby birds did David see?
4. How many children saw trees?

PRACTICE

Solve.

5. How many birds did Eva see?
6. How many birds did David see?
7. Who saw the greater number of birds?
8. How many birds did the children see in all?

Ranger Marcia counted different kinds of birds in Cooper Park. Then she made a drawing to show the number of each kind.

Solve.

9. How many meadowlarks and robins are there in all?

10. What is the total number of jays and robins?

11. How many crows and pheasants are there altogether?

12. About how many crows and flickers are there in all?

★ 13. Which is greater, the number of flickers and robins or the number of quail and jays?

CHECKPOINT 1

Add. *(pages 60–65, 68–71)*

1. $\begin{array}{r} 36 \\ +\ 42 \\ \hline \end{array}$ 2. $\begin{array}{r} 47 \\ +\ 23 \\ \hline \end{array}$ 3. $\begin{array}{r} 68 \\ +\ 57 \\ \hline \end{array}$

Estimate the sum. *(pages 66–67)*

4. $\begin{array}{r} 47 \\ +\ 32 \\ \hline \end{array}$ 5. $\begin{array}{r} 45 \\ +\ 54 \\ \hline \end{array}$ 6. $\begin{array}{r} 63 \\ +\ 25 \\ \hline \end{array}$

Solve. *(pages 72–73)*

7. How many birds are there in all?

Extra practice on page 404

ADDING MORE THAN TWO NUMBERS

How many children are in the play? You can add two numbers at a time until you find the sum.

$$\begin{array}{r} \boxed{9} \\ \boxed{8} \\ +\ 7 \\ \hline \end{array} \Rightarrow \begin{array}{r} 17 \\ +\ 7 \\ \hline 24 \end{array}$$

You can also add from the bottom up and the sum will be the same.

$$\begin{array}{r} 9 \\ \boxed{8} \\ +\ \boxed{7} \\ \hline \end{array} \Rightarrow \begin{array}{r} 9 \\ +\ 15 \\ \hline 24 \end{array}$$

Grouping Property
Changing the grouping of the addends does not change the sum.

You can use parentheses to show which numbers to add first.

$(9 + 8) + 7 = 24$
$9 + (8 + 7) = 24$

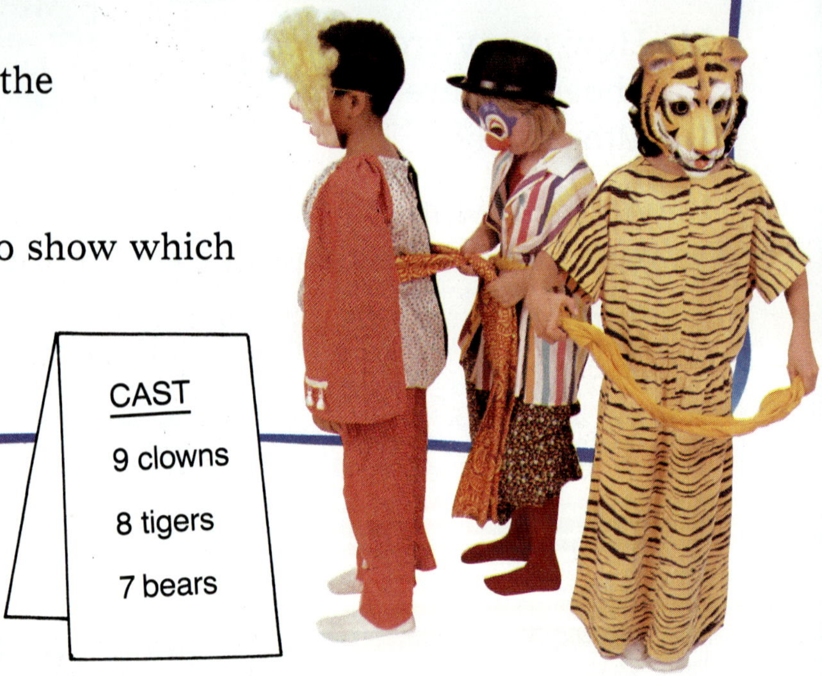

CLASS EXERCISES

What is the sum?

1. $\begin{array}{r} \boxed{5} \\ +\ \boxed{4} \\ \hline \end{array} \Rightarrow \begin{array}{r} 9 \\ +\ 7 \\ \hline \end{array}$

2. $\begin{array}{r} \boxed{3} \\ +\ \boxed{7} \\ \hline \end{array} \Rightarrow \begin{array}{r} 10 \\ +\ 9 \\ \hline \end{array}$

3. $\begin{array}{r} \boxed{1} \\ +\ \boxed{8} \\ \hline \end{array} \Rightarrow \begin{array}{r} 9 \\ +\ 8 \\ \hline \end{array}$

4. $\begin{array}{r} \boxed{9} \\ +\ \boxed{6} \\ \hline \end{array} \Rightarrow \begin{array}{r} 15 \\ +\ 7 \\ \hline \end{array}$

5. $\begin{array}{r} 4 \\ +\ 4 \\ \hline \end{array} \quad \begin{array}{r} 4 \\ 4 \\ +\ 9 \\ \hline \end{array} \quad \begin{array}{r} 4 \\ 4 \\ 9 \\ +\ 5 \\ \hline \end{array}$

6. $\begin{array}{r} 4 \\ +\ 5 \\ \hline \end{array} \quad \begin{array}{r} 4 \\ 5 \\ +\ 9 \\ \hline \end{array} \quad \begin{array}{r} 4 \\ 5 \\ 9 \\ +\ 5 \\ \hline \end{array}$

7. $\begin{array}{r} 3 \\ +\ 4 \\ \hline \end{array} \quad \begin{array}{r} 3 \\ 4 \\ +\ 6 \\ \hline \end{array} \quad \begin{array}{r} 3 \\ 4 \\ 6 \\ +\ 9 \\ \hline \end{array}$

PRACTICE

Add.

8. $\begin{array}{r} 6 \\ 7 \\ +\,4 \\ \hline \end{array}$	**9.** $\begin{array}{r} 5 \\ 5 \\ +\,5 \\ \hline \end{array}$	**10.** $\begin{array}{r} 7 \\ 7 \\ +\,8 \\ \hline \end{array}$	**11.** $\begin{array}{r} 6 \\ 5 \\ +\,9 \\ \hline \end{array}$	**12.** $\begin{array}{r} 6 \\ 5 \\ +\,8 \\ \hline \end{array}$	**13.** $\begin{array}{r} 9 \\ 8 \\ +\,9 \\ \hline \end{array}$
14. $\begin{array}{r} 7 \\ 7 \\ 6 \\ +\,6 \\ \hline \end{array}$	**15.** $\begin{array}{r} 5 \\ 8 \\ 8 \\ +\,5 \\ \hline \end{array}$	**16.** $\begin{array}{r} 9 \\ 2 \\ 9 \\ +\,2 \\ \hline \end{array}$	**17.** $\begin{array}{r} 5 \\ 7 \\ 8 \\ +\,9 \\ \hline \end{array}$	**18.** $\begin{array}{r} 9 \\ 6 \\ 3 \\ +\,2 \\ \hline \end{array}$	**19.** $\begin{array}{r} 4 \\ 2 \\ 9 \\ +\,3 \\ \hline \end{array}$

20. 8 + (4 + 7) **21.** (6 + 9) + 7 **22.** (4 + 9) + 9

23. (7 + 5) + 8 **24.** (4 + 7) + 6 **25.** (5 + 5) + 9

26. 8 + (6 + 4) **27.** 5 + (7 + 3) **28.** 9 + (2 + 8)

MIXED REVIEW

Write the standard form.

29. twenty-four **30.** fifty-two

31. 6000 + 400 + 30 + 2 **32.** 4000 + 500 + 20 + 1

PROBLEM SOLVING APPLICATIONS

Choosing the Operation

Tony sold 7 tickets to the show. Sue sold 5 tickets, Ann sold 8, and Vince sold 4. Solve.

33. Who sold the greatest number of tickets?

34. How many tickets did they sell in all?

35. How many more tickets did Ann sell than Sue?

★ **36.** Which 3 children sold 19 tickets?

ADDING THREE OR MORE TWO-DIGIT NUMBERS

To add more than two numbers, you add the ones first. Then you add the tens.

If you add down, you can check by adding up.

$$\begin{array}{r} {}^{1} \\ 27 \\ 48 \\ +\ 53 \\ \hline 128 \end{array} \downarrow \qquad \begin{array}{r} {}^{1} \\ 27 \\ 48 \\ +\ 53 \\ \hline 128 \end{array} \uparrow$$

E You can estimate to check your answer. Round to the nearest ten, then add.

$$\begin{array}{rcr} 27 & \rightarrow & 30 \\ 48 & \rightarrow & 50 \\ +\ 53 & \rightarrow & +\ 50 \\ \hline & & 130 \end{array}$$

The estimate is close to the sum. The answer makes sense.

CLASS EXERCISES

What is the sum?

1. $\begin{array}{r} 14 \\ 35 \\ +\ 20 \\ \hline \end{array}$ $\quad\begin{array}{r} 14 \\ 35 \\ +\ 28 \\ \hline \end{array}$

2. $\begin{array}{r} 25 \\ 81 \\ +\ 42 \\ \hline \end{array}$ $\quad\begin{array}{r} 25 \\ 81 \\ +\ 49 \\ \hline \end{array}$

3. $\begin{array}{r} 25 \\ 84 \\ +\ 41 \\ \hline \end{array}$ $\quad\begin{array}{r} 25 \\ 84 \\ +\ 47 \\ \hline \end{array}$

PRACTICE

Add down. Check by adding up.

4. $\begin{array}{r} 26 \\ 31 \\ +\ 40 \\ \hline \end{array}$

5. $\begin{array}{r} 36 \\ 22 \\ +\ 19 \\ \hline \end{array}$

6. $\begin{array}{r} 15 \\ 63 \\ +\ 24 \\ \hline \end{array}$

7. $\begin{array}{r} 46 \\ 21 \\ +\ 77 \\ \hline \end{array}$

8. $\begin{array}{r} 62 \\ 10 \\ +\ 28 \\ \hline \end{array}$

9. $\begin{array}{r} 45 \\ 31 \\ +\ 24 \\ \hline \end{array}$ **10.** $\begin{array}{r} 56 \\ 46 \\ +\ 15 \\ \hline \end{array}$ **11.** $\begin{array}{r} 30 \\ 58 \\ +\ 41 \\ \hline \end{array}$ **12.** $\begin{array}{r} 33 \\ 92 \\ +\ 50 \\ \hline \end{array}$ **13.** $\begin{array}{r} 24 \\ 66 \\ +\ 32 \\ \hline \end{array}$

14. $\begin{array}{r} 90 \\ 80 \\ +\ 69 \\ \hline \end{array}$ **15.** $\begin{array}{r} 52 \\ 77 \\ +\ 42 \\ \hline \end{array}$ **16.** $\begin{array}{r} 81 \\ 15 \\ +\ 36 \\ \hline \end{array}$ **17.** $\begin{array}{r} 39 \\ 23 \\ +\ 77 \\ \hline \end{array}$ **18.** $\begin{array}{r} 17 \\ 41 \\ +\ 22 \\ \hline \end{array}$

19. 30 + 75 + 12 **20.** 58 + 19 + 35 **21.** 47 + 28 + 35

22. 22 + 53 + 57 **23.** 36 + 71 + 45 **24.** 27 + 46 + 63

Estimate the sum.

ESTIMATE

25. 23 + 44 + 51 **26.** 56 + 13 + 49

27. 56 + 29 + 12 **28.** 39 + 43 + 62

29. 58 + 73 + 24 **30.** 98 + 96 + 92

PROBLEM SOLVING APPLICATIONS
Using a Table

Solve.

31. Where was the greatest number of crates sent?

32. Where was the least number of crates sent?

33. What was the total number of crates sent to all cities?

★ **34.** One of the cities wants twice as many crates. When doubled, the number of crates will be the same as Monterey's. Which city wants twice as many crates?

CRATES OF ORANGES

NUMBER	PLACE SENT
19	Atlanta
56	Monterey
46	Pittsburgh
28	Des Moines

THREE-DIGIT ADDITION

Sometimes when you add three-digit numbers, you need to rename 10 ones as 1 ten. To add 416 and 248, you rename 14 ones as 1 ten 4 ones.

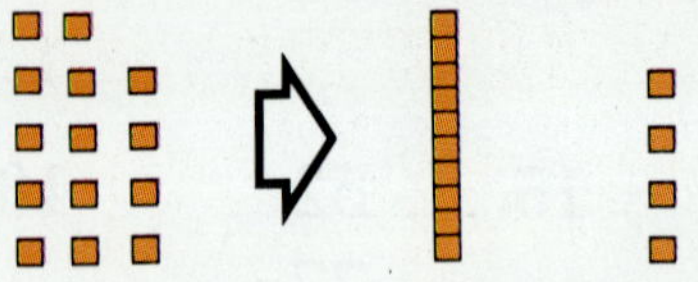

14 ones 1 ten 4 ones

Add the ones. Rename.

	h	t	o
		1	
	4	1	6
+	2	4	8
			4

Add the tens.

	h	t	o
		1	
	4	1	6
+	2	4	8
		6	4

Add the hundreds.

	h	t	o
		1	
	4	1	6
+	2	4	8
	6	6	4

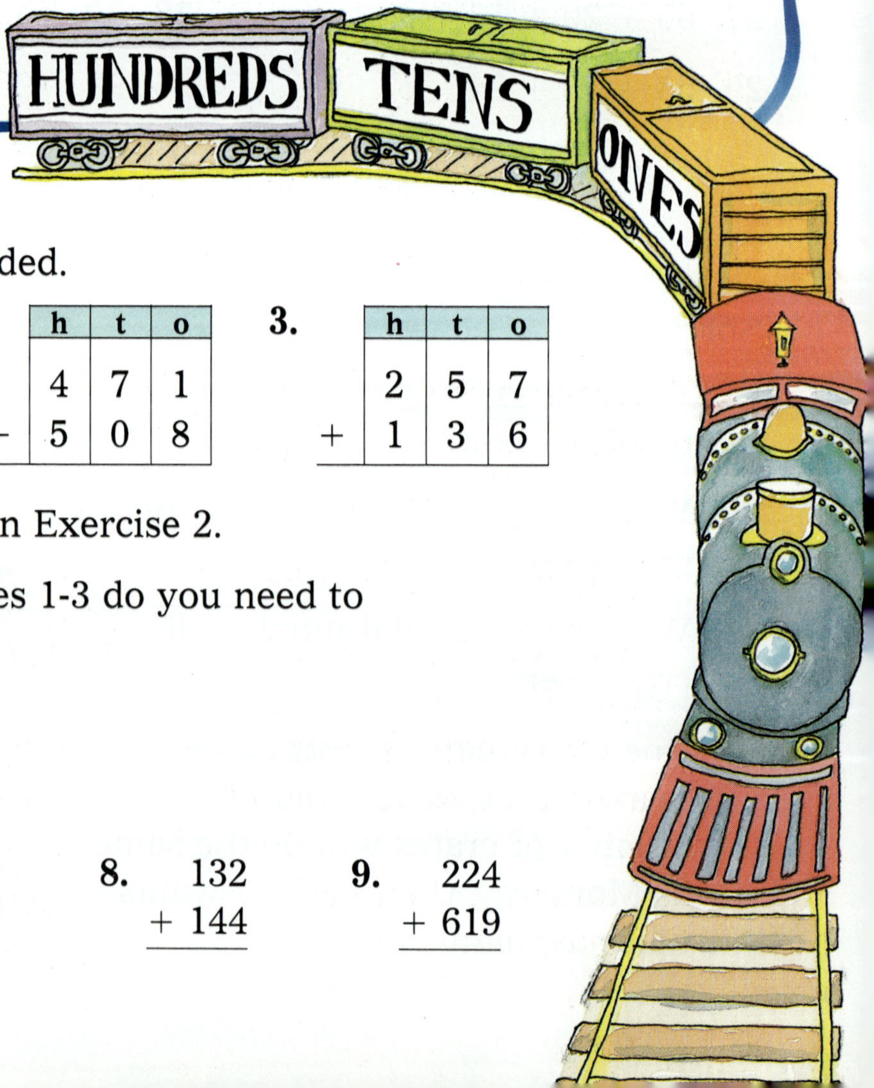

CLASS EXERCISES

Add. Rename when needed.

1.

	h	t	o
	2	6	1
+	3	1	9

2.

	h	t	o
	4	7	1
+	5	0	8

3.

	h	t	o
	2	5	7
+	1	3	6

4. Name the addends in Exercise 2.

5. In which of Exercises 1-3 do you need to rename?

PRACTICE

Add.

6. $516 + 146$

7. $138 + 658$

8. $132 + 144$

9. $224 + 619$

10. 357 + 428	**11.** 416 + 313	**12.** 345 + 315	**13.** 518 + 365	**14.** 319 + 128
15. 126 + 739	**16.** 215 + 257	**17.** 737 + 137	**18.** 673 + 214	**19.** 503 + 358
20. 242 + 325 + 216	**21.** 262 + 213 + 514	**22.** 125 + 513 + 131	**23.** 143 + 624 + 229	**24.** 214 + 431 + 246

25. 207 + 345 **26.** 518 + 26 **27.** 625 + 238 + 125

Write the answer.

MIXED REVIEW

28. 13 − 7	**29.** 12 − 6	**30.** 17 − 8	**31.** 8 + 8	**32.** 14 − 9
33. 15 − 7	**34.** 12 − 8	**35.** 7 + 9	**36.** 13 − 6	**37.** 15 − 6

PROBLEM SOLVING APPLICATIONS
Choosing the Operation

Solve.

38. The Chugga Train Lines sold 115 tickets to Detroit, 67 to Toledo, and 104 to Columbus. How many tickets were sold in all?

39. The Fresno Train makes 14 stops in the morning. In the afternoon the train makes 6 stops. How many more stops does it make in the morning than in the afternoon?

★ **40.** The Goldrush Train picked up 766 passengers at three stops. It picked up 250 passengers at each of the first two stops. How many did it pick up at the third stop?

THREE-DIGIT ADDITION

$$\begin{array}{r} 352 \\ +\ 293 \\ \hline ?5 \end{array}$$

Sometimes when you add, you need to rename 10 tens as 1 hundred. To add 352 and 293, you rename 14 tens as 1 hundred 4 tens.

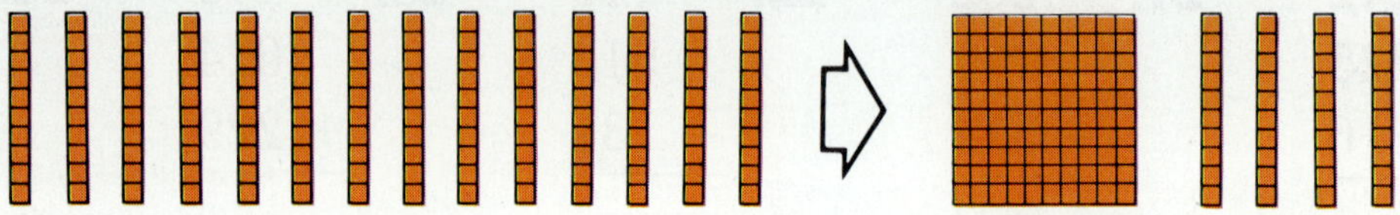

14 tens → 1 hundred 4 tens

Add the ones.

	h	t	o
	3	5	2
+	2	9	3
			5

Add the tens. Rename.

	h	t	o
	1		
	3	5	2
+	2	9	3
		4	5

Add the hundreds.

	h	t	o
	1		
	3	5	2
+	2	9	3
	6	4	5

When you work on a calculator, you do not enter numbers by columns. Instead, you enter one whole number at a time.

352 [+] 293 [=] 645

CLASS EXERCISES

Complete.

1. 10 tens = _?_ hundred 0 tens **2.** 11 tens = _?_ hundred 1 ten

3. 14 tens = 1 hundred _?_ tens **4.** 17 tens = _?_ hundred _?_ tens

Add.

5.

	h	t	o
	3	2	1
+	4	8	5

6.

	h	t	o
	2	7	3
+	1	9	4

7.

	h	t	o
	7	8	4
+	1	6	2

PRACTICE

Add.

8. 598 + 171 **9.** 481 + 232 **10.** 355 + 394 **11.** 431 + 196 **12.** 582 + 393

13. 482 + 364 **14.** 247 + 182 **15.** 291 + 543 **16.** 546 + 253 **17.** 363 + 574

18. 231 + 221 + 193 **19.** 383 + 112 + 221 **20.** 524 + 131 + 242 **21.** 363 + 131 + 344 **22.** 424 + 221 + 184

23. 634 + 285 **24.** 251 + 281 **25.** 123 + 475

26. 361 + 468 **27.** 452 + 465 **28.** 470 + 356

29. 254 + 362 + 153 ★ **30.** 473 + 31 + 124 + 41

Tell whether you would use mental math or a calculator to add. Write *m* or *c*, then add.

CALCULATOR

31. 6 + 7 **32.** 20 + 30 **33.** 500 + 600

34. 573 + 245 **35.** 30 + 40 + 10

36. 342 + 284 **37.** 232 + 345 + 151

PROBLEM SOLVING APPLICATIONS

Using a Picture

Use the picture to solve.

38. In how many different sized boxes are robots packed?

39. How many robots are there in all?

40. How many toys are in boxes?

41. Which is greater, the number of dolls and ducks or the number of robots?

THREE-DIGIT ADDITION

To add 439 and 372, you have to rename twice.

Add the ones. Rename.	Add the tens. Rename.	Add the hundreds.
$\begin{array}{r} {\scriptstyle 1} \\ 439 \\ +\ 372 \\ \hline 1 \end{array}$	$\begin{array}{r} {\scriptstyle 11} \\ 439 \\ +\ 372 \\ \hline 11 \end{array}$	$\begin{array}{r} {\scriptstyle 11} \\ 439 \\ +\ 372 \\ \hline 811 \end{array}$

E You may not always have a pencil when you want to estimate. You may need to estimate mentally.

Round to the nearest hundred.

Think: 439 + 372 → 400 + 400 = 800

The estimate is 800. The sum is close to the estimate. The answer makes sense.

CLASS EXERCISES

What is the sum?

1. $\begin{array}{r} 29 \\ +\ 54 \\ \hline \end{array}$ $\begin{array}{r} 290 \\ +\ 540 \\ \hline \end{array}$ $\begin{array}{r} 296 \\ +\ 545 \\ \hline \end{array}$

2. $\begin{array}{r} 46 \\ +\ 38 \\ \hline \end{array}$ $\begin{array}{r} 460 \\ +\ 38 \\ \hline \end{array}$ $\begin{array}{r} 464 \\ +\ 389 \\ \hline \end{array}$

PRACTICE

Add.

3. $\begin{array}{r} 429 \\ +\ 82 \\ \hline \end{array}$ **4.** $\begin{array}{r} 183 \\ +\ 748 \\ \hline \end{array}$ **5.** $\begin{array}{r} 295 \\ +\ 17 \\ \hline \end{array}$ **6.** $\begin{array}{r} 176 \\ +\ 765 \\ \hline \end{array}$ **7.** $\begin{array}{r} 688 \\ +\ 257 \\ \hline \end{array}$

8. 369 + 199 **9.** 84 + 389 **10.** 247 + 264 **11.** 669 + 246 **12.** 567 + 89

13. 254 + 458 **14.** 95 + 389 **15.** 289 + 563 **16.** 477 + 437 **17.** 396 + 546

18. 124 + 373 + 599 **19.** 221 + 648 + 187 **20.** 233 + 435 + 178 **21.** 376 + 212 + 173 **22.** 316 + 313 + 297

23. 428 + 541 + 195 **24.** 211 + 342 + 346 **25.** 442 + 221 + 185 **26.** 312 + 387 + 355 **27.** 329 + 111 + 448

28. 286 + 613 **29.** 229 + 427 **30.** 167 + 496

31. 248 + 45 **32.** 517 + 95 **33.** 208 + 18

Estimate mentally. Round the numbers to the nearest hundred. Write the answer.

ESTIMATE

34. 461 + 215 **35.** 328 + 479 **36.** 621 + 379 **37.** 615 + 214 **38.** 308 + 285

PROBLEM SOLVING APPLICATIONS
Using Pictures

How many nuts are there altogether?

39. chestnuts and Brazil nuts

40. walnuts and peanuts

41. Brazil nuts and peanuts

42. chestnuts, peanuts, and Brazil nuts

43. walnuts, peanuts, and chestnuts

44. in all four bags

FOUR–DIGIT ADDITION

When you add greater numbers, you sometimes must rename hundreds as thousands.

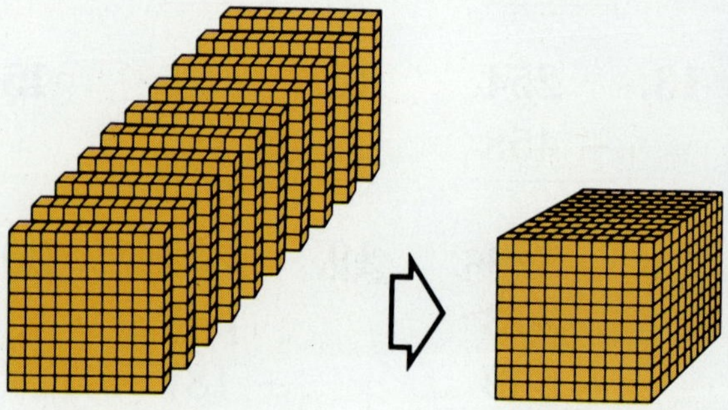

10 hundreds → 1 thousand

This is how you add 3842 and 2834.

Add the ones.	Add the tens.	Add the hundreds. Rename 16 hundreds as 1 thousand 6 hundreds.	Add the thousands.
		1	1
3842	3842	3842	3842
+ 2834	+ 2834	+ 2834	+ 2834
6	76	676	6676

When you add on a calculator, it's easy to push the wrong key by mistake. Be sure to check your answer.

3842 [+] 2834 [=] 6676

CLASS EXERCISES

What is the sum?

1. 4000 + 3000

2. 4600 + 3500

3. 4650 + 3570

4. 4653 + 3578

PRACTICE

Add.

5. 3246 + 1535

6. 1423 + 3253

7. 4237 + 1296

8. 3524 + 2364

9.	3281 + 1128	**10.**	4264 + 3261	**11.**	1260 + 1837	**12.**	6286 + 1042	**13.**	2786 + 2017
14.	6234 + 1426	**15.**	4911 + 3092	**16.**	3458 + 1724	**17.**	1827 + 2849	**18.**	2835 + 4069
19.	1776 + 1016	**20.**	8942 + 1339	**21.**	4806 + 3092	**22.**	7521 + 2543	**23.**	2684 + 3096

24. 5932 + 1081 **25.** 5263 + 3925 **26.** 4761 + 289 **27.** 2396 + 178

The addition below was done on a calculator.
Check the answers. Correct any mistakes.

CALCULATOR

28. 4728 + 2346 [7074] **29.** 5625 + 2154 [9779]

30. 2369 + 3862 [4231] **31.** 4172 + 1891 [6064]

32. 3829 + 2164 [5003] **33.** 1872 + 1124 [2996]

34. Would it be faster to do Exercises 28 to 33 on a calculator or with pencil and paper?

PROBLEM SOLVING APPLICATIONS

Solve.

35. 66 sailors saw 647 fish and 736 swimming seals. How many swimming animals did the sailors see?

36. 7 little boats chugged to the dock. 15 people hopped off. 6 of the boats floated out to sea. How many of the boats were still at the dock?

37. 23 sailors sailed in a ship. 17 of the sailors found a chest. Inside the chest 2474 gold coins gleamed. How many sailors were not there when the chest was found?

PROBLEM SOLVING

Strategy: Using a Pictograph

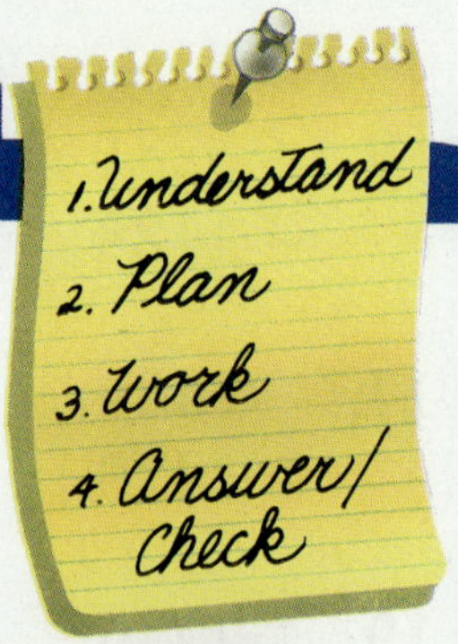

A **pictograph** helps to show numbers. This pictograph shows how many light bulbs Roberto sold in one week. On Saturday Roberto sold 9 light bulbs.

LIGHT BULBS SOLD

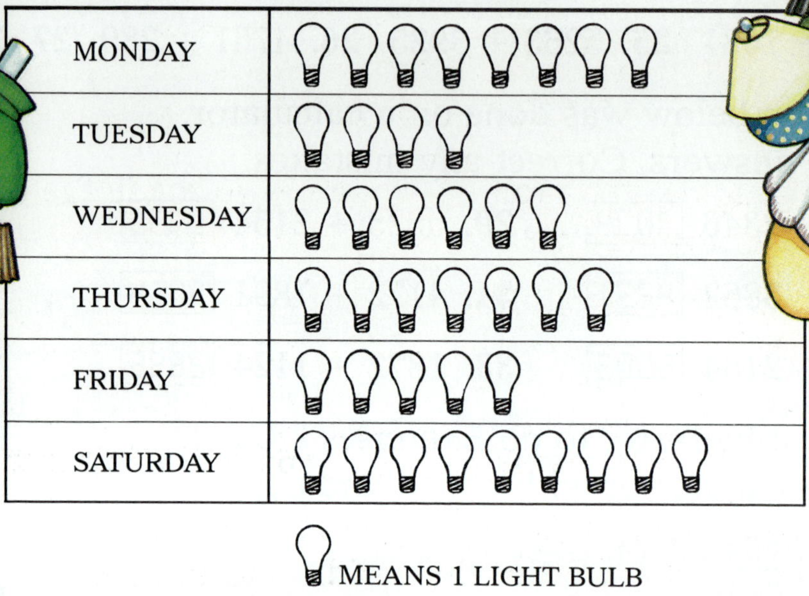

CLASS EXERCISES

What is the answer?

1. On which day were the most light bulbs sold?
2. On which day were the fewest light bulbs sold?

PRACTICE

3. How many light bulbs were sold the first two days?
4. How many light bulbs were sold the first three days?
5. How many more light bulbs were sold on Saturday than on Tuesday?
6. Order the number of light bulbs sold from least to greatest.

This pictograph shows the number of toy trucks made in one day.

TOY TRUCKS MADE

 MEANS 5 TOY TRUCKS

7. Each  stands for how many toy trucks?

8. Who made the greatest number of toy trucks?

9. How many trucks did Rosa make?

10. How many trucks did Sumi and Carol make altogether?

11. Did Antonio make more or fewer trucks than Sam?

★ **12.** Which two workers made 65 trucks altogether?

★ **13.** Make a pictograph. Use  to mean 1 bottle. Show how many bottles the children found. Don Found 5. Sue found 3. Gino found 7.

CHECKPOINT 2

Add. *(pages 74–85)*

1. 8 + 6 + 4

2. 25 + 46 + 38

3. 72 + 55 + 27

4. 534 + 248

5. 372 + 294

6. 5631 + 2729

Solve. *(pages 86–87)*

APPLES PICKED

 MEANS 2 APPLES

7. How many apples did Pam pick?

Extra practice on page 404

CHAPTER 3 TEST

Write the answer. *(pages 60–65, 68–71)*

1. $57 + 41$

2. $65 + 25$

3. $78 + 14$

4. $37 + 86$

Round to the nearest ten. Estimate the sum. *(pages 66–67)*

5. $52 + 37$

6. $63 + 15$

7. $14 + 52$

8. $54 + 35$

Write the answer. *(pages 72–73)*

9. How many pencils and pens are there in all?

10. How many rulers and pens are there altogether?

Write the answer. *(pages 74–85)*

11. $8 + 5 + 9 + 7$

12. $4 + (7 + 3)$

13. $76 + 35 + 41$

14. $247 + 538$

15. $245 + 493$

16. $386 + 24$

17. $196 + 635$

Write the answer. *(pages 86–87)*

NEW CHILDREN IN SCHOOL

Means 1 Child

18. How many more new children are in Grade 1 than in Grade 2?

19. How many new children are there in all?

Extra practice on page 405.

MATHEMATICS and ART

Students in art class make a pictograph to show how they get to school. They make pictures of people to paste on the graph.

WHAT CAN A PICTURE MEAN?

HOW STUDENTS GET TO SCHOOL	
Walk	
Bus	
Bike	

 means 2 students

Copy the pictograph. Use the sentences below to complete the graph.

1. Students make 7 people to show the number of students who walk to school.
2. Students make 4 people to show the number of students who take the bus to school.
3. Students make 6 people to show the number of students who ride bikes to school.

Use your pictograph to solve.

4. How many students walk to school?
5. How many more students walk than take the bus?
6. How do most of the children get to school?
7. How many children are in the art class?

Enrichment

Pretend you are in a city where the streets look like the ones on the map. To find where you are, just look at the street signs.

You are on the corner where Second Street meets D Street.

When you have a *grid*, you can use the grid to help locate *points*.

The jar of paste on the grid below is at the point where 5 crosses 2. The point is called 5,2. You write (5,2). (5,2) is called a **number pair.**

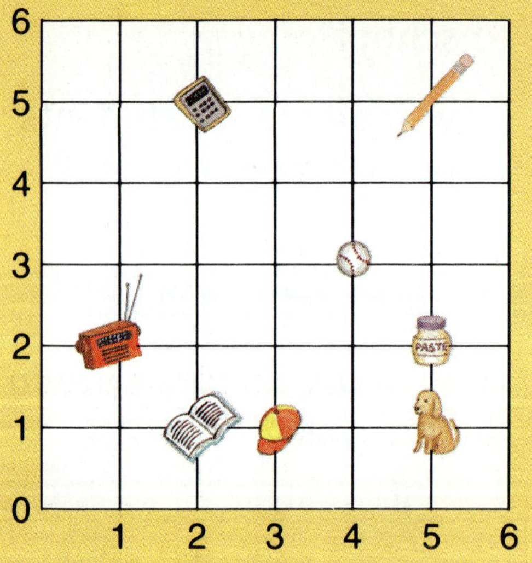

NUMBER PAIRS

Solve.

1. The point (5, 2) is not the same as (2, 5) on the grid at the left. What is at point (5, 2)?
2. What is at point (5, 5)?
3. What is at point (2, 5)?
4. What is at point (2, 1)?

Write the number pair to locate the object.

5. baseball
6. cap
7. dog
8. radio

Look at this grid. The picture was made by connecting dots in order. The points (or places) to put the dots were listed like this:

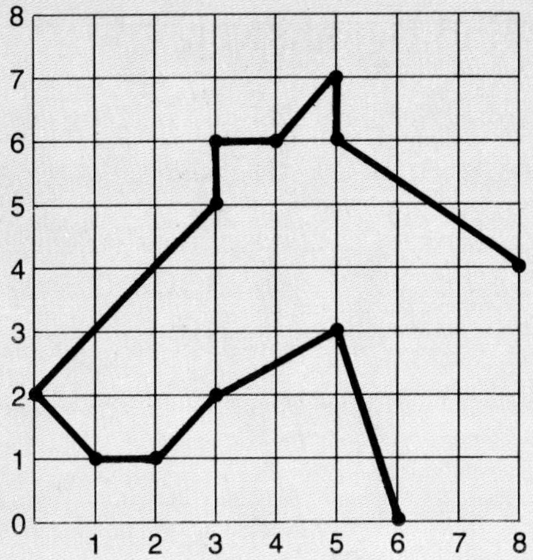

(6, 0) ⇨ (5, 3) ⇨ (3, 2) ⇨ (2, 1) ⇩

⇩ (3, 6) ⇦ (3, 5) ⇦ (0, 2) ⇦ (1, 1)

(4, 6) ⇨ (5, 7) ⇨ (5, 6) ⇨ (8, 4)

Follow the arrows. What picture is it?

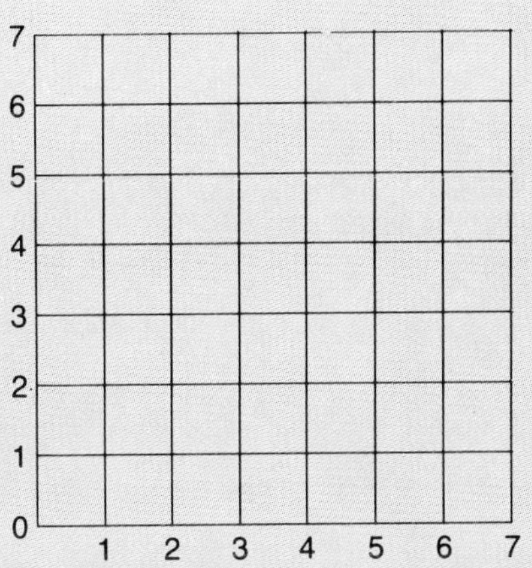

9. Make a grid on your paper. Draw a dot for each number pair. Connect the dots in order.

(1, 4) ⇨ (3, 4) ⇨ (4, 6) ⇨ (5, 4) ⇩

⇩ (4, 2) ⇦ (6, 1) ⇦ (5, 3) ⇦ (7, 4)

(2, 1) ⇨ (3, 3) ⇨ (1, 4)

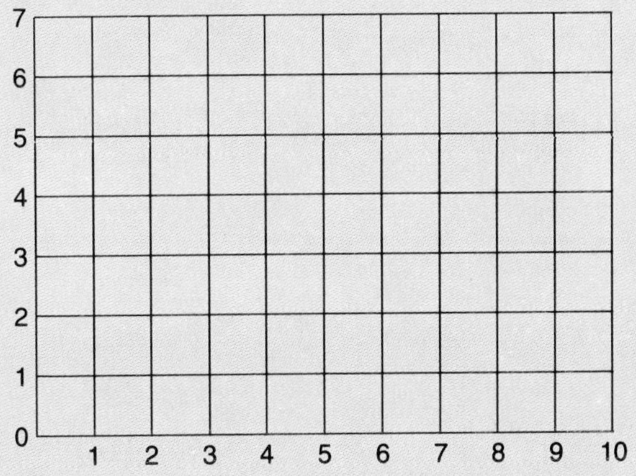

10. Draw another grid on your paper. Draw a dot for each number pair. Connect the dots in order.

(1, 2) ⇨ (1, 6) ⇨ (2, 5) ⇩

⇩ (10, 5) ⇦ (7, 6) ⇦ (4, 6)

(9, 4) ⇨ (10, 3) ⇨ (7, 2) ⇩

(1, 2) ⇦ (2, 3) ⇦ (4, 2)

CUMULATIVE REVIEW

Choose the correct answer. Choose *a*, *b*, *c*, or *d*.

Find the answer.

1. 7 + 5
a. 1
b. 12
c. 14
d. none of these

2. 8 + 9
a. 17
b. 18
c. 19
d. none of these

3. 6 + 6
a. 0
b. 8
c. 12
d. none of these

4. $\begin{array}{r} 0 \\ +\,9 \\ \hline \end{array}$
a. 0
b. 10
c. 9
d. none of these

5. $\begin{array}{r} 6 \\ +\,7 \\ \hline \end{array}$
a. 13
b. 12
c. 11
d. none of these

6. $\begin{array}{r} 5 \\ +\,8 \\ \hline \end{array}$
a. 12
b. 13
c. 14
d. none of these

Find the answer.

7. 14 − 6
a. 6
b. 7
c. 8
d. none of these

8. 16 − 7
a. 9
b. 8
c. 7
d. none of these

9. 13 − 9
a. 3
b. 4
c. 5
d. none of these

10. $\begin{array}{r} 7 \\ -\,7 \\ \hline \end{array}$
a. 7
b. 14
c. 0
d. none of these

11. $\begin{array}{r} 11 \\ -\,8 \\ \hline \end{array}$
a. 5
b. 3
c. 7
d. none of these

12. $\begin{array}{r} 17 \\ -\,9 \\ \hline \end{array}$
a. 12
b. 10
c. 8
d. none of these

Match.

13. 800 + 3
a. 83
b. 830
c. 803
d. none of these

14. 4 hundreds 6 tens
a. 460
b. 4600
c. 406
d. none of these

Compare the numbers.

15. 69 ■ 70
a. $>$
b. $<$
c. $=$
d. none of these

16. 30 ■ 20
a. $>$
b. $<$
c. $=$
d. none of these

Solve.

FRUIT	COST
oranges	25¢
pears	29¢
apples	43¢
bananas	15¢

17. You use dimes and pennies to buy apples. How many coins will you use if only 3 of them are pennies?

a. 4 **b.** 7
c. 3 **d.** none of these

18. Which fruit costs more than 25¢ but less than 30¢?

a. orange **b.** apple
c. banana **d.** none of these

LANGUAGE and VOCABULARY REVIEW

Unscramble the letters to write a math word.

1. ppghtrcioa (a picture that helps show amounts)

2. seon (10 of these equal one ten)

3. ddrhsnue (10 of these equal one thousand)

4. tnse (10 of these equal one hundred)

INPUT, PROCESS, OUTPUT

When you bake bread, you do three steps.

1. Make the dough.

2. Put the dough in the oven.

3. Take out the bread.

The oven did the job of changing the dough to bread.

To change something is to **process** it. A computer processes input. You must tell a computer how to process the input.

After the process, the computer shows an output.

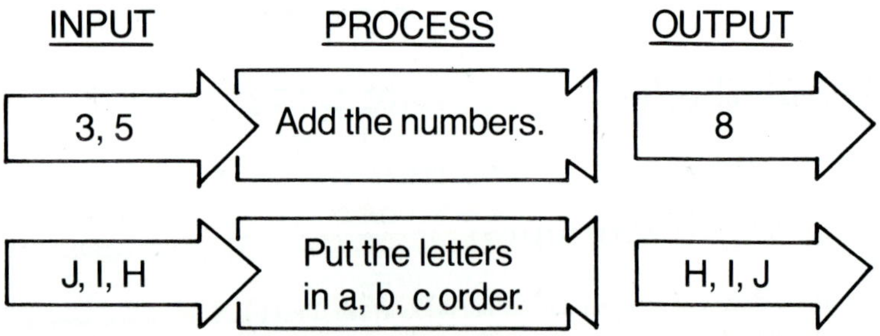

Write the output.

	INPUT	PROCESS
1.	17, 8	Add.
2.	54, 45, 64	Order from least to greatest.
3.	702, 720	Compare to show which is greater.
4.	18, 7	Subtract.

4

57 penguins waddled to the edge of the ice. One by one, 7 penguins dove into the icy water to fish. How many penguins were left on the ice?

SUBTRACTION
GREATER NUMBERS

TWO-DIGIT SUBTRACTION

To subtract 7 from 30, you rename to make more ones. Rename 3 tens 0 ones as 2 tens 10 ones.

$$\begin{array}{r}30\\-\ 7\\\hline\end{array}$$

tens	ones
3	0

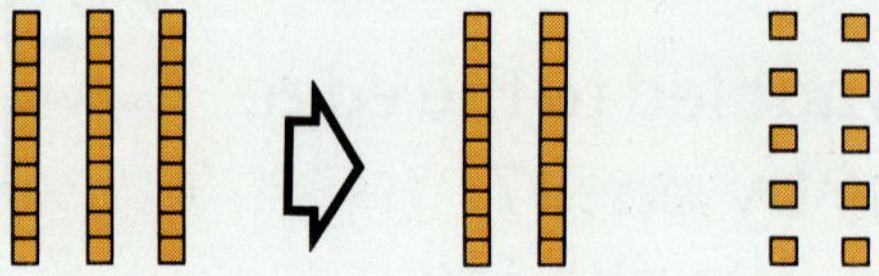

3 tens 2 tens 10 ones

tens	ones
2 ~~3~~	10 ~~0~~

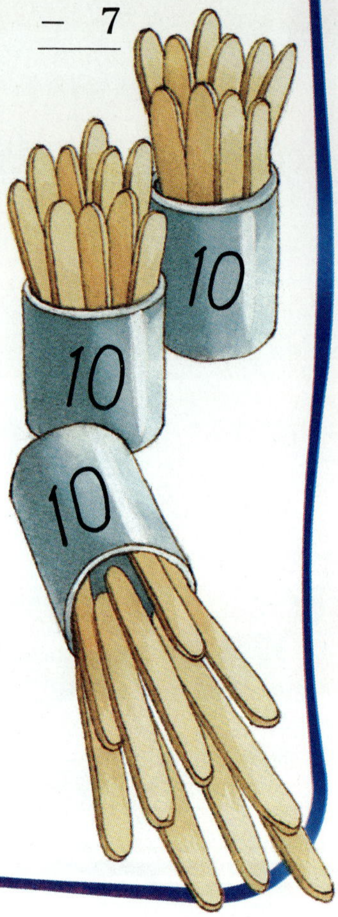

To subtract, line up the ones and line up the tens.

First subtract the ones.

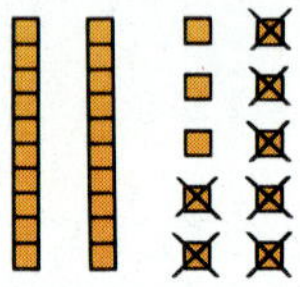

	t	o
	2 ~~3~~	10 ~~0~~
−		7
		3

Then subtract the tens.

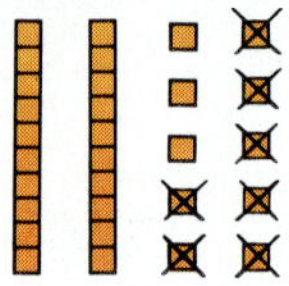

	t	o
	2 ~~3~~	10 ~~0~~
−		7
	2	3

M You can subtract 7 from 30 mentally.
Think: 10 − 7 = 3, so 30 − 7 = 23.

CLASS EXERCISES

Tell how many tens and ones.

1. 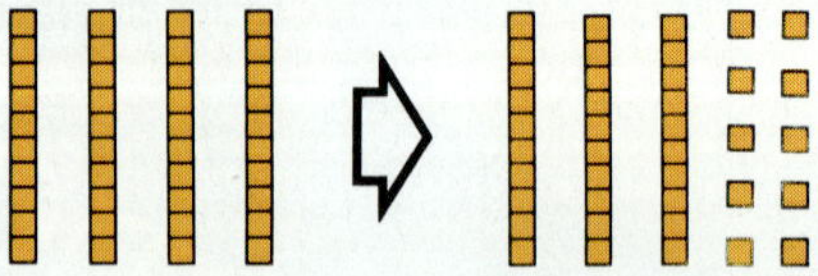

_?_ tens = _?_ tens _?_ ones

2. 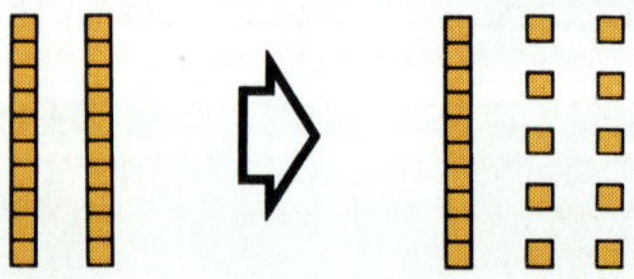

_?_ tens = _?_ ten _?_ ones

Do you need to rename? Subtract.

3.

	t	o
	3	6
−		4

4.

	t	o
	4	0
−		5

5.

	t	o
	2	0
−		6

6.

	t	o
	1	4
−		3

PRACTICE

Subtract.

7. $\begin{array}{r} 30 \\ -\ 4 \\ \hline \end{array}$	8. $\begin{array}{r} 48 \\ -\ 6 \\ \hline \end{array}$	9. $\begin{array}{r} 50 \\ -\ 7 \\ \hline \end{array}$	10. $\begin{array}{r} 80 \\ -\ 1 \\ \hline \end{array}$	11. $\begin{array}{r} 26 \\ -\ 3 \\ \hline \end{array}$
12. $\begin{array}{r} 67 \\ -\ 5 \\ \hline \end{array}$	13. $\begin{array}{r} 60 \\ -\ 0 \\ \hline \end{array}$	14. $\begin{array}{r} 70 \\ -\ 3 \\ \hline \end{array}$	15. $\begin{array}{r} 58 \\ -\ 4 \\ \hline \end{array}$	16. $\begin{array}{r} 90 \\ -\ 8 \\ \hline \end{array}$
17. $\begin{array}{r} 45 \\ -\ 2 \\ \hline \end{array}$	18. $\begin{array}{r} 20 \\ -\ 3 \\ \hline \end{array}$	19. $\begin{array}{r} 40 \\ -\ 8 \\ \hline \end{array}$	20. $\begin{array}{r} 50 \\ -\ 5 \\ \hline \end{array}$	21. $\begin{array}{r} 80 \\ -\ 4 \\ \hline \end{array}$

22. $40 - 7$ **23.** $86 - 4$ **24.** $60 - 2$ **25.** $18 - 3$

Compare. Write < or >.

26. $60 - 6$ ■ 60 **27.** $80 + 6$ ■ 80 **28.** $47 - 5$ ■ 47

Use mental math to subtract.

MENTAL MATH

29. $20 - 8$ **30.** $50 - 6$ **31.** $40 - 3$

32. $70 - 4$ **33.** $30 - 7$ **34.** $90 - 2$

PROBLEM SOLVING APPLICATIONS
Choosing a Strategy

Solve.

35. There are 30 bones in the arm, wrist, and hand. 6 of the bones are in the arm. How many bones are in the wrist and hand?

36. There are 60 bones in the leg, ankle, and foot. The leg has 8 bones. How many bones are in the ankle and foot?

★ **37.** One out of every 20 people has an extra rib. In a group of 60 people, how many people might have an extra rib?

★ **38.** Men have an extra rib 3 times more often than women. If 8 women in a town have an extra rib, how many men in that same town might have an extra rib?

TWO-DIGIT SUBTRACTION

Darla makes 30 popovers. She fills 14 with stew. How many popovers are not filled?

To find out, you can subtract 14 from 30.

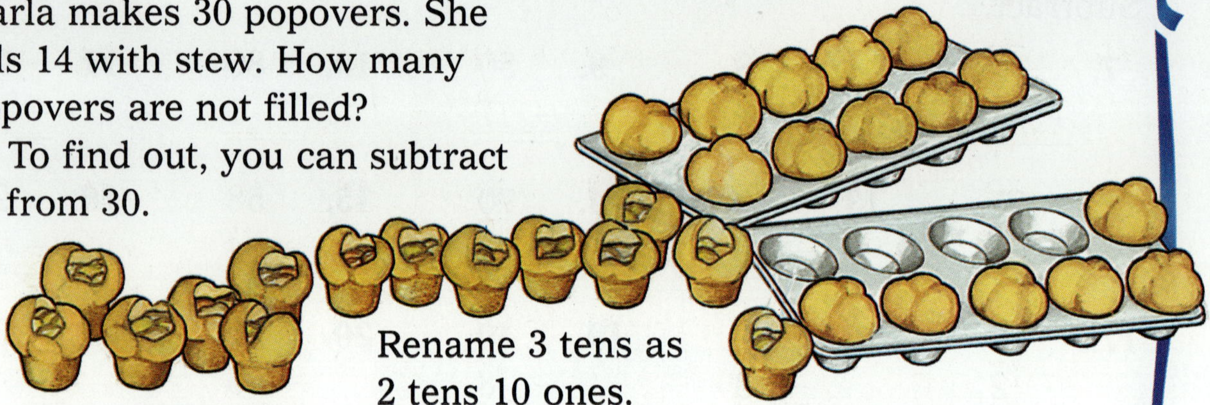

Look at the ones.

	t	o
	3	0
−	1	4

Rename 3 tens as 2 tens 10 ones. Subtract the ones.

	t	o
	2 ~~3~~	10 ~~0~~
−	1	4
		6

Subtract the tens.

	t	o
	2 ~~3~~	10 ~~0~~
−	1	4
	1	6

16 popovers are not filled.

CLASS EXERCISES

What is the missing number?

1. 3 tens = _?_ tens 10 ones
2. 5 tens = _?_ tens 10 ones
3. 6 tens = 5 tens _?_ ones
4. 8 tens = 7 tens _?_ ones

Which column do you subtract first? Subtract.

5.

	t	o
	7	0
−	2	7

6.

	t	o
	6	0
−	3	4

7.

	t	o
	5	8
−		6

8.

	t	o
	8	0
−	5	3

9. **Think:** What might happen if you subtract the tens first?

PRACTICE

Subtract.

10.	70 − 65	**11.**	20 − 12	**12.**	80 − 76	**13.**	60 − 51	**14.**	40 − 10
15.	60 − 47	**16.**	40 − 22	**17.**	90 − 40	**18.**	80 − 33	**19.**	50 − 19
20.	30 − 15	**21.**	70 − 30	**22.**	90 − 47	**23.**	60 − 20	**24.**	80 − 64
25.	50 − 36	**26.**	20 − 15	**27.**	40 − 10	**28.**	90 − 32	**29.**	30 − 11

30. 50 − 27 **31.** 70 − 50 **32.** 30 − 18 **33.** 80 − 47

34. 60 − 38 **35.** 40 − 36 **36.** 90 − 60 **37.** 80 − 73

PROBLEM SOLVING APPLICATIONS
Choosing the Operation

Solve.

The popover pan has room for 10 popovers.

1 pan = 10 popovers
2 pans = 20 popovers
3 pans = 30 popovers

38. Terry baked 3 pans of popovers. She filled 15 popovers with creamed chicken. How many popovers were left?

39. Gus baked a pan of popovers on Saturday. On Sunday 3 popovers were left. How many popovers had been eaten?

40. Lily, Darla, and Jake each baked a pan of popovers. Stefan baked 2 pans of popovers. How many popovers were baked?

TWO-DIGIT SUBTRACTION

To subtract 18 from 32, you must first take 1 ten from 32 and rename it as 10 ones.

	t	o
	3	2
−	1	8

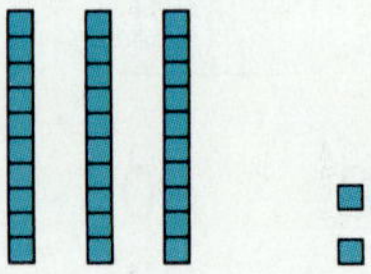

3 tens 2 ones

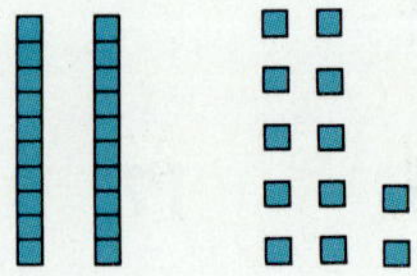

2 tens 12 ones

	t	o
	2 ~~3~~	12 ~~2~~
−	1	8

Subtract the ones.

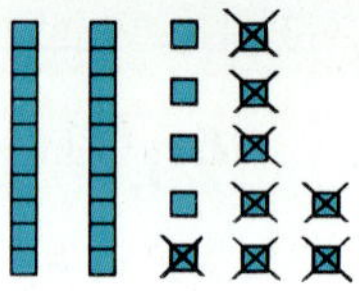

	t	o
	2 ~~3~~	12 ~~2~~
−	1	8
		4

Subtract the tens.

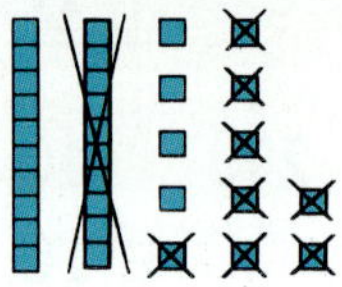

	t	o
	2 ~~3~~	12 ~~2~~
−	1	8
	1	4

M Sometimes you can subtract mentally.

$$\begin{array}{r} 42 \\ -\ 8 \\ \hline \end{array}$$

Think: $12 - 8 = 4.$
So $42 - 8 = 34.$

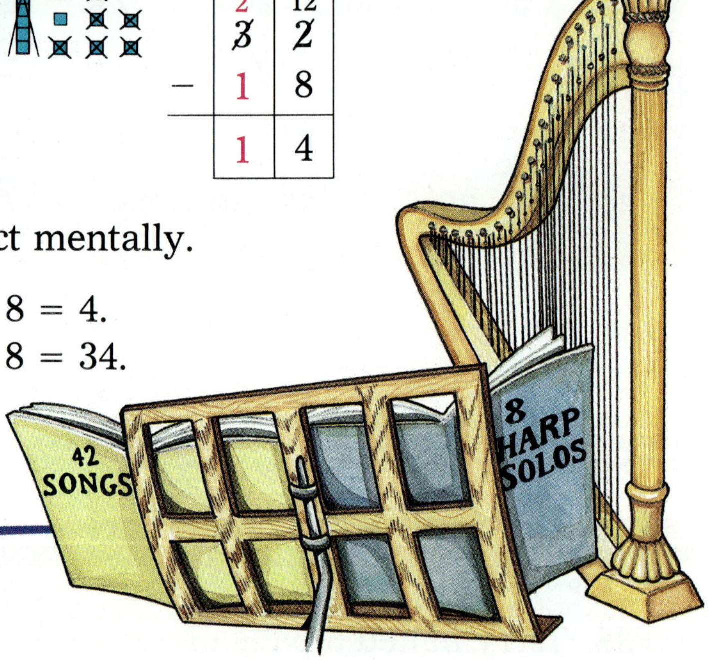

CLASS EXERCISES

What is the difference?

1.

	t	o
	7	0
−	2	8

2.

	t	o
	7	4
−	2	8

3.

	t	o
	3	0
−	1	9

4.

	t	o
	3	7
−	1	9

Do you need to rename? Subtract.

5. $\begin{array}{r} 45 \\ -\ 12 \\ \hline \end{array}$ **6.** $\begin{array}{r} 27 \\ -\ 19 \\ \hline \end{array}$ **7.** $\begin{array}{r} 31 \\ -\ 20 \\ \hline \end{array}$ **8.** $\begin{array}{r} 82 \\ -\ 6 \\ \hline \end{array}$ **9.** $\begin{array}{r} 50 \\ -\ 33 \\ \hline \end{array}$

PRACTICE

Subtract.

10. 87 − 39 **11.** 95 − 26 **12.** 52 − 38 **13.** 46 − 15 **14.** 75 − 36

15. 66 − 24 **16.** 91 − 64 **17.** 83 − 5 **18.** 72 − 55 **19.** 51 − 33

20. 93 − 6 **21.** 47 − 28 **22.** 37 − 14 **23.** 24 − 16 **24.** 52 − 11

25. 53 − 29 **26.** 76 − 5 **27.** 42 − 27 **28.** 64 − 8

Subtract mentally. Write just the answer.

M MENTAL MATH

29. 74 − 26 **30.** 56 − 39 **31.** 45 − 17 **32.** 65 − 48

33. 34 − 15 **34.** 83 − 66 **35.** 74 − 59 **36.** 92 − 26

37. Would it be easier to do Exercises 29-36 mentally or on a calculator?

PROBLEM SOLVING APPLICATIONS
Choosing the Operation

Solve.

38. A harp has 46 strings. Most guitars have 6 strings. How many more strings does a harp have than a guitar?

★ **39.** The 36 black keys on a piano are in groups of one, two, and three. There is 1 group of one. The number of groups of two equals the number of groups of three. How many groups of three are there?

ESTIMATING DIFFERENCES

The Saturday Cinema sold 57 tickets to *Cosmo the Cougar*. Of those, 24 were children's tickets. About how many tickets were sold to adults?

You can estimate since you don't need an exact answer. First, round each number to the nearest ten. Then subtract.

$$\begin{array}{r} 57 \\ -\ 24 \\ \hline \end{array} \rightarrow \begin{array}{r} 60 \\ -\ 20 \\ \hline 40 \end{array} \leftarrow \text{estimated difference}$$

There were about 40 tickets sold to adults.

CLASS EXERCISES

Round to the nearest ten.

1. 48
2. 24
3. 31
4. 16
5. 89
6. 23
7. 45
8. 52
9. 18
10. 85

Estimate the difference.

11. $\begin{array}{r} 76 \\ -\ 23 \\ \hline \end{array} \rightarrow \begin{array}{r} 80 \\ -\ 20 \\ \hline \blacksquare \end{array}$

12. $\begin{array}{r} 86 \\ -\ 43 \\ \hline \end{array} \rightarrow \begin{array}{r} 90 \\ -\ 40 \\ \hline \blacksquare \end{array}$

13. $\begin{array}{r} 48 \\ -\ 24 \\ \hline \end{array} \rightarrow \begin{array}{r} 50 \\ -\ 20 \\ \hline \blacksquare \end{array}$

14. $\begin{array}{r} 92 \\ -\ 48 \\ \hline \end{array} \rightarrow \begin{array}{r} 90 \\ -\ 50 \\ \hline \blacksquare \end{array}$

15. $\begin{array}{r} 58 \\ -\ 32 \\ \hline \end{array} \rightarrow \begin{array}{r} \blacksquare \\ -\ \blacksquare \\ \hline \blacksquare \end{array}$

16. $\begin{array}{r} 31 \\ -\ 19 \\ \hline \end{array} \rightarrow \begin{array}{r} \blacksquare \\ -\ \blacksquare \\ \hline \blacksquare \end{array}$

PRACTICE

Round each number to the nearest ten. Estimate the difference.

17. $36 - 12$	**18.** $48 - 24$	**19.** $57 - 19$	**20.** $45 - 13$	**21.** $49 - 32$
22. $68 - 23$	**23.** $45 - 34$	**24.** $37 - 12$	**25.** $84 - 63$	**26.** $46 - 22$
27. $48 - 14$	**28.** $73 - 32$	**29.** $92 - 69$	**30.** $79 - 53$	**31.** $84 - 60$
32. $78 - 43$	**33.** $65 - 40$	**34.** $88 - 52$	**35.** $75 - 51$	**36.** $91 - 40$

Write the answer.

37. $87 + 25$ **38.** $17 + 22$ **39.** $8 - 2$ **40.** $867 + 75$ **41.** $20 - 14$

MIXED REVIEW

PROBLEM SOLVING APPLICATIONS
Using Estimation

Estimate the sum or difference.

42. Fritz swapped 47 stickers one week. The next week he swapped 28. About how many stickers did he swap in the two weeks?

43. Maria spent 27 minutes at the computer on Monday. She spent 35 minutes on the computer on Wednesday. About how many minutes did she spend on the computer in the two days?

CHECKING SUBTRACTION WITH ADDITION

Jeff subtracted 23 from 41 on his calculator.

41 [−] 23 [=] 18

To check his answer, Jeff added 23 to the difference.

18 [+] 23 [=] 41

Jeff knew the subtraction was right. He got the number with which he started.

It doesn't matter if you use a calculator or pencil and paper. You can still check subtraction with addition.

$$\begin{array}{r} {\scriptstyle 3\,11} \\ \not{4}\,\not{1} \\ -\ 2\,3 \\ \hline 1\,8 \end{array} \qquad \begin{array}{r} {\scriptstyle 1} \\ 1\,8 \\ +\ 2\,3 \\ \hline 4\,1 \end{array}$$

Think: What is another way to check the answer for this subtraction?

CLASS EXERCISES

What number would you add to check the answer?

1. $\begin{array}{r} 46 \\ -\ 15 \\ \hline 31 \end{array}$ $\begin{array}{r} 31 \\ +\ \square \\ \hline \end{array}$ **2.** $\begin{array}{r} 46 \\ -\ 35 \\ \hline 11 \end{array}$ $\begin{array}{r} 11 \\ +\ \square \\ \hline \end{array}$ **3.** $\begin{array}{r} 74 \\ -\ 29 \\ \hline 45 \end{array}$ $\begin{array}{r} 45 \\ +\ \square \\ \hline \end{array}$

PRACTICE

Subtract. Add to check your work.

4. $\begin{array}{r} 62 \\ -\ 18 \\ \hline \end{array}$ **5.** $\begin{array}{r} 74 \\ -\ 26 \\ \hline \end{array}$ **6.** $\begin{array}{r} 44 \\ -\ 19 \\ \hline \end{array}$ **7.** $\begin{array}{r} 91 \\ -\ 20 \\ \hline \end{array}$ **8.** $\begin{array}{r} 53 \\ -\ 32 \\ \hline \end{array}$

9. $76 - 74$

10. $45 - 29$

11. $33 - 25$

12. $80 - 25$

13. $72 - 49$

14. $90 - 53$

15. $68 - 18$

16. $71 - 48$

17. $50 - 38$

18. $62 - 25$

19. $43 - 16$

20. $84 - 75$

21. $55 - 39$

22. $88 - 27$

23. $70 - 49$

The subtraction was done on a calculator. Write what you would enter next to check the answer. Correct the answer if it is wrong.

CALCULATOR

24. $47 - 23 = 14$

25. $73 - 26 = 47$

26. $83 - 25 = 52$

27. $48 - 19 = 29$

28. $54 - 18 = 36$

29. $50 - 39 = 11$

30. $60 - 24 = 46$

31. $53 - 48 = 15$

PROBLEM SOLVING APPLICATIONS
Too Much Information

Find the facts you need. Solve.

32. On Monday, there were 7 puppies, 12 kittens, 14 gerbils, 22 white mice, and 71 fish at Friendly's Pet Shop. If 13 fish are sold, how many fish are left?

33. Aaron sold 29 leashes and 15 bones one day. He sold 82 plants and 17 leashes the next day. How many leashes did he sell?

34. Flea collars cost \$2.98. Dog sweaters cost \$10.95. There are 48 flea collars in each carton. How many flea collars are in 2 cartons?

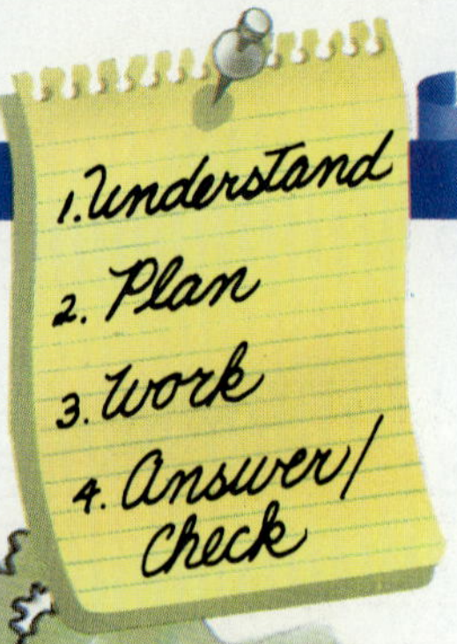

PROBLEM SOLVING

Strategy: Two-Step Problems

John bought two packages of paper plates for a picnic. Each package had 25 plates. If 36 plates were used, how many were left?

This problem takes two steps to solve. Before you can find the number left, you need to know how many plates there were in all.

Add to find out how many plates in all.

$$\begin{array}{r} {}^{1} \\ 25 \\ +\ 25 \\ \hline 50 \end{array}$$

Subtract to find out how many plates were left.

$$\begin{array}{r} {}^{4}\ {}^{10} \\ \not{5}\ \not{0} \\ -\ 3\ 6 \\ \hline 1\ 4 \end{array}$$

There were 14 plates left.

CLASS EXERCISES

Explain the steps you would use to solve the problem.

1. Beth brought 24 apples to the picnic. Phil brought 8. If 12 apples were eaten, how many were left?
2. Yuki grilled 9 fish and boiled 7. She had twice as many buns as fish. How many buns did she have?
3. Jill brought 12 tomatoes. Ernie brought 15. Jill sliced 6 tomatoes to put on hamburgers. How many tomatoes were left for the salad?

PRACTICE

Solve.

4. Pedro caught 18 fish. Bev caught 9. They cooked 7 fish. How many fish were not cooked?

5. 13 children played on one team and 15 on another. 6 children left the game. How many were still playing?

6. 28 children paddled canoes and 19 children rowed boats. The next day twice as many children rode in canoes and in boats. How many children rode the next day?

7. 36 children jumped into the lake. 38 other children waded into the lake. Of all the children in the lake, 13 floated on their backs. How many children did not float on their backs?

8. The children collected 78 logs for a fire. They burned 24 logs during storytelling. They burned 27 other logs during the songs. How many logs were left?

★ 9. Jim brought 50 forks and 37 spoons. Jean brought 75 forks and 46 spoons. How many more forks were there than spoons?

CHECKPOINT 1

Subtract. *(pages 96–101, 104–105)*

1. $50 - 4$
2. $60 - 26$
3. $73 - 49$
4. $59 - 43$
5. $82 - 37$
6. $95 - 28$

Round to the nearest ten. Estimate. *(pages 102–103)*

7. $58 - 32$
8. $61 - 37$
9. $89 - 32$

Solve. *(pages 106–107)*

10. The campers looked for 100 bugs. Ian found 39 bugs. Sandra found 17 more. How many bugs weren't found?

Extra practice on page 406

THREE-DIGIT SUBTRACTION

When you subtract, look at the ones. You may need to rename 1 ten as 10 ones.

	h	t	o
	7	5	2
−	4	3	6

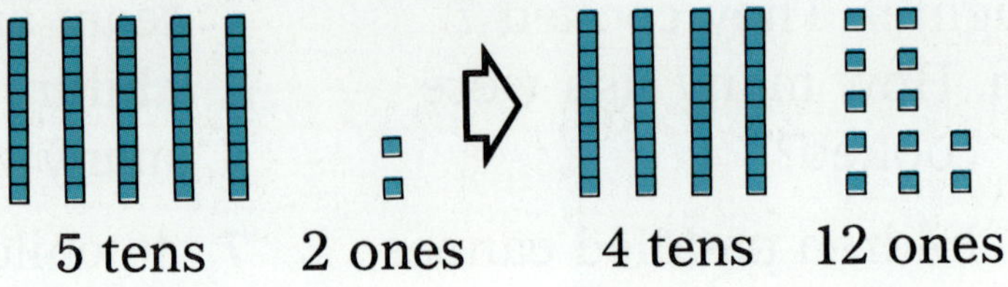

Rename.
Subtract the ones.

	h	t	o
		4	12
	7	~~5~~	~~2~~
−	4	3	6
			6

Subtract the tens.

	h	t	o
		4	12
	7	~~5~~	~~2~~
−	4	3	6
		1	6

Subtract the hundreds.

	h	t	o
		4	12
	7	~~5~~	~~2~~
−	4	3	6
	3	1	6

CLASS EXERCISES

Do you need to rename? Subtract.

1.

	h	t	o
	4	7	8
−	1	4	9

2.

	h	t	o
	2	2	5
−	1	1	6

3.

	h	t	o
	8	8	7
−	5	5	2

4.

	h	t	o
	6	3	3
−	1	1	4

5.

	h	t	o
	9	8	8
−	3	4	5

6.

	h	t	o
	4	7	2
−	2	5	6

PRACTICE

Subtract.

7. $\begin{array}{r} 564 \\ -\ 138 \\ \hline \end{array}$ **8.** $\begin{array}{r} 792 \\ -\ 524 \\ \hline \end{array}$ **9.** $\begin{array}{r} 649 \\ -\ 126 \\ \hline \end{array}$ **10.** $\begin{array}{r} 995 \\ -\ 786 \\ \hline \end{array}$ **11.** $\begin{array}{r} 256 \\ -\ 133 \\ \hline \end{array}$

12. 642 − 223 13. 758 − 117 14. 990 − 367 15. 846 − 517 16. 984 − 735

17. 783 − 256 18. 776 − 329 19. 697 − 345 20. 885 − 469 21. 953 − 137

22. 460 − 125 23. 869 − 146 24. 884 − 326 25. 978 − 542 26. 483 − 156

27. 572 − 254 28. 987 − 645 29. 861 − 322

30. 586 − 179 31. 931 − 415 32. 883 − 457

Find the missing number.

★ 33. 587 − 24□ = 342 ★ 34. 964 − □38 = 726 ★ 35. 651 − 31□ = 332 ★ 36. 724 − 31□ = 406 ★ 37. 126 − 11□ = 14

Write the answer. Add to check your work.

MIXED REVIEW

38. 417 − 105 39. 16 − 9 40. 476 − 220 41. 67 − 35 42. 277 − 66

43. 682 − 544 44. 60 − 8 45. 9 − 3 46. 970 − 865 47. 53 − 15

PROBLEM SOLVING APPLICATIONS
Choosing the Operation

Solve.

48. Dolly planted 125 tulip bulbs. Squirrels ate 19 bulbs. How many tulips can Dolly expect in the spring?

49. Zachary planted 25 crocuses, 30 irises, and 50 tulips. Which is greater, the number of irises or the number of tulips?

THREE-DIGIT SUBTRACTION

To subtract 135 from 429, you first subtract the ones.

$$\begin{array}{r} 429 \\ -\ 135 \\ \hline 4 \end{array}$$

Rename 1 hundred as 10 tens.

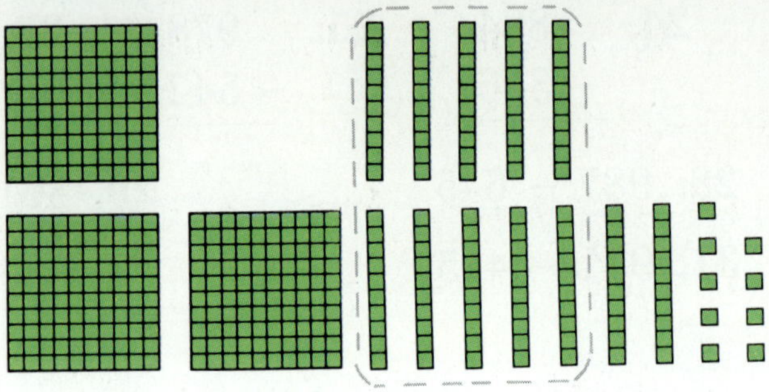

Subtract the tens.

$$\begin{array}{r} {\scriptstyle 3\ 12} \\ \not{4}\,\not{2}\,9 \\ -\ 1\ 3\ 5 \\ \hline 9\ 4 \end{array}$$

Subtract the hundreds.

$$\begin{array}{r} {\scriptstyle 3\ 12} \\ \not{4}\,\not{2}\,9 \\ -\ 1\ 3\ 5 \\ \hline 2\ 9\ 4 \end{array}$$

You can estimate the difference with three-digit numbers. Round each number to the nearest hundred. Then subtract.

$$\begin{array}{r} 429 \\ -\ 135 \\ \hline \end{array} \begin{array}{c} \rightarrow \\ \rightarrow \\ \\ \end{array} \begin{array}{r} 400 \\ -\ 100 \\ \hline 300 \end{array}$$

CLASS EXERCISES

Rename. What is the missing number?

1. 4 hundreds 5 tens = 3 hundreds __?__ tens
2. 3 hundreds 0 tens = 2 hundreds __?__ tens
3. 8 hundreds 3 tens = __?__ hundreds 13 tens

What is the difference?

4. $\begin{array}{r} 852 \\ -\ 352 \\ \hline \end{array}$ 5. $\begin{array}{r} 842 \\ -\ 352 \\ \hline \end{array}$ 6. $\begin{array}{r} 832 \\ -\ 352 \\ \hline \end{array}$ 7. $\begin{array}{r} 822 \\ -\ 352 \\ \hline \end{array}$ 8. $\begin{array}{r} 812 \\ -\ 352 \\ \hline \end{array}$

PRACTICE

Subtract.

9. 782 − 541	10. 845 − 551	11. 904 − 461	12. 569 − 184	13. 942 − 271
14. 407 − 295	15. 916 − 354	16. 758 − 163	17. 698 − 395	18. 708 − 262
19. 609 − 183	20. 826 − 173	21. 593 − 281	22. 518 − 396	23. 849 − 491

24. 872 − 351 **25.** 549 − 265 **26.** 717 − 496

27. 654 − 382 **28.** 438 − 132 **29.** 907 − 770

30. Subtract 356 from 529. **31.** Subtract 75 from 626.

32. Subtract 140 from 832. **33.** Subtract 98 from 209.

Round to the nearest hundred. Estimate the difference. ESTIMATE

34. 921 − 341	35. 817 − 196	36. 436 − 155	37. 880 − 690	38. 920 − 159
39. 621 − 371	40. 869 − 178	41. 937 − 111	42. 859 − 507	43. 907 − 433

PROBLEM SOLVING APPLICATIONS
Function Machine

The difference machine subtracts one number from another.

Complete the chart for a machine that subtracts 72.

	44.	45.	46.	47.	48.
IN	639	458	324	247	566
OUT	?	?	?	?	?

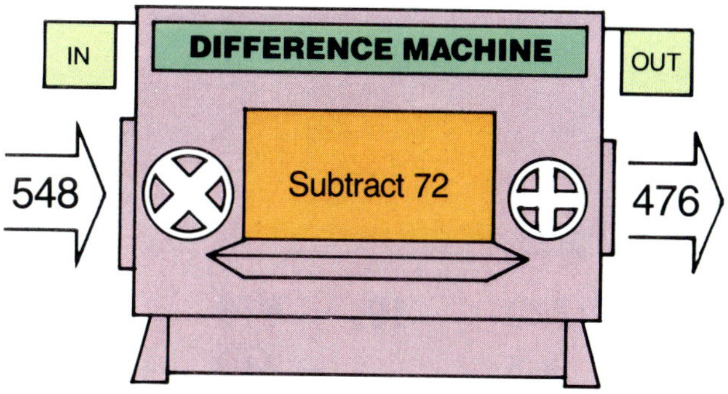

THREE-DIGIT SUBTRACTION

Students planted 435 trees. They planted 189 maple trees. The rest were pine trees. How many pine trees did they plant?

To find out, you can subtract 189 from 435. You need to rename twice.

Rename 3 tens 5 ones as 2 tens 15 ones. Subtract the ones.

$$\begin{array}{r} 2\ 15 \\ 4\ \not{3}\ \not{5} \\ -\ 1\ 8\ 9 \\ \hline 6 \end{array}$$

Rename 4 hundreds 2 tens as 3 hundreds 12 tens. Subtract the tens.

$$\begin{array}{r} 12\ \ \\ 3\ \not{2}\ 15 \\ \not{4}\ \not{3}\ \not{5} \\ -\ 1\ 8\ 9 \\ \hline 4\ 6 \end{array}$$

Subtract the hundreds.

$$\begin{array}{r} 12\ \ \\ 3\ \not{2}\ 15 \\ \not{4}\ \not{3}\ \not{5} \\ -\ 1\ 8\ 9 \\ \hline 2\ 4\ 6 \end{array}$$

The students planted 246 pine trees.

CLASS EXERCISES

Subtract. How many times do you need to rename?

1. $\begin{array}{r} 538 \\ -\ 214 \\ \hline \end{array}$
2. $\begin{array}{r} 538 \\ -\ 219 \\ \hline \end{array}$
3. $\begin{array}{r} 538 \\ -\ 244 \\ \hline \end{array}$
4. $\begin{array}{r} 538 \\ -\ 249 \\ \hline \end{array}$
5. $\begin{array}{r} 356 \\ -\ 143 \\ \hline \end{array}$
6. $\begin{array}{r} 356 \\ -\ 148 \\ \hline \end{array}$
7. $\begin{array}{r} 356 \\ -\ 173 \\ \hline \end{array}$
8. $\begin{array}{r} 356 \\ -\ 178 \\ \hline \end{array}$

PRACTICE

Subtract.

9. $\begin{array}{r} 732 \\ -\ 365 \\ \hline \end{array}$
10. $\begin{array}{r} 676 \\ -\ 342 \\ \hline \end{array}$
11. $\begin{array}{r} 418 \\ -\ 129 \\ \hline \end{array}$
12. $\begin{array}{r} 533 \\ -\ 246 \\ \hline \end{array}$
13. $\begin{array}{r} 726 \\ -\ 239 \\ \hline \end{array}$

14. 641 − 169

15. 855 − 342

16. 831 − 456

17. 412 − 236

18. 752 − 364

19. 543 − 378

20. 651 − 495

21. 632 − 289

22. 926 − 389

23. 841 − 588

24. 317 − 158

25. 924 − 513

26. 741 − 597

27. 637 − 302

28. 812 − 649

29. Find the difference between 952 and 786.

30. Subtract 479 from 763.

31. Which is greater, 947 or 689? How much greater?

Write the answer.

MIXED REVIEW

32. 846 + 319

33. 775 + 38

34. 615 − 406

35. 70 − 59

36. 198 + 217

37. 465 − 288

38. 67 + 39

39. 280 − 95

40. 77 + 33

41. 550 − 275

PROBLEM SOLVING APPLICATIONS
Logical Thinking

Find the number for each leaf.

42. I am 113 less than 159.

43. I am 121 less than 350.

44. I am 204 less than 350.

45. I am 183 less than 229.

46. I am the sum of 46 and 154.

★ 47. I am the sum of 46, 159, 350, and 224.

SUBTRACTING WITH ZEROS

Three hundred people flew in a jet. The plane landed in Chicago and 178 people got off. How many people were still on the plane?

To find out, you can subtract 178 from 300. You must rename. There are no tens that you can rename to give you some ones. You must first rename a hundred to give you some tens.

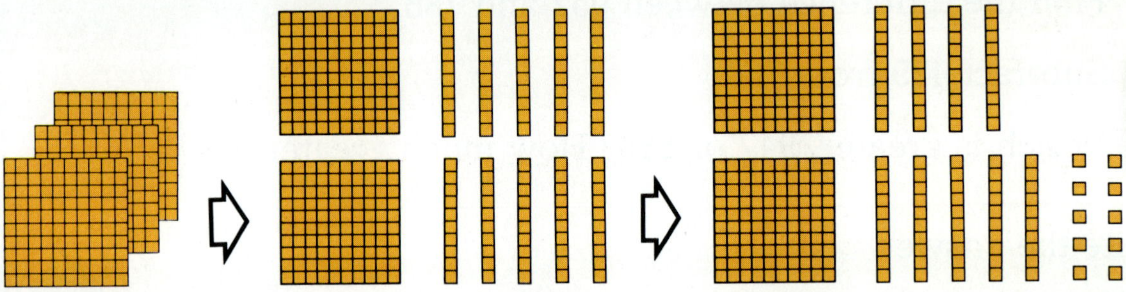

Rename the hundreds.

```
 2 10
 3̸ 0̸ 0
− 1 7 8
```

Rename 10 tens as 9 tens 10 ones.

```
    9
 2 1̸0̸ 10
 3̸ 0̸ 0̸
− 1 7 8
```

Subtract.

```
    9
 2 1̸0̸ 10
 3̸ 0̸ 0̸
− 1 7 8
  1 2 2
```

CLASS EXERCISES

What is the difference?

1. $200 - 155$ $\quad$ $203 - 155$
2. $400 - 342$ $\quad$ $401 - 342$
3. $500 - 366$ $\quad$ $502 - 366$
4. $900 - 27$ $\quad$ $903 - 27$
5. $100 - 86$ $\quad$ $105 - 86$
6. $700 - 435$ $\quad$ $701 - 435$

PRACTICE

7. $800 - 608$
8. $100 - 74$
9. $600 - 103$
10. $300 - 99$
11. $900 - 819$
12. $400 - 106$
13. $204 - 36$
14. $500 - 206$
15. $700 - 496$
16. $300 - 7$
17. $300 - 6$
18. $600 - 3$
19. $705 - 8$
20. $900 - 2$
21. $200 - 5$
22. $505 - 8$
23. $600 - 17$
24. $403 - 121$
25. $800 - 23$
26. $709 - 105$
27. $100 - 23$
28. $703 - 304$
29. $600 - 56$
30. $400 - 75$
31. $800 - 76$
32. $502 - 4$
33. $200 - 9$
34. $700 - 7$

PROBLEM SOLVING APPLICATIONS

The table shows the number of people that can ride at one time. Use the table to solve.

VEHICLE	NUMBER OF PEOPLE
Taxi 	4
Bus 	43
747 Jet 	500

35. How many more people can ride in a 747 than in a bus?
36. How many more people can ride in a 747 than in a taxi?
37. How many people can ride in a taxi and a bus altogether?

★ 38. About how many bus loads would it take to fill a 747?

FOUR-DIGIT SUBTRACTION

When you subtract greater numbers, you may need to rename the thousands. To subtract 1899 from 6383, you have to rename three times.

Rename the tens. Subtract the ones.	Rename the hundreds. Subtract the tens.	Rename the thousands. Subtract the hundreds.	Subtract the thousands.
7 13	17 2 7 13	12 17 5 2 7 13	12 17 5 2 7 13
6 3 8 3	6 3 8 3	6 3 8 3	6 3 8 3
− 1 8 9 9	− 1 8 9 9	− 1 8 9 9	− 1 8 9 9
4	8 4	4 8 4	4 4 8 4

CLASS EXERCISES

Subtract. How many times do you need to rename?

1.	4658 − 3600	4658 − 3700	**2.**	7359 − 1830	7359 − 1860	**3.**	5466 − 2972	5466 − 2977

PRACTICE

Subtract.

4. 4325 − 2101	**5.** 3061 − 1829	**6.** 7115 − 498	**7.** 4723 − 4445	**8.** 5783 − 2462
9. 7846 − 5294	**10.** 4923 − 68	**11.** 4269 − 1826	**12.** 6347 − 3475	**13.** 7638 − 2599
14. 5648 − 2357	**15.** 7086 − 4328	**16.** 6729 − 3459	**17.** 5248 − 3159	**18.** 7603 − 3429

19.	6767 − 913	**20.**	5835 − 3245	**21.**	7562 − 2349	**22.**	8923 − 3837	**23.**	5387 − 3142
24.	7115 − 504	**25.**	8990 − 3576	**26.**	4115 − 523	**27.**	5329 − 2477	**28.**	7301 − 1528
29.	8145 − 6368	**30.**	7423 − 4607	**31.**	4938 − 3417	**32.**	5867 − 1442	**33.**	9539 − 7427
34.	7263 − 4102	**35.**	8062 − 5214	**36.**	5326 − 1429	**37.**	9728 − 1656	**38.**	6439 − 2354

39. 2450 − 1785

40. 4524 − 2845

41. 5672 − 2899

42. 3983 − 1852

43. 7603 − 5919

44. 1042 − 879

PROBLEM SOLVING APPLICATIONS

Use the table to answer the question.

45. How many clay pots are in the history museum?

46. How many chairs and rugs are there altogether?

47. How many more hats are there than tools?

48. How many more tools are there than chairs?

★ **49.** Two of the items in the table have a total number of 2441. Which items are they?

HISTORY MUSEUM

ITEM	NUMBER
clay pots	1246
hats	1899
rugs	797
chairs	846
tools	1595

PROBLEM SOLVING

Strategy: Reasonable Answers

1. Understand
2. Plan
3. Work
4. Answer/Check

Burt works at Harlequin's Costume Shop. Burt had 537 costumes. In one week he rented 194 of the costumes. Burt's boss asked him how many costumes were left.

Burt subtracted to find out.

$$\begin{array}{r} {\scriptstyle 13} \\ 5\not{3}7 \\ -194 \\ \hline 443 \end{array}$$

Next, he estimated to check his answer.

$$\begin{array}{r} 500 \\ -200 \\ \hline 300 \end{array}$$

Burt's estimate wasn't close. He knew his answer wasn't reasonable.

Burt went back to check his subtraction. Burt forgot to rename the hundreds. He corrected his work.

$$\begin{array}{r} {\scriptstyle 4\,13} \\ \not{5}\not{3}7 \\ -194 \\ \hline 343 \text{ costumes} \end{array}$$

CLASS EXERCISES

Is the answer reasonable? Use estimation to check. If the answer is not reasonable, tell what went wrong.

1. Jane needs 315 tree costumes. She only has 196. How many more tree costumes does Jane need?

$$\begin{array}{r} {\scriptstyle 1\,1} \\ 315 \\ -196 \\ \hline 511 \text{ costumes} \end{array}$$

2. Ace Delivery Service delivers 150 pirate masks, 185 ballerina masks, and 225 butterfly masks. How many masks does Ace deliver in all?

$$\begin{array}{r} {\scriptstyle 1} \\ 150 \\ 185 \\ +225 \\ \hline 460 \text{ masks} \end{array}$$

PRACTICE

If the answer is reasonable, write *R*. If not, give the correct answer.

3. Peter got an order for 63 dinosaur tails. Last week he made 13 tails. How many more tails does Peter need?
   Answer: 40 tails

4. Sue Ellen counted 482 fake ears, 119 curly wigs, and 267 clown noses. How many items did she count?
   Answer: 868 items

5. Rose sewed 388 stars on a princess gown and 509 stars on a wizard robe. How many stars did she sew on in all?
   Answer: 121 stars

6. There were 28 parts in a play. 72 people tried out. How many people didn't get parts?
   Answer: 44 people

7. The shop rented 315 alligator costumes and 183 lion costumes. How many more alligator than lion costumes did they rent?
   Answer: 232 more

★ 8. Pat sewed 38 tails on lion costumes, 19 tails on dragon costumes, and 61 tails on cat costumes. He had 22 tails left. With how many tails did Pat start?
   Answer: 120 tails

CHECKPOINT 2

Write the answer. *(pages 108–117)*

1. $\begin{array}{r} 528 \\ -\ 246 \\ \hline \end{array}$

2. $\begin{array}{r} 423 \\ -\ 184 \\ \hline \end{array}$

3. $\begin{array}{r} 600 \\ -\ 237 \\ \hline \end{array}$

4. $\begin{array}{r} 8462 \\ -\ 4398 \\ \hline \end{array}$

Write *R* if the answer is reasonable or give the correct answer. *(pages 118–119)*

5. The costume shop had 568 masks. 257 masks were sold. How many masks were left?
   Answer: 411 masks

Extra practice on page 406

CHAPTER 4 TEST

Write the answer. *(pages 96–101, 104–105)*

1. $40 - 8$ **2.** $60 - 23$ **3.** $58 - 34$ **4.** $53 - 28$ **5.** $84 - 59$

Round to the nearest ten. Estimate the difference. *(pages 102–103)*

6. $39 - 11$ **7.** $87 - 41$ **8.** $38 - 12$ **9.** $67 - 32$ **10.** $62 - 48$

Solve. *(pages 106–107)*

11. Beth has 17 stamps. She buys 25 more. She uses 35 stamps on her party invitations. How many stamps does Beth have left?

12. Bert picked 13 peaches. Carrie picked 9. They ate 6 peaches and saved the rest. How many peaches did they save?

Write the answer. *(pages 108–117)*

13. $903 - 651$ **14.** $614 - 156$ **15.** $700 - 382$ **16.** $4225 - 2318$

If the answer is reasonable, write *R*. If the answer is not reasonable, give the correct answer. *(pages 118–119)*

17. For the class party, there were 23 red balloons, 31 green balloons, and 14 blue balloons. How many balloons were there in all?
Answer: 58 balloons

Extra practice on page 407

MATHEMATICS and MUSIC

Over 200 years ago Wolfgang Mozart wrote music. People still love to listen to his works.

Mozart was born in Austria in 1756. He loved music when he was 3 years old. In 1760 he learned to play musical instruments. Mozart wrote his first music in 1761.

WHEN DID MOZART START?

Use the dates above to solve.

1. What was Mozart's age when he first played an instrument?
2. How old was Mozart when he wrote his first music?
3. Mozart was 14 years older than Beethoven. When was Beethoven born?
4. Mozart met Beethoven in 1787. How old was Mozart then?
5. Dates from 1900 to 1999 are in the 20th Century. Dates from 1800 to 1899 are in the 19th Century. In what century was Mozart born?
6. How many years ago was Mozart born?

Enrichment

Look at the number path. The rules are above the arrows. Add or subtract to complete.

1.

Copy the path. Pick another number between 50 and 99 for the first number. Follow the rules.

2.

3. What can you say about the first and last numbers?

Make three copies of the number path below. Pick three numbers from 1 to 49 for the first numbers in the three copies. Follow the rules.

4.

FOLLOWING NUMBER PATHS

5. What can you say about the first and last numbers?

Copy the path. Write the rules to go from start to finish.

6.

7.

Copy the path. Write your own rules. Fill the number path using only one-digit numbers. Start at the beginning and add or subtract a different number at each step.

8.

9.

Copy the path. Fill in the number path using 1, 5, 10, 25, or 50 for each rule.

10.

11.

CUMULATIVE REVIEW

Choose the correct answer. Choose *a*, *b*, *c*, or *d*.

Find the matching value.

1. 694¢
- **a.** $69.4
- **b.** $694
- **c.** $6.94
- **d.** none of these

2. 1 dollar 3 pennies
- **a.** $10.30
- **b.** $1.03
- **c.** $1.30
- **d.** none of these

3. eight dollars and fifty cents
- **a.** $8.50
- **b.** $850.
- **c.** $85.00
- **d.** none of these

Compare the numbers.

4. 57 ▢ 56
- **a.** $>$
- **b.** $<$
- **c.** $=$
- **d.** none of these

5. 671 ▢ 722
- **a.** $>$
- **b.** $<$
- **c.** $=$
- **d.** none of these

6. 477 ▢ 493
- **a.** $>$
- **b.** $<$
- **c.** $=$
- **d.** none of these

Round to the nearest ten or hundred.
Estimate the sum.

7. 38 + 46
- **a.** 40
- **b.** 50
- **c.** 90
- **d.** 60

8. 612 + 123
- **a.** 400
- **b.** 900
- **c.** 700
- **d.** 500

9. 488 + 224
- **a.** 700
- **b.** 200
- **c.** 900
- **d.** 500

Find the answer.

10. 4 + 1 + 5 + 7
- **a.** 17
- **b.** 16
- **c.** 15
- **d.** none of these

11. 6 + 3 + (5 + 5)
- **a.** 29
- **b.** 19
- **c.** 18
- **d.** none of these

12. 2 + 4 + 6 + 8
- **a.** 16
- **b.** 20
- **c.** 18
- **d.** none of these

13. $\begin{array}{r} 20 \\ 34 \\ +\ 17 \\ \hline \end{array}$

a. 70
b. 61
c. 71
d. none of these

14. $\begin{array}{r} 46 \\ 26 \\ +\ 13 \\ \hline \end{array}$

a. 75
b. 74
c. 85
d. none of these

15. $\begin{array}{r} 39 \\ 45 \\ +\ 18 \\ \hline \end{array}$

a. 102
b. 92
c. 100
d. none of these

Find the answer.

16. $\begin{array}{r} 372 \\ +\ 419 \\ \hline \end{array}$

a. 781
b. 791
c. 891
d. none of these

17. $\begin{array}{r} 2407 \\ +\ 5846 \\ \hline \end{array}$

a. 8243
b. 8353
c. 7253
d. none of these

18. $\begin{array}{r} 7873 \\ +\ 1458 \\ \hline \end{array}$

a. 9331
b. 9221
c. 9231
d. none of these

LANGUAGE and VOCABULARY REVIEW

Read each sentence. On your paper, write *true* or *false*.

1. You read $5 > 2$ as "5 is less than 2."
2. You read $2 < 5$ as "2 is greater than 5."
3. 23 can be renamed as two tens and three ones.
4. 217 rounded to the nearest hundred is 200.
5. 500¢ has the same value as five dollars.

MEMORY

A computer can remember things. Suppose you give the computer words and numbers to remember. The computer will store them in its **memory**.

Each number, letter, and sign is given a special place in the computer's memory. The special place is called an **address.**

You can see that the address of N is 5.

Write the input that is stored at the address.

Example: Address: 3 2

Input: H I

1. Address: 2 7 8

Input: ? ? ?

2. Address: 7 3 8 7 11

Input: ? ? ? ? ?

3. Address: 12 6 4 1 10

Input: ? ? ? ? ?

4. Address: 12 4 10 7 3 2 7 11 8 5 9

Input: ? ? ? ? ? ? ? ? ? ? ?

5

How many pennies equal a dime? How many dimes equal a dollar? How many one dollar bills equal a ten dollar bill?

MONEY AND TIME

RECOGNIZING MONEY

To write amounts of money, you can use the cents sign (¢) or you can use a dollar sign ($) and decimal point (.).

Here are the coins and bills you should know.

penny	**nickel**	**dime**	**quarter**	**half dollar**
1¢ or \$.01	5¢ or \$.05	10¢ or \$.10	25¢ or \$.25	50¢ or \$.50

one dollar	**five dollars**	**ten dollars**
100¢ or \$1.00	500¢ or \$5.00	1000¢ or \$10.00

CLASS EXERCISES

Answer the question. Use ¢ and then use \$ and . to write the amount two ways.

1. Count by 5's. How many nickels are in 25¢?

2. Count by 25's. How many quarters are in \$1.00?

3. Count by 50's. How many half dollars are in \$1.00?

PRACTICE

Use $ and . to write the value.

4. 5¢ **5.** 871¢ **6.** 1704¢ **7.** 85¢ **8.** 1090¢

9. 5 dollars 4 nickels

10. 4 dollars 5 quarters

11. 6 dollars 1 half dollar

12. 18 dollars 6 half dollars

Write the number of coins needed to make the amount.

13. _?_ pennies make $.50

14. _?_ quarters make $.50

15. _?_ dimes make $.50

16. _?_ nickels make $.50

17. _?_ half dollars make $2.00.

18. _?_ dimes make $1.00

Compare the values. Write < or >.

19. 1 half dollar ■ 1 quarter

20. 1 nickel ■ 1 dime

21. 5 nickels ■ 3 quarters

22. 1 dime 4 nickels ■ 1 quarter

Write the answer.

MIXED REVIEW

23.	36 − 17	**24.**	347 + 526	**25.**	457 − 165	**26.**	78 − 49	**27.**	4865 + 3527
28.	637 − 275	**29.**	487 − 298	**30.**	603 − 471	**31.**	700 − 534	**32.**	7349 − 2685

PROBLEM SOLVING APPLICATIONS
Using Money

Solve.

33. Ellis put a five dollar bill and 4 quarters into his piggy bank. The next day he took out 2 quarters. How much money was left in the piggy bank?

★ **34.** Sherm had 4 half dollars. He used 1 half dollar to pay for an apple. He got a dime back in change. How much money did Sherm have left?

COUNTING MONEY

It's often easier to count money if you first order the values from greatest to least.

$1 25¢ 25¢ 10¢ 5¢ 1¢

Now, count mentally.

Think: $1.00 . . . $1.25 . . . $1.50 . . . $1.60 . . . $1.65 . . . $1.66

The total is $1.66.

CLASS EXERCISES

What is the total value?

1.

2.

3.

4.

Complete.

5. 2 nickels = ? ¢ **6.** 1 quarter = ? ¢ **7.** 5 nickels = ? ¢

8. 5 dimes = ? ¢ **9.** 10 dimes = ? ¢ **10.** 60 pennies = ? ¢

PRACTICE

MENTAL MATH

Count mentally. Use $ and . to write the total value.

11.

12.

13.

14.

15.

16.

PROBLEM SOLVING APPLICATIONS
Using a Table

Use the table to solve.

17. How much money does the pig have?

18. How much money does the bear have?

★ **19.** What is the greatest number of coins the pig can have and still have the same amount of money?

★ **20.** What is the least number of coins the bear can have and still have the same amount of money?

COINS IN POCKET

PIG	BEAR
2 half dollars	1 quarter
1 quarter	2 dimes
1 dime	1 nickel
1 nickel	2 pennies

MAKING CHANGE

A clerk makes change by counting. The cost of an airplane is 29¢. You give the clerk 50¢. Starting with the cost, the clerk counts out coins from 29¢ to 50¢.

Count: *twenty-nine, thirty, forty, fifty*

The clerk gives one penny and two dimes, or 21¢, for change.

Estimate to make sure you get the correct change. Round the amounts to the nearest ten cents and subtract mentally.

Think: 50¢ − 30¢ = 20¢

Since 20¢ is close to 21¢, you probably have the correct change.

CLASS EXERCISES

Choose the correct change. Write *a* or *b*.

1. You spend 38¢. You give the clerk 40¢.

a. 

b. 

2. You spend 69¢. You give the clerk 75¢.

a. 

b. 

PRACTICE

Match. Write the letter for the correct change.

3. cost: 13¢
you give: 25¢
change: ?

4. cost: 31¢
you give: 50¢
change: ?

5. cost: 27¢
you give: 35¢
change: ?

A. 

B. 

C. 

List the coins you would get as change.
Use as few coins as possible.

6. cost: 11¢
you give: 20¢
change: ?

7. cost: 28¢
you give: 50¢
change: ?

8. cost: 74¢
you give: $1.00
change: ?

Estimate. Write *yes* or *no* to tell if the correct change is given.

ESTIMATE

9. cost: 79¢
you give: 90¢
change: 11¢

10. cost: 31¢
you give: 50¢
change: 45¢

11. cost: 69¢
you give: 75¢
change: 30¢

PROBLEM SOLVING APPLICATIONS
Nonroutine Problems

When Gil makes change he likes to use as few coins as possible. One day Gil runs out of dimes and quarters. List the coins Gil uses to make change.

12. A sports car costs 32¢. Gil is given a dollar.

13. A squeaky duck costs 64¢. Gil is given a dollar.

ADDING AND SUBTRACTING MONEY

Jean has $10.00. She buys a kite for $4.78. She gets 5 dollars, 2 dimes, and 2 pennies in change.

To find the total amount of change, Jean can count the change or she can add.

5 dollars →	$5.00	
2 dimes →	.20	
2 pennies →	+ .02	
	$5.22	

Jean lines up the decimal points and adds. Then she writes a dollar sign and decimal point in the answer.

Jean can also subtract the price of the kite from the amount she gives the clerk.

```
    9 10
  9 1̶0̶
$1̶ 0̶.0̶ 0̶
−   4.7 8
---------
$   5.2 2
```

Line up the decimal points.

Most calculators don't have a $ key. You have to remember to write $ when you copy the answer.

10.00 [−] 4.78 [=] 5.22

CLASS EXERCISES

What is the sum or difference?

1. 49 + 24

2. 49¢ + 24¢

3. $.49 + .24

4. $3.49 + 2.24

5. $23.49 + 12.24

6. 72 − 34

7. 72¢ − 34¢

8. $.72 − .34

9. $5.72 − 3.34

10. $65.72 − 23.34

PRACTICE

Add or subtract. Watch the signs!

11. $.48 + .37

12. $28.61 − 13.72

13. $20.00 − 3.73

14. $64.16 + 22.37

15. $65.37 + 31.59

16. $50.00 − 13.85

17. $26.12 + 72.97

18. $86.33 − 44.28

19. $40.00 + 41.49

20. $16.22 + 71.49

21. $10.00 − 7.97

22. $.49 + .56

23. $19.21 − 8.38

24. $67.46 − 14.89

25. $ 9.51 + 35.64

26. $88.42 − 64.78

27. $9.37 + $3.42

28. $31.73 − $9.24

29. $74.43 − $8.85

30. $86.18 − $9.97

31. $21.45 − $7.79

32. $11.32 + $5.48

★ **33.** $14.95 + $.07 + $3.64

★ **34.** $63.56 + $14.08 + $5.99

Write the answer you would get if you entered this on a calculator.

CALCULATOR

35. 7.67 [+] 15.43 [=]

36. 67.05 [−] 0.96 [=]

PROBLEM SOLVING APPLICATIONS
Choosing the Operation

Solve.

37. Paul has $5.00 to spend. He buys red paint for $1.98. How much money does he have left?

38. Bernice buys a chair for $48.95 and a matching rug for $14.50. How much money does she spend in all?

★ **39.** Phil buys a $4.25 word game and a $3.69 puzzle. How much change does he get from $10.00?

PROBLEM SOLVING

Strategy: Estimating with Money

Richard stops at a hobby shop to buy paint and a piece of track. Before he pays, he estimates the cost.

$.89	→	$.90	Round amounts less than a dollar to the nearest ten cents.
+ .42	→	+ .40	
		$1.30	

The clerk asks Richard for $1.31. The cost is reasonable.

Richard sees two train engines. One engine costs $35.96. The other costs $24.14. Richard estimates the difference in price.

$35.96	→	$36.00	Round amounts greater than a dollar to the nearest dollar.
− 24.14	→	− 24.00	
		$12.00	

Richard's estimate is $12.00. The exact difference is $11.82.

CLASS EXERCISES

Round to the nearest ten cents or dollar.

1. $.15 **2.** $.32 **3.** $.89 **4.** $.21 **5.** $.45 **6.** $.36

7. $1.15 **8.** $1.89 **9.** $5.39 **10.** $12.98 **11.** $48.50 **12.** $10.75

Match. Write the letter. Solve the problem.

13. Loren had $15.34. She bought sunglasses for $12.98. About how much money did she have left?

A. $15.00 − 13.00

B. $13.00 + 15.00

PRACTICE

Estimate to solve.

14. Can you buy Monticello and Blue Ridge Mountains for $20.00?

15. About how much do a paint brush and a tube of glue cost altogether?

16. About how much more does the Golden Gate Bridge cost than Monticello?

17. About how much less does the Golden Gate Bridge cost than the United Nations building?

18. About how much do Monticello and the Blue Ridge Mountains cost altogether?

★ **19.** If you had $55.00, what is the greatest number of different kits you could buy? What are they?

★ **20.** About how much more is the United Nations buildings than the Monticello and Blue Ridge Mountains kits altogether?

CHECKPOINT 1

Use $ and . to write the value. *(pages 128–133)*

1. 3 dimes 2 nickels = ___?___

2. 4 nickels 1 quarter = ___?___

Write the answer. *(pages 134–135)*

3. $\begin{array}{r} \$.95 \\ +\ .27 \\ \hline \end{array}$ **4.** $\begin{array}{r} \$4.08 \\ -\ 1.28 \\ \hline \end{array}$

Estimate to solve. *(pages 136–137)*

5. Louisa bought a jump rope for $2.50 and a puzzle for $1.89. About how much did she spend?

6. A model ship costs $21.86. A model plane costs $14.19. About how much more does the ship cost than the plane?

Extra practice on page 408

TELLING TIME TO FIVE MINUTES

There are two hands on a clock. The short hand tells the hour. The long hand tells the minute. The long hand takes 5 minutes to move from one number to the next.

4 o'clock

5 minutes after 4

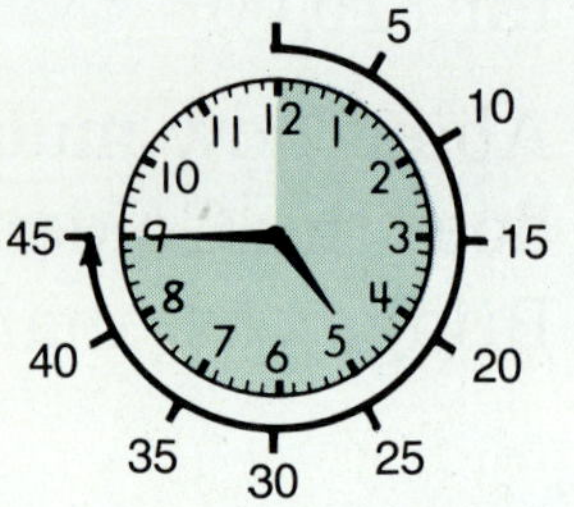

45 minutes after 4

You can read some times different ways.

15 minutes after 4
or
quarter past 4

30 minutes after 4
or
half past 4

CLASS EXERCISES

Count by fives. Complete the pattern.

1.

0	5	10	?	20	25	?	?	40	45	?	?	60

PRACTICE

Write the time.

2. 

_?_ o'clock

3. 

_?_ minutes after 4

4. 

_?_ minutes after 4

5. 

? minutes after ?

6. 

? minutes after ?

7. 

? minutes after ?

8. 

? minutes after ?

9. 

? minutes after ?

10. 

? minutes after ?

11. 

? minutes after ?

12. 

? minutes after ?

13. 

? minutes after ?

14. What's another way to read the time in Exercise 12?

15. What's another way to read the time in Exercise 13?

Write the answer.

MIXED REVIEW

16. 5 + 3 **17.** 15 + 3 **18.** 35 + 3 **19.** 55 + 3

20. 60 − 9 **21.** 60 − 12 **22.** 60 − 7 **23.** 60 − 35

PROBLEM SOLVING APPLICATIONS
Time of Day

Write the letter to match.

24. 12 o'clock noon

25. 30 minutes after 3 in the afternoon

26. 8 o'clock at night

27. 7 o'clock in the morning

A. 

Get up.

B. 

Eat lunch.

C. 

Go home from school.

D. 

Go to bed.

28. Using the letters, order the activities from early in the day to late in the day.

TELLING TIME TO THE MINUTE

There are 60 minutes in an hour.

It takes 1 minute for the long hand to move from one short mark to the next short mark.

You can say *17 minutes after 8* or *eight seventeen.*

You can write 8:17.

On this clock, the last number changes every minute.

You can say *17 minutes after 8* or *eight seventeen.*

You can write 8:17.

Sometimes you see times written with A.M. or P.M. A.M. means before noon. P.M. means after noon.

6 minutes after 5 in the morning ⟶ 5:06 A.M.

CLASS EXERCISES

Complete.

1. 

22 minutes after ___?___
7 : ___?___

2. 

29 minutes after ___?___
10 : ___?___

3. 

___?___ minutes after 10
___?___ : 50

PRACTICE

Complete.

4. 

___?___ minutes after ___?___
___?___ : ___?___

5. 

___?___ minutes after ___?___
___?___ : ___?___

6. 

___?___ minutes after ___?___
___?___ : ___?___

7. 

? : ?

8. 

? : ?

9. 

? : ?

Write the time in words.

10. 

11. 

12. 

Write the time using A.M. or P.M.

13. 13 minutes past 2 in the afternoon

14. 24 minutes past 8 in the evening

15. 7 minutes past 9 in the morning

16. 38 minutes past 11 at night

PROBLEM SOLVING APPLICATIONS
Using Time

Solve.

17. Caryl wants to leave for her uncle's house in 30 minutes. It is 1:00 P.M. When will Caryl leave?

18. The time is 5 o'clock in the afternoon. Caryl plans to eat in 18 minutes. When will Caryl eat?

19. Caryl falls asleep on the sofa. When she wakes up the sun is setting. Her clock shows 6:15. Write the time Caryl wakes up using A.M. or P.M.

20. Caryl must leave for piano practice at 20 minutes after 6 in the evening. Caryl's clock shows 6:32 P.M. Is Caryl early, late, or on time?

TELLING TIME BEFORE AND AFTER THE HOUR

Mike and Jemma want to be at band practice by 2:00 P.M. Mike plans to leave at 40 minutes after 1. Jemma plans to leave 20 minutes before 2. Who is going to leave first?

To find out, you can count on a clock.

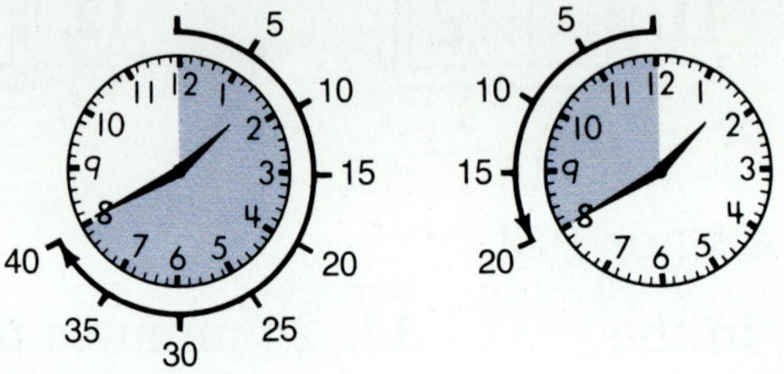

40 minutes after 1
1:40

20 minutes before 2
1:40

Mike and Jemma leave at the same time.

If you have this kind of clock, you may have to subtract. ⇨

$$\begin{array}{r} 60 \text{ minutes in an hour} \\ - \ 40 \text{ minutes after 1} \\ \hline 20 \text{ minutes before 2} \end{array}$$

You can round time to the nearest five minutes. This clock shows 3:08. The minute hand is closer to 2 than 1.

3:08 ⟶ 3:10 The time is about 10 minutes after 3.

CLASS EXERCISES

Complete.

1. 

_?_ minutes after _?_
_?_ minutes before _?_

2. 

_?_ minutes after _?_
_?_ minutes before _?_

3. 

_?_ minutes after _?_
_?_ minutes before _?_

PRACTICE

Complete.

4. 

? minutes before ?

5. 

? minutes before ?

6. 

? minutes before ?

7. 

? minutes after ?

8. 

? minutes after ?

9. 

? minutes before ?

10. 

? minutes before ?

11. 

? minutes before ?

12. 

? minutes before ?

Round to the nearest five minutes. Complete.

ESTIMATE

13. 

about ? minutes after ?

14. 

about ? minutes before ?

PROBLEM SOLVING APPLICATIONS

Solve.

15. Dale plans to meet Maureen at 10:35. Dale arrives at 25 minutes before 11. Is Dale early, late, or on time?

★ 16. Lowell ate at 26 minutes before 5. Sharon ate at 16 minutes before 5. Maureen ate at 34 minutes after 4. Who ate at the same time?

PROBLEM SOLVING
Elapsed Time

Sergio plays tennis from 3:30 to 4:10. From 3:30 to 4:00 is 30 minutes. From 4:00 to 4:10 is 10 minutes.

$$30 + 10 = 40$$

Sergio plays tennis for 40 minutes.

Carol practiced her backhand from 3:30 to 4:40. Did she practice for more or less than an hour? **Think:** From 3:30 to 4:30 is one hour. Since 4:40 comes after 4:30, Carol practiced for more than an hour.

CLASS EXERCISES

Use the clock to help you. Solve.

1. At the track meet, Ed signs up to run in two races. He finishes the first race at 3:50. His next race begins in 20 minutes. At what time does Ed's next race begin?

2. George can walk to the playground in 15 minutes. He wants to meet his friends by the swings at 2:00. At what time should George start walking?

3. On Saturday Daniel plays soccer from 10:30 A.M. to 11:15 A.M. How many minutes does Daniel play soccer?

PRACTICE

Solve.

4. Charles wants to play tennis for 1 hour and 15 minutes. He starts at 10:45. At what time must he stop?

5. Jody starts playing tennis at 2:45. She must stop at 3:25. How long can Jody play?

6. Michael and Glen stop playing at 12:00 to eat lunch. Michael takes 30 minutes to eat lunch. Glen takes 45 minutes. At what time can Michael and Glen begin playing together again?

7. Harlin begins ice skating at 1:50. He skates for 20 minutes, then gets cold. He warms up by the fire for 5 minutes. Then he begins skating again. At what time does Harlin begin skating again?

8. Karatol has 35 minutes to get ready for a tennis match. If it's 1:30 now, at what time is her tennis match?

9. Robert missed the 4:10 bus to the swimming pool by 5 minutes. The next bus comes at 4:40. How long will Robert have to wait?

★ 10. Pearl plays tennis for 2 hours and 15 minutes. She stops at 4 o'clock. When did Pearl start to play tennis?

★ 11. Jerry plays tennis for 2 hours and 35 minutes. He stops at 6:30. When did Jerry start?

Estimate the amount of time.

ESTIMATE

12. June swam from 12:15 to 1:00. Did she swim more or less than an hour?

13. Simon had a skiing lesson from 3:30 to 4:00. Then he skied for 40 more minutes. Did Simon ski for more or less than an hour?

DAYS OF THE WEEK

There are 7 days in a week.

CLASS EXERCISES

Write the day of the week.

1. 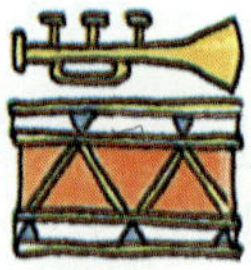

2. 

3. 

4. first
5. second
6. third
7. seventh
8. sixth
9. fifth

PRACTICE

Write the day that comes just after and the day that comes just before the day shown.

10. Monday
11. Wednesday
12. Tuesday
13. Saturday
14. Thursday
15. Sunday

Write the day that is two days after the day shown.

16. Monday
17. Thursday
18. Saturday

Write the day that is two days before the day shown.

19. Sunday
20. Friday
21. Tuesday

Write the number of days from Monday to the day shown.

22. 

23. 

24. 

Write the number of days from Tuesday to this day.

25. Wednesday **26.** Saturday **27.** Friday

28. Monday of the next week **29.** Sunday of the next week

Write the answer.

MIXED REVIEW

30.	**31.**	**32.**	**33.**	**34.**
23	754	61	62	824
+ 38	− 28	+ 20	+ 39	− 629

PROBLEM SOLVING APPLICATIONS

Solve.

35. There are 7 days in a week. How many days are there in 2 weeks? in 3 weeks? in 4 weeks?

36. One week the sun shone for 57 hours, the next week for 68. How many hours did the sun shine in the two weeks?

37. The school nurse saw Bill on Monday. She wants to see him again in 10 days. On what day of the week will Bill see the nurse?

38. Ben usually had band practice on Thursday. One week it was put off until the next Monday. How many days was it put off?

★ **39.** On which day of the week does July 4 come this year?

★ **40.** Thanksgiving is always on which day of the week?

MONTHS OF THE YEAR

January	February	March	April	May	June
July	August	September	October	November	December

There are 31 days in the months in color. There are 30 in all the others, except February. February can have either 28 or 29 days.

The month shown begins on Tuesday and ends on Thursday. The date of the last Thursday is December 31. We say *December thirty-first.*

DECEMBER

SUN	MON	TUE	WED	THU	FRI	SAT
		1	2	3	4	5
6	7	8	9	10	11	12
13	14	15	16	17	18	19
20	21	22	23	24	25	26
27	28	29	30	31		

M A week has seven days. You can use this fact to figure the date a week before or after a given date. **Think:** One week after July 4 is July 11 because $4 + 7 = 11$.

CLASS EXERCISES

Read the date.

1. April 21 **2.** January 18 **3.** May 29 **4.** July 3

5. November 8 **6.** March 10 **7.** August 4 **8.** December 31

PRACTICE

Write the month that comes just after the month shown.

9. January **10.** March **11.** November **12.** April

Write the month that comes just before the month shown.

13. May **14.** June **15.** August **16.** December

Look at the calendar page on page 148. How many are in the month? Write the number.

17. Mondays **18.** Fridays **19.** Wednesdays **20.** Saturdays

Write the date.

21. first Friday **22.** first Monday **23.** first Sunday

24. second Tuesday **25.** second Saturday **26.** third Wednesday

Add or subtract mentally. Write the date.

MENTAL MATH

27. one week before October 17

28. one week after October 11

29. one week after October 16

30. one week before October 29

31. Would it be faster to solve Exercises 27-30 with mental math or a calculator?

PROBLEM SOLVING APPLICATIONS
Using a Calendar

Solve.

32. John saw his dentist May 9th and May 26th. How many days were between his visits?

★**33.** Leo sees the dentist 17 days after Tuesday. On which day of the week is that?

CHECKPOINT 2

Complete. *(pages 138–143)*

1. 

$\underline{?}$: $\underline{?}$

2. 

$\underline{?}$: $\underline{?}$

Solve. *(pages 144–149)*

3. Which month comes just after November?

4. Dale started to swim at 8:15 A.M. She stopped 25 minutes later. What time was it when Dale stopped?

Extra practice on page 408

CHAPTER 5 TEST

Use $ and . to write the value. *(pages 128–131)*

1. 4 nickels 2 dimes

2. 2 half dollars 6 pennies

Write the answer. *(pages 134–135)*

3. $.26 + .35

4. $20.00 − 4.91

5. $22.37 + 58.64

6. $74.21 − 32.75

Estimate to solve. *(pages 136–137)*

7. Kate bought a notebook for $2.17 and a book bag for $7.45. About how much did she spend?

8. Marcus got $12.75 from shoveling snow. He spent $9.29 on a new soccer ball. About how much did he have left?

Write the time. *(pages 138–143)*

9. 

_?_ minutes after _?_
_?_ minutes before _?_

10. 

_?_ minutes after _?_
_?_ minutes before _?_

Solve. *(pages 144–149)*

11. Betty's dance class began at 9:05 A.M. and ended at 9:55 A.M. How long did Betty's dance class last?

12. Ann and Rita played tennis on Tuesday. They planned to play again in eleven days. On what day of the week will they play?

Extra practice on page 409

MATHEMATICS and SCIENCE

Earth is one of nine planets that travel in a path around the sun. The path is called an *orbit*. The table shows the length of time it takes the planets to make 1 orbit.

LENGTH OF TIME TO ORBIT

NAME	TIME
Mercury	about 88 days
Venus	about 225 days
Earth	about 365 days
Mars	about 687 days
Jupiter	about 12 years
Saturn	about 29 years
Uranus	about 84 years
Neptune	about 165 years
Pluto	about 248 years

HOW LONG IS THE TRIP?

Use the table to solve.

1. Which planet takes the longest time to orbit the sun? the shortest?
2. Which planet or planets take about one year to orbit the sun? less than one year?
3. How much longer does it take Neptune to orbit the sun than Saturn?
4. Suppose each planet based its calendar year on the time it takes to orbit the sun. On which planet would you have the greatest number of birthdays?

Enrichment

Tina's father bought three metal numbers at a hardware store. What could their house number be?

Using 1 first	123 or 132
Using 2 first	213 or 231
Using 3 first	312 or 321

Now we know Tina's house number is one of these: 123, 132, 213, 231, 312, or 321.

Write the answer.

1. Andy, Josie, and Hank are lined up at the school door. Make a list of the different ways they could be standing in line.

2. Three cars are parked along the street, one behind the other. List the ways they could be parked.

3. You have 2 moon pictures exactly the same and 2 star pictures exactly the same. How many different ways can you arrange them in a row?

UNDERSTANDING ARRANGEMENTS

Sometimes it's not easy to find all the combinations. Luckily there is an easier way of finding them. It is called a **tree diagram.**

You have 2 pairs of jeans (1 blue and 1 brown) and 3 tops (1 red, 1 blue, and 1 green). How many different outfits can you wear?

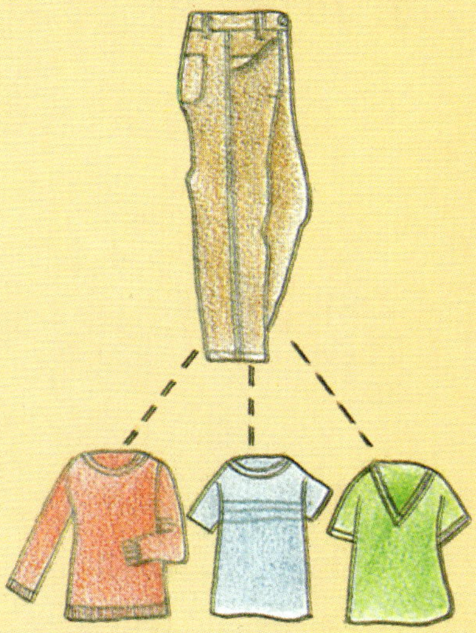

OUTFITS

blue jeans—blue top
blue jeans—red top
blue jeans—green top
brown jeans—blue top
brown jeans—red top
brown jeans—green top

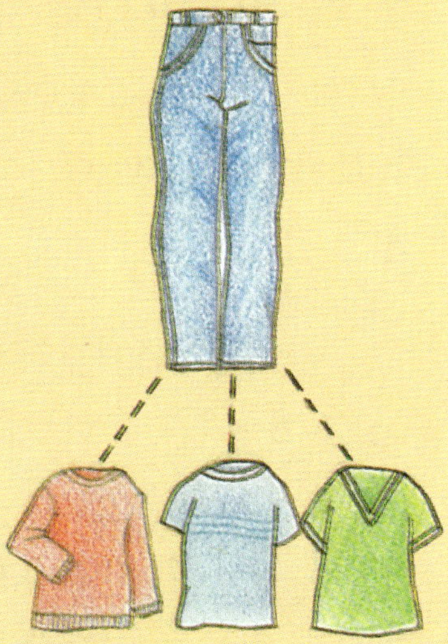

You can wear 6 different outfits. Draw a tree diagram to solve the problem.

4. Jody has 2 skirts and 5 blouses. How many different outfits can she wear using these clothes?

5. How many different ways can you pass out 4 books to 2 people so that each person gets only 1 book?

6. Pete went to the store to buy a new bicycle. The store had 2 models. Each model came in either red, green, or blue. From how many different bicycles could Pete choose?

CUMULATIVE REVIEW

Choose the correct answer. Choose *a*, *b*, *c*, or *d*.

Estimate the sum.

1. $51 + 33$

a. 100 **b.** 90
c. 80 **d.** 70

2. $65 + 24$

a. 90 **b.** 50
c. 70 **d.** 60

3. $40 + 16$

a. 80 **b.** 60
c. 70 **d.** 40

Find the answer.

4. $3 + 5 + 7 + 8$

a. 13 **b.** 25
c. 26 **d.** none of these

5. $25 + 64 + 34$

a. 123 **b.** 113
c. 133 **d.** none of these

6. $41 + 89 + 15$

a. 125 **b.** 145
c. 135 **d.** none of these

Find the answer.

7. $312 + 486$

a. 808 **b.** 708
c. 798 **d.** none of these

8. $489 + 73$

a. 552 **b.** 562
c. 462 **d.** none of these

9. $648 + 263$

a. 811 **b.** 901
c. 911 **d.** none of these

10. $2361 + 5327$

a. 7688 **b.** 6778
c. 7048 **d.** none of these

11. $6087 + 2596$

a. 8673 **b.** 8683
c. 8583 **d.** none of these

12. $3774 + 3686$

a. 6350 **b.** 7460
c. 7450 **d.** none of these

Use the pictograph to answer questions 13–16.

KITES SOLD

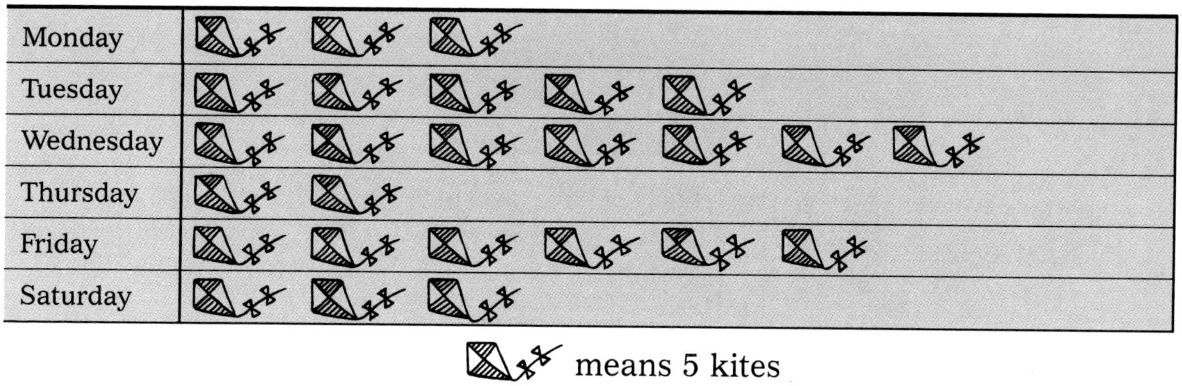

13. On which day were the most kites sold?
    a. Wednesday **b.** Thursday
    c. Friday **d.** none of these

14. How many kites were sold on Tuesday and Saturday?
    a. 8 kites **b.** 5 kites
    c. 40 kites **d.** none of these

15. How many kites were sold on Monday?
    a. 3 kites **b.** 5 kites
    c. 40 kites **d.** none of these

16. On which day were 10 kites sold?
    a. Friday **b.** Wednesday
    c. Thursday **d.** none of these

LANGUAGE and VOCABULARY REVIEW

Use the clues to unscramble the words. Write the words on your paper.

1. kinelc: five cents
2. tearrqu: twenty-five cents
3. sady: seven of these in a week
4. mide: ten cents
5. stonmh: twelve of these in a year
6. findecefer: the answer in subtraction

FLOWCHART

A flowchart is a picture. It shows the correct steps for doing a job or solving a problem.

A flowchart uses shapes for each step.
▭ tells what to do.
⬭ means start or stop.

What does this flowchart tell?

START

Step 1 Take out a bottle of milk.

Step 2 Open the bottle.

Step 3 Get a glass.

Step 4 Pour the milk into the glass.

Step 5 Drink the milk.

STOP

Write what happens.

1. You do step 2 first.

2. You don't do step 2.

3. You do step 4 first.

4. You don't do step 4.

5. Draw a flowchart. Use 2 ⬭ and 3 ▭. Show how to wash your hands.

6

The yellow crayons are in 2 rows. If there are 3 yellow crayons in each row, how many yellow crayons are there altogether?

MULTIPLICATION FACTS

ADDING THE SAME NUMBER

To find the total number of cubes, you can add 4 twos or you can multiply.

$$2 + 2 + 2 + 2 = 8$$
$$\text{or } 4 \times 2 = 8$$

4 times 2 equals 8.

If there were 2 more cubes, there would be 5 twos. You can say that 5 twos is greater than 4 twos.

$$5 \times 2 > 4 \times 2$$

4 groups of 2

CLASS EXERCISES

Complete.

1. 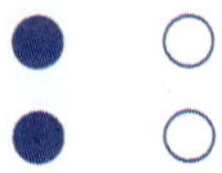

$2 + 2 =$?

$2 \times 2 =$?

2. 

$2 + 2 + 2 =$?

$3 \times 2 =$?

3. 

$2 + 2 + 2 + 2 =$?

$4 \times 2 =$?

Match. Write the letter.

4. $2 + 2 + 2 + 2 + 2$

5. $2 + 2 + 2 + 2 + 2 + 2$

6. $2 + 2 + 2 + 2 + 2 + 2 + 2$

7. $2 + 2 + 2 + 2 + 2 + 2 + 2 + 2$

8. $2 + 2 + 2 + 2 + 2 + 2 + 2 + 2 + 2$

A. $7 \times 2 = 14$

B. $8 \times 2 = 16$

C. $5 \times 2 = 10$

D. $9 \times 2 = 18$

E. $6 \times 2 = 12$

PRACTICE

Solve.

9. $2 + 2 + 2 + 2 + 2 + 2 + 2 + 2 + 2 = \underline{?}$
$9 \times 2 = \underline{?}$

10. $2 + 2 + 2 = \underline{?}$
$3 \times 2 = \underline{?}$

11. $2 + 2 + 2 + 2 + 2 + 2 + 2 = \underline{?}$
$7 \times 2 = \underline{?}$

12. $2 + 2 + 2 + 2 = \underline{?}$
$4 \times 2 = \underline{?}$

13. $2 + 2 + 2 + 2 + 2 + 2 = \underline{?}$
$6 \times 2 = \underline{?}$

14. $2 \times 2 = \underline{?}$

15. $8 \times 2 = \underline{?}$

16. $5 \times 2 = \underline{?}$

Which is greater? Write < or >.

ESTIMATE

17. 4×2 ■ 3×2

18. 7×2 ■ 6×2

19. 3×2 ■ 4×2

20. 5×2 ■ 7×2

PROBLEM SOLVING APPLICATIONS
Using a Pictograph

The pictograph shows the number of bicycle tires fixed at Kerry's Fix-It Shop. Use the pictograph to solve the problem.

BICYCLE TIRES FIXED

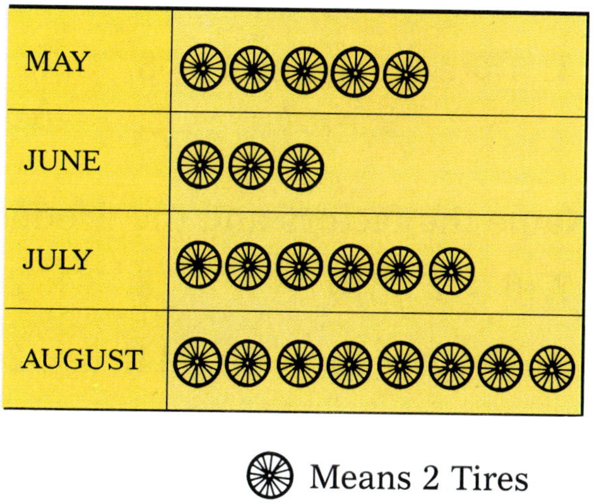

21. How many tires were fixed in May?

22. How many tires were fixed in June?

23. How many tires were fixed in August?

★ **24.** How many tires were fixed in July and August altogether?

★ **25.** How many more tires were fixed in August than in June?

MULTIPLYING TWOS

Counting by twos can help you multiply two.

3 hops of 2

$3 \times 2 = 6$

factor, factor, product

You say, *three times two equals six* or *three twos are six.*

CLASS EXERCISES

Complete.

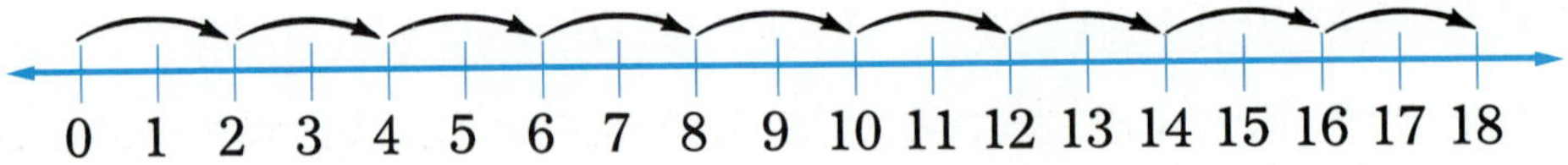

1. Take 3 hops of 2.
   $3 \times 2 = \underline{?}$
2. Take 4 hops of 2.
   $4 \times 2 = \underline{?}$
3. Take 5 hops of 2.
   $5 \times 2 = \underline{?}$
4. Take 2 hops of 2.
   $2 \times 2 = \underline{?}$
5. Take 6 hops of 2.
   $6 \times 2 = \underline{?}$
6. Take 7 hops of 2.
   $7 \times 2 = \underline{?}$

Name the factors and the product.

7. $5 \times 2 = 10$
8. $3 \times 2 = 6$
9. $8 \times 2 = 16$
10. $7 \times 2 = 14$
11. $6 \times 2 = 12$
12. $2 \times 2 = 4$

PRACTICE

Write the multiplication fact.

13. 3 twos
14. 6 times 2
15. 4 twos
16. 7 times 2
17. 5 twos
18. 9 times 2

Multiply.

19. 3×2 **20.** 2×2 **21.** 4×2 **22.** 5×2

23. 8×2 **24.** 7×2 **25.** 6×2 **26.** 9×2

27. What is the product when you multiply 7 and 2?

28. What is the product when the factors are 5 and 2?

Write the answer.

MIXED REVIEW

29.	**30.**	**31.**	**32.**	**33.**	**34.**
26	4	54	1	32	33
35	2	25	4	27	23
+ 28	+ 2	+ 37	+ 5	+ 45	+ 78

PROBLEM SOLVING APPLICATIONS
Choosing the Operation

Solve.

35. Lee got two pairs of shoes from Dad. Tell how many shoes Lee had.

36. How many children in all are there in 3 sets of twins with curly hair?

37. If there are 5 sets of twins in Grade 3, how many children would that be?

38. 6 boys and 2 girls walk down the hall. How many children are there in all?

★ **39.** My product is 14. One factor is 2. I know the other factor. Do you?

★ **40.** One factor is 2. The product is 10. What is the other factor, then?

MULTIPLYING THREES

How many boxes do the children have?

You can add 4 threes or you can multiply.

$$3 + 3 + 3 + 3 = 12$$
$$4 \times 3 = 12$$

4 times 3 equals 12.

M Counting by threes can help you remember the facts.

Think: 4×3 is 4 threes.
Count 3, 6, 9, 12.
$4 \times 3 = 12$

CLASS EXERCISES

Name the sum and the product.

1. 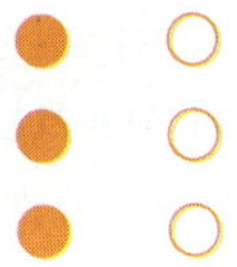

$3 + 3 =$?
$2 \times 3 =$?

2. 

$3 + 3 + 3 =$?
$3 \times 3 =$?

3. 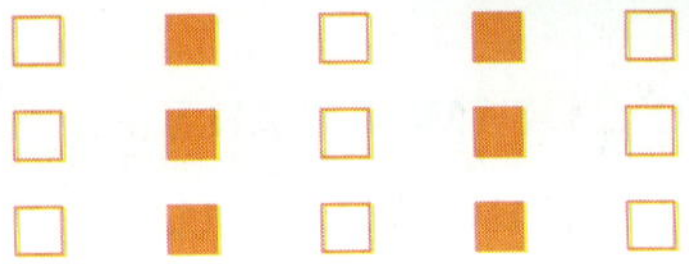

$3 + 3 + 3 + 3 + 3 =$?
$5 \times 3 =$?

Add, then multiply.

4. $3 + 3 + 3 =$? $\quad 3 \times 3 =$?

5. $3 + 3 + 3 + 3 =$? $\quad 4 \times 3 =$?

6. $3 + 3 + 3 + 3 + 3 =$? $\quad 5 \times 3 =$?

7. $3 + 3 + 3 + 3 + 3 + 3 =$? $\quad 6 \times 3 =$?

8. $3 + 3 + 3 + 3 + 3 + 3 + 3 =$? $\quad 7 \times 3 =$?

9. $3 + 3 + 3 + 3 + 3 + 3 + 3 + 3 =$? $\quad 8 \times 3 =$?

10. $3 + 3 + 3 + 3 + 3 + 3 + 3 + 3 + 3 =$? $\quad 9 \times 3 =$?

PRACTICE

Multiply.

11. 2 × 3	**12.** 5 × 3	**13.** 4 × 3	**14.** 7 × 3
15. 3 × 3	**16.** 9 × 3	**17.** 8 × 3	**18.** 6 × 3
19. 7 × 2	**20.** 6 × 2	**21.** 4 × 2	**22.** 2 × 2
23. 3 × 2	**24.** 5 × 2	**25.** 8 × 2	**26.** 9 × 2

Match. Write the letter. Then write the product.

MENTAL MATH

27. 5 × 3	**A.** 3, 6, 9
28. 3 × 3	**B.** 2, 4, 6, 8, 10
29. 5 × 2	**C.** 3, 6, 9, 12
30. 4 × 3	**D.** 3, 6, 9, 12, 15

PROBLEM SOLVING APPLICATIONS
Math and Language

Tri at the beginning of a word can mean three. Use the word to solve.

31. *Triplets* are three brothers or sisters born together. How many children are in 4 sets of triplets?

33. A *tricycle* has 3 wheels. How many wheels do 3 tricycles have?

32. A *triplane* is an airplane with 3 levels of wings. How many levels of wings are on 7 triplanes?

34. If 3 people sing together they are called a *trio*. How many people are in 4 trios?

35. A *triangle* is a shape having 3 sides. How many sides do 6 triangles have?

36. A *tripod* is a 3-legged stool. How many legs do 5 tripods have?

THE ORDER PROPERTY OF MULTIPLICATION

5 threes = 15
$5 \times 3 = 15$

3 fives = 15
$3 \times 5 = 15$

Order Property Changing the order of the factors does not change the product.

The Order Property can help you remember facts. If you know $5 \times 3 = 15$, then you know that $3 \times 5 = 15$.

You can compare factors to see if a product makes sense. You know $5 \times 3 = 15$. So you know 5×2 is less than 15, and 2×5 is less than 15.

CLASS EXERCISES

What is the product?

1. 2 threes = ?
   $2 \times 3 =$?

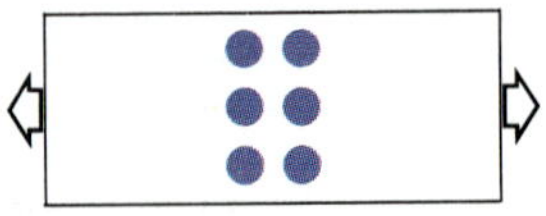

2. 3 twos = ?
   $3 \times 2 =$?

3. 4 threes = ?
   $4 \times 3 =$?

4. 3 fours = ?
   $3 \times 4 =$?

5. 5 threes = ?
   $5 \times 3 =$?

6. 3 fives = ?
   $3 \times 5 =$?

PRACTICE

Multiply.

7. 4×2
   2×4
8. 4×3
   3×4
9. 7×2
   2×7
10. 6×3
    3×6

11. 5×3
3×5

12. 5×2
2×5

13. 2×8
8×2

14. 3×7
7×3

Write the related fact.

15. 9×3	**16.** 3×8	**17.** 6×2	**18.** 2×9

Multiply.

19. 2×3	**20.** 3×6	**21.** 4×2	**22.** 2×7
23. 4×3	**24.** 5×2	**25.** 9×2	**26.** 5×3
27. 6×2	**28.** 7×3	**29.** 3×8	**30.** 9×3

Look at the factors. Write $<$ or $>$.

ESTIMATE

31. $5 \times 2 = 10$,
so 6×2 ▢ 10

32. $5 \times 4 = 20$,
so 5×5 ▢ 20

33. $2 \times 7 = 14$,
so 2×8 ▢ 14

34. $2 \times 4 = 8$,
so 3×4 ▢ 8

PROBLEM SOLVING APPLICATIONS
Choosing the Operation

Solve.

35. There are 6 camels with 3 boxes on each camel. How many boxes are there in all?

36. Joe throws 3 balls to one seal and 7 balls to another. How many balls does Joe throw?

★ **37.** What number is greater than 2×6 but less than 2×7?

★ **38.** What is the difference between 2 nines and 3 eights?

A NEW FORM OF MULTIPLICATION

You know how to write addition two ways.

$$9 + 3 = 12 \qquad \begin{array}{r} 9 \\ +\ 3 \\ \hline 12 \end{array}$$

You can also write multiplication in two ways.

$$4 \times 3 = 12 \qquad \begin{array}{r} 3 \\ \times 4 \\ \hline 12 \end{array}$$

Either way, you say *four threes are twelve* or *four times three equals twelve.*

You can multiply 4×3 on a calculator.

4 [×] 3 [=] 12

CLASS EXERCISES

Name the letter that matches.

1. $8 \times 2 = 16$
2. $7 \times 2 = 14$
3. 2 times 3 equals 6
4. $2 \times 4 = 8$
5. $9 \times 3 = 27$
6. 9 times 2 equals 18

A. $\begin{array}{r} 3 \\ \times 2 \\ \hline 6 \end{array}$ **B.** $\begin{array}{r} 2 \\ \times 9 \\ \hline 18 \end{array}$ **C.** $\begin{array}{r} 4 \\ \times 2 \\ \hline 8 \end{array}$ **D.** $\begin{array}{r} 3 \\ \times 9 \\ \hline 27 \end{array}$ **E.** $\begin{array}{r} 2 \\ \times 8 \\ \hline 16 \end{array}$ **F.** $\begin{array}{r} 2 \\ \times 7 \\ \hline 14 \end{array}$

PRACTICE

Multiply.

7. $\begin{array}{r} 2 \\ \times 2 \\ \hline \end{array}$ **8.** $\begin{array}{r} 3 \\ \times 4 \\ \hline \end{array}$ **9.** $\begin{array}{r} 3 \\ \times 7 \\ \hline \end{array}$ **10.** $\begin{array}{r} 2 \\ \times 9 \\ \hline \end{array}$ **11.** $\begin{array}{r} 2 \\ \times 4 \\ \hline \end{array}$ **12.** $\begin{array}{r} 3 \\ \times 5 \\ \hline \end{array}$

13. $\begin{array}{r} 3 \\ \times 2 \\ \hline \end{array}$ **14.** $\begin{array}{r} 2 \\ \times 7 \\ \hline \end{array}$ **15.** $\begin{array}{r} 4 \\ \times 2 \\ \hline \end{array}$ **16.** $\begin{array}{r} 4 \\ \times 3 \\ \hline \end{array}$ **17.** $\begin{array}{r} 3 \\ \times 3 \\ \hline \end{array}$ **18.** $\begin{array}{r} 2 \\ \times 3 \\ \hline \end{array}$

19. $\begin{array}{r} 3 \\ \times 6 \\ \hline \end{array}$ **20.** $\begin{array}{r} 2 \\ \times 5 \\ \hline \end{array}$ **21.** $\begin{array}{r} 3 \\ \times 9 \\ \hline \end{array}$ **22.** $\begin{array}{r} 2 \\ \times 8 \\ \hline \end{array}$ **23.** $\begin{array}{r} 2 \\ \times 6 \\ \hline \end{array}$ **24.** $\begin{array}{r} 3 \\ \times 8 \\ \hline \end{array}$

CALCULATOR

Suppose you cannot multiply on your calculator.
Draw the keys you would push to find the answer.

25. 2×6 **26.** 3×4 **27.** 4×2 **28.** 3×5

PROBLEM SOLVING APPLICATIONS

Solve.

29. Jason puts 3 cans on each shelf. How many cans does he put on 5 shelves?

30. Lorraine puts 2 jars on each shelf. How many jars does she put on 6 shelves?

31. Jason puts out 27 cans. Gina puts out 36. How many do they put out in all?

★ **32.** Jason fills 18 shelves in 2 hours. How many shelves will he have filled in 3 hours?

CHECKPOINT 1

Write the answer.

(pages 158–167)

1. 4×2 **2.** 7×2

3. 5×2 **4.** 8×2

5. 2×3 **6.** 5×3

7. 8×3 **8.** 6×3

9. 3×9 **10.** 2×6

11. 3×7 **12.** 2×9

13. $\begin{array}{r} 3 \\ \times 4 \\ \hline \end{array}$ **14.** $\begin{array}{r} 3 \\ \times 3 \\ \hline \end{array}$ **15.** $\begin{array}{r} 8 \\ \times 2 \\ \hline \end{array}$

Extra practice on page 410

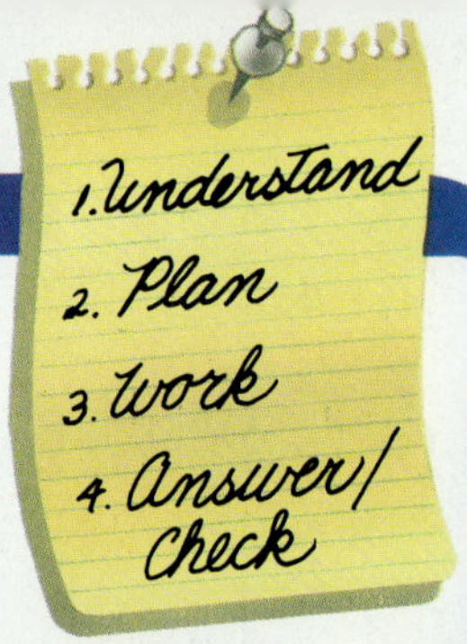

PROBLEM SOLVING

Strategy: Too Little Information

Jill wants to make bracelets for her friends. She uses 9 beads for each bracelet. How many beads does Jill need in all?

One fact is missing. You need to know how many bracelets Jill plans to make. Once you know the number, you can multiply to find how many beads she needs.

CLASS EXERCISES

Is there enough information to solve the problem? If not, tell what is missing.

1. Donna uses 4 strips of cloth to make each flag. Donna makes 2 flags. How many strips of cloth does she use?

2. Bill makes 5 clay bowls. He sets them on a shelf to dry. How many bowls does Bill make?

3. The art teacher has 3 pieces of clay for each student. How many pieces of clay does the teacher have for the class?

4. The art class plans to make pencil holders from cans. Each student brings 2 empty cans. How many cans are brought to class?

PRACTICE

Which fact is missing? Write the letter. Solve the problem.

5. Rosa needs 35 beads for a bracelet. How many more beads does she need?

a. Beads cost 4¢ each.
b. Rosa likes red beads.
c. Rosa has 26 beads.

Match the missing fact to the problem. Solve the problem.

6. Bob makes toy animals. He uses 2 balls of yarn for each animal. How many balls of yarn does Bob use to make the animals?

7. Sue buys a jar of paint and a paintbrush. The brush costs $2.98. How much does Sue spend in all?

8. Elida folds a paper hat in 2 minutes. How long does it take her to fold hats for all the children at the party?

9. The art teacher gives each student 2 sheets of red paper. How many sheets does the teacher give to the class?

10. Tom sews 2 rows of buttons on a puppet. How many buttons does he sew on in all?

★ 11. Martha sews 2 rows of buttons onto each puppet. How many buttons does she sew in all?

A. The paint costs $2.50.

B. There are 9 students.

C. He makes 8 animals.

D. There are 5 puppets.

E. There will be 8 children at the party.

F. There are 3 buttons in each row.

Write the answer.

MIXED REVIEW

12. 1542 + 2719

13. 5749 − 1873

14. $37.95 − 9.07

15. $35.65 + 14.95

16. 609 − 436

17. 387 + 452

MULTIPLYING FOURS

In a race Roberta Rabbit takes 4 hops of 3. Freddie Frog takes 3 hops of 4. Who's ahead?

The race is tied.

×	4
2	8
3	12
4	16
5	20
6	24
7	28
8	32
9	36

4 hops of 3 = 12   3 hops of 4 = 12

$3 + 3 + 3 + 3 = 12$ $4 + 4 + 4 = 12$

$$\begin{array}{r} 3 \\ \times 4 \\ \hline 12 \end{array} \qquad \begin{array}{r} 4 \\ \times 3 \\ \hline 12 \end{array}$$

Roberta and Freddie both hop to 12.

You can press either 4 [×] 3 or 3 [×] 4 on your calculator to get 12. The product is the same because the factors are the same.

CLASS EXERCISES

Count by fours. Complete the pattern.

1.

4	8	?	16	?	24	?	32	?

What is the product?

2. 4 hops of 4 = ?
$4 \times 4 =$?

3. 5 hops of 4 = ?
$5 \times 4 =$?

4. 6 hops of 4 = ?
$6 \times 4 =$?

5. 7 hops of 4 = ?
$7 \times 4 =$?

6. 8 hops of 4 = ?
$8 \times 4 =$?

7. 9 hops of 4 = ?
$9 \times 4 =$?

PRACTICE

Multiply.

8. 2×4
4×2

9. 3×4
4×3

10. 5×4
4×5

11. 6×4
4×6

12. 7×4 **13.** 8×4 **14.** 5×4 **15.** 9×4

16. 3×4 **17.** 6×4 **18.** 4×4 **19.** 2×4

20. $\begin{array}{r} 2 \\ \times 6 \\ \hline \end{array}$ **21.** $\begin{array}{r} 3 \\ \times 4 \\ \hline \end{array}$ **22.** $\begin{array}{r} 4 \\ \times 4 \\ \hline \end{array}$ **23.** $\begin{array}{r} 3 \\ \times 6 \\ \hline \end{array}$ **24.** $\begin{array}{r} 2 \\ \times 9 \\ \hline \end{array}$ **25.** $\begin{array}{r} 3 \\ \times 7 \\ \hline \end{array}$

26. $\begin{array}{r} 3 \\ \times 8 \\ \hline \end{array}$ **27.** $\begin{array}{r} 3 \\ \times 5 \\ \hline \end{array}$ **28.** $\begin{array}{r} 2 \\ \times 8 \\ \hline \end{array}$ **29.** $\begin{array}{r} 3 \\ \times 9 \\ \hline \end{array}$ **30.** $\begin{array}{r} 4 \\ \times 8 \\ \hline \end{array}$ **31.** $\begin{array}{r} 2 \\ \times 7 \\ \hline \end{array}$

CALCULATOR

Write two facts with the same factors that could have been entered to get the product on the calculator.

32. 8 **33.** 12 **34.** 32

35. 20 **36.** 36 **37.** 28

PROBLEM SOLVING APPLICATIONS

Solve.

38. Which rabbit goes the greatest distance?

39. Which rabbit goes the least distance?

40. Which rabbits go the same distance?

★ **41.** Which rabbit goes a distance of 15 more than 21?

MULTIPLYING BY ZERO AND ONE

What happens when you multiply with 1 or 0?

When you multiply 1 and another number, the product is the other number.

When you multiply 0 and another number, the product is always 0.

1 dog + 1 dog + 1 dog

$3 \times 1 = 3$

0 dogs + 0 dogs + 0 dogs

$3 \times 0 = 0$

M Knowing these properties can help you multiply mentally.

CLASS EXERCISES

What is the sum and the product?

1. $0 + 0 = \underline{?}$
$2 \times 0 = \underline{?}$

2. $0 + 0 + 0 + 0 = \underline{?}$
$4 \times 0 = \underline{?}$

3. $0 + 0 + 0 + 0 + 0 = \underline{?}$
$5 \times 0 = \underline{?}$

4. $1 + 1 = \underline{?}$
$2 \times 1 = \underline{?}$

5. $1 + 1 + 1 + 1 = \underline{?}$
$4 \times 1 = \underline{?}$

6. $1 + 1 + 1 + 1 + 1 = \underline{?}$
$5 \times 1 = \underline{?}$

PRACTICE

Multiply.

7. 6×0
0×6

8. 8×0
0×8

9. 9×0
0×9

10. 7×0
0×7

11. 6×1 1×6	**12.** 8×1 1×8	**13.** 9×1 1×9	**14.** 7×1 1×7

15. $\begin{array}{r} 0 \\ \times 2 \\ \hline \end{array}$	**16.** $\begin{array}{r} 0 \\ \times 8 \\ \hline \end{array}$	**17.** $\begin{array}{r} 1 \\ \times 5 \\ \hline \end{array}$	**18.** $\begin{array}{r} 0 \\ \times 4 \\ \hline \end{array}$	**19.** $\begin{array}{r} 1 \\ \times 9 \\ \hline \end{array}$	**20.** $\begin{array}{r} 1 \\ \times 7 \\ \hline \end{array}$
21. $\begin{array}{r} 6 \\ \times 0 \\ \hline \end{array}$	**22.** $\begin{array}{r} 0 \\ \times 5 \\ \hline \end{array}$	**23.** $\begin{array}{r} 3 \\ \times 0 \\ \hline \end{array}$	**24.** $\begin{array}{r} 1 \\ \times 4 \\ \hline \end{array}$	**25.** $\begin{array}{r} 7 \\ \times 0 \\ \hline \end{array}$	**26.** $\begin{array}{r} 0 \\ \times 9 \\ \hline \end{array}$
27. $\begin{array}{r} 1 \\ \times 0 \\ \hline \end{array}$	**28.** $\begin{array}{r} 7 \\ \times 1 \\ \hline \end{array}$	**29.** $\begin{array}{r} 2 \\ \times 1 \\ \hline \end{array}$	**30.** $\begin{array}{r} 1 \\ \times 1 \\ \hline \end{array}$	**31.** $\begin{array}{r} 3 \\ \times 1 \\ \hline \end{array}$	**32.** $\begin{array}{r} 0 \\ \times 6 \\ \hline \end{array}$
33. $\begin{array}{r} 8 \\ \times 0 \\ \hline \end{array}$	**34.** $\begin{array}{r} 0 \\ \times 0 \\ \hline \end{array}$	**35.** $\begin{array}{r} 1 \\ \times 6 \\ \hline \end{array}$	**36.** $\begin{array}{r} 0 \\ \times 7 \\ \hline \end{array}$	**37.** $\begin{array}{r} 1 \\ \times 2 \\ \hline \end{array}$	**38.** $\begin{array}{r} 8 \\ \times 1 \\ \hline \end{array}$

MENTAL MATH

Multiply mentally. Write just the answer.

39. $2 \times 4 \times 0$ **40.** $3 \times 8 \times 1$ **41.** $0 \times 4 \times 7$

42. $5 \times 0 \times 3$ **43.** $4 \times 1 \times 3$ ★**44.** $0 \times 2 \times 3 \times 4$

45. Is it easier to do Exercises 39–44 mentally or with paper and pencil?

PROBLEM SOLVING APPLICATIONS
Choosing a Strategy

Solve.

46. Pam gets a letter from her pen pal each day for 9 days. How many letters does Pam get in all?

47. Pam writes 0 letters a day for 9 days. How many letters does Pam write?

48. A letter carrier delivers 7 letters on Main Street. Then she delivers 4 letters on Barker Avenue. How many letters does she deliver on 3 streets?

PROBLEM SOLVING
Strategy: Logical Thinking

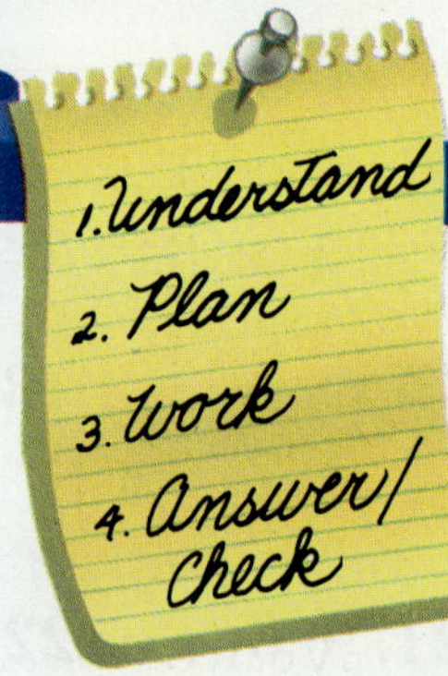

John writes a number on a piece of paper. The number is between 9 and 13. The number is an odd number. What number does John write?

To solve, think: the numbers between 9 and 13 are 10, 11, and 12. The number 11 is the only odd number greater than 9 and less than 13.

~~10~~ 11 ~~12~~

John's number must be 11.

CLASS EXERCISES

What is the number? Write and cross out numbers to help.

1. Jean writes an odd number greater than 5 and less than 21. The number ends in 3.

2. Bill writes an even number between 0 and 10. The number times 2 equals the next even number.

PRACTICE

Solve.

3. Barb writes two different odd numbers between 9 and 19. Their sum is 30. What are the numbers?

4. Pablo writes two different even numbers greater than 8. Their sum is 24. What are the numbers?

5. Bill multiplies two odd numbers. Is the product even or odd?

6. Barb adds two odd numbers. Is the sum even or odd?

7. John multiplies two even numbers. Is the product even or odd?

8. Jean adds two even numbers. Is the sum even or odd?

Write the number.

9. To write the odd number that comes just after any even number, you add ___?___.

10. All of the even numbers are the product of a number and ___?___.

★ 11. If you want to write the odd number that comes just after any odd number, you add ___?___.

★ 12. If you want to write the even number that comes just before an even number, you subtract ___?___.

CHECKPOINT 2

Which fact is missing? Write the letter. Solve the problem. *(pages 168–169)*

1. Each of Bill's rose bushes had 3 flowers. How many flowers were there in all?
   - **A.** John picked 5 roses.
   - **B.** There were 2 in each row.
   - **C.** There were 4 rose bushes.

Write the answer. *(pages 170–173)*

2. 4×8 **3.** 4×6 **4.** 0×4

5. 3×1 **6.** 8×0

Solve. *(pages 174–175)*

7. Pam adds an even number and an odd number. Is the sum even or odd?

Extra practice on page 410

CHAPTER 6 TEST

Write the answer. *(pages 158–167)*

1. 2×6 **2.** 3×3 **3.** 9×2 **4.** 8×3

5. $\begin{array}{r} 2 \\ \times 7 \\ \hline \end{array}$ **6.** $\begin{array}{r} 5 \\ \times 3 \\ \hline \end{array}$ **7.** $\begin{array}{r} 8 \\ \times 2 \\ \hline \end{array}$ **8.** $\begin{array}{r} 4 \\ \times 3 \\ \hline \end{array}$ **9.** $\begin{array}{r} 3 \\ \times 7 \\ \hline \end{array}$

Which fact is needed to solve each problem? Write *A*, *B*, or *C*. *(pages 168–169)*

10. Cara used 3 packages of nuts in each batch of party mix. How many packages of nuts did she use?

A. Cara also used 2 lb raisins in each batch.
B. Cara made 4 batches of party mix.
C. Each package weighed 1 kg.

11. Each child in the class got 4 pencils. How many pencils were handed out?

A. 2 teachers gave out the pencils.
B. Each pencil was 13 cm long.
C. 26 children were in the class.

Write the answer. *(pages 170–173)*

12. 4×6 **13.** 0×8 **14.** 5×0 **15.** 1×9

16. $\begin{array}{r} 8 \\ \times 4 \\ \hline \end{array}$ **17.** $\begin{array}{r} 4 \\ \times 7 \\ \hline \end{array}$ **18.** $\begin{array}{r} 0 \\ \times 2 \\ \hline \end{array}$ **19.** $\begin{array}{r} 7 \\ \times 1 \\ \hline \end{array}$ **20.** $\begin{array}{r} 4 \\ \times 9 \\ \hline \end{array}$

Solve. *(pages 174–175)*

21. Elise writes an odd number greater than 3 and less than 9. The number times 2 equals 14. What is the number?

Extra practice on page 411

MATHEMATICS and PHYSICAL EDUCATION

In school basketball, a goal made as a free throw adds 1 point to the score. All other goals, called *field goals*, add 2 points.

WHAT'S YOUR GOAL?

Complete the table.

THE EAGLES

	PLAYER'S NAME	FREE THROWS	FIELD GOALS	TOTAL POINTS
1.	Raoul	2	4	?
2.	Theresa	3	3	?
3.	John	1	2	?
4.	Frank	3	4	?
5.	Pam	0	3	?
6.	Ellen	4	1	?

7. What was the total team score for the Eagles?

8. The Tigers made 7 free throws and 8 field goals in the first part of the game. In the last part the Tigers made 9 free throws and 6 field goals. How many points did the Tigers score in the game?

Enrichment

What's the animal in the picture?

Look at the picture to the right.

1. If it's not a lion, a tiger, or a camel, then it's a ?.
2. If it's not a camel, a tiger, or a giraffe, then it's a ?.

Look at the picture to the left.

3. If it's not a horse, a goat, or a dog, then it's a ?.
4. If it's not a goat, a cow, or a horse, then it's a ?.

Write the name of the object to complete.

LOGICAL THINKING

5. If it's not a saucer, plate, or spoon, then it's a ?.
6. If it's not a plate, spoon, or cup, then it's a ?.

Write the number to solve.

7. If it's not 7, 23, or 31, then it's ? .

8. If it's not 7, 23, or 18, then it's ? .

9. If it's not 19, 41, or 17, then it's ? .

10. If it's not 17, 41, or 12, then it's ? .

11. If it's not the sum of 8 and 4, then it's ? .

12. If it's not the product of 5 and 3, then it's ? .

13. If it's not 4 times 4, then it's ? .

14. If it's not 9 twos, then it's ? .

15. If it's not less than 6, then it's ? .

16. If it's not even, then it's ? .

17. If it's not 3 times some number, then it's ? .

18. If it's not odd, then it's ? .

CUMULATIVE REVIEW

Choose the correct answer. Choose *a*, *b*, *c*, or *d*.

Estimate the difference.

1. $73 - 39$
- **a.** 20
- **b.** 110
- **c.** 30
- **d.** 50

2. $666 - 451$
- **a.** 200
- **b.** 100
- **c.** 300
- **d.** 500

3. $803 - 299$
- **a.** 700
- **b.** 500
- **c.** 400
- **d.** 300

Find the answer.

4. 876 − 523
- **a.** 353
- **b.** 343
- **c.** 359
- **d.** none of these

5. 712 − 322
- **a.** 380
- **b.** 394
- **c.** 390
- **d.** none of these

6. 612 − 238
- **a.** 384
- **b.** 374
- **c.** 373
- **d.** none of these

7. $900 - 305$
- **a.** 605
- **b.** 695
- **c.** 505
- **d.** none of these

8. $7823 - 572$
- **a.** 7251
- **b.** 7351
- **c.** 7395
- **d.** none of these

9. $9341 - 6463$
- **a.** 3888
- **b.** 3878
- **c.** 2878
- **d.** none of these

Use estimation to choose the most reasonable answer.

10. 56 third graders and 67 fourth graders signed up for the field trip. How many children in all signed up for the trip?
- **a.** 13 children
- **b.** 123 children
- **c.** 103 children
- **d.** 11 children

11. On Tuesday, 115 tuna sandwiches were sold in the cafeteria. 264 cheese sandwiches were also sold. How many sandwiches were sold altogether?
   a. 379 sandwiches
   b. 656 sandwiches
   c. 266 sandwiches
   d. 149 sandwiches

12. Michael O'Malley has 123 stamps. He needs 175 stamps for his letters. How many more stamps does Michael need?
   a. 10 stamps
   b. 52 stamps
   c. 198 stamps
   d. 298 stamps

13. Dottie has 29 stuffed animals and 42 dolls. How many more dolls does she have than animals?
   a. 33 more dolls
   b. 3 more dolls
   c. 73 more dolls
   d. 13 more dolls

14. Sharon drew 39 pictures of horses and 27 pictures of goats. How many pictures did she draw?
   a. 16 pictures
   b. 66 pictures
   c. 26 pictures
   d. 86 pictures

LANGUAGE and VOCABULARY REVIEW

Use the words to complete the sentences.

odd estimate even properties total factor

1. Order and Grouping are _?_.
2. To make a good guess is to _?_.
3. A number that is multiplied is a _?_.
4. 1, 3, and 5 are _?_ numbers.
5. 2, 4, and 6 are _?_ numbers.
6. A sum is the _?_ amount.

FLOWCHART WITH A QUESTION

You can use a flowchart to help you do some things in a special order.

Here is another shape you can use in a flowchart.

◇ shows a question.

Follow the arrows in this flowchart. When you reach the ◇ shape you must answer the question.

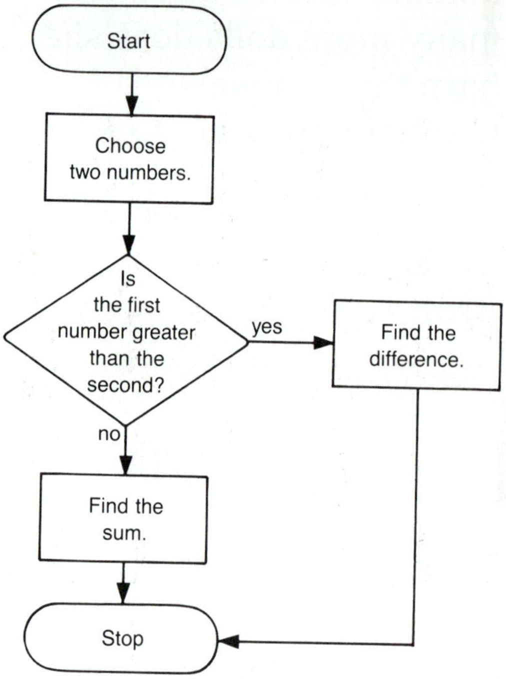

Use the flowchart.

1. What do you do if the first number is 6 and the second is 9?

2. What do you do if the first number is 12 and the second is 8?

3. Find the answers. Remember to use the flowchart.

FIRST NUMBER	SECOND NUMBER	ANSWER
29	42	a. ?
172	170	b. ?

7

Laces go through eyelets. There are 2 rows of 5 eyelets on each sneaker. How many eyelets are on each sneaker? on both?

MULTIPLICATION FACTS

MULTIPLYING FIVES

Suppose you save 6 nickels.

5 + 5 + 5 + 5 + 5 + 5

To find the total value, you count by fives or multiply 6×5.

$$\begin{array}{r} 5¢ \\ \times 6 \\ \hline 30¢ \end{array}$$

6 fives are 30.
Six times five equals 30.

$0 \times 5 = 0$
$1 \times 5 = 5$
$2 \times 5 = 10$
$3 \times 5 = 15$
$4 \times 5 = 20$

$5 \times 5 = 25$
$6 \times 5 = 30$
$7 \times 5 = 35$
$8 \times 5 = 40$
$9 \times 5 = 45$

M You can use the facts you know to help you learn new facts. If you know that $4 \times 5 = 20$, then 5×5 is 1 more five, or 5 more.

$$20 + 5 = 25$$
$$\text{so, } 5 \times 5 = 25$$

CLASS EXERCISES

Count by fives. What are the missing numbers?

1.

5	10	?	20	25	?	?	40	?

What is the product?

2. 4×5 / 5×4 **3.** 7×5 / 5×7 **4.** 8×5 / 5×8 **5.** 9×5 / 5×9

6. 3×5 / 5×3 **7.** 6×5 / 5×6 **8.** 2×5 / 5×2 **9.** 5×5

PRACTICE

Multiply.

10. 3×5 **11.** 0×5 **12.** 7×5 **13.** 5×5

14. 2×5 **15.** 8×5 **16.** 6×5 **17.** 9×5

18. $\begin{array}{r} 4 \\ \times 6 \\ \hline \end{array}$ **19.** $\begin{array}{r} 5 \\ \times 3 \\ \hline \end{array}$ **20.** $\begin{array}{r} 3 \\ \times 4 \\ \hline \end{array}$ **21.** $\begin{array}{r} 5 \\ \times 6 \\ \hline \end{array}$ **22.** $\begin{array}{r} 5 \\ \times 9 \\ \hline \end{array}$ **23.** $\begin{array}{r} 5 \\ \times 4 \\ \hline \end{array}$

24. $\begin{array}{r} 3 \\ \times 9 \\ \hline \end{array}$ **25.** $\begin{array}{r} 5 \\ \times 1 \\ \hline \end{array}$ **26.** $\begin{array}{r} 3 \\ \times 6 \\ \hline \end{array}$ **27.** $\begin{array}{r} 1 \\ \times 5 \\ \hline \end{array}$ **28.** $\begin{array}{r} 5 \\ \times 3 \\ \hline \end{array}$ **29.** $\begin{array}{r} 5 \\ \times 7 \\ \hline \end{array}$

30. $\begin{array}{r} 5 \\ \times 8 \\ \hline \end{array}$ **31.** $\begin{array}{r} 4 \\ \times 9 \\ \hline \end{array}$ **32.** $\begin{array}{r} 5 \\ \times 5 \\ \hline \end{array}$ **33.** $\begin{array}{r} 4 \\ \times 5 \\ \hline \end{array}$ **34.** $\begin{array}{r} 4 \\ \times 8 \\ \hline \end{array}$ **35.** $\begin{array}{r} 5 \\ \times 2 \\ \hline \end{array}$

Use mental math patterns. Write the number.

MENTAL MATH

36. If $3 \times 5 = 15$, then $4 \times 5 = \underline{\ ?\ }$.

37. If $5 \times 5 = 25$, then $6 \times 5 = \underline{\ ?\ }$.

38. If $7 \times 5 = 35$, then $8 \times 5 = \underline{\ ?\ }$.

39. If $6 \times 5 = 30$, then $7 \times 5 = \underline{\ ?\ }$.

PROBLEM SOLVING APPLICATIONS
Choosing the Operation

Solve.

40. Lee saw 3 groups of 5 deer. How many deer did he see?

41. Ty saw 5 groups of 5 deer. How many deer did he see?

42. Brad went for a walk at 5:15 P.M. He saw a group of deer 20 minutes later. At what time did Brad see the deer?

★ **43.** Carlos saw 5 deer families. The families had the same number of members. If Carlos saw 20 deer, how many deer were in each family?

MULTIPLYING SIXES

How many apples are in the rows?
You can count by six.

$0 \times 6 = 0$
$1 \times 6 = 6$
$2 \times 6 = 12$
$3 \times 6 = 18$
$4 \times 6 = 24$
$5 \times 6 = 30$

$6 \times 6 = 36$
$7 \times 6 = 42$
$8 \times 6 = 48$
$9 \times 6 = 54$

Counting by six can take a long time. You can find answers much faster if you know the facts.

5 rows of 6 apples
$5 \times 6 = 30$

Watch your factors to make sure your products make sense. If you know that $6 \times 6 = 36$, then you know that 7×6 is greater than 36. You also know that 5×6 is less than 36.

CLASS EXERCISES

What is the product?

1. 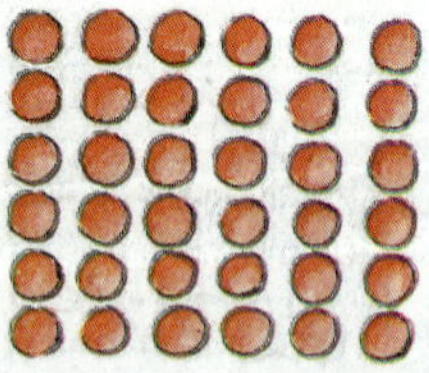

6 rows of 6 apples
$6 \times 6 = \underline{\ ?\ }$

$$\begin{array}{r} 6 \\ \times 6 \\ \hline \end{array}$$

2. 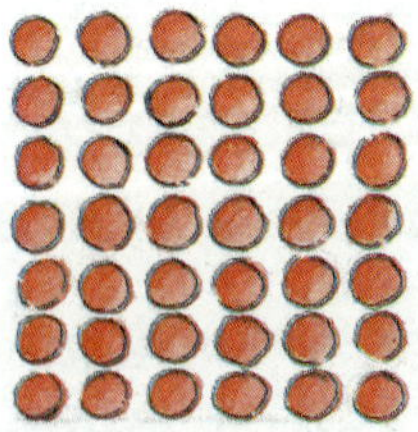

7 rows of 6 apples
$7 \times 6 = \underline{\ ?\ }$

$$\begin{array}{r} 6 \\ \times 7 \\ \hline \end{array}$$

3. 8 rows of 6 apples
$8 \times 6 = \underline{\ ?\ }$

$$\begin{array}{r} 6 \\ \times 8 \\ \hline \end{array}$$

4. 9 rows of 6 apples
$9 \times 6 = \underline{\ ?\ }$

$$\begin{array}{r} 6 \\ \times 9 \\ \hline \end{array}$$

PRACTICE

Multiply.

5. 6×2	**6.** 6×3	**7.** 6×6	**8.** 6×5	**9.** 6×4	**10.** 6×9
11. 6×1	**12.** 6×7	**13.** 6×8	**14.** 6×0	**15.** 5×6	**16.** 4×6
17. 8×6	**18.** 2×6	**19.** 9×6	**20.** 7×6	**21.** 3×6	**22.** 0×6
23. 1×6	**24.** 2×9	**25.** 5×3	**26.** 3×7	**27.** 5×5	**28.** 4×7

★ **29.** $2 \times 1 \times 4$ ★ **30.** $3 \times 2 \times 5$ ★ **31.** $4 \times 2 \times 6$ ★ **32.** $6 \times 1 \times 6$

Look at the factors. Then write <, >, or =.

ESTIMATE

33. 5×4 ▢ 25 **34.** 5×5 ▢ 25 **35.** 5×7 ▢ 25

36. 5×6 ▢ 25 **37.** 3×4 ▢ 25 **38.** 6×7 ▢ 25

PROBLEM SOLVING APPLICATIONS
Using Number Sentences

Write a number sentence. Then solve.

39. There are 8 rows of plants in the garden. How many plants are there if there are 6 plants in a row?

40. Rosa has 6 groups of 5 apples. How many groups of 6 apples can she make?

41. Claire has 72 pears. She washes 47 pears. How many pears does Claire still have to wash?

MULTIPLICATION TABLES

The table shows the facts you have learned so far. Look across the top and down the side for factors. Look in the rest of the table for the products.

4 × 5 = 20

5 × 4 = 20

×	2	3	4	5	6	7	8	9
2	4	6	8	10	12	14	16	18
3	6	9	12	15	18	21	24	27
4	8	12	16	20	24	28	32	36
5	10	15	20	25	30	35	40	45
6	12	18	24	30	36	42	48	54
7	14	21	28	35	42			
8	16	24	32	40	48			
9	18	27	36	45	54			

CLASS EXERCISES

Multiply.

			1.	**2.**	**3.**	**4.**	**5.**
×	4	3	6	8	5	7	9
3	12	9	?	?	?	?	?

			6.	**7.**	**8.**	**9.**	**10.**
×	4	3	6	7	5	8	9
4	16	12	?	?	?	?	?

			11.	**12.**	**13.**	**14.**	**15.**
×	2	3	9	6	8	5	7
5	10	15	?	?	?	?	?

			16.	**17.**	**18.**	**19.**	**20.**
×	4	3	5	7	8	9	6
6	24	18	?	?	?	?	?

PRACTICE

Multiply.

21. $\begin{array}{r} 5 \\ \times 5 \\ \hline \end{array}$ **22.** $\begin{array}{r} 6 \\ \times 6 \\ \hline \end{array}$ **23.** $\begin{array}{r} 4 \\ \times 4 \\ \hline \end{array}$ **24.** $\begin{array}{r} 4 \\ \times 8 \\ \hline \end{array}$ **25.** $\begin{array}{r} 8 \\ \times 4 \\ \hline \end{array}$ **26.** $\begin{array}{r} 9 \\ \times 5 \\ \hline \end{array}$

27. $\begin{array}{r} 9 \\ \times 4 \\ \hline \end{array}$	**28.** $\begin{array}{r} 7 \\ \times 4 \\ \hline \end{array}$	**29.** $\begin{array}{r} 7 \\ \times 6 \\ \hline \end{array}$	**30.** $\begin{array}{r} 6 \\ \times 9 \\ \hline \end{array}$	**31.** $\begin{array}{r} 7 \\ \times 5 \\ \hline \end{array}$	**32.** $\begin{array}{r} 5 \\ \times 9 \\ \hline \end{array}$
33. $\begin{array}{r} 6 \\ \times 3 \\ \hline \end{array}$	**34.** $\begin{array}{r} 5 \\ \times 6 \\ \hline \end{array}$	**35.** $\begin{array}{r} 3 \\ \times 4 \\ \hline \end{array}$	**36.** $\begin{array}{r} 6 \\ \times 5 \\ \hline \end{array}$	**37.** $\begin{array}{r} 6 \\ \times 7 \\ \hline \end{array}$	**38.** $\begin{array}{r} 4 \\ \times 6 \\ \hline \end{array}$
39. $\begin{array}{r} 4 \\ \times 5 \\ \hline \end{array}$	**40.** $\begin{array}{r} 7 \\ \times 3 \\ \hline \end{array}$	**41.** $\begin{array}{r} 8 \\ \times 5 \\ \hline \end{array}$	**42.** $\begin{array}{r} 4 \\ \times 7 \\ \hline \end{array}$	**43.** $\begin{array}{r} 0 \\ \times 9 \\ \hline \end{array}$	**44.** $\begin{array}{r} 5 \\ \times 8 \\ \hline \end{array}$
45. $\begin{array}{r} 9 \\ \times 6 \\ \hline \end{array}$	**46.** $\begin{array}{r} 5 \\ \times 3 \\ \hline \end{array}$	**47.** $\begin{array}{r} 6 \\ \times 8 \\ \hline \end{array}$	**48.** $\begin{array}{r} 5 \\ \times 7 \\ \hline \end{array}$	**49.** $\begin{array}{r} 8 \\ \times 6 \\ \hline \end{array}$	**50.** $\begin{array}{r} 4 \\ \times 9 \\ \hline \end{array}$

Complete.

★ **51.** $6 \times 5 = 5 \times \underline{?} = \underline{?}$

★ **52.** $7 \times 6 = 6 \times \underline{?} = \underline{?}$

★ **53.** $8 \times 5 = 5 \times \underline{?} = \underline{?}$

★ **54.** $6 \times 9 = 9 \times \underline{?} = \underline{?}$

MIXED REVIEW

Write the answer.

55. $\begin{array}{r} 24 \\ 48 \\ +\ 17 \\ \hline \end{array}$	**56.** $\begin{array}{r} 19 \\ 20 \\ +\ 14 \\ \hline \end{array}$	**57.** $\begin{array}{r} 17 \\ 18 \\ +\ 29 \\ \hline \end{array}$	**58.** $\begin{array}{r} 36 \\ 16 \\ +\ 27 \\ \hline \end{array}$	**59.** $\begin{array}{r} 63 \\ 12 \\ +\ 7 \\ \hline \end{array}$
60. $\begin{array}{r} 41¢ \\ -\ 18¢ \\ \hline \end{array}$	**61.** $\begin{array}{r} 67¢ \\ -\ 48¢ \\ \hline \end{array}$	**62.** $\begin{array}{r} 69¢ \\ -\ 15¢ \\ \hline \end{array}$	**63.** $\begin{array}{r} 54¢ \\ -\ 25¢ \\ \hline \end{array}$	**64.** $\begin{array}{r} 66¢ \\ -\ 38¢ \\ \hline \end{array}$

PROBLEM SOLVING APPLICATIONS
Nonroutine Problems

Use the math you know to find the number of dots. Do not count all the dots.

65. 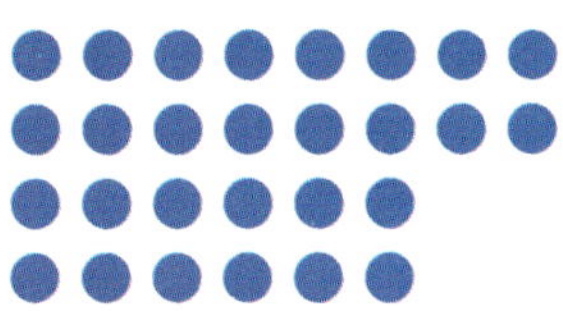

66. 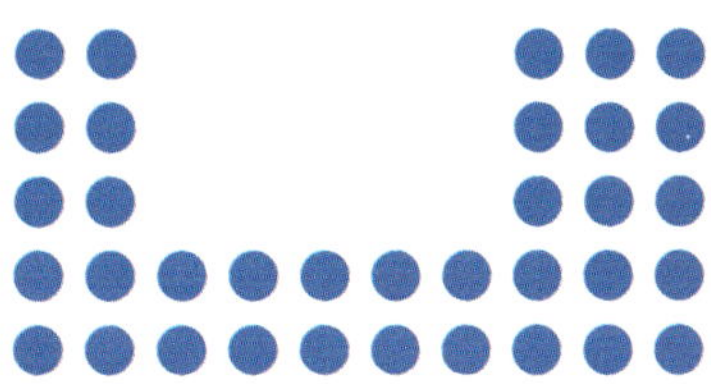

67. 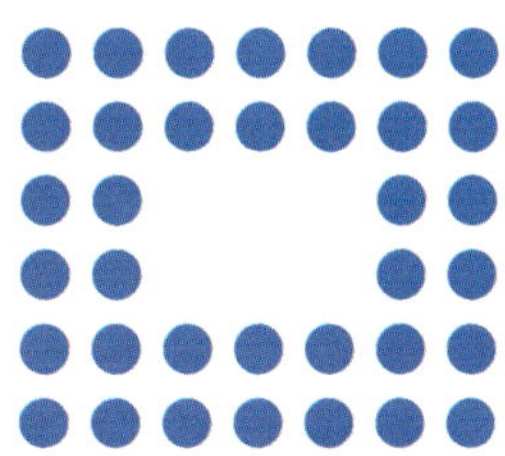

PROBLEM SOLVING

Strategy: Reasonable Answers

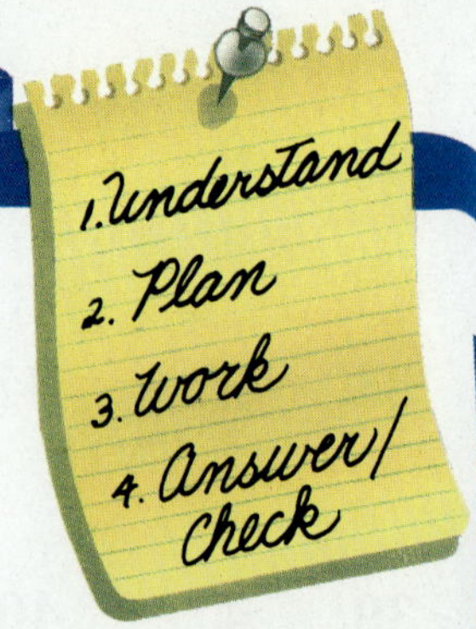

Two people answered a problem. What's wrong with their answers?

Six cows graze in a field. Each cow has 3 bells. How many bells are there altogether?

Answer: 18 cows   *Answer*: 9 bells

The first answer has the wrong label. The problem asks how many bells, not cows.

The second answer has the right label, but the number must be greater than 9. The person may have used addition instead of multiplication.

When you check your answer, make sure the number and the label make sense.

CLASS EXERCISES

Which answer makes sense?

1. Horses parade down the street in 6 rows. There are 4 horses in each row. How many horses are there?
a. 24 horses **b.** 24 rows

2. Five horses wait in the barn. Each horse needs 4 new shoes. How many shoes are needed in all?
a. 9 shoes **b.** 20 shoes

3 Jean bought horseshoes for her 6 horses. Each horse got 4 shoes. How many did she buy?
a. 24 horses **b.** 24 horseshoes

4. Bill's 7 pet hens each laid 4 eggs. How many eggs did the hens lay in all?
a. 11 eggs **b.** 28 eggs

PRACTICE

Solve. Check to make sure your answer is reasonable.

5. Nine horses each get 2 bales of hay. How many bales of hay do the horses get in all?

6. A farmer plants 3 strips of corn on 5 different hills. How many strips of corn does the farmer plant?

7. Eight pups each buried 6 bones. How many bones did the pups bury?

8. A farmer has 40 cows. 35 cows are in the barn. How many are not in the barn?

9. Bob, Rita, and Chris each brought 3 lambs to the fair. How many lambs did they bring in all?

10. Seven heads of lettuce grow in each of 3 rows. A rabbit eats 2 heads. How many are left?

11. A tractor pulls a drill. The drill can plant 12 rows of seeds at a time. How many rows does the drill plant if it is pulled across the field 3 times?

★ 12. Bob has 5 buckets of corn. Each bucket has 9 ears of corn. Bob puts 8 ears in the refrigerator. He freezes the rest. How many ears of corn does Bob freeze?

CHECKPOINT 1

Write the answer.

(pages 184–189)

1. 5×6
2. 5×8
3. 4×5
4. 6×4
5. 6×7
6. 6×6

Solve. Check to make sure your answer is reasonable.

(pages 190–191)

7. Jan plants 8 rows of bulbs. There are 5 bulbs in each row. How many bulbs does Jan plant?

Extra practice on page 412

MULTIPLYING SEVENS

Luisa is having a party on January 20. She buys 4 bags of balloons. There are 7 balloons in each bag. How many balloons does Luisa buy?

Think: 4 bags of 7 balloons
4 sevens = 28
$4 \times 7 = 28$

Luisa buys 28 balloons.

Luisa can skip count using her calculator. She presses 0 [+] 7 [=] to get 7. When she presses [=] again, she gets 14. Each time she presses [=], the calculator counts by 7.

To find 4 sevens, Luisa must be careful to press the [=] only 4 times.

CLASS EXERCISES

Count by sevens. What are the missing numbers?

1.

7	14	?	?	35	?	49	?	?

What is the product?

2. $1 \times 7 =$? **3.** $2 \times 7 =$? **4.** $3 \times 7 =$?

5. $4 \times 7 =$? **6.** $5 \times 7 =$? **7.** $6 \times 7 =$?

8. $7 \times 7 =$? **9.** $8 \times 7 =$? **10.** $9 \times 7 =$?

PRACTICE

Multiply.

11. $\begin{array}{r} 7 \\ \times 3 \\ \hline \end{array}$ **12.** $\begin{array}{r} 6 \\ \times 4 \\ \hline \end{array}$ **13.** $\begin{array}{r} 5 \\ \times 6 \\ \hline \end{array}$ **14.** $\begin{array}{r} 7 \\ \times 5 \\ \hline \end{array}$ **15.** $\begin{array}{r} 7 \\ \times 7 \\ \hline \end{array}$ **16.** $\begin{array}{r} 6 \\ \times 5 \\ \hline \end{array}$

17. $\begin{array}{r} 6 \\ \times 7 \\ \hline \end{array}$	**18.** $\begin{array}{r} 7 \\ \times 1 \\ \hline \end{array}$	**19.** $\begin{array}{r} 5 \\ \times 4 \\ \hline \end{array}$	**20.** $\begin{array}{r} 0 \\ \times 7 \\ \hline \end{array}$	**21.** $\begin{array}{r} 7 \\ \times 8 \\ \hline \end{array}$	**22.** $\begin{array}{r} 4 \\ \times 6 \\ \hline \end{array}$
23. $\begin{array}{r} 4 \\ \times 7 \\ \hline \end{array}$	**24.** $\begin{array}{r} 6 \\ \times 9 \\ \hline \end{array}$	**25.** $\begin{array}{r} 1 \\ \times 7 \\ \hline \end{array}$	**26.** $\begin{array}{r} 7 \\ \times 6 \\ \hline \end{array}$	**27.** $\begin{array}{r} 7 \\ \times 0 \\ \hline \end{array}$	**28.** $\begin{array}{r} 7 \\ \times 2 \\ \hline \end{array}$
29. $\begin{array}{r} 7 \\ \times 4 \\ \hline \end{array}$	**30.** $\begin{array}{r} 7 \\ \times 9 \\ \hline \end{array}$	**31.** $\begin{array}{r} 2 \\ \times 7 \\ \hline \end{array}$	**32.** $\begin{array}{r} 3 \\ \times 7 \\ \hline \end{array}$	**33.** $\begin{array}{r} 6 \\ \times 8 \\ \hline \end{array}$	**34.** $\begin{array}{r} 5 \\ \times 7 \\ \hline \end{array}$

Solve. Write *c* or *m* to tell whether you use a calculator or mental math.

CALCULATOR

35. $25 + 4 + 12 + 18 + 36$ **36.** 5×3

37. $5243 + 3857$ **38.** $7 + 7 + 7 + 7 + 7$

39. $531 - 279$ **40.** 4×7

PROBLEM SOLVING APPLICATIONS
Working with Time

Write the date. Remember, there are 7 days in a week.

41. 2 weeks after January 2 **42.** 3 weeks after January 6

43. 2 weeks after April 4 **44.** 2 weeks after February 9

Solve.

45. The date is November 3. You are going to visit friends in 3 weeks. Name the date you will see your friends.

46. For 3 days in September and 7 days in October you help at Children's Hospital. How many days do you help in all?

★ **47.** In the first week you save 5¢ a day. In the second week you save 6¢ a day. How much money do you save in 2 weeks?

★ **48.** You put $2.59 in your piggy bank. Then you saved 3¢ a day for 2 weeks. How much money did you save altogether?

MULTIPLYING EIGHTS

How many dots?

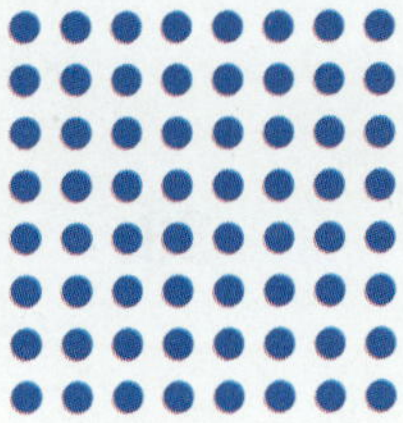

8 eights = 64
$8 \times 8 = 64$

9 eights = 72
$9 \times 8 = 72$

$0 \times 8 = 0$
$1 \times 8 = 8$
$2 \times 8 = 16$
$3 \times 8 = 24$
$4 \times 8 = 32$
$5 \times 8 = 40$
$6 \times 8 = 48$
$7 \times 8 = 56$
$8 \times 8 = 64$
$9 \times 8 = 72$

M Memorizing your facts helps you multiply quickly.

CLASS EXERCISES

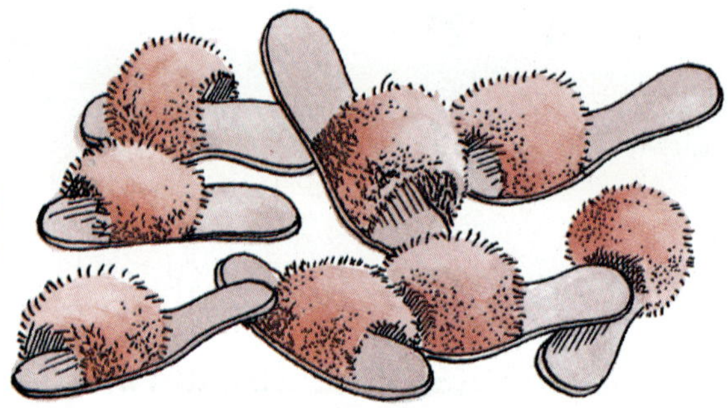

Count by eights.

1.

8	16	?	32	?	48	?	64	?

What is the product?

2. 0×8, 8×0
3. 1×8, 8×1
4. 2×8, 8×2
5. 3×8, 8×3
6. 4×8, 8×4
7. 5×8, 8×5
8. 6×8, 8×6
9. 7×8, 8×7
10. 8×8
11. 9×8, 8×9

PRACTICE

Multiply.

12. 8×2
13. 8×7
14. 8×3
15. 5×8
16. 8×9
17. 8×5
18. 8×0
19. 3×8
20. 8×8
21. 8×4
22. 8×6
23. 7×5

24. $\begin{array}{r}7\\ \times 8\\ \hline\end{array}$	**25.** $\begin{array}{r}6\\ \times 6\\ \hline\end{array}$	**26.** $\begin{array}{r}7\\ \times 4\\ \hline\end{array}$	**27.** $\begin{array}{r}8\\ \times 1\\ \hline\end{array}$	**28.** $\begin{array}{r}5\\ \times 7\\ \hline\end{array}$	**29.** $\begin{array}{r}6\\ \times 5\\ \hline\end{array}$
30. $\begin{array}{r}0\\ \times 8\\ \hline\end{array}$	**31.** $\begin{array}{r}7\\ \times 3\\ \hline\end{array}$	**32.** $\begin{array}{r}5\\ \times 5\\ \hline\end{array}$	**33.** $\begin{array}{r}7\\ \times 6\\ \hline\end{array}$	**34.** $\begin{array}{r}5\\ \times 4\\ \hline\end{array}$	**35.** $\begin{array}{r}5\\ \times 9\\ \hline\end{array}$
36. $\begin{array}{r}2\\ \times 8\\ \hline\end{array}$	**37.** $\begin{array}{r}6\\ \times 7\\ \hline\end{array}$	**38.** $\begin{array}{r}1\\ \times 8\\ \hline\end{array}$	**39.** $\begin{array}{r}7\\ \times 7\\ \hline\end{array}$	**40.** $\begin{array}{r}4\\ \times 8\\ \hline\end{array}$	**41.** $\begin{array}{r}6\\ \times 9\\ \hline\end{array}$
42. $\begin{array}{r}7\\ \times 9\\ \hline\end{array}$	**43.** $\begin{array}{r}5\\ \times 6\\ \hline\end{array}$	**44.** $\begin{array}{r}4\\ \times 9\\ \hline\end{array}$	**45.** $\begin{array}{r}6\\ \times 8\\ \hline\end{array}$	**46.** $\begin{array}{r}2\\ \times 9\\ \hline\end{array}$	**47.** $\begin{array}{r}6\\ \times 4\\ \hline\end{array}$

Multiply and add mentally. Work from left to right. Write just the answer.

MENTAL MATH

48. $3 \times 4 + 1$ **49.** $5 \times 2 + 4$ **50.** $6 \times 7 + 2$

51. $8 \times 5 + 2$ **52.** $2 \times 8 + 1$ **53.** $6 \times 8 + 3$

PROBLEM SOLVING APPLICATIONS
Choosing the Operation

The Spider family needs to buy new shoes. Each family member has 8 feet to fit.

54. The Spiders have 9 family members. How many feet are in the family?

55. Sabrina Spider tried on 7 pairs of tennis shoes. How many shoes did she try on?

56. On each foot, Sammy Spider tried on a tennis shoe, then a running shoe, and then a loafer. Sammy tried on how many shoes?

★ **57.** The Spiders' bill is \$2462 for play shoes and \$5731 for dress shoes. The Spiders have \$9000. How much money is left for socks?

★ **58.** Shelly buys a slipper for each foot. How many pairs of slippers does Shelly buy?

MULTIPLYING NINES

The computer screen shows 9 rows of 9 stars.

9 nines = 81
$9 \times 9 = 81$

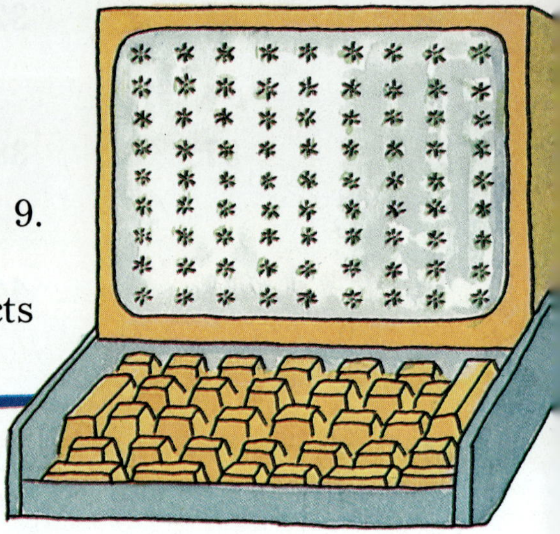

You could use a calculator to find 9×9.

9 ⊠ 9 ⊟ 81

It's much faster to remember your facts than to use a calculator.

CLASS EXERCISES

Count by nines. What are the missing numbers?

1.

9	18	?	36	?	54	63	?	?

How many stars are there? Use the picture if you need help.

2. 7 rows of 9 stars
$7 \times 9 =$?

3. 8 rows of 9 stars
$8 \times 9 =$?

4. 9 rows of 9 stars
$9 \times 9 =$?

5. 6 rows of 9 stars
$6 \times 9 =$?

6. 5 rows of 9 stars
$5 \times 9 =$?

7. 4 rows of 9 stars
$4 \times 9 =$?

PRACTICE

Multiply.

8. 9×7	**9.** 9×0	**10.** 9×6	**11.** 9×3	**12.** 9×8	**13.** 9×2
14. 9×5	**15.** 9×9	**16.** 9×1	**17.** 9×4	**18.** 0×9	**19.** 7×9
20. 6×9	**21.** 2×9	**22.** 5×9	**23.** 8×9	**24.** 4×9	**25.** 3×9

26. $\begin{array}{r} 1 \\ \times 9 \\ \hline \end{array}$	**27.** $\begin{array}{r} 8 \\ \times 7 \\ \hline \end{array}$	**28.** $\begin{array}{r} 6 \\ \times 8 \\ \hline \end{array}$	**29.** $\begin{array}{r} 8 \\ \times 5 \\ \hline \end{array}$	**30.** $\begin{array}{r} 4 \\ \times 8 \\ \hline \end{array}$	**31.** $\begin{array}{r} 6 \\ \times 4 \\ \hline \end{array}$
32. $\begin{array}{r} 8 \\ \times 8 \\ \hline \end{array}$	**33.** $\begin{array}{r} 7 \\ \times 6 \\ \hline \end{array}$	**34.** $\begin{array}{r} 6 \\ \times 5 \\ \hline \end{array}$	**35.** $\begin{array}{r} 7 \\ \times 8 \\ \hline \end{array}$	**36.** $\begin{array}{r} 8 \\ \times 6 \\ \hline \end{array}$	**37.** $\begin{array}{r} 5 \\ \times 7 \\ \hline \end{array}$

Multiply the numbers in the parentheses first.
Write the product.

★ **38.** $(2 \times 4) + 3$ ★ **39.** $7 + (3 \times 2)$ ★ **40.** $(3 \times 3) + 5$

Match. You may use some letters more than once.

CALCULATOR

41. 0 [×] 8 [=] **42.** 9 [×] 8 [=] **A.** 0 **B.** 72

43. 6 [×] 4 [=] **44.** 6 [×] 0 [=] **C.** 24 **D.** 8

45. 8 [×] 9 [=] **46.** 3 [×] 8 [=] **E.** 56 **F.** 64

47. 8 [×] 1 [=] **48.** 3 [×] 7 [+] 3 [=] **G.** 1 **H.** 6

PROBLEM SOLVING APPLICATIONS
Choosing the Operation

Solve.

49. Seven teams enter the relay race. Three of the teams win ribbons. How many teams do not win ribbons?

50. Eight teams enter the volleyball finals. Each team has 8 players. How many players will be playing in the finals?

51. Which race has the greater number of players, a race with 7 teams of 9 or a race with 8 teams of 8?

★ **52.** How many runners run in two races? The first race has 8 teams of 8. The second race has 7 teams of 8.

★ **53.** Write the products in order from least to greatest.

7×4 6×5 3×9 6×6 8×4 7×5

PRACTICE MULTIPLYING 0–9

The multiplication machine changes numbers. Here's how it works. First you give it a rule. Then the machine uses the rule to change every number you enter.

The rule for this machine is multiply by 5. Every number that goes in comes out five times greater.

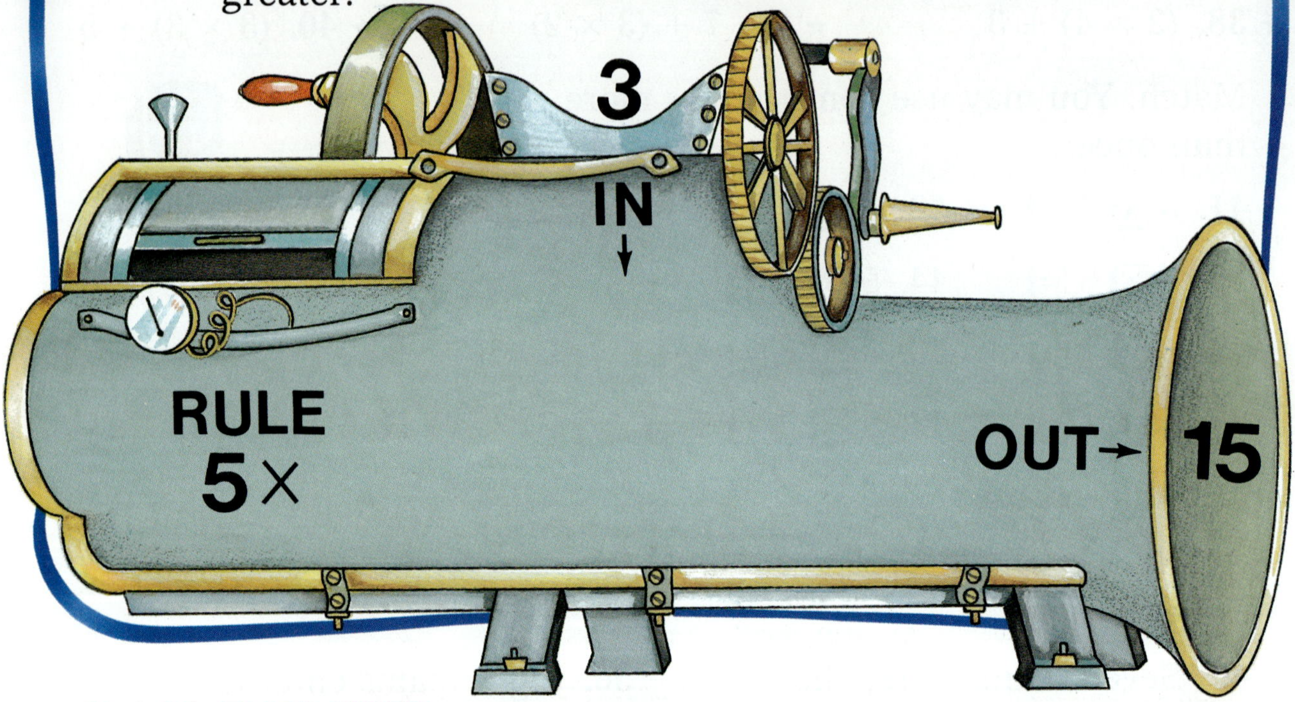

CLASS EXERCISES

Look at the rule for each machine. Tell what number will come out if the given number goes in.

	Rule 7 ×	
	In	Out
1.	1	?
2.	5	?
3.	3	?
4.	9	?
5.	0	?

	Rule 2 ×	
	In	Out
6.	5	?
7.	7	?
8.	1	?
9.	2	?
10.	9	?

	Rule 6 ×	
	In	Out
11.	4	?
12.	6	?
13.	0	?
14.	?	48
15.	?	6

PRACTICE

Multiply.

16. 3×5	**17.** 6×4	**18.** 7×2	**19.** 5×9	**20.** 7×6	**21.** 8×8
22. 0×6	**23.** 4×3	**24.** 9×6	**25.** 8×5	**26.** 5×5	**27.** 7×4
28. 7×9	**29.** 6×3	**30.** 9×9	**31.** 8×5	**32.** 4×4	**33.** 9×8
34. 8×7	**35.** 6×6	**36.** 8×9	**37.** 4×7	**38.** 3×7	**39.** 8×6

MIXED REVIEW

Write the answer.

40. 2×3 **41.** $6 + 4$ **42.** 6×3 **43.** $9 - 6$

44. 4×3 **45.** 3×9 **46.** $5 + 4$ **47.** $18 - 9$ **48.** 4×4

PROBLEM SOLVING APPLICATIONS
Using Money

What do you pay?

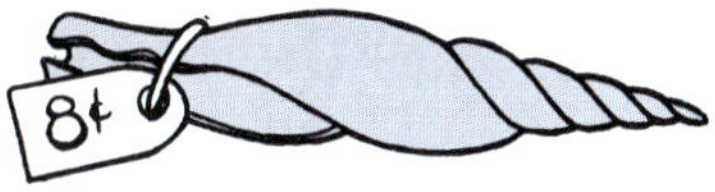

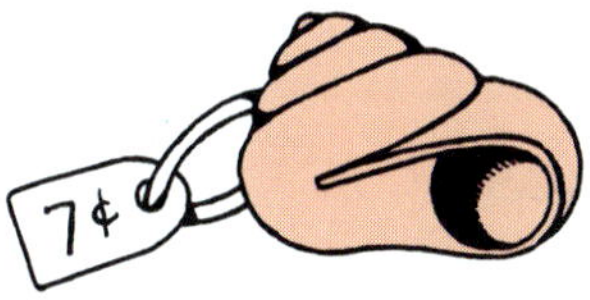

49. for 7 

50. for 5 

51. for 4 

52. for 5 

53. for 9 

54. for 5 

★ **55.** for one of each

★ **56.** for 6  and 6 

★ **57.** for 2  and 4 

★ **58.** for 6 of each , , and 

PROBLEM SOLVING
Strategy: Using a Bar Graph

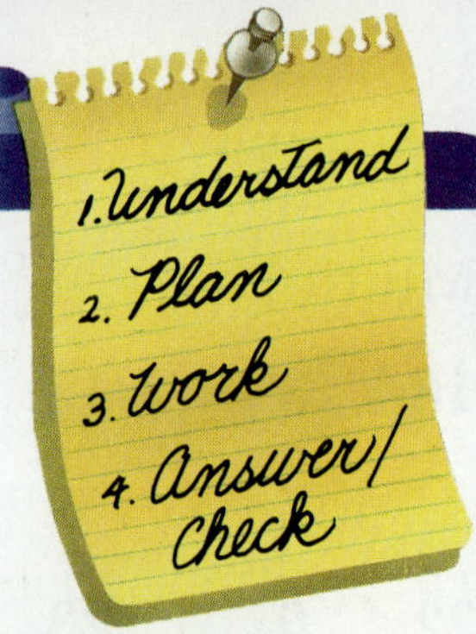

A **bar graph** helps you see and compare numbers. This graph shows the number of students in each class at Clown School.

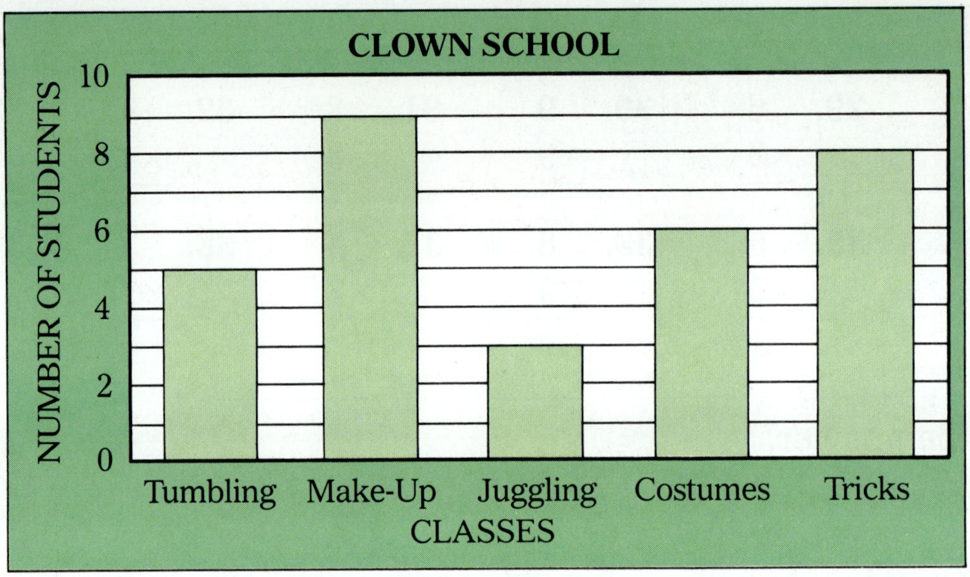

CLASS EXERCISES

Use the bar graph to solve.

1. How many students are learning to juggle?

2. How many students are learning about tumbling?

3. Which class has the most students?

4. Which class has the fewest students?

PRACTICE

Use the bar graph to solve.

5. Which class has twice as many students as the Juggling class?

6. How many students are in all of the classes?

Use the bar graph to solve.

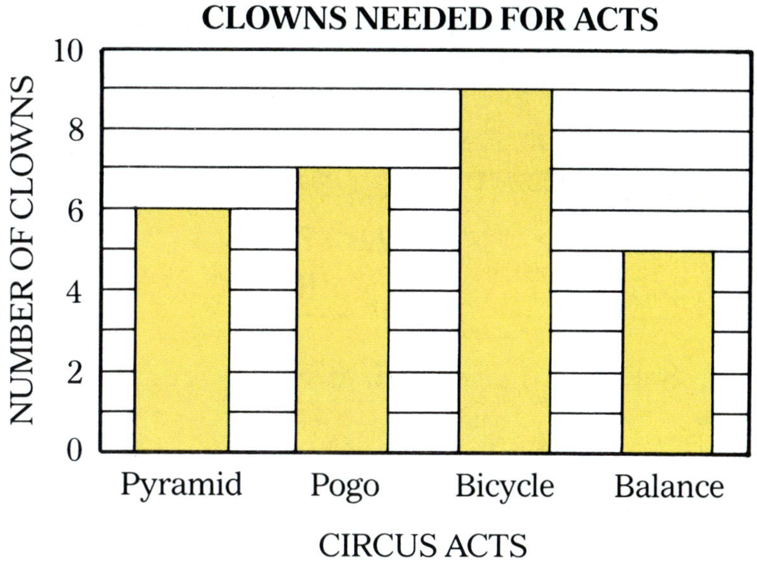

7. Write the acts in order from fewest clowns needed to the most clowns needed.

8. Nine times as many clowns tried out for the Bicycle Act as were needed. How many clowns tried out for the Bicycle Act?

9. How many more clowns are needed for the Pogo Act than the Balance Act?

10. How many clowns are needed for all four acts?

★ 11. Each week Smiley practices head stands for 6 hours, Boo for 4 hours, and Lazy for 2 hours. Make a bar graph to show the numbers of hours the clowns practice each week.

CHECKPOINT 2

Write the answer.
(pages 192–199)

1. $\begin{array}{r} 7 \\ \times 6 \\ \hline \end{array}$ 2. $\begin{array}{r} 8 \\ \times 8 \\ \hline \end{array}$ 3. $\begin{array}{r} 9 \\ \times 9 \\ \hline \end{array}$

Use the bar graph above to solve. *(pages 200–201)*

4. How many clowns are needed for both the Pogo and Bicycle Acts?

Extra practice on page 412

CHAPTER 7 TEST

Write the answer. *(pages 184–189)*

1. 6×5 **2.** 7×6 **3.** 6×6 **4.** 5×9

5. 8 × 5 **6.** 6 × 0 **7.** 5 × 5 **8.** 8 × 6

Solve. Check your answer. *(pages 190–191)*

9. Chris wrapped 6 gifts. Each gift had 2 bows. How many bows did Chris make?

10. There were 6 turtles. Each turtle laid 4 eggs. How many eggs were laid?

Write the answer. *(pages 192–195)*

11. 1×7 **12.** 7×8 **13.** 5×7 **14.** 8×8

Write the answer. *(pages 196–199)*

15. 9 × 0 **16.** 8 × 9 **17.** 9 × 6 **18.** 9 × 9

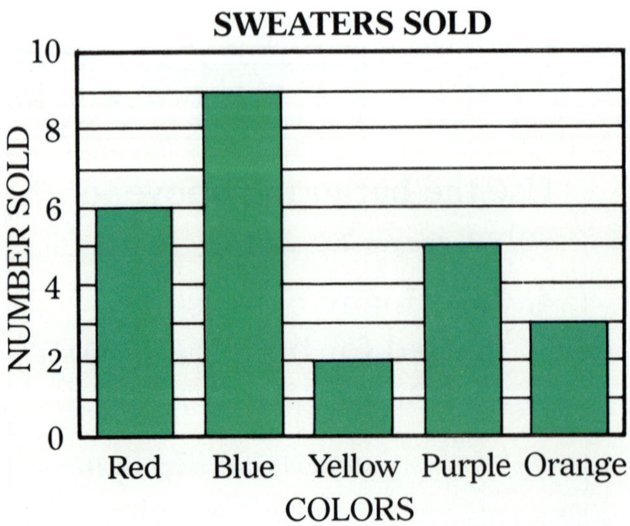

Use the bar graph to answer the questions. *(pages 200–201)*

19. How many more blue sweaters were sold than purple sweaters?

20. How many red, blue, and yellow sweaters were sold altogether?

Extra practice on page 413

MATHEMATICS and LANGUAGE ARTS

Knowing where words come from can make it easier to figure out what they mean. The word *twenty* was shortened from *two tens*.

What do the following words mean?

1. thirty

2. fifty

3. ninety

Sometimes words can have different meanings. The word *score* can be used for points in games or tests. It can also be used to mean *twenty*.

WHAT DOES IT MEAN?

How many years are the following?

4. four score

5. two score and three

Prefixes are word parts that sometimes give clues to a word's meaning. The chart shows some number prefixes and their meanings.

Prefix	bi	hex	oct	dec
Meaning	2	6	8	10

Complete.

6. A hexagon has ? sides.

7. A decade is ? years.

8. A bicycle has ? wheels.

9. An octopus has ? legs.

Enrichment

Linda likes to sleep late. She wants school to start at 9:00 A.M. rather than at 8:00 A.M.

Before Linda tells the principal about her idea, she takes a *survey* of teachers and students. Her survey looks like the one at the right.

When Linda gets the surveys back, she uses *tallies* to keep track of the answers. Each tally mark stands for one answer. Linda writes the tally marks in groups of five. Then she counts by five or multiplies to find the number.

	Tallies	Number
8:00 A.M.	𝍸𝍸𝍸𝍸 ||	22
8:30 A.M.	𝍸𝍸 |||	13
9:00 A.M.	𝍸 ||	7

Linda found out that most students wanted to start school at 8:00 A.M.

SURVEYS AND TALLIES

Write the standard form for the tallies.

1. 𝍸 ||　　**2.** 𝍸𝍸𝍸 |||

3. 𝍸𝍸 ||||　　**4.** 𝍸𝍸𝍸𝍸 |

Write the tallies for the standard form.

5. 11　　**6.** 23　　**7.** 14

8. 36　　**9.** 53

Bill's class sells notebooks at the school fair. Bill wonders whether more students or more adults buy the notebooks. To find out, Bill makes a list of the buyers.

Write the answer.

10. Use tallies to show how many students bought notebooks.

11. Use tallies to show how many adults bought notebooks.

12. Count your tallies. In standard form, write the number of students, then the number of adults.

13. Who bought more notebooks, students or adults?

CUMULATIVE REVIEW

Choose the correct answer. Choose *a*, *b*, *c*, or *d*.

Order the numbers from greatest to least.

1. 7893 9416 7516 8793

a. 9416 8793 7893 7516
b. 7893 9416 8793 7516
c. 7516 7893 8793 9416
d. none of these

2. 5871 5824 5817 5842

a. 5817 5824 5842 5871
b. 5842 5871 5817 5824
c. 5871 5842 5824 5817
d. none of these

Find the matching value.

3. 95¢

a. $9.50
b. $95.99
c. $.95
d. none of these

4. 392¢

a. $392
b. $3.92
c. $39.2
d. none of these

5. 3 dollars 6 quarters

a. $4.50
b. $3.50
c. $3.25
d. none of these

Find the answer.

6.
```
   $.55
 +  .26
```

a. $.71
b. $.72
c. $.29
d. none of these

7.
```
   $30.00
 −   4.83
```

a. $34.83
b. $26.27
c. $25.17
d. none of these

8.
```
   $43.96
 +  35.13
```

a. $18.83
b. $79.09
c. $78.09
d. none of these

Estimate to solve.

9. Cliff's new bike horn cost $6.93 and a small can of oil cost $1.09. About how much money did Cliff spend?

a. $6.00
b. $5.00
c. $8.00
d. $4.00

10. Sara received $15.00 as a gift. She bought a puzzle for $3.76. About how much money does she have left?

a. $10.00
b. $11.00
c. $18.00
d. $19.00

Find the correct time.

11. 

a. 8:17
b. 8:23
c. 7:23
d. none of these

12. 

a. 5 minutes before 11
b. 5 minutes before 10
c. 5 minutes after 11
d. none of these

13. 

a. a quarter to three
b. a quarter past three
c. a quarter to four
d. none of these

14. 

a. 7 minutes after 5
b. 5 minutes after 7
c. 7 minutes before 5
d. none of these

LANGUAGE and VOCABULARY REVIEW

Use the words to complete the sentences. Write the words on your own paper.

facts　　equals
calculator　　multiplication table　　bar graph

1. A _?_ has factors across the top and side with the products written in between.

2. A _?_ is a tool you can use to add, subtract, multiply, or divide quickly.

3. Another way to say "means the same as" is _?_.

4. $2 + 3 = 5$ and $7 + 8 = 15$ are examples of addition _?_.

5. A _?_ helps you see and compare numbers.

PROGRAMS

A **program** is a list of steps that tells the computer what to do.

Line numbers are used to tell the computer the order of the steps.

Here are steps that are like a program. They tell how to brush your teeth.

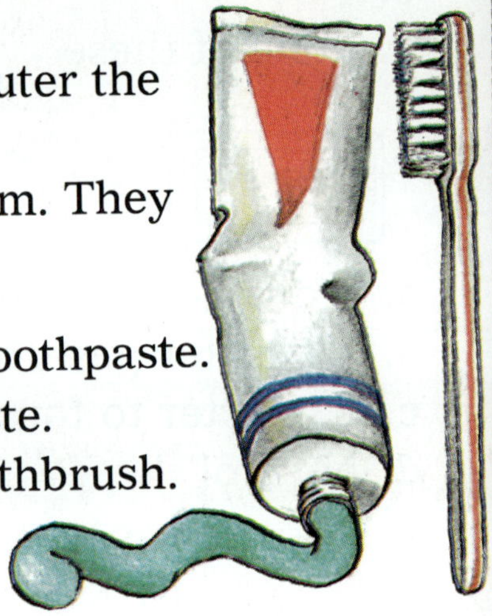

Count by tens to write line numbers.

10 Get toothbrush and toothpaste.
20 Take cap off toothpaste.
30 Put toothpaste on toothbrush.
40 Brush teeth.
50 Rinse mouth.

Put each program in order. Use 10, 20, 30, and so on as line numbers.

1. Put on shoes.
Put on socks.
Tie shoes.

2. Eat an orange.
Get an orange.
Peel an orange.

3. Read a book.
Open a book.
Go to the library.
Choose a book.

4. Pay for bread.
Go home.
Go to the store.
Choose the bread.

5. Fill bathtub with water.
Turn off the water.
Take a bath.
Turn on the water.

6. Add the two numbers.
Write the second addend.
Write the sum.
Write the first addend.

8

Little rooms were built on a beach. A painter painted 2 rooms each hour. How long did it take to paint 6 rooms? Think of the rooms grouped by twos.

DIVISION FACTS

SUBTRACTING THE SAME NUMBER

To find out how many cubes are in 4 twos, you can add or multiply.

Add.

$2 + 2 + 2 + 2 = 8$

Multiply.

$4 \times 2 = 8$

To find out how many twos are in 8, you can subtract or divide.

Subtract.

$$\begin{array}{r} 8 \\ -\,2 \\ \hline 6 \\ -\,2 \\ \hline 4 \\ -\,2 \\ \hline 2 \\ -\,2 \\ \hline 0 \end{array}$$

Divide.

$8 \div 2 = 4$

You say, *eight divided by two equals four.*

CLASS EXERCISES

Tell how many twos.

1. $$\begin{array}{r} 4 \\ -\,2 \\ \hline 2 \\ -\,2 \\ \hline 0 \end{array}$$

_?_ twos are in 4.
$4 \div 2 =$ _?_

2. $$\begin{array}{r} 6 \\ -\,2 \\ \hline 4 \\ -\,2 \\ \hline 2 \\ -\,2 \\ \hline 0 \end{array}$$

_?_ twos are in 6.
$6 \div 2 =$ _?_

PRACTICE

Complete.

3. ? twos are in 4.
   $4 \div 2 =$?

4. ? twos are in 10.
   $10 \div 2 =$?

5. ? twos are in 12.
   $12 \div 2 =$?

6. ? twos are in 6.
   $6 \div 2 =$?

7. ? twos are in 8.
   $8 \div 2 =$?

8. ? twos are in 16.
   $16 \div 2 =$?

9. ? twos are in 14.
   $14 \div 2 =$?

10. ? twos are in 18.
    $18 \div 2 =$?

PROBLEM SOLVING APPLICATIONS
Choosing a Strategy

Solve.

11. There are 10 boys in a class. How many groups of 2 can they form?

12. There are 12 people on a team. How many groups of 2 can they form?

13. There are 10 girls in one class, 12 in the next, and 18 in the next. How many girls are there in all?

14. There are 43 people watching a football game. At half time, 29 leave. About how many people are left?

15. In this lesson you subtracted twos from 2, 4, 6, 8, 10, 12, 14, 16, and 18. Are these numbers even or odd?

★ 16. Can you subtract twos from an odd number and get zero?

DIVIDING BY TWO

There are 14 counters placed in groups of two. To find the number of groups, you can subtract twos or you can divide.

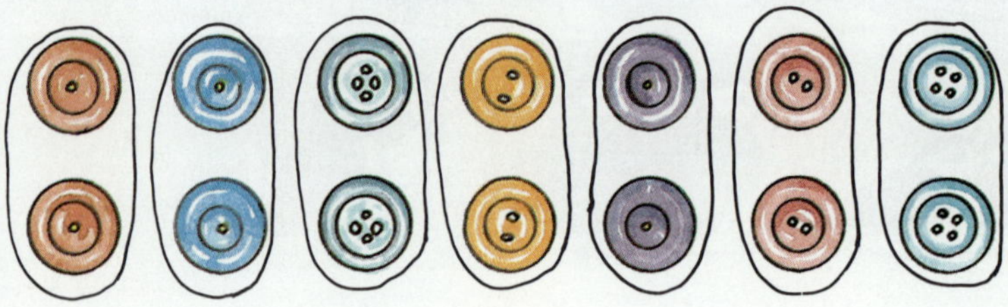

14 divided by 2 equals 7

$14 \div 2 = 7$

↑

quotient

There are 7 groups of counters.

CLASS EXERCISES

Divide.

1. 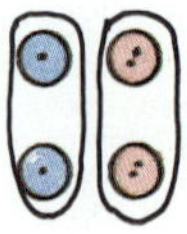

$4 \div 2$

2. 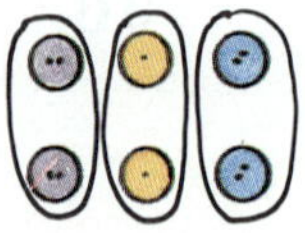

$6 \div 2$

3. 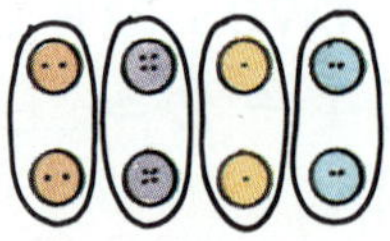

$8 \div 2$

4. 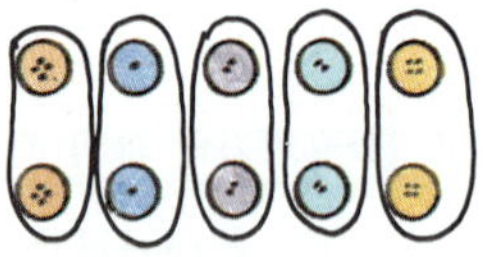

$10 \div 2$

5. 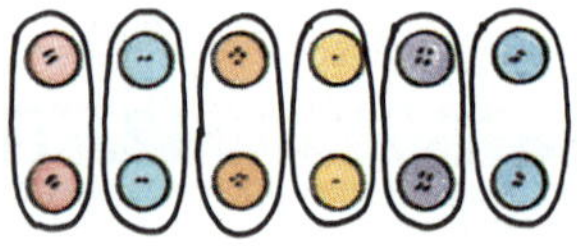

$12 \div 2$

6. 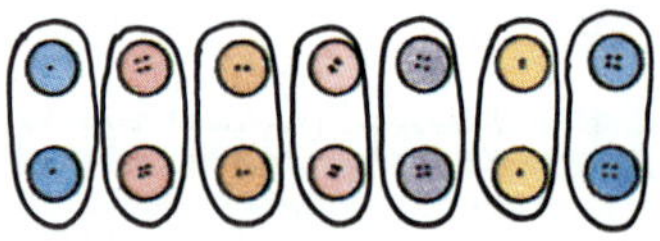

$14 \div 2$

7. 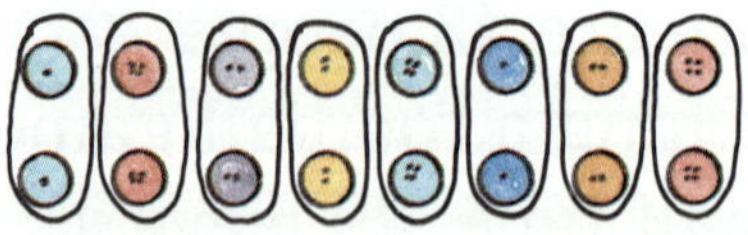

$16 \div 2$

8. 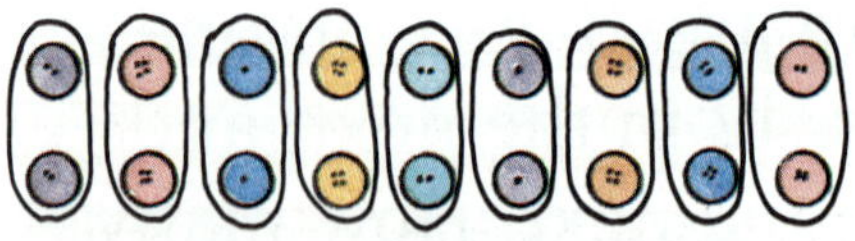

$18 \div 2$

Which number is the quotient?

9. $6 \div 2 = 3$ **10.** $8 \div 2 = 4$ **11.** $18 \div 2 = 9$

12. $14 \div 2 = 7$ **13.** $10 \div 2 = 5$ **14.** $16 \div 2 = 8$

PRACTICE

Divide.

15. 4 ÷ 2 **16.** 12 ÷ 2 **17.** 18 ÷ 2 **18.** 8 ÷ 2

19. 14 ÷ 2 **20.** 6 ÷ 2 **21.** 16 ÷ 2 **22.** 10 ÷ 2

Divide by 2.

23. 16 **24.** 4 **25.** 8 **26.** 12 **27.** 10 **28.** 18

MIXED REVIEW

Complete.

29. 2 dollars, 2 quarters, 1 dime, and 1 nickel equals $ __?__.

30. 1 half dollar, 3 dimes, 5 nickels, and 1 penny equals $ __?__.

31. 45 minutes after 2:00 is the same as __?__ minutes before 3:00.

32. 10 minutes before 4:00 is the same as __?__ minutes after 3:00.

PROBLEM SOLVING APPLICATIONS
Choosing the Operation

Solve.

33. Michael buys 18 buttons. Two buttons are in each package. How many packages does he buy?

34. Joel has 8 shirts. Each shirt has 4 buttons. How many buttons in all are on the shirts?

35. Pearl's Coat Shop has 16 coats in stock. If Pearl sells 2 coats a day, can she sell all the coats in a week?

★ **36.** Sue can sew 5 buttons on a dress in 18 minutes. How long does it take Sue to sew 15 buttons?

★ **37.** Bob can sew one button in 5 minutes. Jim can sew one button in 10 minutes. How many buttons can they sew together in 40 minutes?

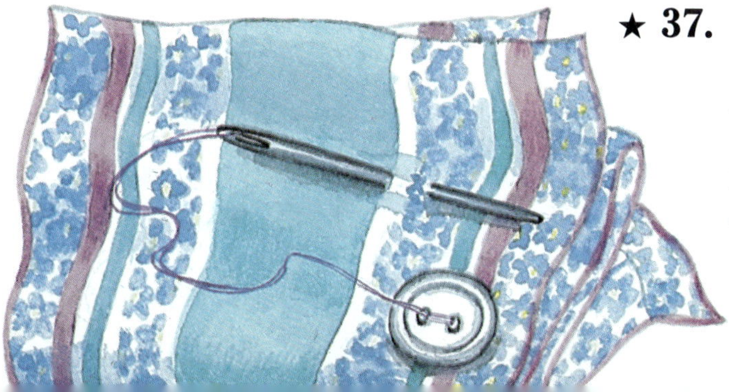

DIVIDING BY THREE

To divide 12 by 3, you can count backwards by threes.

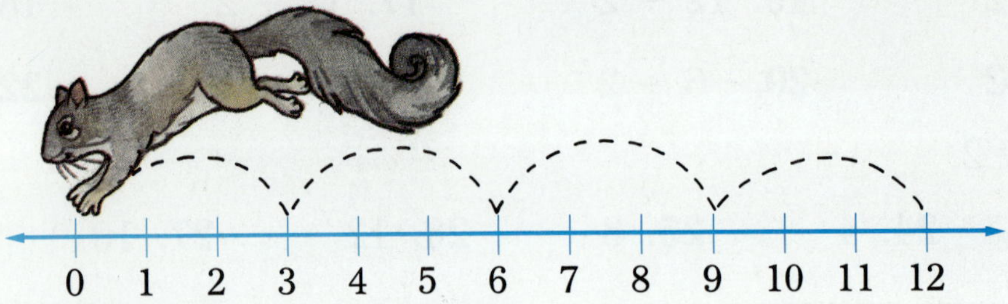

There are 4 threes in 12. $12 \div 3 = 4$

Here are two ideas that can help you remember some facts.

When you divide a number by itself, the quotient is 1.

$3 \div 3 = 1$

When you divide a number by 1, the quotient is the number.

$3 \div 1 = 3$

CLASS EXERCISES

Count back by threes.

1.

27	24	?	18	?	12	9	?	?	0

What is the quotient?

2. 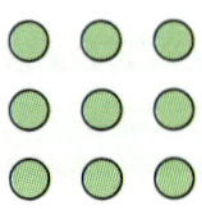

_?_ threes in 9

$9 \div 3 =$ _?_

3. 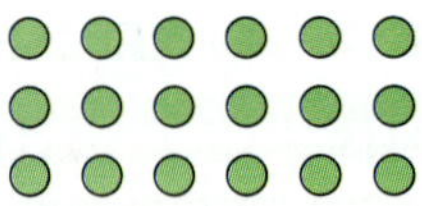

_?_ threes in 18

$18 \div 3 =$ _?_

4. 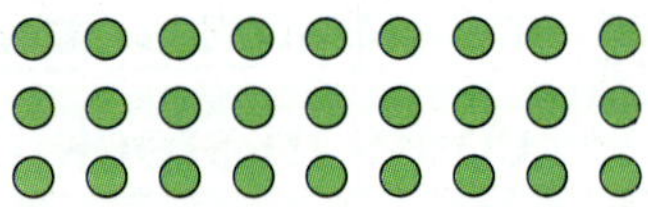

_?_ threes in 27

$27 \div 3 =$ _?_

5. 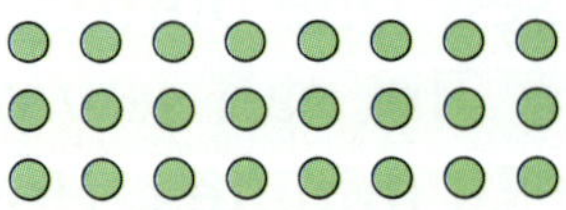

_?_ threes in 24

$24 \div 3 =$ _?_

6. 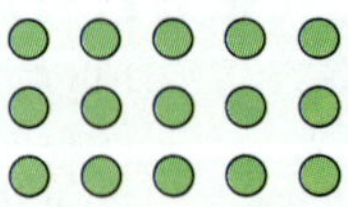

_?_ threes in 15

$15 \div 3 =$ _?_

7. 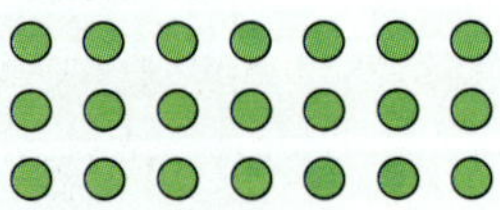

_?_ threes in 21

$21 \div 3 =$ _?_

PRACTICE

Divide.

8. 6 ÷ 3	**9.** 9 ÷ 3	**10.** 12 ÷ 3	**11.** 6 ÷ 2
12. 15 ÷ 3	**13.** 3 ÷ 3	**14.** 18 ÷ 3	**15.** 21 ÷ 3
16. 12 ÷ 2	**17.** 2 ÷ 1	**18.** 3 ÷ 3	**19.** 3 ÷ 1
20. 2 ÷ 2	**21.** 24 ÷ 3	**22.** 14 ÷ 2	**23.** 27 ÷ 3
24. 4 ÷ 2	**25.** 10 ÷ 2	**26.** 16 ÷ 2	**27.** 18 ÷ 2

Divide the number by 3.

28. 21 **29.** 12 **30.** 24 **31.** 15 **32.** 27 **33.** 18

PROBLEM SOLVING APPLICATIONS
Choosing a Strategy

Solve.

34. Ed found 15 acorns. Mary found 24 acorns. Susan found 21 acorns. About how many acorns did they find altogether?

35. A squirrel has 27 acorns. It eats 3 acorns a day. How many days will the acorns last?

36. Ed hid 5 acorns in each of 4 trees. How many acorns did he hide?

★ **37.** Susan hides 18 acorns. She puts 3 acorns under each rock. A squirrel takes the acorns from under 2 rocks. How many acorns are still hidden?

DIVIDING BY FOUR

You have 24 strawberries. You put 4 in each bowl. How many bowls do you fill?

You can use a multiplication fact to answer this division problem.

M **Think:** What number times 4 equals 24?

6 fours are 24.

$6 \times 4 = 24$ so $24 \div 4 = 6$

You fill 6 bowls.

CLASS EXERCISES

What is the product and the quotient?

1. 

2×4
$8 \div 4$

2. 

3×4
$12 \div 4$

3. 

4×4
$16 \div 4$

4. 

5×4
$20 \div 4$

5. 6×4
$24 \div 4$

6. 7×4
$28 \div 4$

7. 8×4
$32 \div 4$

8. 9×4
$36 \div 4$

PRACTICE

Divide.

9. $4 \div 4$	**10.** $12 \div 3$	**11.** $6 \div 2$	**12.** $18 \div 3$
13. $8 \div 2$	**14.** $6 \div 3$	**15.** $16 \div 4$	**16.** $21 \div 3$
17. $20 \div 4$	**18.** $14 \div 2$	**19.** $24 \div 4$	**20.** $18 \div 2$
21. $12 \div 4$	**22.** $4 \div 1$	**23.** $12 \div 2$	**24.** $32 \div 4$
25. $24 \div 4$	**26.** $15 \div 3$	**27.** $16 \div 2$	**28.** $28 \div 4$
29. $27 \div 3$	**30.** $8 \div 4$	**31.** $10 \div 2$	**32.** $36 \div 4$

Write the missing factor.

MENTAL MATH

33. $\underline{?} \times 3 = 12$ **34.** $\underline{?} \times 7 = 28$ **35.** $\underline{?} \times 4 = 16$

36. $\underline{?} \times 5 = 15$ **37.** $\underline{?} \times 4 = 32$ **38.** $\underline{?} \times 9 = 36$

39. Would it have been faster to do Exercises 33-38 with paper and pencil?

PROBLEM SOLVING APPLICATIONS
Choosing the Operation

Solve.

40. Lucie bought 5 baskets of strawberries. Each basket has 9 strawberries. How many strawberries did Lucie buy?

41. Steve has 36 plums to put in jars. Each jar holds 4 plums. How many jars does Steve need?

★ **42.** Edna bought a bunch of carrots for $.59 and a head of lettuce for $.85. How much change did Edna get from a five-dollar bill?

★ **43.** Ralph serves 4 chunks of carrots in each serving of his carrot stew. For a pot of stew, Ralph cuts 3 carrots into 8 chunks each. How many servings are in a pot of Ralph's carrot stew?

DIVIDING BY FIVE

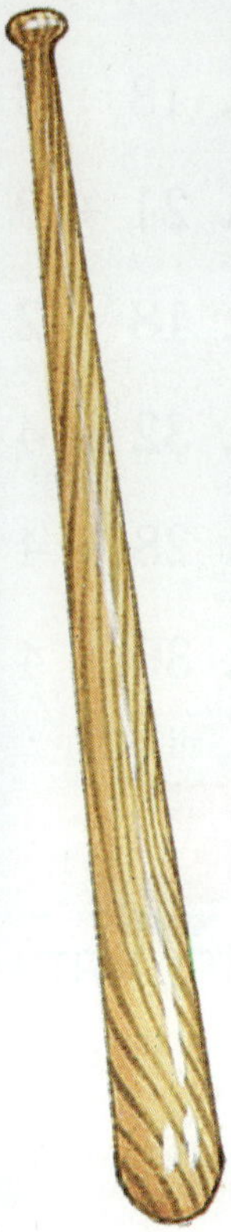

A coach has 20 baseballs. He gives 5 baseballs to each team. How many teams get baseballs?

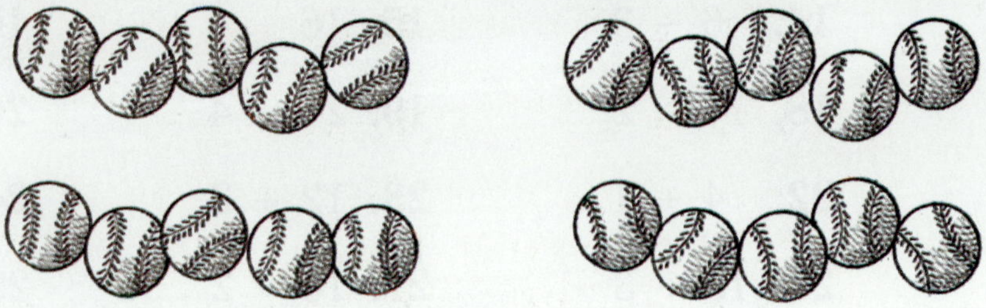

To solve, you need to know how many fives there are in 20.

You can use a multiplication fact to find the quotient.

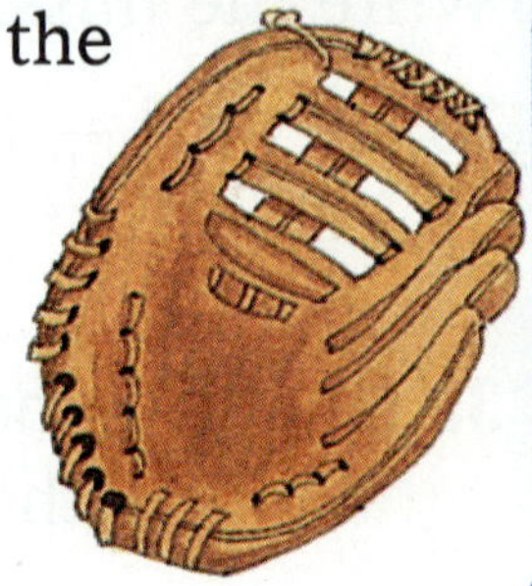

Think: What number times 5 equals 20?

$$4 \times 5 = 20 \text{ so } 20 \div 5 = 4$$

Four teams get baseballs.

CLASS EXERCISES

What is the product and the quotient?

1. 2×5 $10 \div 5$

2. 3×5 $15 \div 5$

3. 4×5 $20 \div 5$

4. 5×5 $25 \div 5$

5. 6×5 $30 \div 5$

6. 7×5 $35 \div 5$

7. 8×5 $40 \div 5$

8. 9×5 $45 \div 5$

PRACTICE

Divide.

9. $10 \div 5$ **10.** $25 \div 5$ **11.** $20 \div 5$ **12.** $40 \div 5$

13. $15 \div 5$ **14.** $35 \div 5$ **15.** $45 \div 5$ **16.** $30 \div 5$

17. 16 ÷ 4	**18.** 18 ÷ 2	**19.** 27 ÷ 3	**20.** 14 ÷ 2
21. 24 ÷ 4	**22.** 12 ÷ 4	**23.** 16 ÷ 2	**24.** 21 ÷ 3
25. 5 ÷ 5	**26.** 28 ÷ 4	**27.** 15 ÷ 3	**28.** 5 ÷ 1
29. 32 ÷ 4	**30.** 18 ÷ 3	**31.** 12 ÷ 2	**32.** 20 ÷ 4
33. 10 ÷ 2	**34.** 36 ÷ 4	**35.** 24 ÷ 3	**36.** 12 ÷ 3

Complete. Write ÷, +, or −.

37. 25 ▒ 5 = 5 **38.** 35 ▒ 5 = 30 **39.** 45 ▒ 5 = 50 **40.** 15 ▒ 5 = 3

★ **41.** (40 ▒ 5) ▒ 8 = 0 ★ **42.** (25 ▒ 5) ▒ 5 = 6

PROBLEM SOLVING APPLICATIONS
Nonroutine Problems

Write the player's number.

43. *Beth*: This number multiplied by 4 is 32.

44. *John*: This number multiplied by 5 is 45.

45. *Chris*: This number multiplied by itself is 16.

46. *Frank*: This number multiplied by itself is 25.

★ **47.** *Pete*: The product of its two digits equals the sum of the digits.

★ **48.** *Rosa*: The sum of its two digits is 10. The ones' digit divided by the tens' digit is 4.

TWO FORMS OF DIVISION

The band has 10 players. The players form rows of 2. How many rows are there?

To find the answer, you divide.

You can use either of two forms to divide.

$10 \div 2 = 5$ ← quotient

$\begin{array}{r} 5 \\ 2\overline{)10} \end{array}$ ← quotient (5)

There are 5 rows of players.

CLASS EXERCISES

Which number is the quotient?

1. $12 \div 2 = 6$ **2.** $10 \div 2 = 5$ **3.** $18 \div 2 = 9$ **4.** $14 \div 2 = 7$

5. $\begin{array}{r} 2 \\ 3\overline{)6} \end{array}$ **6.** $\begin{array}{r} 5 \\ 3\overline{)15} \end{array}$ **7.** $\begin{array}{r} 7 \\ 3\overline{)21} \end{array}$ **8.** $\begin{array}{r} 8 \\ 3\overline{)24} \end{array}$

Match. Name the letter.

9. $2\overline{)12}$ **10.** $5\overline{)25}$ **11.** $3\overline{)18}$ **12.** $2\overline{)16}$ **13.** $3\overline{)27}$

A. $16 \div 2$ **B.** $12 \div 2$ **C.** $25 \div 5$ **D.** $27 \div 3$ **E.** $18 \div 3$

Write another form for the division.

14. $12 \div 3 = 4$ **15.** $16 \div 4 = 4$ **16.** $14 \div 2 = 7$ **17.** $8 \div 2 = 4$

18. $\begin{array}{r} 2 \\ 3\overline{)6} \end{array}$ **19.** $\begin{array}{r} 3 \\ 4\overline{)12} \end{array}$ **20.** $\begin{array}{r} 6 \\ 5\overline{)30} \end{array}$ **21.** $\begin{array}{r} 8 \\ 4\overline{)32} \end{array}$

PRACTICE

Divide.

22. $3\overline{)9}$	**23.** $1\overline{)4}$	**24.** $5\overline{)10}$	**25.** $4\overline{)20}$	**26.** $3\overline{)18}$
27. $2\overline{)16}$	**28.** $3\overline{)24}$	**29.** $5\overline{)15}$	**30.** $4\overline{)24}$	**31.** $3\overline{)12}$
32. $2\overline{)18}$	**33.** $5\overline{)5}$	**34.** $3\overline{)21}$	**35.** $5\overline{)40}$	**36.** $4\overline{)16}$
37. $5\overline{)35}$	**38.** $4\overline{)28}$	**39.** $2\overline{)14}$	**40.** $5\overline{)25}$	**41.** $4\overline{)32}$
42. $4\overline{)12}$	**43.** $2\overline{)10}$	**44.** $4\overline{)36}$	**45.** $5\overline{)45}$	**46.** $3\overline{)15}$
47. $3\overline{)27}$	**48.** $5\overline{)30}$	**49.** $2\overline{)12}$	**50.** $5\overline{)20}$	**51.** $1\overline{)9}$

PROBLEM SOLVING APPLICATIONS
Choosing the Operation

Solve.

52. Twenty players in the school band divide into groups of 5. How many groups do they make?

53. A ticket to the band concert costs $1.25. Laura needs 2 tickets. How much money does she need?

54. There are 327 adults and 584 students at the band concert. Everyone has a chair. What is the least number of chairs at the concert?

55. A band uniform costs $38.92. How much do 2 uniforms cost?

★ **56.** There are 6 more trumpet players than tuba players. If there are 15 tuba players, how many players are there in all?

PROBLEM SOLVING
Strategy: Choosing the Operation

Before you solve a problem, you need to decide whether to add, subtract, multiply, or divide. Look at these examples of multiplication and division.

There are 5 seats in a row. How many seats are in 4 rows?

Multiply to find the total when the groups are equal.

$5 \times 4 = 20$
20 seats

There are 20 seats. If you put 5 seats in a row, how many rows would you make?

Divide to find how many groups when the groups are equal.

$20 \div 5 = 4$
4 rows

CLASS EXERCISES

Tell if you *add, subtract, multiply,* or *divide.* Solve.

1. Bill made 12 posters. He hung 4 posters in each school. In how many schools did Bill hang posters?

2. Erin placed chairs in 5 rows for the show. She put 7 chairs in each row. How many chairs were there in all?

3. The Comedy Group sold 28 tickets to the first show. They sold 32 tickets to the second show and 35 tickets to the third show. How many tickets did they sell?

4. The Comedy Group made \$190 by selling tickets. They spent \$119 to put on the shows. How much money did the Comedy Group have left?

PRACTICE

Solve.

5. The first show starts at 1:00. It lasts for 1 hour and 15 minutes. When does it end?

6. Rod stands on his head 7 times in each show. How many times does he stand on his head in all 3 shows?

7. Twenty-five ballet dancers trip over one another. They fall into piles of 5. How many piles of dancers are there?

8. Dan juggles 4 objects at a time. He juggles balls, then rolling pins, then hats. How many objects does Dan juggle in all?

9. Bob forgot his lines 16 times during the first show, 15 times during the second show, and 18 times during the third show. How many times did he forget his lines?

10. The band's 15 players sit in 3 rows. Six players sit in the first row and 5 in the second row. How many players sit in the third row?

★ **11.** Ruth sang 3 songs in each of the 3 shows. She sang 3 of the songs with the band. How many songs did she sing without the band?

★ **12.** Twelve dancers wore red masks and 6 wore green masks. They formed 2 equal lines. How many dancers were in each line?

CHECKPOINT 1

Divide. *(pages 210–221)*

1. $16 \div 2$ **2.** $15 \div 3$

3. $24 \div 4$ **4.** $35 \div 5$

5. $4\overline{)32}$ **6.** $5\overline{)30}$

Solve. *(pages 222–223)*

7. There are 16 children. Four children sit at each table. How many tables are there?

Extra practice on page 414

DIVIDING BY SIX

There are 24 swim fins with 6 in each row. How many rows of fins are there?

You want to know how many rows of 6 are in 24. You can divide to find out. Knowing your multiplication facts helps.

$4 \times 6 = 24$ so $24 \div 6 = 4$

There are 4 rows of swim fins.

If you divide 30 by 6, will the quotient be greater than 4?

Think: You are dividing a greater number by 6.
The quotient will be greater than 4.

CLASS EXERCISES

What is the product and the quotient?

1. 3×6
 $18 \div 6$

2. 4×6
 $24 \div 6$

3. 6×6
 $36 \div 6$

4. 1×6
 $6 \div 6$

5. 7×6
 $42 \div 6$

6. 8×6
 $48 \div 6$

7. 9×6
 $54 \div 6$

8. 2×6
 $12 \div 6$

PRACTICE

Divide.

9. $5\overline{)20}$	**10.** $6\overline{)18}$	**11.** $4\overline{)28}$	**12.** $6\overline{)30}$	**13.** $5\overline{)35}$	**14.** $3\overline{)24}$
15. $6\overline{)42}$	**16.** $3\overline{)21}$	**17.** $4\overline{)36}$	**18.** $5\overline{)30}$	**19.** $6\overline{)36}$	**20.** $4\overline{)20}$
21. $5\overline{)40}$	**22.** $6\overline{)24}$	**23.** $4\overline{)32}$	**24.** $6\overline{)54}$	**25.** $5\overline{)25}$	**26.** $6\overline{)6}$
27. $5\overline{)45}$	**28.** $4\overline{)12}$	**29.** $4\overline{)24}$	**30.** $6\overline{)48}$	**31.** $3\overline{)27}$	**32.** $6\overline{)12}$

Estimate. Write < or >.

ESTIMATE

33. $12 \div 4$ ▒ $16 \div 4$ **34.** $25 \div 5$ ▒ $15 \div 5$

35. $36 \div 6$ ▒ $48 \div 6$ **36.** $40 \div 5$ ▒ $45 \div 5$

37. $42 \div 6$ ▒ $30 \div 6$ **38.** $35 \div 5$ ▒ $40 \div 5$

PROBLEM SOLVING APPLICATIONS
Choosing the Operation

Solve.

39. The Stony Point Swim Club had a race. The 8 teams each had 6 swimmers. How many swimmers were there?

40. A group of 6 people can ride on the water slide at one time. There are 36 people in line. How many groups will ride?

★ **41.** Out of 30 swimmers, 18 swam in groups of 3. The others swam in groups of 4. How many groups were swimming?

★ **42.** A line of 36 students waited to tour a submarine. Every 5 minutes 6 people went on board. How many minutes was it before everyone was on board?

DIVIDING BY SEVEN

How many weeks are in 21 days?

You know there are 7 days in a week. How many sevens equal 21?

$3 \times 7 = 21$, so $21 \div 7 = 3$.

There are 3 weeks in 21 days.

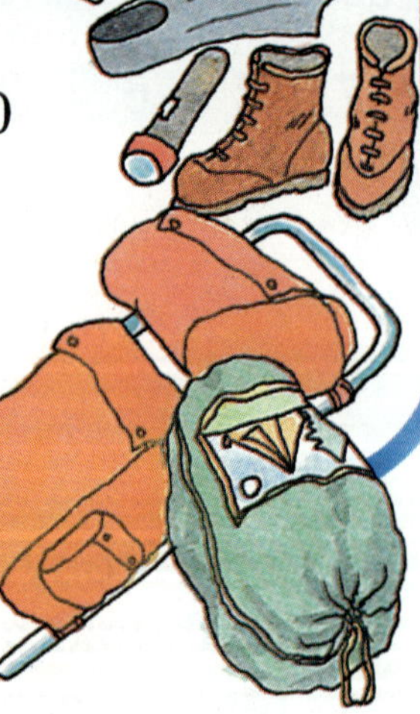

M What is the quotient when you divide 0 by 7?
Think: What number times 7 equals 0? $0 \times 7 = 0$

What is the quotient when you divide 7 by 0?
Think: What number times 0 equals 7? There is no number. You can't divide by zero.

CLASS EXERCISES

What is the product and the quotient?

1. 4×7
$28 \div 7$

2. 5×7
$35 \div 7$

3. 6×7
$42 \div 7$

4. 7×7
$49 \div 7$

5. 0×7
$0 \div 7$

6. 8×7
$56 \div 7$

7. 9×7
$63 \div 7$

8. 2×7
$14 \div 7$

PRACTICE

Divide.

9. $3\overline{)9}$ **10.** $5\overline{)20}$ **11.** $7\overline{)28}$ **12.** $7\overline{)14}$ **13.** $4\overline{)0}$ **14.** $5\overline{)25}$

15. $6\overline{)30}$ **16.** $7\overline{)21}$ **17.** $6\overline{)42}$ **18.** $7\overline{)7}$ **19.** $6\overline{)18}$ **20.** $5\overline{)30}$

21. $4\overline{)24}$ 22. $5\overline{)40}$ 23. $3\overline{)24}$ 24. $7\overline{)56}$ 25. $4\overline{)20}$ 26. $7\overline{)42}$

27. $6\overline{)36}$ 28. $4\overline{)28}$ 29. $7\overline{)49}$ 30. $4\overline{)16}$ 31. $5\overline{)45}$ 32. $3\overline{)27}$

33. $7\overline{)35}$ 34. $5\overline{)45}$ 35. $7\overline{)0}$ 36. $6\overline{)48}$ 37. $5\overline{)35}$ 38. $7\overline{)63}$

Decide quickly if you can divide. Write *yes* or *no*.

MENTAL MATH

39. $0 \div 5$ 40. $15 \div 0$ 41. $0\overline{)21}$ 42. $7\overline{)0}$ 43. $0\overline{)8}$

PROBLEM SOLVING APPLICATIONS
Choosing the Operation

Solve.

44. Roberto's family went on a fishing trip. They were gone 14 days. How many weeks were they gone?

45. Pearl's family drove to California. They were gone 28 days. How many weeks were they gone?

46. Roberto has 63 days of summer vacation. How many weeks of vacation does he have?

47. Pearl drives to the lake in 2 days. She fishes for 7 days. Then she drives home in 1 day. How many days is Pearl away from home?

★ 48. Pearl gave 3 fish to each of her 7 friends. She kept 4 fish for herself. How many fish did she have at the start?

★ 49. Roberto estimated that he would catch 3 fish an hour for 5 hours. If Roberto caught 18 fish, how far off was his estimate?

DIVIDING BY EIGHT

Before Alaska and Hawaii joined the Union in 1959, 48 stars were on the United States' flag. There were 8 stars in each row. How many rows of stars were there?

$6 \times 8 = 48$ so $48 \div 8 = 6$

There were 6 rows of stars.

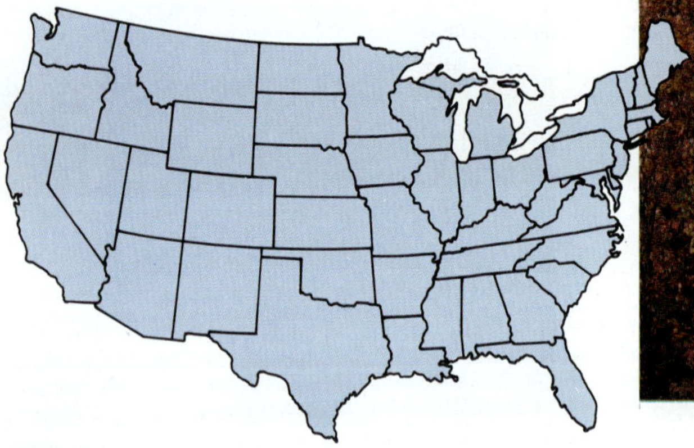

CLASS EXERCISES

What is the product and the quotient?

1. 6×8
 $48 \div 8$

2. 7×8
 $56 \div 8$

3. 8×8
 $64 \div 8$

4. 9×8
 $72 \div 8$

5. 4×8
 $32 \div 8$

6. 3×8
 $24 \div 8$

7. 5×8
 $40 \div 8$

8. 2×8
 $16 \div 8$

PRACTICE

Divide.

9. $8\overline{)8}$ **10.** $6\overline{)24}$ **11.** $4\overline{)20}$ **12.** $8\overline{)24}$ **13.** $5\overline{)25}$ **14.** $3\overline{)15}$

15. $7\overline{)35}$ **16.** $6\overline{)36}$ **17.** $5\overline{)30}$ **18.** $8\overline{)40}$ **19.** $8\overline{)0}$ **20.** $6\overline{)18}$

21. $8\overline{)16}$ 22. $5\overline{)35}$ 23. $4\overline{)16}$ 24. $6\overline{)48}$ 25. $5\overline{)45}$ 26. $8\overline{)56}$

27. $6\overline{)42}$ 28. $5\overline{)40}$ 29. $6\overline{)54}$ 30. $7\overline{)42}$ 31. $8\overline{)64}$ 32. $4\overline{)32}$

33. $3\overline{)24}$ 34. $2\overline{)16}$ 35. $7\overline{)49}$ 36. $7\overline{)56}$ 37. $4\overline{)28}$ 38. $8\overline{)72}$

39. $8\overline{)48}$ 40. $1\overline{)8}$ 41. $8\overline{)32}$ 42. $4\overline{)36}$ 43. $7\overline{)63}$ 44. $7\overline{)28}$

MIXED REVIEW

Round to the nearest ten. Estimate the answer.

45. $\begin{array}{r} 71 \\ -\ 29 \\ \hline \end{array}$ 46. $\begin{array}{r} 22 \\ +\ 28 \\ \hline \end{array}$ 47. $\begin{array}{r} 43 \\ -\ 19 \\ \hline \end{array}$ 48. $\begin{array}{r} 82 \\ +\ 69 \\ \hline \end{array}$ 49. $\begin{array}{r} 23 \\ +\ 81 \\ \hline \end{array}$

50. $\begin{array}{r} 51 \\ -\ 28 \\ \hline \end{array}$ 51. $\begin{array}{r} 78 \\ +\ 39 \\ \hline \end{array}$ 52. $\begin{array}{r} 91 \\ -\ 37 \\ \hline \end{array}$ 53. $\begin{array}{r} 62 \\ -\ 49 \\ \hline \end{array}$ 54. $\begin{array}{r} 83 \\ +\ 68 \\ \hline \end{array}$

PROBLEM SOLVING APPLICATIONS
Logical Thinking

Write the number of stars on the state flag. Use the clues to find the answer.

A. Arizona, California, and North Carolina each have the same number of stars.

B. Tennessee has 3 stars.

C. Missouri has 8 times as many stars as Tennessee.

D. Arkansas has 5 more stars than Missouri.

E. Missouri has 23 more stars than California.

55. Tennessee **56.** Missouri **57.** Arkansas

★ **58.** Arizona ★ **59.** California ★ **60.** North Carolina

★ **61.** Write your own problem about a state flag.

DIVIDING BY NINE

A farmer picked 81 pineapples. She has 9 boxes. She wants the same number of pineapples in each box. How many does she put in each box?

Think: How many would there be in 9 equal groups? To answer, you can divide by 9.

$9 \times 9 = 81$ so $81 \div 9 = 9$

She can put 9 pineapples in each box.

When you divide 81 by 9 on a calculator, you get 9. On some calculators, if you push the equals sign again, you get 1. What happened?

Each time you push the equals sign on this type of calculator, the quotient is divided by 9.

CLASS EXERCISES

What is the product and the quotient?

1. 2×9 / $18 \div 9$

2. 3×9 / $27 \div 9$

3. 4×9 / $36 \div 9$

4. 5×9 / $45 \div 9$

5. 6×9 / $54 \div 9$

6. 7×9 / $63 \div 9$

7. 8×9 / $72 \div 9$

8. 9×9 / $81 \div 9$

PRACTICE

Divide.

9. $9\overline{)0}$ **10.** $8\overline{)16}$ **11.** $7\overline{)28}$ **12.** $4\overline{)36}$ **13.** $6\overline{)42}$ **14.** $9\overline{)63}$

15. $8\overline{)40}$	**16.** $7\overline{)42}$	**17.** $8\overline{)24}$	**18.** $5\overline{)25}$	**19.** $7\overline{)63}$	**20.** $1\overline{)9}$
21. $9\overline{)18}$	**22.** $7\overline{)49}$	**23.** $5\overline{)45}$	**24.** $2\overline{)18}$	**25.** $9\overline{)9}$	**26.** $9\overline{)54}$
27. $8\overline{)32}$	**28.** $3\overline{)27}$	**29.** $9\overline{)72}$	**30.** $4\overline{)32}$	**31.** $9\overline{)36}$	**32.** $9\overline{)45}$
33. $8\overline{)72}$	**34.** $8\overline{)56}$	**35.** $9\overline{)81}$	**36.** $8\overline{)64}$	**37.** $9\overline{)27}$	**38.** $6\overline{)48}$

CALCULATOR

Write the number that would be shown on the calculator if you pushed the keys.

39. 36 ÷ 6 = =

40. 25 ÷ 5 = =

41. 49 ÷ 7 = =

42. 64 ÷ 8 = =

★ **43.** 8 ÷ 2 = = =

★ **44.** 27 ÷ 3 = =

PROBLEM SOLVING APPLICATIONS

Solve.

45. A farmer puts 72 carrots in 9 bags. He puts the same number in each bag. How many carrots are in each bag?

46. Ted bought 23 green apples and 49 red apples at the farm stand. How many apples did Ted buy?

★ **47.** A grocer emptied 30 apples from one box and 15 from another box. He placed all of the apples in 9 rows. How many apples were in each row?

★ **48.** A grocer had a bag of 18 carrots and a bag of 24 carrots. She took out the carrots. How many bunches of 6 can she make?

FACT FAMILIES

Multiplication and division facts may share the same numbers. Related facts are called a fact family.

$72 \div 9 = 8 \qquad 72 \div 8 = 9$

$8 \times 9 = 72 \qquad 9 \times 8 = 72$

You can see how these four facts are related by looking at the fact table. You can read the table either from the outside to the inside *or* from the inside to the outside.

×	1	2	3	4	5	6	7	8	9
1	1	2	3	4	5	6	7	8	9
2	2	4	6	8	10	12	14	16	18
3	3	6	9	12	15	18	21	24	27
4	4	8	12	16	20	24	28	32	36
5	5	10	15	20	25	30	35	40	45
6	6	12	18	24	30	36	42	48	54
7	7	14	21	28	35	42	49	56	63
8	8	16	24	32	40	48	56	64	72
9	9	18	27	36	45	54	63	72	81

CLASS EXERCISES

Complete.

1. $12 \div 4 =$?
$3 \times 4 =$?
$12 \div 3 =$?
$4 \times 3 =$?

2. $10 \div 2 =$?
$5 \times 2 =$?
$10 \div 5 =$?
$2 \times 5 =$?

3. $42 \div 6 =$?
$7 \times 6 =$?
$42 \div 7 =$?
$6 \times 7 =$?

4. $72 \div 8 =$?
$9 \times 8 =$?
$72 \div 9 =$?
$8 \times 9 =$?

5. $54 \div 9 =$?
$6 \times 9 =$?
$54 \div 6 =$?
$9 \times 6 =$?

PRACTICE

Divide.

6. $7\overline{)28}$	**7.** $9\overline{)27}$	**8.** $9\overline{)0}$	**9.** $9\overline{)54}$	**10.** $7\overline{)49}$	**11.** $8\overline{)48}$
12. $6\overline{)42}$	**13.** $8\overline{)64}$	**14.** $9\overline{)63}$	**15.** $6\overline{)54}$	**16.** $9\overline{)81}$	**17.** $8\overline{)32}$
18. $6\overline{)36}$	**19.** $9\overline{)45}$	**20.** $7\overline{)21}$	**21.** $4\overline{)24}$	**22.** $7\overline{)56}$	**23.** $9\overline{)9}$
24. $8\overline{)40}$	**25.** $7\overline{)63}$	**26.** $3\overline{)24}$	**27.** $5\overline{)35}$	**28.** $8\overline{)56}$	**29.** $9\overline{)72}$
30. $9\overline{)36}$	**31.** $7\overline{)35}$	**32.** $8\overline{)72}$	**33.** $7\overline{)42}$	**34.** $6\overline{)48}$	**35.** $4\overline{)32}$

36. What is 49 divided by 7?

★ **37.** What is $64 \div 8 \div 8$?

★ **38.** Divide 72 by 9. Then divide the answer by 4. What is the answer?

★ **39.** Add 12 and 13. Divide by 5. What is the answer?

MIXED REVIEW

Write the standard form.

40. 6 hundreds 8 tens 3 ones

41. four thousand three hundred twelve

42. 9000 + 800 + 30 + 2

43. four hundred sixty-five thousand

44. 9 thousands 7 hundreds 4 ones

PROBLEM SOLVING APPLICATIONS
Nonroutine Problems

45. Philip's pet moth ate holes in his homework. Help Philip. Find the missing numbers.

×	4	6	?	9
5	?	?	40	?
?	?	24	?	?
3	?	?	?	27
?	?	42	?	?

PROBLEM SOLVING

Strategy: Two-Step Problems

Sue is packing party decorations. She packs 4 stars in each box. If she packs 4 full boxes and 1 box with 3 stars, how many stars does she pack in all?

To solve this problem, you first multiply $4 \times 4 = 16$. Then you add $16 + 3 = 19$.

Sue packs 19 stars in all.

CLASS EXERCISES

Name the two operations you would use to solve the problem. Then solve.

1. Sue packs 5 candles in each box. She packs 3 full boxes and a box with 2 candles. How many candles does she pack in all?

2. Bob packs 4 boxes with 4 party hats in each box. He takes 2 of the hats out of 1 box because they are torn. How many hats does he have left?

3. Sue has 17 bells. Two are broken, so she doesn't pack them. How many boxes does she pack with 3 bells in each?

4. Bob packs 8 whistles in each box. If he packs 3 full boxes and 5 in another box, how many whistles does he pack in all?

PRACTICE

Solve.

5. Phyllis wants to bike for 13 minutes. She bikes 5 minutes along the river. She bikes 2 minutes through the park. How much longer does she have to bike?

6. Bob buys 8 cans of soup and 6 cans of fruit. He divides the cans equally between his knapsack and his basket. How many cans are in his basket?

7. Bill has 15 apples. Sally has 13. How many plates can they set out with 4 apples on each plate?

8. Rosa bikes 2 blocks to the library. Then she bikes twice as far from there to the store. How far does she bike altogether?

9. Bill buys 3 apples at 9¢ each and a pear at 8¢. How much does he spend in all?

10. Sally has 35¢. Can she buy 4 apples at 9¢ each?

11. Brenda puts air in tires. She fills the tires on 3 bicycles and 4 tricycles. How many tires does she fill?

★ 12. Bill buys 4 apples at 9¢ each and 5 pears at 8¢ each. How much change does he get from $1.00?

CHECKPOINT 2

Divide. *(pages 224–233)*

1. $42 \div 6$
2. $54 \div 6$
3. $49 \div 7$
4. $28 \div 7$
5. $8\overline{)56}$
6. $8\overline{)64}$
7. $9\overline{)36}$
8. $9\overline{)81}$

Solve. *(pages 234–235)*

9. Susan put 8 plums in each jar. She filled 6 jars and had 2 plums left over. How many plums did she have in all?

Extra practice on page 414

CHAPTER 8 TEST

Write the answer. *(pages 210–215)*

1. $16 \div 2$ **2.** $27 \div 3$ **3.** $12 \div 2$ **4.** $15 \div 3$

Write the answer. *(pages 216–221)*

5. $4\overline{)28}$ **6.** $5\overline{)45}$ **7.** $4\overline{)20}$ **8.** $5\overline{)35}$

Solve. *(pages 222–223)*

9. Mr. Johnson delivered 3 bags of groceries to each of 5 customers. How many bags of groceries did he deliver altogether?

10. Mr. Johnson unpacked 40 cans of tomatoes. He put an equal number of cans on each of 5 shelves. How many cans did he put on each shelf?

Write the answer. *(pages 224–227)*

11. $18 \div 6$ **12.** $36 \div 6$

13. $35 \div 7$ **14.** $63 \div 7$

Write the answer. *(pages 228–231)*

15. $9\overline{)0}$ **16.** $8\overline{)56}$

17. $8\overline{)64}$ **18.** $9\overline{)72}$

Solve. *(pages 234–235)*

19. Sandy buys 3 pencils at 7¢ each and a ruler for 15¢. How much does she spend in all?

20. Ed packs 4 toys in each box. He has 13 toy trucks and 19 puppets. How many boxes does Ed fill?

Extra practice on page 415

MATHEMATICS and HISTORY

The table shows the dates on which the first thirteen states joined the United States.

1. Write the states in order by the dates they entered the Union. Compare the year, then the month. If they are both the same, compare the days.

STATE	DATE JOINED
Connecticut	January 9, 1788
Delaware	December 7, 1787
Georgia	January 2, 1788
Maryland	April 28, 1788
Massachusetts	February 6, 1788
New Hampshire	June 21, 1788
New Jersey	December 18, 1787
New York	July 26, 1788
North Carolina	November 21, 1789
Pennsylvania	December 12, 1787
Rhode Island	May 29, 1790
South Carolina	May 23, 1788
Virginia	June 26, 1788

ORDER IN THE STATES!

2. What year did your state enter the Union? How long ago was that?

3. Florida and Texas were the only states to enter the Union in 1845. Florida entered on March 3. Texas entered on December 29. If Florida is twenty-seventh, what is Texas?

4. California entered the Union on September 9, 1850. Idaho entered the Union thirty years later. What year was that?

5. North Dakota was the thirty-ninth state to enter the Union. It entered on November 2, 1889. South Dakota entered later on that same day. What rank is South Dakota?

Enrichment

The flowers sell for 8¢ each. To find the cost of more than one flower, you can multiply.

2 flowers → 2 × 8 = 16¢
3 flowers → 3 × 8 = 24¢
4 flowers → 4 × 8 = 32¢

You can write a rule to show how to find the total cost.

■ × 8

The ■ stands for a missing number.

Rule: ■ × 8

Number of Flowers	5	6	7	8	9
Cost of Flowers	40¢	48¢	56¢	64¢	72¢

You can use a table to show the numbers you use for ■ and the answers.

Complete the table.

Rule: ■ ÷ 2

			1.	2.	3.	4.
Number for	2	4	6	8	?	12
Answer	1	2	?	?	5	?

FUNCTIONS

Rule: 15 + ■

		5.	6.	7.	8.	9.
Number for ■	4	5	6	7	?	?
Answer	19	?	?	?	23	24

When you write a rule it's often easier to use a letter instead of a ▮. A letter that stands for a missing number is called a **variable.**

Match the rule to the table. Write the letter.

A. $x \div 6$ **B.** $x \times 6$ **C.** $x - 6$ **D.** $x + 6$

10.

x	1	2	3	4
Answer	6	12	18	24

11.

x	12	13	14	15
Answer	18	19	20	21

12.

x	36	42	48	54
Answer	6	7	8	9

13.

x	28	29	30	31
Answer	22	23	24	25

Make x equal 3. Write the answer.

14. $x \div 1$ **15.** $x - 2$ **16.** $17 + x$ **17.** $5 \times x$

18. $x \times 4$ **19.** $x + 39$ **20.** $50 - x$ **21.** $21 \div x$

22. $5 + 4 + x$ **23.** $(x + 5) + 7$ **24.** $(x \div 3) \times 9$

25. $x + x + 18$ **26.** $x - x + 6$ **27.** $(x \times 6) + 48$

CUMULATIVE REVIEW

Choose the correct answer. Choose *a, b, c,* or *d.*
Find the answer.

1. 2×5
- **a.** 8 **b.** 10
- **c.** 7 **d.** none of these

2. 3×6
- **a.** 9 **b.** 12
- **c.** 18 **d.** none of these

3. 9×3
- **a.** 12 **b.** 27
- **c.** 21 **d.** none of these

Choose the fact you need to solve the problem.

4. Each plant had 3 new flowers on Monday. How many new flowers were there on Monday?
- **a.** There were 2 new flowers on Tuesday.
- **b.** Plants are watered 3 times a week.
- **c.** There are 4 plants.
- **d.** none of these

5. Michael can plant 1 flower in 2 minutes. How long will it take him to plant all the flowers?
- **a.** The garden is 180 cm long.
- **b.** Each flower is 5 cm tall.
- **c.** There are 25 flowers to be planted.
- **d.** none of these

Find the answer.

6. 4×9
- **a.** 32 **b.** 13
- **c.** 36 **d.** none of these

7. 6×0
- **a.** 6 **b.** 60
- **c.** 0 **d.** none of these

8. 1×8
- **a.** 7 **b.** 8
- **c.** 9 **d.** none of these

Find the answer.

9. Maria writes an odd number that is greater than 7 and less than 15. The number times 4 is 36.
- **a.** 9 **b.** 11
- **c.** 7 **d.** none of these

10. Hank writes 2 even numbers between 4 and 18. Their sum is 28.
- **a.** 12 and 14 **b.** 13 and 15
- **c.** 12 and 16 **d.** none of these

Find the answer.

11. $\begin{array}{r} 1 \\ \times 5 \\ \hline \end{array}$

a. 1 **b.** 5
c. 6 **d.** none of these

12. $\begin{array}{r} 4 \\ \times 6 \\ \hline \end{array}$

a. 10 **b.** 12
c. 24 **d.** none of these

13. $\begin{array}{r} 6 \\ \times 9 \\ \hline \end{array}$

a. 54 **b.** 45
c. 15 **d.** none of these

Find the answer.

14. 7×9

a. 16 **b.** 54
c. 72 **d.** none of these

15. 8×0

a. 0 **b.** 1
c. 8 **d.** none of these

16. 5×8

a. 3 **b.** 13
c. 40 **d.** none of these

Find the answer.

17. $\begin{array}{r} 9 \\ \times 1 \\ \hline \end{array}$

a. 8 **b.** 9
c. 10 **d.** none of these

18. $\begin{array}{r} 8 \\ \times 9 \\ \hline \end{array}$

a. 17 **b.** 64
c. 72 **d.** none of these

19. $\begin{array}{r} 3 \\ \times 9 \\ \hline \end{array}$

a. 12 **b.** 27
c. 21 **d.** none of these

LANGUAGE and VOCABULARY REVIEW

Choose the correct word to complete each sentence.

1. A product is the answer in (multiplication, division).

2. You can think of division as (adding, subtracting) the same number over and over.

3. Knowing the multiplication facts helps you to learn the (subtraction, division) facts.

4. You can think of multiplication as (adding, subtracting) the same number over and over.

5. A quotient is the answer in (multiplication, division).

DATA BASE

The numbers, letters, and signs used by the computer are called **data.**

You can tell a computer to put the data in order. Then you can find what you need quickly.

Jenny puts data about her books into the computer. She lists each book's subject, title, and author.

She decides to put the books in order by subject. So, Jenny tells the computer to put the subjects in A, B, C order. She gets this list.

SUBJECT	TITLE	AUTHOR
Cats	Your Pet Cat	Tina More
Cooking	How To Cook	Kim Yee
Magic Tricks	Guess The Number	Abe Fisher
Making Things	Make A Table	Carlos Lopez
Stories	The Longest Tail	Niki Papas

Write the data in order.

1. Write the names in A, B, C order.
Robert
Jim
Angela
Mariko

2. Write the numbers in order from least to greatest.
250 Pine Lane
205 Pine Lane
255 Pine Lane
225 Pine Lane

9

Some fire trucks carry ladders that reach 4 stories high. This ladder can stretch 3 times as far. How many stories is that?

MEASUREMENT

INFORMAL UNITS

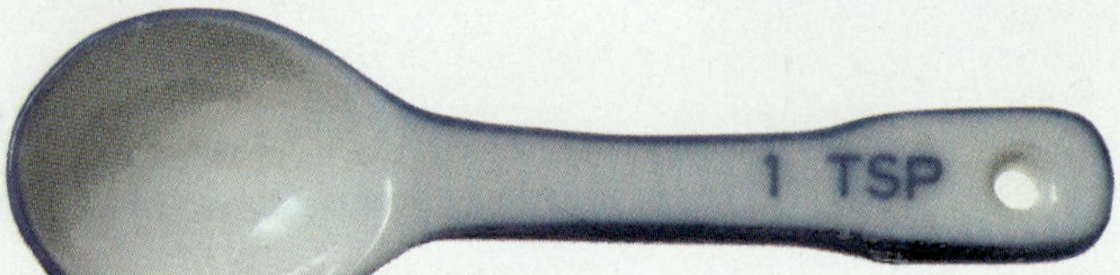

1 unit

The spoon is 4 units long.

The fork is between 4 and 5 units long. It is nearer to 5 units. The length is *about* 5 units.

CLASS EXERCISES

About how many units long is each object?

1.

2.

3.

4.

PRACTICE

Estimate the length. Then count the number of units.

1 unit

5. 

6. 

7. 

8. 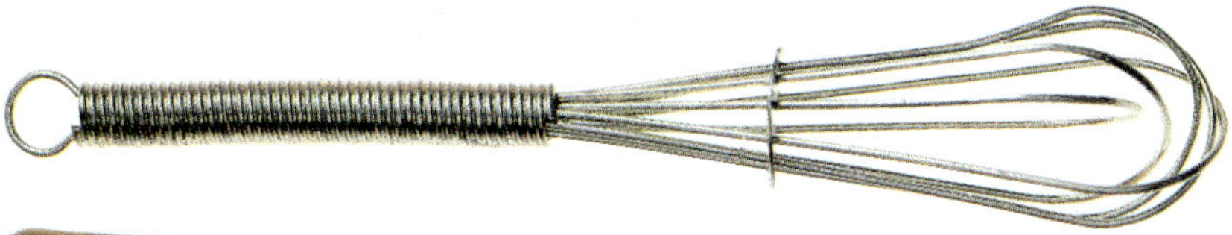

9. 

10. 

PROBLEM SOLVING APPLICATIONS
Reasonable Answers

Choose the best estimate.
Write *a*, *b*, or *c*.

1 unit 

11. 

a. 10 units **b.** 3 units
c. 25 units

12. 

a. 2 units **b.** 8 units
c. 15 units

13. 

a. 10 units **b.** 1 unit
c. 4 units

14. 

a. 10 units **b.** 1 unit
c. 20 units

MEASURING IN CENTIMETERS

In the metric system, you can measure lengths in **centimeters** (cm). This is one centimeter.

1 cm

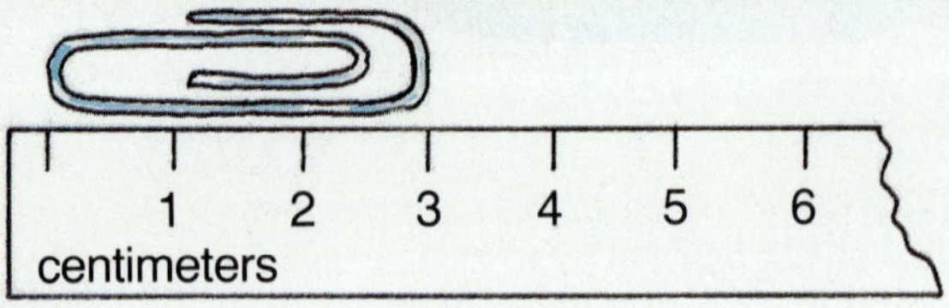

This paper clip is 3 cm long.

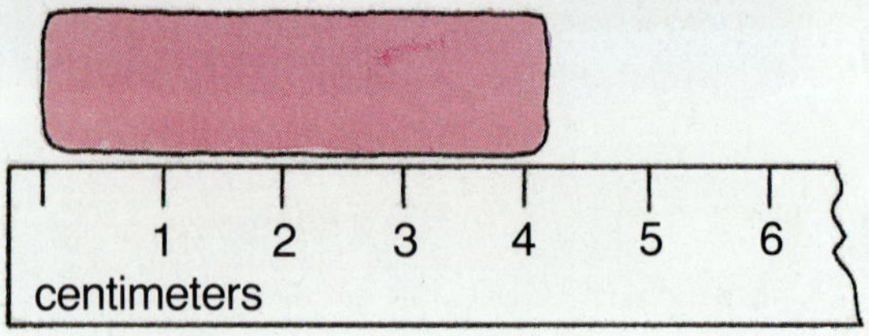

The eraser is between 4 and 5 cm. It is nearer 4 cm. Its length is 4 cm to the nearest centimeter.

The width of the chalk is about 1 cm. You can use this idea to estimate length.

CLASS EXERCISES

What is the length?

1. 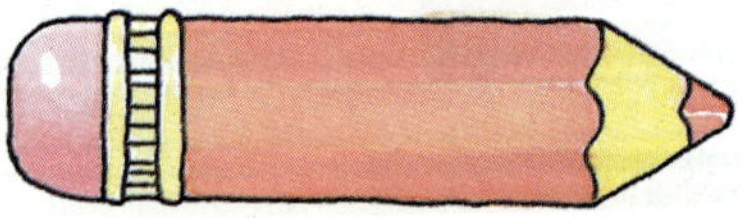

_?_ cm

2. 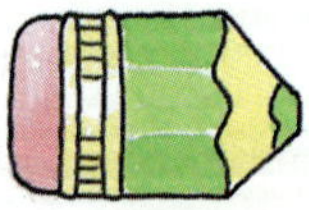

_?_ cm

3. 

between _?_ and _?_ cm
_?_ cm to the nearest centimeter

PRACTICE

Measure to the nearest centimeter.

4. 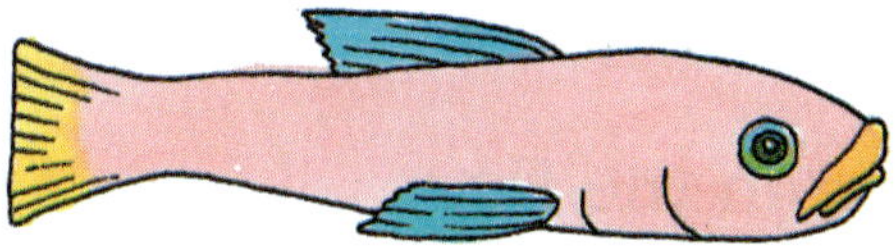

5. 

6. 

7. 

Use a centimeter ruler to draw something that is this length.

8. 9 cm **9.** 7 cm **10.** 6 cm **11.** 8 cm **12.** 5 cm

Estimate the length in centimeters. Then measure to check your estimate.

ESTIMATE

13. ____________

14. ______________________

15. _________________

16. _________________________

PROBLEM SOLVING APPLICATIONS
Choosing a Strategy

Solve.

17. Alicia caught 4 fish in 2 hours. Barb caught 3 times as many fish as Alicia in 3 hours. How many fish did Barb catch?

18. A 5 cm fishing fly costs \$3.50. An 8 cm fly costs \$4.75. About how much more does an 8 cm fly cost?

19. Jesse's fish is 25 cm long. Sandy's fish is 7 cm longer. How long is Sandy's fish?

★ **20.** Raoul caught 7 fish and Alan caught 5 fish. Bill and Ed caught 8 fish together. They divided the fish equally among themselves. How many fish did each one get?

METER, KILOMETER

Longer lengths in the metric system can be measured in **meters** (m) and **kilometers** (km).

A doorknob is about 1 m from the floor.

100 centimeters (cm) = 1 meter (m)

A line of 100 school buses is about 1 km long.

1000 meters (m) = 1 kilometer (km)

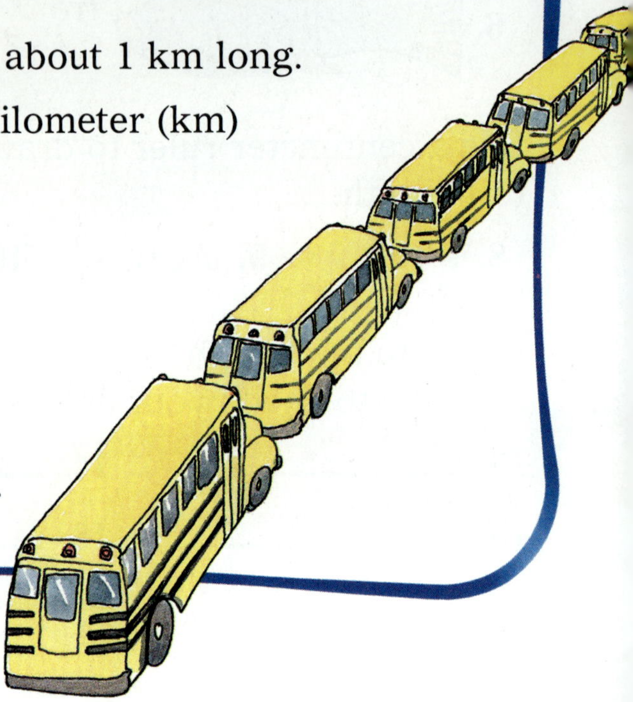

M You can use what you know about counting to change meters to centimeters. How many centimeters are in 6 m? Since 1 m equals 100 cm, you can count mentally by hundreds.

Think: 100, 200, 300, 400, 500, 600. There are 600 cm in 6 m.

CLASS EXERCISES

Which is the better unit for measuring, *centimeter*, *meter*, or *kilometer*? Explain why.

5. Name something near you that you can measure in centimeters.

PRACTICE

Complete. Write *cm, m,* or *km.*

6. A bus is about 10 __?__ long.

7. A door is about 1 __?__ wide.

8. A shovel is about 2 __?__ long.

9. A pencil is about 20 __?__ long.

10. It is about 1000 __?__ from St. Louis to Dallas.

11. Road maps show distances in __?__.

12. A book is about 25 __?__ high.

13. A comb is about 13 __?__ long.

14. A banana is about 20 __?__ long.

15. A giraffe is about 6 __?__ high.

Complete. Remember 100 cm = 1 m.

MENTAL MATH

16. 3 m = __?__ cm

17. 4 m = __?__ cm

18. 5 m = __?__ cm

19. 6 m = __?__ cm

PROBLEM SOLVING APPLICATIONS
Choosing the Operation

Solve.

20. Bob Beamon set a long jump record in 1968. He jumped about 11 m. This was 1 m farther than the record he broke. What was the earlier long jump record?

21. Mac Wilkins broke the Olympic record for discus throwing. He threw the discus about 82 m. The earlier record was 79 m set by Al Oerter. How much farther did Wilkins throw?

★ **22.** In 1960 Wilma Rudolph ran the 100 m race in about 11 seconds. If she ran this fast in a longer race, how long would it take her to run 200 m?

LITER

You can measure amounts of liquid in **liters** (L).

There is about 1 L of juice in this bottle.

There are about 4 glasses of juice in 1 L.

CLASS EXERCISES

Which is the better estimate, *a* or *b*?

1. 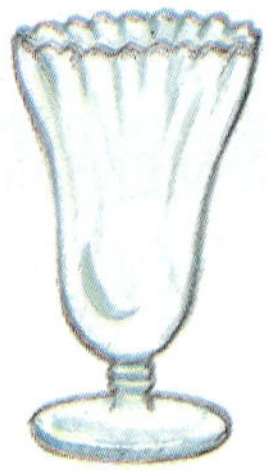

a. 1 L
b. 10 L

2. 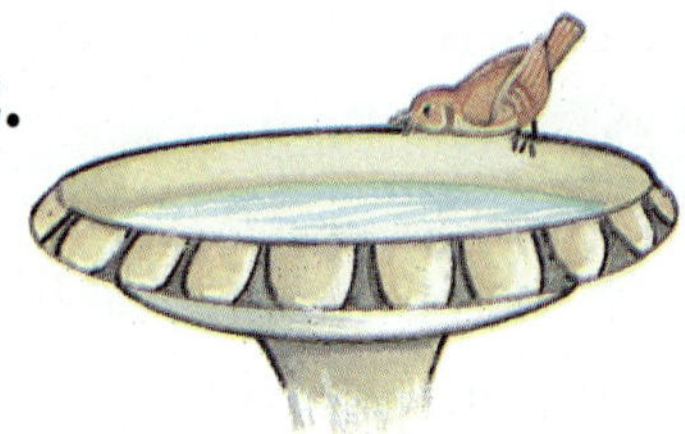

a. 4 L
b. 40 L

3. 

a. 9 L
b. 90 L

4. 

a. 20 L
b. 200 L

PRACTICE

Choose the better estimate. Write *a* or *b*.

5. How much water can a watering can hold?
a. 30 L **b.** 3 L

6. How much milk can a pitcher hold?
a. 1 L **b.** 15 L

PRACTICE

Complete.

7. A bathtub holds about ___?___.
   a. 3 pt **b.** 3 c **c.** 30 gal

8. A pitcher holds about ___?___.
   a. 1 c **b.** 3 gal **c.** 2 qt

9. A can of paint holds about ___?___.
   a. 1 c **b.** 100 gal **c.** 1 gal

10. A saucepan holds about ___?___.
    a. 1 qt **b.** 5 gal **c.** 1 c

11. A milk carton holds about ___?___.
    a. 5 gal **b.** 10 qt **c.** 1 qt

12. A serving of yogurt is about ___?___.
    a. 1 qt **b.** 1 c **c.** 1 gal

Complete.

MENTAL MATH

13. 4 pt = ___?___ c
14. 2 c = ___?___ pt
15. 8 pt = ___?___ qt
16. 8 qt = ___?___ gal
17. 4 qt = ___?___ gal
18. 8 c = ___?___ qt

PROBLEM SOLVING APPLICATIONS
Using Measurement

Solve.

19. A soup recipe calls for 3 c of milk. How many cups of milk would you need if you wanted to double the recipe?

20. Aletha needs 4 c of sliced apples for one salad. If she is making 3 salads, how many cups of apples will she need?

★ 21. If 1 qt of milk has 4 servings, how many quarts will be needed for 36 people?

★ 22. Parents are making stew for Family Night at school. If 1 qt of stew will feed 5 people, how many quarts will they need for 45 people?

FAHRENHEIT TEMPERATURE

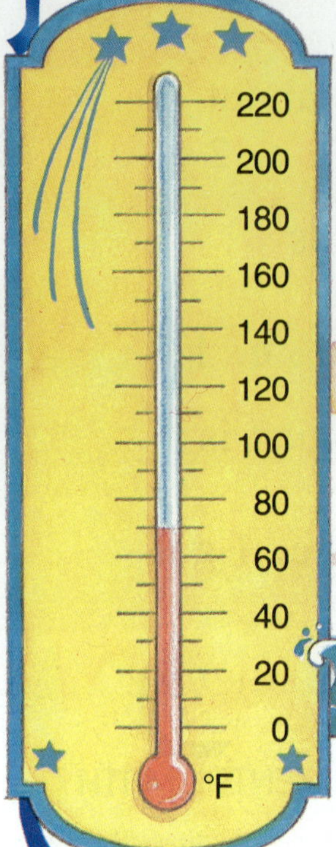

You can measure temperature on a Fahrenheit thermometer. It measures the temperature in degrees **Fahrenheit** (°F). The thermometer on the left shows 70°F.

water boils	212°F
hot cider	160°F
hot tap water	140°F
very hot day	100°F
room temperature	68°F
water freezes	32°F
very cold day	20°F

To find the difference between 95°F and 78°F on a calculator, press these keys. 95 [−] 78 [=] 17

CLASS EXERCISES

What is the temperature?

1. 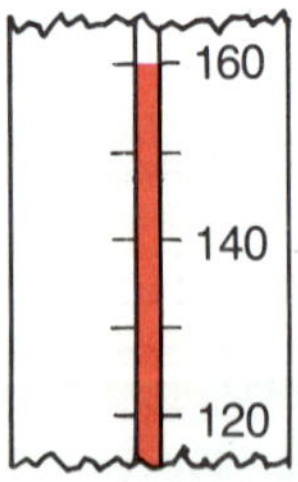

?

2. 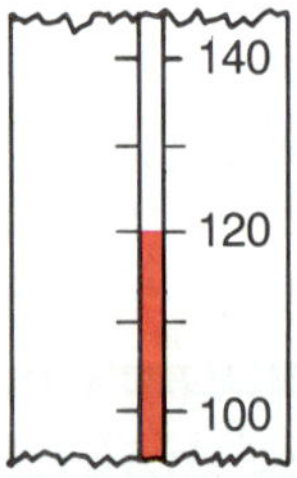

?

3. 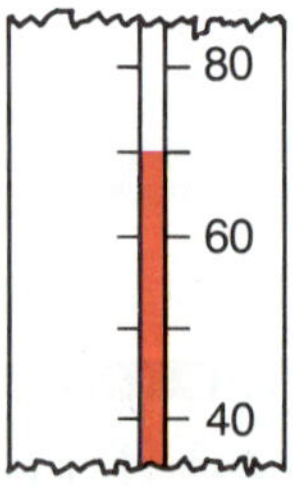

?

4. 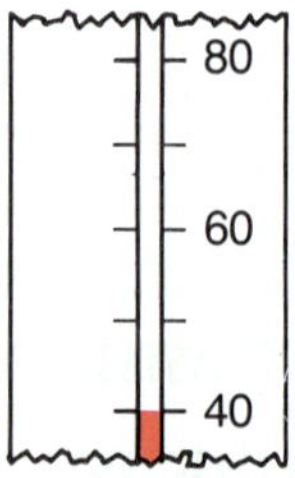

?

What is the temperature? Use the facts in the table.

5. water freezes ?

6. water boils ?

7. very cold day ?

8. very hot day ?

PRACTICE

Draw a thermometer showing the temperature.

9. 50°F **10.** 100°F **11.** 140°F **12.** 20°F

Choose the best estimate. Write *a*, *b*, or *c*.

13. a cold day
a. 75°F **b.** 28°F **c.** 90°F

14. a warm day
a. 72°F **b.** 20°F **c.** 120°F

15. soup boils
a. 90°F **b.** 0°F **c.** 212°F

16. in a freezer
a. 100°F **b.** 25°F **c.** 250°F

17. a cool day
a. 120°F **b.** 0°F **c.** 45°F

18. bath water
a. 10°F **b.** 120°F **c.** 240°F

Find the difference between the temperatures.
Use a calculator if you have one.

CALCULATOR

19. high: 43°F
low: 33°F

20. high: 63°F
low: 38°F

21. high: 45°F
low: 0°F

22. Which of Exercises 19–21 would be easier to do with mental math than with a calculator?

PROBLEM SOLVING APPLICATIONS

Use the table to answer the question.

23. Which city had the highest temperature?

24. Which city had the lowest temperature?

25. What is the difference between the high temperatures in Boston and Anchorage?

26. Write the cities in order from the coolest to the warmest.

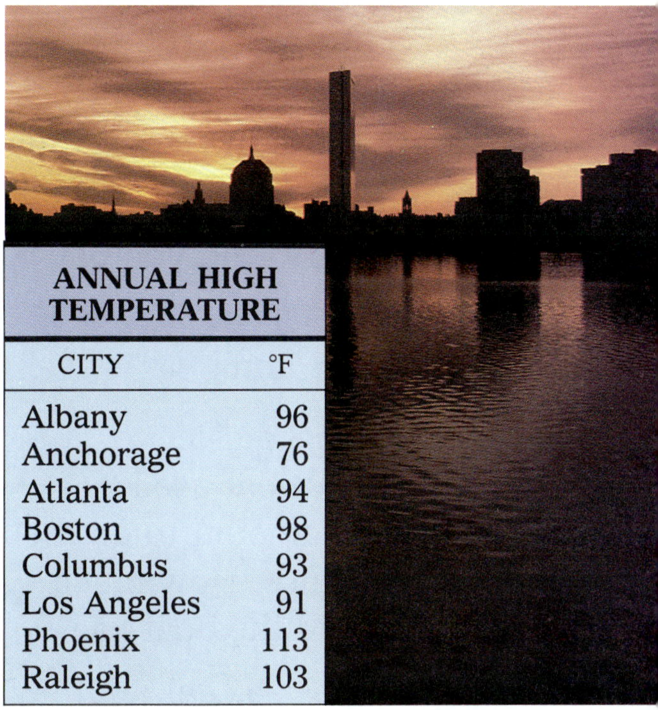

ANNUAL HIGH TEMPERATURE

CITY	°F
Albany	96
Anchorage	76
Atlanta	94
Boston	98
Columbus	93
Los Angeles	91
Phoenix	113
Raleigh	103

PROBLEM SOLVING
Strategy: Reasonable Answers

It is 240 mi to the campground. The Andersons have driven 178 mi in 4 hours. How much farther do they have to drive?

$$\begin{array}{r} 240 \\ -\ 178 \\ \hline 62 \end{array}$$

Think: Should my answer be in hours or in miles?

Since you want to know a distance, you should answer in miles.

They must drive 62 mi farther to the campground.

CLASS EXERCISES

Solve and choose the correct label.

1. A 5 lb bag of ice costs 79¢. How much would you pay for 2 bags?

a. lb **b.** $ and .

2. The water jug holds 4 gal. If it is filled 6 times, how much water is used?

a. gal **b.** times

3. A car used 8 gal of gasoline. A boat used 3 times that amount to go the same distance. How much gasoline did the boat use?

a. gasoline **b.** gal

4. Eric swam 150 yd to the raft. Then he swam 100 yd to the dock. How far did he swim in all?

a. mi **b.** yd

PRACTICE

Solve. Check the label.

5. The Andersons hiked 3 miles each day for 5 days. How far did they hike?

6. Rope sells for 8¢ a yard. Kerry buys 9 yd. How much does she spend?

7. Joan's backpack holds 35 lb. Anne's pack holds 42 lb. How much more does Anne's backpack hold?

8. Joan caught a fish 18 in. long. Her father's longest fish was 12 in. How much longer was Joan's fish?

9. The Andersons bought 4 lb of apples. There are about 5 apples in a pound. How many apples did they buy?

10. Eric biked 12 mi in 2 hours. If he rode the same distance each hour, how far did he ride in 1 hour?

★ 11. A red board is 18 in. long. A blue board is 1 yd long. How much longer is the blue board?

CHECKPOINT 2

Complete. Write *in.*, *ft*, *yd*, or *mi*. *(pages 258–261)*

1. A sled is about 4 __?__ long.

2. A creek is about 1 __?__ long.

Choose the better estimate. Write *a* or *b*. *(pages 262–267)*

3. bucket of water
   a. 4 qt **b.** 4 c

4. weight of a car
   a. 2000 oz **b.** 2000 lb

5. water boils
   a. 20°F **b.** 212°F

Solve. Check the label. *(pages 268–269)*

6. There are 15 ft of rope in one coil and 7 ft of rope in another. How much rope is there in all?

Extra practice on page 416

CHAPTER 9 TEST

Complete. Write *cm*, *m*, or *km*. *(pages 246–249)*

1. A book is about 2 __?__ thick.
2. A bed is about 1 __?__ wide.

Choose the better estimate. Write *a* or *b*. *(pages 250–255)*

3. water in a bucket
   a. 3 L **b.** 30 L
4. mass of a penny
   a. 1 g **b.** 1 kg
5. temperature of cold milk
   a. 50°C **b.** 5°C
6. mass of a book
   a. 2 g **b.** 2 kg

Use the map to find the distance. *(pages 256–257)*

7. from Salt Lake City to Cheyenne
8. From Cheyenne to Denver to Santa Fe

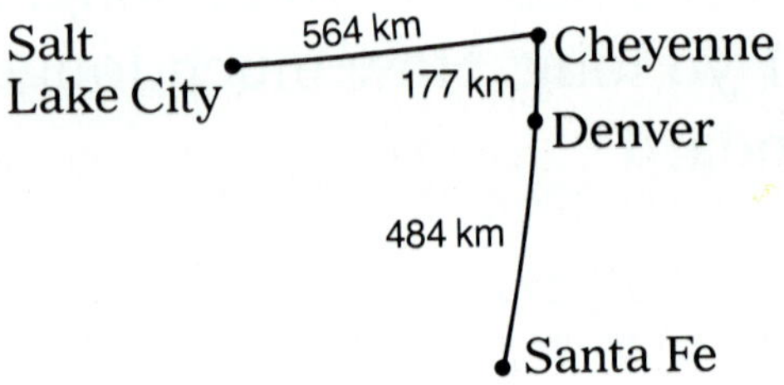

Estimate the length to complete. Write *in.*, *ft*, *yd*, or *mi*. *(pages 258–261)*

9. A caterpillar is about 4 __?__ long.
10. The Nile River is about 3500 __?__ long.

Estimate the most likely measurement. Write *a*, *b*, or *c*. *(pages 262–267)*

11. A child weighs about __?__.
    a. 55 oz **b.** 55 lb **c.** 15 lb
12. A mug holds about __?__.
    a. 1 c **b.** 1 pt **c.** 1 qt

Solve. *(pages 268–269)*

13. Ribbon costs 9¢ a foot. Pat buys 7 ft. How much does Pat pay?

Extra practice on page 417

MATHEMATICS and SCIENCE

A pendulum is an object that swings back and forth.

Use an eraser and a piece of string to set up a pendulum like the one in the picture.

HOW MANY SWINGS?

Now follow these steps:

a. Start the pendulum swinging.

b. Count the swings for 1 minute while someone else keeps time.

c. Write down the number of swings.

d. Repeat steps a–c two more times.

1. How many swings did you count for each of the three times?
2. Suppose you repeated steps a–c again. How many swings do you think you would count?
3. Set up another pendulum using a shorter string. Do you think there will be more or fewer swings in 1 minute? Use the steps to test your guess.

Enrichment

Line graphs help you see changes. This line graph shows you the growth of a marigold plant over a period of 11 weeks.

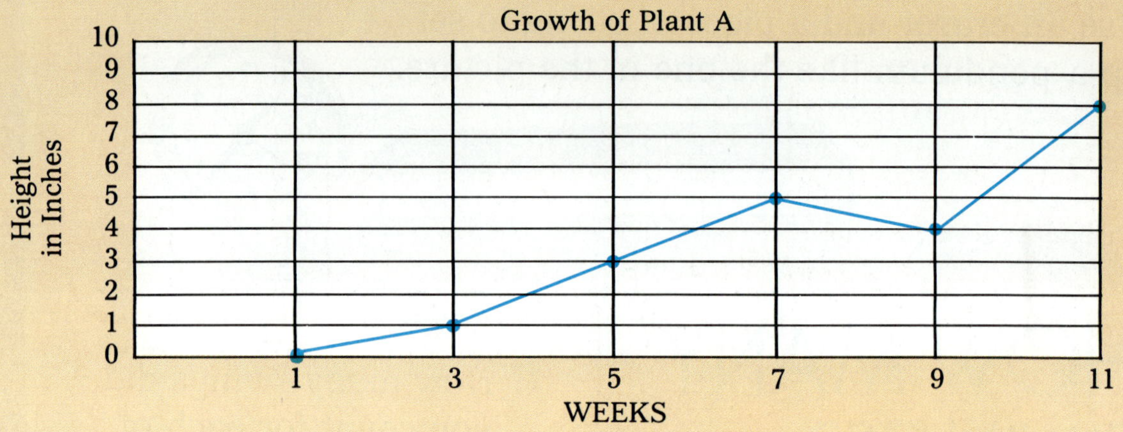

The height of the plant increased every week except from Week 7 to Week 9 when it was pinched back.

LINE GRAPHS

Use the line graph above to answer.

How tall was Plant A in the given week?

1. Week 1 **2.** Week 3
3. Week 5 **4.** Week 7
5. Week 9 **6.** Week 11

How much did Plant A grow in the given time?

7. from Week 1 to Week 3
8. from Week 3 to Week 5
9. from Week 5 to Week 7
10. from Week 9 to Week 11

This line graph shows the growth of another marigold plant. This plant has not received enough water and sunlight.

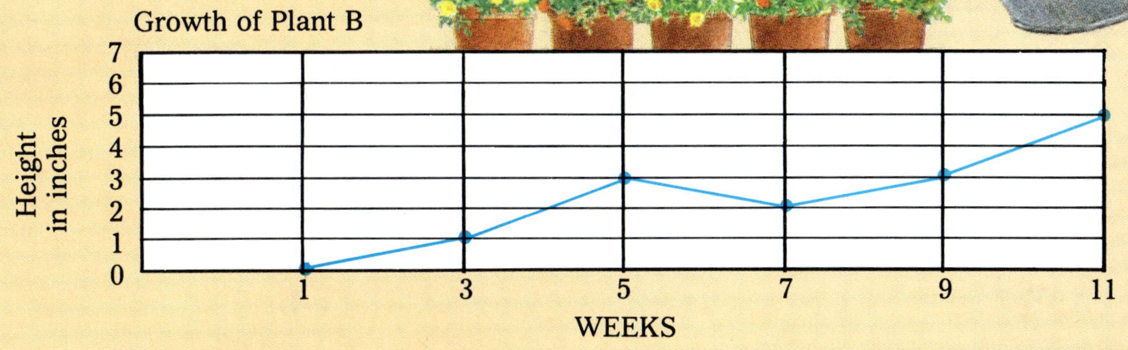

Use the line graph above to answer.

How tall was Plant B in the given week?

11. Week 1 **12.** Week 3
13. Week 5 **14.** Week 7
15. Week 9 **16.** Week 11

How much did Plant B grow in the given time?

17. from Week 1 to Week 3
18. from Week 3 to Week 5
19. from Week 7 to Week 9
20. from Week 9 to Week 11

Compare the two graphs. How much taller was Plant A than Plant B in the given week?

21. Week 1 **22.** Week 3
23. Week 5 **24.** Week 7
25. Week 9 **26.** Week 11

***27.** Use the information to make a line graph.

CONDITIONS	MAXIMUM HEIGHT
Little Sun	5 in.
Underwatered	7 in.
Very Sunny	8 in.
Overwatered	6 in.
Sunny Watered	8 in.

CUMULATIVE REVIEW

Choose the correct answer. Choose *a*, *b*, *c*, or *d*.

Find the answer.

1. 5×6
- **a.** 18
- **b.** 36
- **c.** 30
- **d.** none of these

2. 7×6
- **a.** 42
- **b.** 49
- **c.** 36
- **d.** none of these

3. 8×7
- **a.** 64
- **b.** 49
- **c.** 56
- **d.** none of these

Find the answer.

4. 9×6
- **a.** 54
- **b.** 15
- **c.** 45
- **d.** none of these

5. 7×9
- **a.** 63
- **b.** 81
- **c.** 72
- **d.** none of these

6. 9×8
- **a.** 81
- **b.** 72
- **c.** 64
- **d.** none of these

Use the bar graph to solve.

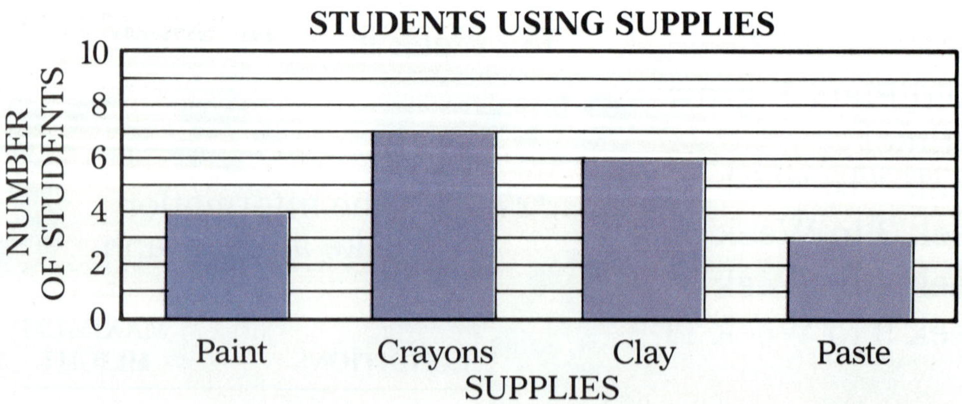

7. How many students are working with clay?
- **a.** 7
- **b.** 6
- **c.** 5
- **d.** none of these

8. Which supply is being used the least?
- **a.** pencils
- **b.** paint
- **c.** paste
- **d.** none of these

Find the answer.

9. $2\overline{)6}$
   a. 4
   b. 12
   c. 3
   d. none of these

10. $4\overline{)16}$
   a. 4
   b. 2
   c. 8
   d. none of these

11. $5\overline{)35}$
   a. 5
   b. 9
   c. 7
   d. none of these

Find the answer.

12. $24 \div 6$
   a. 6
   b. 4
   c. 8
   d. none of these

13. $48 \div 6$
   a. 8
   b. 6
   c. 4
   d. none of these

14. $49 \div 7$
   a. 9
   b. 5
   c. 7
   d. none of these

Find the answer.

15. $8\overline{)40}$
   a. 8
   b. 6
   c. 5
   d. none of these

16. $9\overline{)27}$
   a. 5
   b. 3
   c. 7
   d. none of these

17. $9\overline{)72}$
   a. 9
   b. 8
   c. 7
   d. none of these

LANGUAGE and VOCABULARY REVIEW

Match the symbol to the word. Write the letter.

1. centimeter
2. before noon
3. liter
4. equals
5. kilometer
6. after noon
7. degrees Celsius
8. gram
9. meter
10. kilogram

a. L
b. °C
c. kg
d. cm
e. g
f. km
g. =
h. m
i. A.M.
j. P.M.

PRINT

A language that you use is English. A computer uses a language too. One language it uses is BASIC.

PRINT is a word in BASIC. It tells the computer to do a process, then show an output.

Suppose you tell the computer PRINT 9 + 7. The computer adds the two numbers. Then it shows only the answer.

OUTPUT

```
PRINT 9 + 7 ⇨
```

Here is a program in BASIC. It uses PRINT.

Push the RETURN key after each line.

```
10 PRINT 9 - 7        2
20 PRINT 3 + 1        4
30 PRINT 2 * 3        6
40 PRINT 16/2         8
```

* means multiply / means divide

This program made the computer show an output. Write the output.

1.
```
10 PRINT 1 * 10
20 PRINT 42 - 33
30 PRINT 48/6
40 PRINT 63/9
```

2.
```
10 PRINT 18 + 18
20 PRINT 76 - 40
30 PRINT 64/8
40 PRINT 6 * 6
```

3.
```
10 PRINT 3 * 8
20 PRINT 12 + 12
30 PRINT 36/9
40 PRINT 88 - 79
```

10

Grapes are grown in almost every state. If each bin holds 100 lb, how many pounds would 4 bins hold?

MULTIPLICATION
GREATER NUMBERS

MULTIPLYING TENS AND HUNDREDS

If you know your multiplication facts, it's easy to multiply tens and hundreds.

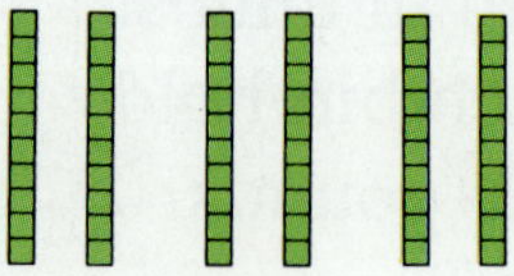

2 tens	20
× 3	× 3
6 tens	60

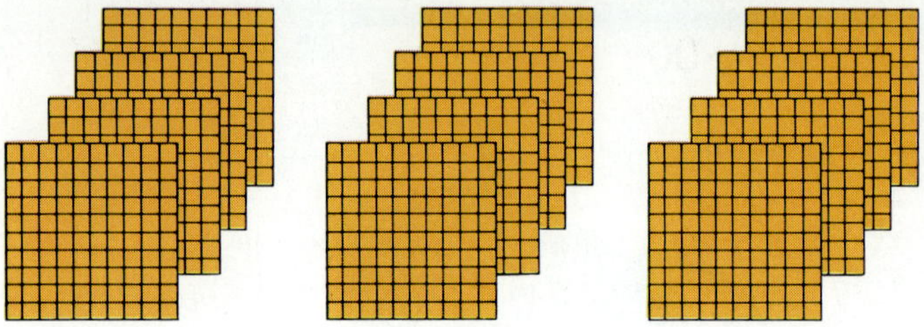

4 hundreds	400
× 3	× 3
12 hundreds	1200

When you multiply, remember the zeros.

$$3 \times 4 = 12$$
$$3 \times 40 = 120$$
$$3 \times 400 = 1200$$

CLASS EXERCISES

Count by tens.

1.

10	20	?	40	?	?	70	?	?	100

Count by hundreds.

2.

100	200	?	400	?	600	?	?	?	1000

Complete.

3. 3 × 3 tens = ? tens
3 × 30 = ?

4. 4 × 2 hundreds = ? hundreds
4 × 200 = ?

5. 6 × 7 tens = ? tens
6 × 70 = ?

6. 4 × 8 hundreds = ? hundreds
4 × 800 = ?

PRACTICE

MENTAL MATH

Multiply mentally.
Write just the product.

7. 20×5	**8.** 70×3	**9.** 90×7	**10.** 30×4	**11.** 90×2
12. 800×4	**13.** 600×7	**14.** 900×5	**15.** 300×8	**16.** 700×4
17. 100×9	**18.** 50×5	**19.** 400×7	**20.** 80×4	**21.** 60×6
22. 40×8	**23.** 800×5	**24.** 40×9	**25.** 90×3	**26.** 500×4
27. 700×6	**28.** 200×5	**29.** 80×9	**30.** 90×6	**31.** 400×6

★ **32.** $5 \times \blacksquare = 350$ ★ **33.** $8 \times \blacksquare = 720$ ★ **34.** $4 \times \blacksquare = 2400$

PROBLEM SOLVING APPLICATIONS

The table shows how fast some animals can travel. Use the table to solve.

ANIMAL	MILES EACH HOUR
Cheetah	70
Dragonfly	60
Lion	50
Zebra	40
Cat	30

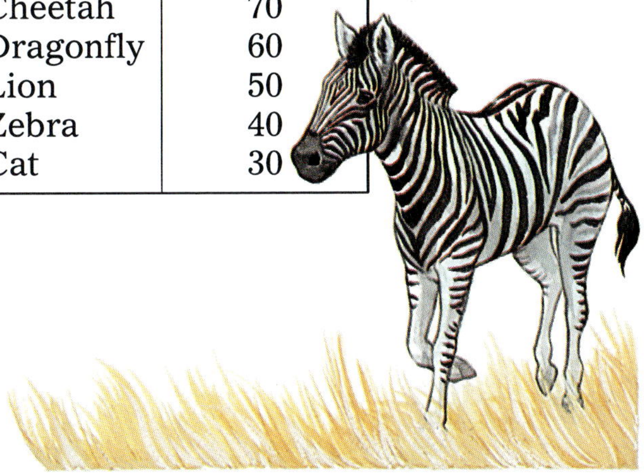

35. Which animal can travel the fastest?

36. How much faster can a lion travel than a zebra?

37. If a dragonfly could fly for 3 hours without stopping, how far could it go?

★ **38.** A dragonfly can travel twice as fast as which animal?

ESTIMATING PRODUCTS

Ming practices her ballet steps for 45 minutes a day. About how many minutes does she practice in 7 days?

The word *about* tells you that an exact answer is not needed. If you don't need an exact answer, you can estimate. Round the factor greater than 10, then multiply.

$$\begin{array}{r} 45 \\ \times\ 7 \\ \hline \end{array} \rightarrow \begin{array}{r} 50 \\ \times\ 7 \\ \hline 350 \end{array}$$

Ming practices for about 350 minutes.

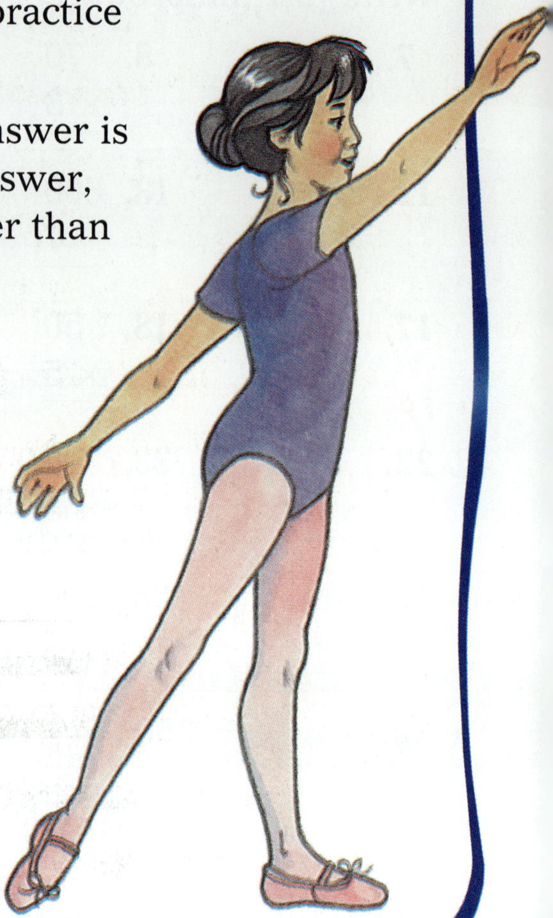

When you estimate with a 3-digit number, round to the nearest hundred. Then multiply.

$$\begin{array}{r} 473 \\ \times\ 7 \\ \hline \end{array} \rightarrow \begin{array}{r} 500 \\ \times\ 7 \\ \hline 3500 \end{array}$$

CLASS EXERCISES

What is the estimate?

1. $\begin{array}{r} 48 \\ \times\ 5 \\ \hline \end{array} \rightarrow \begin{array}{r} 50 \\ \times\ 5 \\ \hline \blacksquare \end{array}$

2. $\begin{array}{r} 57 \\ \times\ 7 \\ \hline \end{array} \rightarrow \begin{array}{r} 60 \\ \times\ 7 \\ \hline \blacksquare \end{array}$

3. $\begin{array}{r} 92 \\ \times\ 4 \\ \hline \end{array} \rightarrow \begin{array}{r} \blacksquare \\ \times\ 4 \\ \hline \blacksquare \end{array}$

4. $\begin{array}{r} 538 \\ \times\ 9 \\ \hline \end{array} \rightarrow \begin{array}{r} 500 \\ \times\ 9 \\ \hline \blacksquare \end{array}$

5. $\begin{array}{r} 362 \\ \times\ 8 \\ \hline \end{array} \rightarrow \begin{array}{r} 400 \\ \times\ 8 \\ \hline \blacksquare \end{array}$

6. $\begin{array}{r} 719 \\ \times\ 6 \\ \hline \end{array} \rightarrow \begin{array}{r} \blacksquare \\ \times\ 6 \\ \hline \blacksquare \end{array}$

PRACTICE

Round to the nearest ten or hundred. Estimate the product.

7. 51 × 6	**8.** 82 × 5	**9.** 78 × 3	**10.** 63 × 7	**11.** 59 × 8
12. 681 × 9	**13.** 621 × 7	**14.** 486 × 5	**15.** 793 × 4	**16.** 370 × 6

17. 9 × 57 **18.** 4 × 514 **19.** 3 × 674 **20.** 3 × 88

21. 7 × 456 **22.** 2 × 884 **23.** 6 × 85 **24.** 4 × 569

MIXED REVIEW

Write the answer.

25. 14 + 29 + 48 **26.** 823 + 491 + 335

27. 547 − 239 **28.** 436 + 273 **29.** 507 − 243

PROBLEM SOLVING APPLICATIONS
Using Estimation

Estimate to solve.

30. Ming practices dance for 18 minutes each day. About how many minutes does she practice in 5 days?

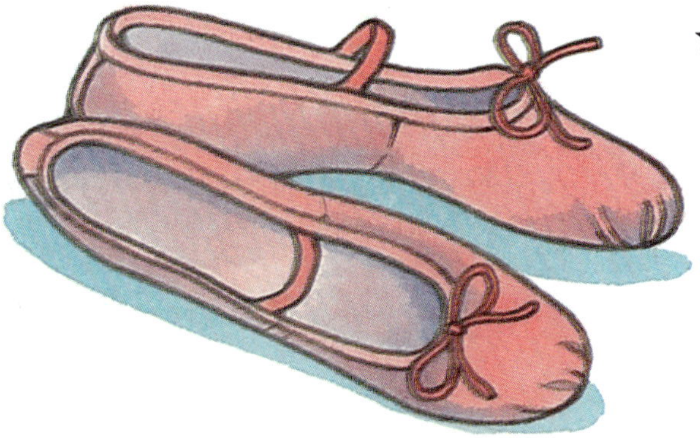

31. Ming's ballet class put on a show 48 miles from home. About how far did Ming travel to and from the show?

★ **32.** Bruce traveled 211 miles through New Mexico. Then he traveled twice as far through Arizona. About how far did Bruce travel in all?

MULTIPLYING A TWO-DIGIT NUMBER, NO RENAMING

Students collected 24 folk songs and 24 show songs. How many songs did they collect?

To find out, you can add.

$24 + 24 = 48$

You can also multiply.

Multiply the ones by 2.

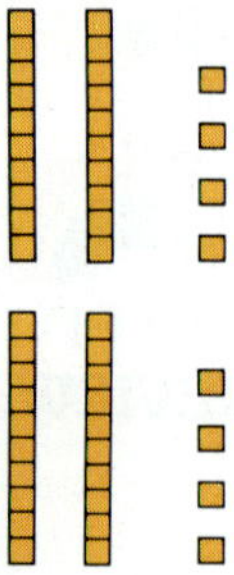

	tens	ones
	2	4
×		2
		8

Then multiply the tens by 2.

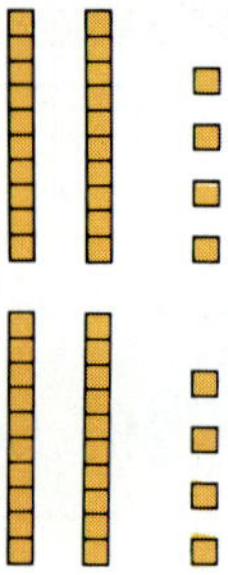

	tens	ones
	2	4
×		2
	4	8

They collected 48 songs.

Here is how you multiply 2 × 24 on a calculator.

2 [×] 24 [=] 48

A calculator is sometimes a handy way to check answers.

CLASS EXERCISES

What is the product?

1.

	t	o
	3	2
×		2

2.

	t	o
	2	1
×		2

3.

	t	o
	3	3
×		3

4.

	t	o
	1	3
×		2

PRACTICE

Multiply.

5. 12×4	**6.** 22×4	**7.** 23×3	**8.** 14×2	**9.** 42×2	**10.** 32×3
11. 34×2	**12.** 43×2	**13.** 11×4	**14.** 31×2	**15.** 12×3	**16.** 41×2
17. 23×2	**18.** 21×3	**19.** 22×3	**20.** 33×2	**21.** 11×3	**22.** 21×4

23. 2×22 **24.** 3×33 **25.** 3×31 **26.** 3×13

Multiply. If you can find all your answers on the calculator displays, your answers are correct.

CALCULATOR

27. 11×2	**28.** 44×2	**29.** 32×2	**30.** 14×2

64 22 88 28

PROBLEM SOLVING APPLICATIONS
Choosing the Operation

Solve.

31. The Music Club makes 42 green programs and 23 yellow ones. How many programs do they make?

32. At the concert there are 4 rows with 21 seats in each row. How many seats are there in all 4 rows?

33. Students sold 156 tickets before the concert and 18 tickets at the door. How many tickets did they sell?

★ **34.** There are 3 rows of 23 seats each and 4 rows of 21 seats each. How many seats are there in all?

MULTIPLYING A TWO-DIGIT NUMBER WITH RENAMING

To add 19 + 19 + 19,
you rename 27 ones as
2 tens 7 ones.

$$\begin{array}{r} {}^{2} \\ 19 \\ 19 \\ +\ 19 \\ \hline 57 \end{array}$$

When you multiply 19 by 3, you have to rename, too.

Multiply the 9 ones by 3.
Rename the 27 ones as 2 tens 7 ones.
Write the 2 in the tens' place.

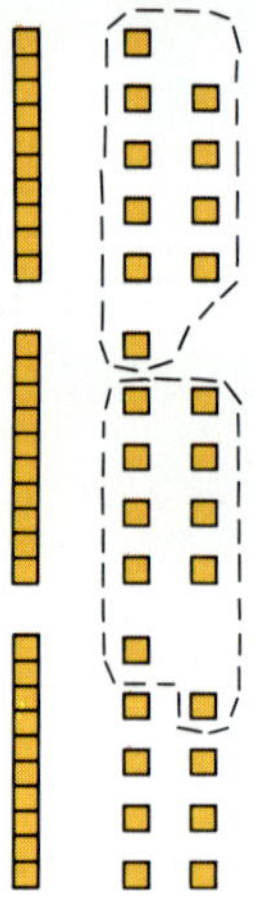

	tens	ones
	2	
	1	9
×		3
		7

Multiply the 1 ten by 3.
Add the 2 tens.

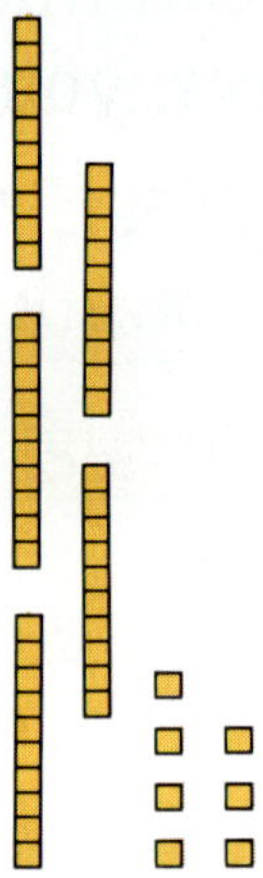

	tens	ones
	2	
	1	9
×		3
	5	7

M When you multiply ones and tens, you must know your facts.

CLASS EXERCISES

Complete the renaming.

1. 42 = ? tens 2 ones

2. 25 = ? tens 5 ones

3. 49 = ? tens 9 ones

4. 36 = ? tens 6 ones

5. 5 × 7 = ? tens 5 ones

6. 6 × 6 = ? tens 6 ones

7. 9 × 8 = ? tens 2 ones

8. 6 × 9 = ? tens 4 ones

PRACTICE

Multiply.

9. $\begin{array}{r} 12 \\ \times 6 \\ \hline \end{array}$ **10.** $\begin{array}{r} 19 \\ \times 2 \\ \hline \end{array}$ **11.** $\begin{array}{r} 18 \\ \times 5 \\ \hline \end{array}$ **12.** $\begin{array}{r} 13 \\ \times 4 \\ \hline \end{array}$ **13.** $\begin{array}{r} 15 \\ \times 6 \\ \hline \end{array}$ **14.** $\begin{array}{r} 13 \\ \times 5 \\ \hline \end{array}$

15. $\begin{array}{r} 14 \\ \times 4 \\ \hline \end{array}$ **16.** $\begin{array}{r} 15 \\ \times 3 \\ \hline \end{array}$ **17.** $\begin{array}{r} 16 \\ \times 4 \\ \hline \end{array}$ **18.** $\begin{array}{r} 18 \\ \times 3 \\ \hline \end{array}$ **19.** $\begin{array}{r} 12 \\ \times 8 \\ \hline \end{array}$ **20.** $\begin{array}{r} 19 \\ \times 4 \\ \hline \end{array}$

21. 2×16 **22.** 2×15 **23.** 5×17 **24.** 6×16

Write + or × to make the sentence true.

★ **25.** $7 \ \square \ 14 = 98$ ★ **26.** $3 \ \square \ 17 = 20$ ★ **27.** $5 \ \square \ 14 = 7 \ \square \ 10$

Multiply and add mentally. Work from left to right. Write just the answer.

M MENTAL MATH

28. $4 \times 2 + 2$ **29.** $3 \times 2 + 2$ **30.** $5 \times 1 + 3$

31. $6 \times 1 + 4$ **32.** $2 \times 4 + 1$ **33.** $3 \times 3 + 2$

PROBLEM SOLVING APPLICATIONS
Using Pictures

Use the picture to solve.

34. How many crayons are in 17 boxes?

35. How many pens are in 3 boxes?

36. How many brushes are in a dozen boxes?

★ **37.** How many more pens than crayons are there in 5 boxes of pens and 5 boxes of crayons?

MULTIPLYING A TWO-DIGIT NUMBER WITH RENAMING

Sumi picked 2 baskets of peaches. She counted 27 peaches in each basket. How many peaches did Sumi pick?

Multiply the 7 ones by 2. Rename the 14 ones as 1 ten 4 ones. Write the 1 in the tens' place.

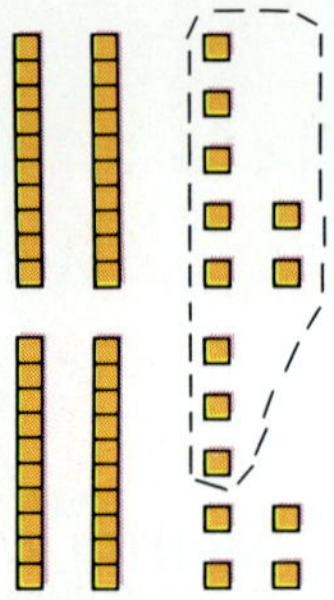

	tens	ones
	1	
	2	7
×		2
		4

Multiply the 2 tens by 2. Add the 1 ten.

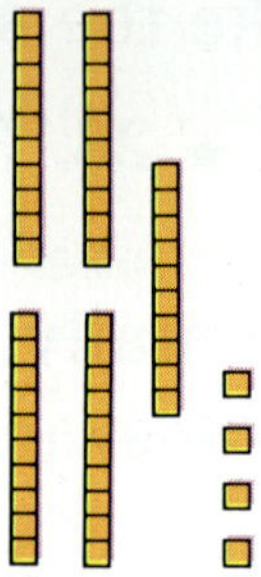

	tens	ones
	1	
	2	7
×		2
	5	4

Sumi picked 54 peaches.

M You can multiply 2×27 mentally.

Think: $2 \times 20 = 40$ and
$2 \times 7 = 14$.
$40 + 14 = 54$

CLASS EXERCISES

What is the product? Explain how the multiplications are related.

1. $\begin{array}{r} 4 \\ \times\ 3 \\ \hline \end{array} \longrightarrow \begin{array}{r} 24 \\ \times\ 3 \\ \hline \end{array}$

2. $\begin{array}{r} 5 \\ \times\ 3 \\ \hline \end{array} \longrightarrow \begin{array}{r} 25 \\ \times\ 3 \\ \hline \end{array}$

3. $\begin{array}{r} 6 \\ \times\ 3 \\ \hline \end{array} \longrightarrow \begin{array}{r} 26 \\ \times\ 3 \\ \hline \end{array}$

4. $\begin{array}{r} 7 \\ \times\ 3 \\ \hline \end{array} \longrightarrow \begin{array}{r} 27 \\ \times\ 3 \\ \hline \end{array}$

5. $\begin{array}{r} 8 \\ \times\ 3 \\ \hline \end{array} \longrightarrow \begin{array}{r} 28 \\ \times\ 3 \\ \hline \end{array}$

6. $\begin{array}{r} 9 \\ \times\ 3 \\ \hline \end{array} \longrightarrow \begin{array}{r} 29 \\ \times\ 3 \\ \hline \end{array}$

PRACTICE

Multiply.

7. $\begin{array}{r} 36 \\ \times\ 2 \\ \hline \end{array}$	**8.** $\begin{array}{r} 29 \\ \times\ 3 \\ \hline \end{array}$	**9.** $\begin{array}{r} 47 \\ \times\ 2 \\ \hline \end{array}$	**10.** $\begin{array}{r} 25 \\ \times\ 2 \\ \hline \end{array}$	**11.** $\begin{array}{r} 28 \\ \times\ 2 \\ \hline \end{array}$	**12.** $\begin{array}{r} 26 \\ \times\ 3 \\ \hline \end{array}$
13. $\begin{array}{r} 46 \\ \times\ 2 \\ \hline \end{array}$	**14.** $\begin{array}{r} 37 \\ \times\ 2 \\ \hline \end{array}$	**15.** $\begin{array}{r} 48 \\ \times\ 2 \\ \hline \end{array}$	**16.** $\begin{array}{r} 24 \\ \times\ 4 \\ \hline \end{array}$	**17.** $\begin{array}{r} 18 \\ \times\ 3 \\ \hline \end{array}$	**18.** $\begin{array}{r} 23 \\ \times\ 4 \\ \hline \end{array}$
19. $\begin{array}{r} 29 \\ \times\ 2 \\ \hline \end{array}$	**20.** $\begin{array}{r} 18 \\ \times\ 2 \\ \hline \end{array}$	**21.** $\begin{array}{r} 45 \\ \times\ 2 \\ \hline \end{array}$	**22.** $\begin{array}{r} 16 \\ \times\ 4 \\ \hline \end{array}$	**23.** $\begin{array}{r} 26 \\ \times\ 2 \\ \hline \end{array}$	**24.** $\begin{array}{r} 25 \\ \times\ 3 \\ \hline \end{array}$

25. 2×49 **26.** 2×38 **27.** 2×40 **28.** 2×27

★ **29.** $(2 \times 4) \times 20$ ★ **30.** $(3 \times 2) \times 800$ ★ **31.** $500 \times (3 \times 3)$

Multiply mentally. Write just the product.

M
MENTAL MATH

32. 3×32 **33.** 2×43 **34.** 4×12
35. 2×23 **36.** 3×25 **37.** 4×18

PROBLEM SOLVING APPLICATIONS
Choosing the Operation

Solve.

38. You use 9 apples to make a quart of spiced apples. How many quarts can you make with 72 apples?

★ **39.** You pick 3 bags of peaches. There are 27 peaches in each bag. How many peaches did you pick?

★ **40.** You have a recipe that calls for 27 turnips. You double the recipe. Then you add 3 more turnips. How many turnips do you use?

MULTIPLYING A TWO-DIGIT NUMBER WITH RENAMING

To find out how many balloons are in 2 bunches of 68, multiply 68 by 2.

Multiply the 8 ones by 2. Rename the 16 ones as 1 ten 6 ones. Write the 1 in the tens' place.

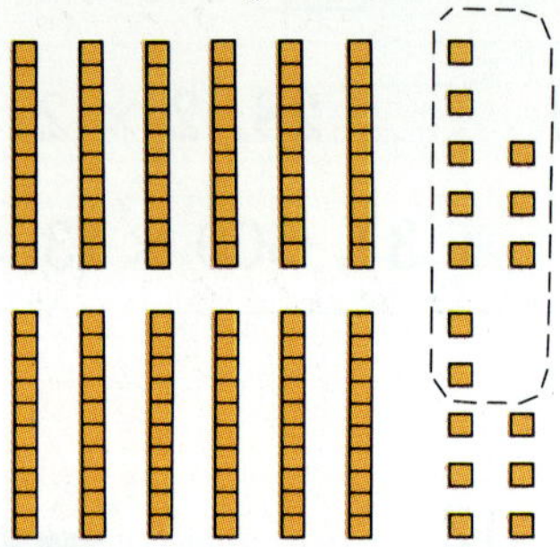

$$\begin{array}{r} {\scriptstyle 1} \\ 68 \\ \times\ 2 \\ \hline 6 \end{array}$$

Multiply the 6 tens by 2. Add the 1 ten.

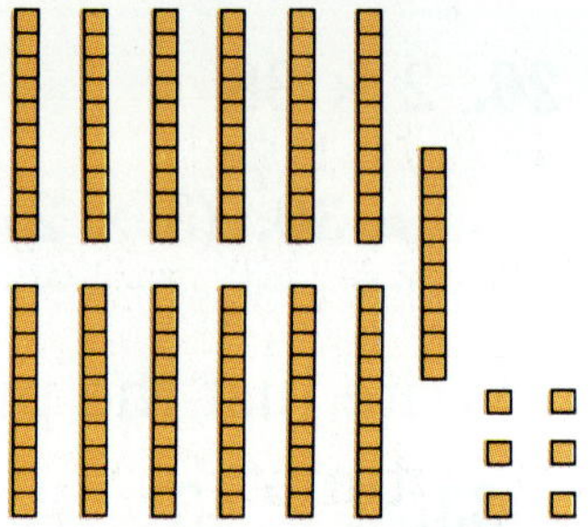

$$\begin{array}{r} {\scriptstyle 1} \\ 68 \\ \times\ 2 \\ \hline 136 \end{array}$$

There are 136 balloons.

You know that $2 \times 50 = 100$. You can estimate that 2×68 is greater than 100.

CLASS EXERCISES

What is the product?

1. $\begin{array}{r} 38 \\ \times\ 3 \\ \hline \end{array}$	**2.** $\begin{array}{r} 48 \\ \times\ 3 \\ \hline \end{array}$	**3.** $\begin{array}{r} 58 \\ \times\ 3 \\ \hline \end{array}$	**4.** $\begin{array}{r} 68 \\ \times\ 3 \\ \hline \end{array}$	**5.** $\begin{array}{r} 78 \\ \times\ 3 \\ \hline \end{array}$	**6.** $\begin{array}{r} 88 \\ \times\ 3 \\ \hline \end{array}$

PRACTICE

Multiply.

7. $\begin{array}{r} 27 \\ \times\ 6 \\ \hline \end{array}$	**8.** $\begin{array}{r} 38 \\ \times\ 4 \\ \hline \end{array}$	**9.** $\begin{array}{r} 47 \\ \times\ 3 \\ \hline \end{array}$	**10.** $\begin{array}{r} 29 \\ \times\ 7 \\ \hline \end{array}$	**11.** $\begin{array}{r} 37 \\ \times\ 5 \\ \hline \end{array}$	**12.** $\begin{array}{r} 78 \\ \times\ 2 \\ \hline \end{array}$

13. $\begin{array}{r}24\\ \times\ 9\\ \hline\end{array}$	**14.** $\begin{array}{r}33\\ \times\ 4\\ \hline\end{array}$	**15.** $\begin{array}{r}28\\ \times\ 7\\ \hline\end{array}$	**16.** $\begin{array}{r}45\\ \times\ 6\\ \hline\end{array}$	**17.** $\begin{array}{r}95\\ \times\ 5\\ \hline\end{array}$	**18.** $\begin{array}{r}38\\ \times\ 9\\ \hline\end{array}$
19. $\begin{array}{r}44\\ \times\ 8\\ \hline\end{array}$	**20.** $\begin{array}{r}87\\ \times\ 4\\ \hline\end{array}$	**21.** $\begin{array}{r}75\\ \times\ 3\\ \hline\end{array}$	**22.** $\begin{array}{r}84\\ \times\ 9\\ \hline\end{array}$	**23.** $\begin{array}{r}27\\ \times\ 8\\ \hline\end{array}$	**24.** $\begin{array}{r}56\\ \times\ 8\\ \hline\end{array}$
25. $\begin{array}{r}32\\ \times\ 3\\ \hline\end{array}$	**26.** $\begin{array}{r}74\\ \times\ 6\\ \hline\end{array}$	**27.** $\begin{array}{r}16\\ \times\ 4\\ \hline\end{array}$	**28.** $\begin{array}{r}43\\ \times\ 2\\ \hline\end{array}$	**29.** $\begin{array}{r}56\\ \times\ 7\\ \hline\end{array}$	**30.** $\begin{array}{r}13\\ \times\ 3\\ \hline\end{array}$

31. 3×74 **32.** 3×67 **33.** 7×76 **34.** 4×84

35. 6×63 **36.** 9×94 **37.** 8×47 **38.** 5×55

Solve. Work from left to right.

★ **39.** $4 \times 20 + 6$ ★ **40.** $5 \times 15 - 2$ ★ **41.** $3 \times 24 - 6$ ★ **42.** $4 \times 52 - 9$

ESTIMATE

Since $2 \times 50 = 100$, estimate whether the product will be less than or greater than 100. Write *less* or *greater*.

43. 2×52 **44.** 2×49 **45.** 2×36 **46.** 2×63

47. 3×50 **48.** 1×50 **49.** 4×49 **50.** 1×51

PROBLEM SOLVING APPLICATIONS
Choosing a Strategy

Solve.

51. Each box holds 24 toys. How many toys are in 6 boxes?

52. There are 36 toy robots in each box. About how many robots are in 7 boxes?

53. How many bags of 5 balloons can you make from 45 balloons?

54. Which is the greater amount, 7 bags of 9 balloons or 8 bags of 8 balloons?

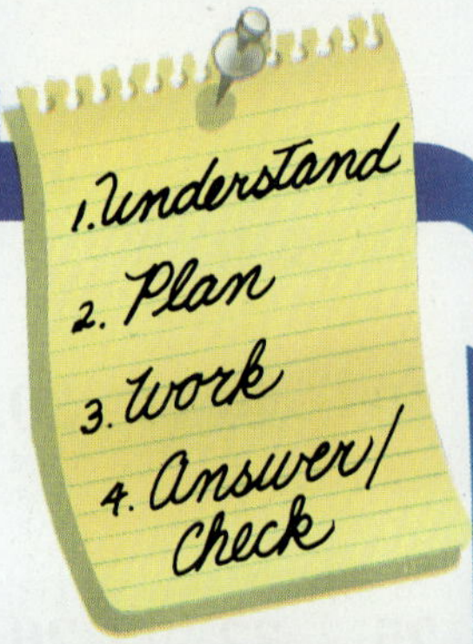

PROBLEM SOLVING

Strategy: Using Estimation

Eva can jog around the track in 13 minutes. Joe can jog around the track in 15 minutes. They estimate to find out about how long it will take each of them to jog 3 times around the track.

Eva estimates by rounding 13 down to 10. Then she multiplies.

$$\begin{array}{r} 13 \\ \times\ 3 \\ \hline \end{array} \rightarrow \begin{array}{r} 10 \\ \times\ 3 \\ \hline 30 \end{array}$$

Since 13 is more than 10, the exact answer is more than the estimate of 30. It takes more than 30 minutes.

Joe estimates by rounding 15 up to 20. Then he multiplies.

$$\begin{array}{r} 15 \\ \times\ 3 \\ \hline \end{array} \rightarrow \begin{array}{r} 20 \\ \times\ 3 \\ \hline 60 \end{array}$$

Since 15 is less than 20, it takes Joe less than 60 minutes.

CLASS EXERCISES

Is the estimate reasonable? Tell why or why not.

1. On Monday Eva jogs around the track in 14 minutes. She estimates that she can jog around the track 4 times *in less than 40 minutes*.

$$\begin{array}{r} 14 \\ \times\ 4 \\ \hline \end{array} \rightarrow \begin{array}{r} 10 \\ \times\ 4 \\ \hline 40 \end{array}$$

2. Joe plans to go jogging 15 times each month. He estimates that he will jog *more than 80 times* in 4 months.

$$\begin{array}{r} 15 \\ \times\ 4 \\ \hline \end{array} \rightarrow \begin{array}{r} 20 \\ \times\ 4 \\ \hline 80 \end{array}$$

3. Eva spends 12 minutes setting up her paints. Then she spends 31 minutes painting. She spends *more than 40 minutes altogether*.

$$\begin{array}{r} 12 \\ +\ 31 \\ \hline \end{array} \rightarrow \begin{array}{r} 10 \\ +\ 30 \\ \hline 40 \end{array}$$

PRACTICE

Estimate to solve. Write *more than* or *less than* with your answer.

4. Eva ran twice as fast to school today as she did a month ago. Today she ran to school in 14 minutes. About how long did it take her one month ago?

5. Joe practices the piano every day for 45 minutes. About how many minutes does he spend practicing in 7 days?

6. Eva spent 52¢ for a jar of red paint and 23¢ for a brush. About how much did she spend?

7. Joe delivers 17 papers on each street. About how many papers does he deliver on 3 streets?

8. Eva bought 7 puzzles. Each has 43 pieces. About how many pieces are there altogether?

★ **9.** Joe rode his bike 4 km in 82 minutes. About how long would it take him to ride 8 km?

CHECKPOINT 1

Estimate the product. *(pages 280–281)*

1. $\begin{array}{r} 54 \\ \times\ 6 \\ \hline \end{array}$ **2.** $\begin{array}{r} 48 \\ \times\ 8 \\ \hline \end{array}$ **3.** $\begin{array}{r} 35 \\ \times\ 3 \\ \hline \end{array}$

Multiply. *(pages 278–279, 282–289)*

4. $\begin{array}{r} 32 \\ \times\ 3 \\ \hline \end{array}$ **5.** $\begin{array}{r} 14 \\ \times\ 6 \\ \hline \end{array}$ **6.** $\begin{array}{r} 36 \\ \times\ 7 \\ \hline \end{array}$

Estimate. Write *more than* or *less than* with your answer. *(pages 290–291)*

7. Bill bought 3 bags of apples. There were 28 apples in each bag. About how many apples did Bill buy in all?

Extra practice on page 418

MULTIPLYING A THREE-DIGIT NUMBER WITH RENAMING

Let's multiply 116 by 2.

Multiply the 6 ones by 2. Rename the 12 ones as 1 ten and 2 ones. Write the 1 in the tens' place.

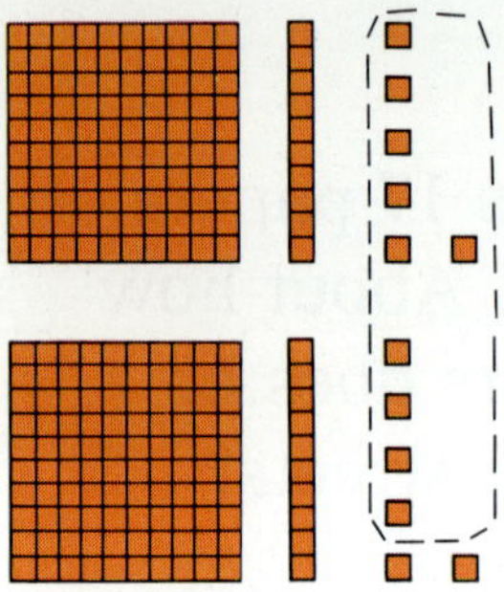

$$\begin{array}{r} {\scriptstyle 1} \\ 116 \\ \times\ 2 \\ \hline 2 \end{array}$$

Multiply the 1 ten by 2. Add the 1 ten.

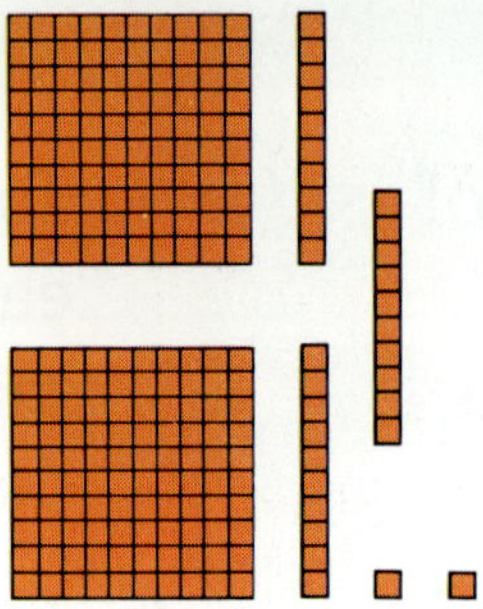

$$\begin{array}{r} {\scriptstyle 1} \\ 116 \\ \times\ 2 \\ \hline 32 \end{array}$$

Multiply the 1 hundred by 2.

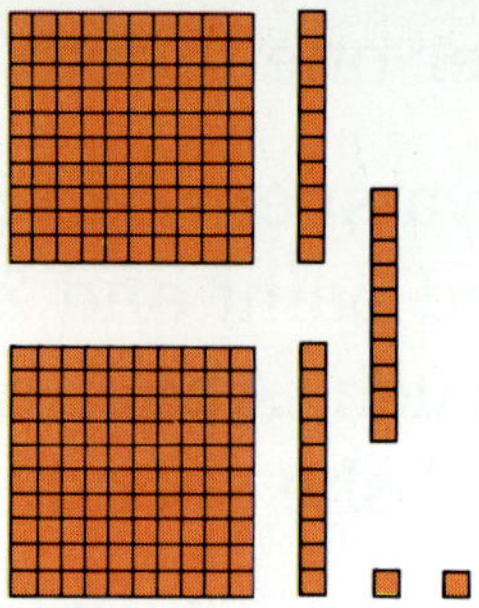

$$\begin{array}{r} {\scriptstyle 1} \\ 116 \\ \times\ 2 \\ \hline 232 \end{array}$$

The product is 232.

CLASS EXERCISES

Multiply. Build on what you know.

1. $\begin{array}{r} 24 \\ \times\ 2 \\ \hline \end{array} \rightarrow \begin{array}{r} 424 \\ \times\ 2 \\ \hline \end{array}$
2. $\begin{array}{r} 23 \\ \times\ 3 \\ \hline \end{array} \rightarrow \begin{array}{r} 323 \\ \times\ 3 \\ \hline \end{array}$
3. $\begin{array}{r} 12 \\ \times\ 4 \\ \hline \end{array} \rightarrow \begin{array}{r} 112 \\ \times\ 4 \\ \hline \end{array}$
4. $\begin{array}{r} 14 \\ \times\ 3 \\ \hline \end{array} \rightarrow \begin{array}{r} 214 \\ \times\ 3 \\ \hline \end{array}$
5. $\begin{array}{r} 48 \\ \times\ 2 \\ \hline \end{array} \rightarrow \begin{array}{r} 348 \\ \times\ 2 \\ \hline \end{array}$
6. $\begin{array}{r} 26 \\ \times\ 3 \\ \hline \end{array} \rightarrow \begin{array}{r} 326 \\ \times\ 3 \\ \hline \end{array}$

PRACTICE

Multiply.

7. $\begin{array}{r} 139 \\ \times\ 2 \\ \hline \end{array}$
8. $\begin{array}{r} 114 \\ \times\ 5 \\ \hline \end{array}$
9. $\begin{array}{r} 103 \\ \times\ 8 \\ \hline \end{array}$
10. $\begin{array}{r} 113 \\ \times\ 7 \\ \hline \end{array}$
11. $\begin{array}{r} 221 \\ \times\ 3 \\ \hline \end{array}$

12. 123 × 4

13. 436 × 2

14. 448 × 2

15. 118 × 5

16. 112 × 8

17. 106 × 6

18. 246 × 2

19. 102 × 9

20. 223 × 3

21. 106 × 9

22. 115 × 6

23. 114 × 7

24. 244 × 2

25. 112 × 4

26. 109 × 8

MIXED REVIEW

Write the answer.

27. 41 − 27

28. 38 + 19

29. 47 − 26

30. 38 + 20

31. $4\overline{)36}$

32. $3\overline{)15}$

33. $7\overline{)49}$

34. $9\overline{)27}$

PROBLEM SOLVING APPLICATIONS

Two-Step Problems

Solve.

35. Jan has 451 leaves. Rob has 1000 leaves. Rob gives 220 leaves to Jan. How many leaves does each person have?

36. Miki collects 145 leaves one day and 263 the next day. Of the leaves, 26 are torn. How many are not torn?

37. Miki's big scrapbook can hold 8 leaves on each of the 113 pages. Miki has 1000 leaves. If Miki fills the scrapbook, how many leaves will be left over?

★ **38.** A scrapbook holds 124 leaves. Yuki fills 3 scrapbooks with maple leaves. She fills 5 scrapbooks with oak leaves. How many more oak leaves than maple leaves are there?

MULTIPLYING A THREE-DIGIT NUMBER WITH RENAMING

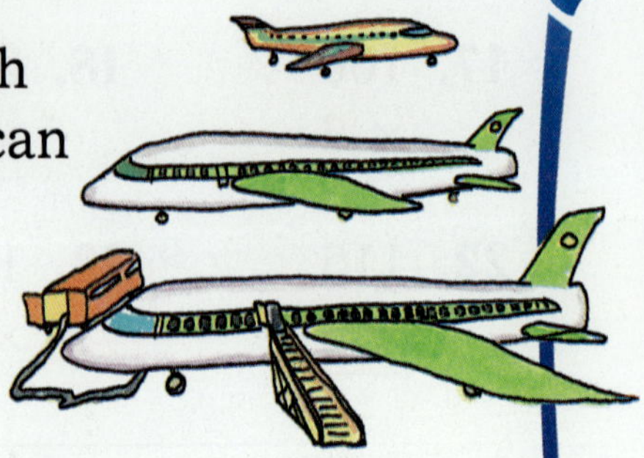

At a small airport, 5 planes land each day. Each plane can hold 231 people. How many people can land there each day?

To find the answer, you multiply 231 by 5.

Multiply the 1 one by 5.	Multiply the 3 tens by 5. Rename the 15 tens as 1 hundred 5 tens. Write the 1 in the hundreds' place.	Multiply the 2 hundreds by 5. Add the 1 hundred.
$\begin{array}{r} 231 \\ \times\ 5 \\ \hline 5 \end{array}$	$\begin{array}{r} ^{1}\ \ \ \\ 231 \\ \times\ 5 \\ \hline 55 \end{array}$	$\begin{array}{r} ^{1}\ \ \ \\ 231 \\ \times\ 5 \\ \hline 1155 \end{array}$

Each day 1155 people can land at the airport.

Remember, to estimate the answer you can round to the nearest hundred and multiply.

$$\begin{array}{rcr} 231 & \longrightarrow & 200 \\ \times\ 5 & \longrightarrow & \times\ 5 \\ \hline & & 1000 \end{array}$$

Think: Why is the estimate less than the actual answer?

CLASS EXERCISES

What are the products?

1. $\begin{array}{r} 222 \\ \times\ 4 \\ \hline \end{array}$ → $\begin{array}{r} 242 \\ \times\ 4 \\ \hline \end{array}$

2. $\begin{array}{r} 323 \\ \times\ 3 \\ \hline \end{array}$ → $\begin{array}{r} 353 \\ \times\ 3 \\ \hline \end{array}$

3. $\begin{array}{r} 454 \\ \times\ 2 \\ \hline \end{array}$ → $\begin{array}{r} 554 \\ \times\ 2 \\ \hline \end{array}$

4. $\begin{array}{r} 140 \\ \times\ 6 \\ \hline \end{array}$ → $\begin{array}{r} 440 \\ \times\ 6 \\ \hline \end{array}$

PRACTICE

Multiply.

5. 351×3	**6.** 232×4	**7.** 143×3	**8.** 242×4	**9.** 141×7
10. 212×6	**11.** 341×8	**12.** 627×3	**13.** 907×8	**14.** 724×3
15. 929×2	**16.** 417×5	**17.** 813×7	**18.** 352×4	**19.** 208×6
20. 243×2	**21.** 705×4	**22.** 283×4	**23.** 621×8	**24.** 526×3

ESTIMATE

You know that $6 \times 400 = 2400$. Will the product be greater than 2400? Write *yes* or *no*.

25. 423×6	**26.** 481×6	**27.** 357×6	**28.** 400×7

PROBLEM SOLVING APPLICATIONS

Mental Math or Pencil

Solve. Tell whether you used pencil and paper or mental math. Write *p* or *m*.

29. Each of the 3 waiting rooms has 5 windows. The hallway has 10 windows. How many windows are there in all?

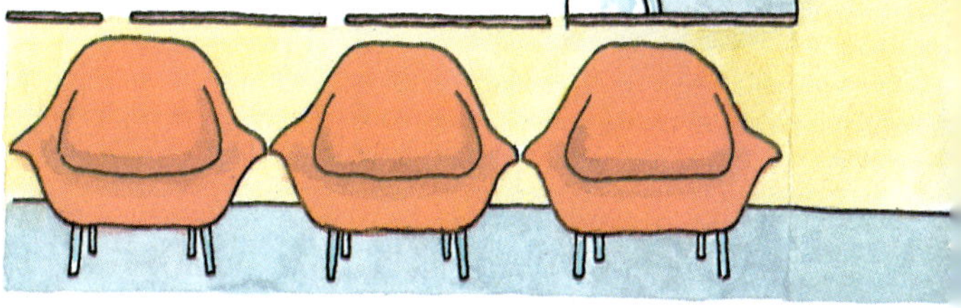

30. An airport has 3 waiting rooms. Each room has 114 seats. How many seats are there in all?

★ **31.** There are 29 windows on each side of the airplane. If there are 3 airplanes, how many windows are there?

MULTIPLYING MONEY

Multiplying money is like multiplying two-digit and three-digit numbers. You must remember to write the decimal point and the dollar sign in the answer.

$$\begin{array}{r} {}^{2} \\ \$.16 \\ \times\ 4 \\ \hline \$.64 \end{array} \qquad \begin{array}{r} \$3.21 \\ \times\ 8 \\ \hline \$25.68 \end{array}$$

Remember the decimal point.

Calculators don't have dollar signs, but they *do* have decimal points. Be sure to enter a point where you need one. Otherwise your answer will be wrong.

$$\begin{array}{r} \$3.21 \\ \times\ 8 \\ \hline \end{array}$$

$3.21 → 3 [.] 21	[×] →	3.21
	8 →	8
	[=] →	25.68

Write the dollar sign when you copy the product. $25.68

CLASS EXERCISES

Write the product using . and $.

1. $\begin{array}{r} {}^{2} \\ \$.15 \\ \times\ 5 \\ \hline 75 \end{array}$ **2.** $\begin{array}{r} {}^{3} \\ \$.49 \\ \times\ 4 \\ \hline 196 \end{array}$ **3.** $\begin{array}{r} {}^{1} \\ \$1.52 \\ \times\ 3 \\ \hline 456 \end{array}$ **4.** $\begin{array}{r} {}^{1} \\ \$.27 \\ \times\ 2 \\ \hline 54 \end{array}$ **5.** $\begin{array}{r} {}^{1} \\ \$3.20 \\ \times\ 7 \\ \hline 2240 \end{array}$

PRACTICE

Multiply.

6. $.34 × 6
7. $.18 × 7
8. $.94 × 2
9. $.55 × 4
10. $.27 × 8
11. $1.31 × 6
12. $3.24 × 4
13. $5.25 × 2
14. $9.15 × 3
15. $8.14 × 5
16. $.32 × 9
17. $.15 × 7
18. $2.15 × 4
19. $.25 × 5
20. $1.16 × 5
21. $4.80 × 4
22. $.60 × 7
23. $.75 × 6
24. $6.82 × 4
25. $.48 × 7
26. 3 × $1.93
27. 6 × $.56
28. 3 × $7.28
29. 9 × $.88

The multiplication was done on a calculator. If it is correct, write *o.k.* If it is not, correct it.

CALCULATOR

30. $.49 × 7 = 34.3
31. $3.54 × 4 = 1.416
32. $.19 × 5 = .95
33. $5.32 × 4 = 2128.

PROBLEM SOLVING APPLICATIONS
Using Money

Solve.

34. A bus ticket for an adult costs $4.45. How much do 2 adult tickets cost?

35. A bus ticket for a student costs $2.46. How much do 5 student tickets cost?

★ 36. A bus ticket costs $2.46. How many tickets can you buy with $15?

★ 37. How much will you save by buying 2 round-trip tickets at $11.48 each rather than 4 single trip tickets at $6.18 each?

PROBLEM SOLVING

Strategy: Open Ended Problems

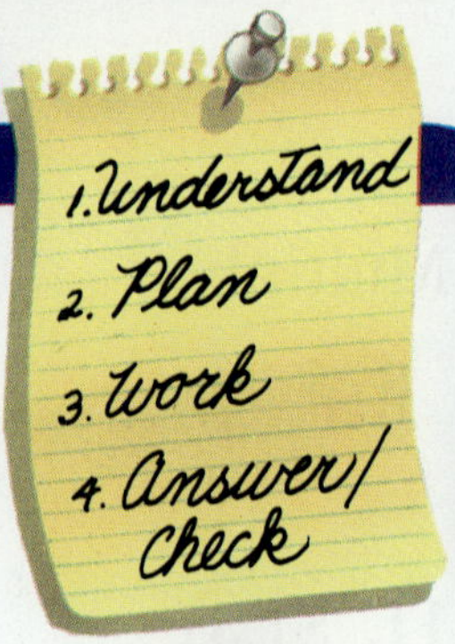

Some problems have more than one answer. Here is an example.

Party favors come in bags of 4 or 6. Arlene needs 12 favors. How many bags should she buy?

One way: $3 \times 4 = 12$
Arlene could buy 3 bags of 4 favors.

Another way: $2 \times 6 = 12$
Arlene could buy 2 bags of 6 favors.

Both ways are correct.

CLASS EXERCISES

Use the pictures to answer the question. Write 2 letters to show the possible answers.

1. Arnie wants to buy 30 balloons. How many bags should he buy?
   a. 2 bags of 15 **b.** 2 bags of 30 **c.** 1 bag of 30
2. Alice has 94¢. What can she buy?
   a. 15 balloons **b.** a yo-yo **c.** a horn
3. Ted gives the clerk $1.00 for the horn. The clerk is out of pennies. Which coins might Ted get as change?
   a. 1 quarter **b.** 2 nickels **c.** 1 dime
4. Rosa returns a yo-yo. What 2 things can she buy for the price of a yo-yo?
   a. 2 bags of 15 balloons **b.** a horn and 1 bag of 15 balloons **c.** a horn and 1 bag of 30 balloons

PRACTICE

Write two possible answers for the problem.

5. Marie buys a paper hat for \$.95. She gives the clerk a one dollar bill. What coins does Marie get back in change?

6. A class needs 40 balloons for a party. Eric has 23. Brad has 16. Kirk has 25. Which 2 students have enough balloons?

7. Ted has 8 bean seeds. He wants to put the same number in each pot. How many pots does he need?

8. Party napkins come 75 to a pack or 150 to a pack. You need 150 napkins. How many packs do you buy?

Solve. There may be 1, 2, or 3 answers.

★ 9. Bob needs 50 cups. A bag of 25 costs \$.79. A bag of 50 costs \$1.49. How many bags should Bob buy?

★ 10. A blue card is worth 2 points. A red card is worth 1 point. Rosa has 5 points. Which cards does she have?

CHECKPOINT 2

Write the answer.

(pages 292–295)

1. $\begin{array}{r} 124 \\ \times 3 \\ \hline \end{array}$

2. $\begin{array}{r} 118 \\ \times 6 \\ \hline \end{array}$

3. $\begin{array}{r} 251 \\ \times 4 \\ \hline \end{array}$

4. $\begin{array}{r} 623 \\ \times 3 \\ \hline \end{array}$

Write the answer.

(pages 296–297)

5. $\begin{array}{r} \$.56 \\ \times 5 \\ \hline \end{array}$

6. $\begin{array}{r} \$.39 \\ \times 8 \\ \hline \end{array}$

7. $\begin{array}{r} \$1.23 \\ \times 7 \\ \hline \end{array}$

8. $\begin{array}{r} \$5.18 \\ \times 6 \\ \hline \end{array}$

9. $\begin{array}{r} \$.98 \\ \times 4 \\ \hline \end{array}$

10. $\begin{array}{r} \$3.51 \\ \times 8 \\ \hline \end{array}$

Extra practice on page 418

CHAPTER 10 TEST

Round to the nearest ten or hundred. Estimate the product.
(pages 280–281)

1. 7×62 **2.** 2×858 **3.** 6×430 **4.** 5×571

Write the answer. *(pages 278–279, 282–289)*

5. 60×3 **6.** 42×2 **7.** 28×3 **8.** 51×8

9. 26×3 **10.** 14×7 **11.** 64×5 **12.** 38×6

Estimate to solve. Write *more than* or *less than* with your answer.
(pages 290–291)

13. Jeff bought 4 bags of marbles. There were 26 marbles in each bag. About how many marbles did Jeff buy?

14. Linda had 3 bags of beads. There were 32 beads in each bag. About how many beads did Linda have?

Write the answer. *(pages 292–295)*

15. 315×3 **16.** 409×2 **17.** 262×3 **18.** 617×5

Write the answer. *(pages 296–297)*

19. $\$.43 \times 6$ **20.** $\$.71 \times 8$ **21.** $\$1.25 \times 3$ **22.** $\$8.70 \times 4$

Extra practice on page 419

MATHEMATICS and LANGUAGE ARTS

To complete this puzzle, you need to know word names for numbers.
Write the standard forms.

■	1 ?	2 ?	3 ?	■
4 ?	?	?	?	■
5 ?	?	?	■	6 ?
7 ?	?	■	8 ?	?
■	■	■	9 ?	?

ACROSS

1. nine times eighty-one
4. four thousand, six hundred seventy
5. nine hundred minus fifty-six
7. two times forty-six
8. sixty minus fifty
9. twenty-nine plus eighteen

DOWN

1. seven thousand, six hundred plus forty-two
2. two times one hundred thirty-seven
3. eighty-six rounded to the nearest ten
4. three-times one hundred sixty-three
6. twenty-three multiplied by nine
8. five plus six plus three

ARE YOU PUZZLED?

Enrichment

Ralph cleans out his button box. He groups buttons that are alike. He draws a red ring around the round buttons. He draws a blue ring around the white buttons.

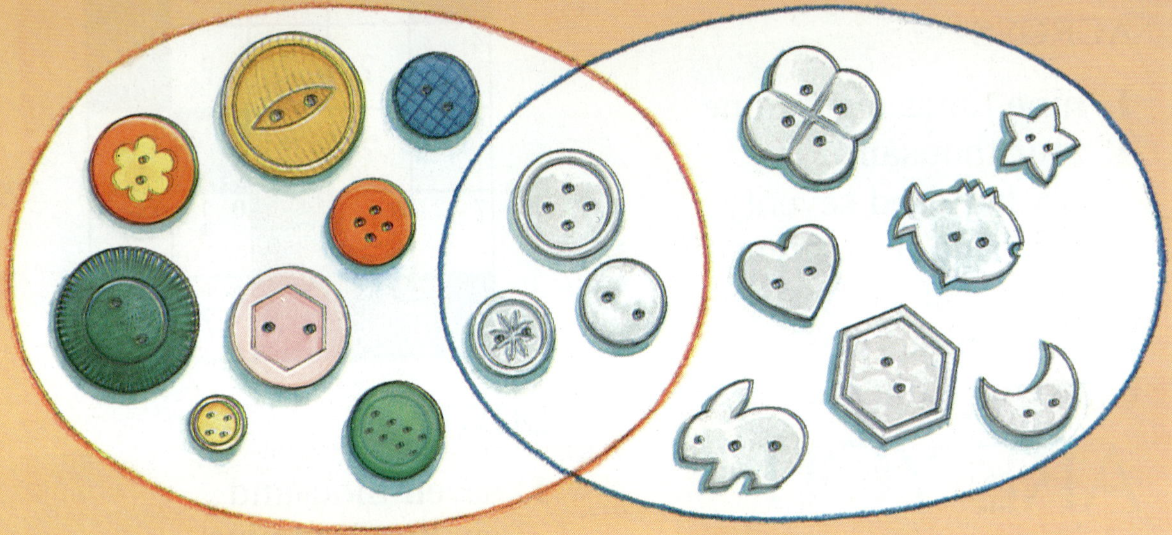

Use the picture to solve.

1. How many buttons are in the red ring?
2. How many buttons are in the blue ring?
3. How many buttons are in the red ring but not the blue ring?

LOGIC DIAGRAMS

4. How many buttons are in the blue ring but not the red ring?
5. How many buttons are in both the red ring and blue ring?
6. Why do the rings overlap?

In which part of the rings does the object belong? Write the letter.

7. bed
8. giraffe
9. goldfish in a bowl
10. baby
11. elephant
12. kitchen chair
13. lion
14. apple tree
15. dog sleeping on couch
16. oven
17. kitchen sink
18. plant on a table

Draw, then solve.

19. Copy the boxes. Write the numbers where they belong.

20. Which numbers are in the red box but not the blue box?

21. Which numbers are in the blue box but not in the red box?

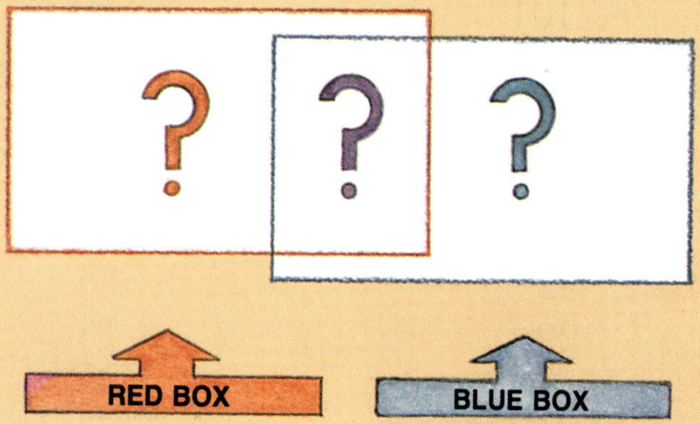

RED BOX: even numbers greater than 1 and less than 10

BLUE BOX: even numbers greater than 5 and less than 20

CUMULATIVE REVIEW

Choose the correct answer. Choose *a*, *b*, *c*, or *d*.

Round to the nearest ten or hundred. Estimate the sum.

1. $38 + 42$

a. 60
b. 80
c. 90
d. 50

2. $61 + 27$

a. 90
b. 70
c. 60
d. 30

3. $509 + 180$

a. 500
b. 700
c. 300
d. 900

Find the answer.

4. $7 + 5 + 4 + 7$

a. 22
b. 13
c. 24
d. none of these

5. $22 + 87 + 16$

a. 125
b. 115
c. 126
d. none of these

6. $4077 + 3846$

a. 7813
b. 7913
c. 7923
d. none of these

7. $463 + 651$

a. 212
b. 1114
c. 1013
d. 1014

8. $807 + 139$

a. 936
b. 668
c. 563
d. none of these

9. $5432 + 2769$

a. 8201
b. 8101
c. 7291
d. 7101

Round to the nearest ten or hundred. Estimate the difference.

10. $42 - 29$

a. 10
b. 60
c. 30
d. 70

11. $65 - 18$

a. 70
b. 50
c. 40
d. 60

12. $731 - 457$

a. 500
b. 200
c. 270
d. 1100

Find the answer.

13. $\begin{array}{r} 786 \\ -\ 461 \\ \hline \end{array}$

a. 235
b. 315
c. 325
d. none of these

14. $\begin{array}{r} 9162 \\ -\ 343 \\ \hline \end{array}$

a. 8819
b. 8829
c. 8719
d. none of these

15. $\begin{array}{r} 4310 \\ -\ 1637 \\ \hline \end{array}$

a. 2773
b. 2683
c. 2673
d. none of these

Find the answer.

16. $6\overline{)42}$

a. 6
b. 7
c. 8
d. none of these

17. $7\overline{)56}$

a. 6
b. 8
c. 9
d. none of these

18. $9\overline{)63}$

a. 7
b. 6
c. 8
d. none of these

Solve.

19. Eddie has 25¢ and Sid has 17¢. How many oranges can they buy at 7¢ each?

a. 25 oranges
b. 6 oranges
c. 7 oranges
d. none of these

20. Jenny bought 2 tickets at \$4 each and 1 ticket at \$3. How much did she spend in all?

a. \$4
b. \$8
c. \$7
d. none of these

LANGUAGE and VOCABULARY REVIEW

Match each word with its sign.

1. divide **2.** multiply

3. dollar **4.** cent

5. equals **6.** degrees Celsius

A. \$ **B.** °C

C. ÷ **D.** ×

E. ¢ **F.** =

QUOTATION MARKS

When you tell the computer **PRINT 35 + 14** it does the arithmetic. Then the computer shows the answer.

When you use PRINT with quotation marks, the computer does not do arithmetic. It shows exactly what is between the marks.

```
10 PRINT "THIRTY-FIVE PLUS FOURTEEN"
20 PRINT "IS THE SAME AS"
30 PRINT "35 + 14"
```

```
THIRTY-FIVE PLUS FOURTEEN
IS THE SAME AS
35 + 14
```

Write the output for the program.

1.
```
10 PRINT "HELLO"
20 PRINT "THIS IS A"
30 PRINT "COMPUTER"
```

2.
```
10 PRINT "SIX TIMES SEVEN"
20 PRINT "IS THE SAME AS"
30 PRINT "6 * 7"
```

3.
```
10 PRINT "ADD 5 AND 6"
20 PRINT "TO GET"
30 PRINT "A SUM OF"
40 PRINT 5 + 6
```

4.
```
10 PRINT "28/4"
20 PRINT "IS"
30 PRINT 28/4
```

5.
```
10 PRINT 178 + 12
20 PRINT "CARS WENT"
30 PRINT "IN THE"
40 PRINT "TUNNEL"
```

6.
```
10 PRINT "THE"
20 PRINT 81/9
30 PRINT "PLAYERS"
40 PRINT "WON THE GAME"
```

11

About 6 hundred people make each flag. If a flag has 3 equal parts, about how many hundred people make each part?

DIVISION
GREATER NUMBERS

DIVIDING BY 1 THROUGH 9

You can use division to find out how many groups of 3 spools there are in 15.

$15 \div 3 = 5$

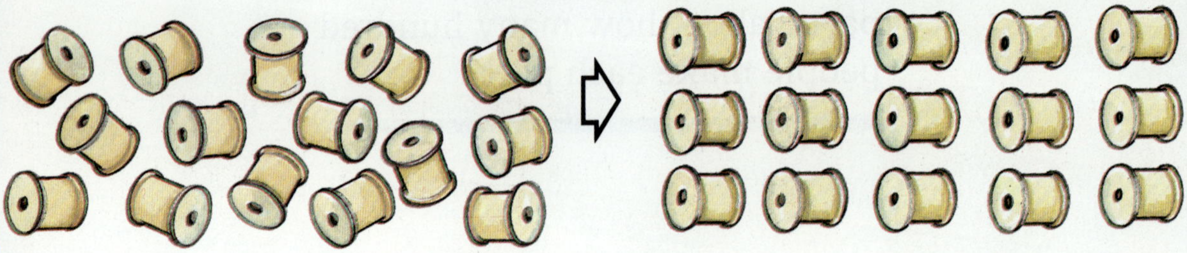

There are 5 threes in 15.
The quotient is 5.

When you divide 15 by 3, the answer will be less than 15.

When you multiply 15 by 3, the answer will be greater than 15.

CLASS EXERCISES

What is the quotient?

1. $24 \div 4$	**2.** $36 \div 6$	**3.** $32 \div 4$	**4.** $56 \div 8$	**5.** $36 \div 9$
6. $28 \div 7$	**7.** $18 \div 2$	**8.** $48 \div 8$	**9.** $35 \div 7$	**10.** $72 \div 9$
11. $9 \div 3$	**12.** $14 \div 2$	**13.** $30 \div 6$	**14.** $32 \div 8$	**15.** $12 \div 6$
16. $10 \div 5$	**17.** $8 \div 1$	**18.** $16 \div 8$	**19.** $56 \div 7$	**20.** $64 \div 8$

PRACTICE

Divide.

21. $9\overline{)63}$	**22.** $2\overline{)16}$	**23.** $4\overline{)4}$	**24.** $4\overline{)16}$	**25.** $7\overline{)63}$

26. $3\overline{)21}$ **27.** $4\overline{)36}$ **28.** $7\overline{)35}$ **29.** $6\overline{)42}$ **30.** $3\overline{)6}$

31. $8\overline{)56}$ **32.** $3\overline{)12}$ **33.** $6\overline{)0}$ **34.** $9\overline{)72}$ **35.** $4\overline{)32}$

36. $6\overline{)48}$ **37.** $3\overline{)18}$ **38.** $9\overline{)36}$ **39.** $5\overline{)40}$ **40.** $8\overline{)0}$

41. $2\overline{)12}$ **42.** $4\overline{)24}$ **43.** $5\overline{)35}$ **44.** $8\overline{)40}$ **45.** $9\overline{)27}$

46. $1\overline{)6}$ **47.** $5\overline{)30}$ **48.** $6\overline{)54}$ **49.** $8\overline{)72}$ **50.** $5\overline{)25}$

Compare. Write < or >.

★ **51.** $36 \div 6$ ▒ $56 \div 8$ ★ **52.** $20 \div 5$ ▒ $42 \div 6$ ★ **53.** $32 \div 8$ ▒ $27 \div 9$

★ **54.** $56 \div 7$ ▒ $54 \div 6$ ★ **55.** $28 \div 7$ ▒ $18 \div 6$ ★ **56.** $64 \div 8$ ▒ $42 \div 6$

Will the answer be greater than or less than the underlined number? Write *greater* or *less*.

ESTIMATE

57. $8 \times \underline{4}$ **58.** $\underline{27} \div 3$ **59.** $7 \times \underline{5}$ **60.** $\underline{64} \div 8$ **61.** $5 \times \underline{6}$

62. $9 \times \underline{8}$ **63.** $\underline{49} \div 7$ **64.** $7 \times \underline{8}$ **65.** $\underline{8} \times 9$ **66.** $\underline{45} \div 9$

PROBLEM SOLVING APPLICATIONS
Choosing the Operation

Solve.

67. It takes Kim 2 hours to make a basket. How many baskets can he make in 8 hours?

68. The third grade is having a Craft Fair. They have 4 weeks to complete their projects. How many days do they have?

★ **69.** Three children make an equal number of baskets. Each basket has 2 hoops. There are 48 hoops. How many baskets does each child make?

DIVISION WITH REMAINDERS

When you divide 23 greeting cards into 7 groups, you have 2 cards left over. A number left over is called a **remainder.**

Divide 23 by 7.

$$\begin{array}{rrl} & 3 & \leftarrow \text{quotient} \\ & 7\overline{)23} & \\ \text{Subtract } 3 \times 7. & -\ 21 & \\ \hline & 2 & \leftarrow \text{remainder} \end{array}$$

Write the remainder with the quotient.

$$\begin{array}{r} 3 \text{ R2} \\ 7\overline{)23} \\ -\ 21 \\ \hline 2 \end{array}$$

Think: What is the greatest remainder you can have when you divide by 7?

CLASS EXERCISES

Divide.

1. $3\overline{)12}$ $3\overline{)13}$ **2.** $4\overline{)16}$ $4\overline{)17}$ **3.** $5\overline{)25}$ $5\overline{)26}$

4. $3\overline{)18}$ $3\overline{)20}$ **5.** $7\overline{)49}$ $7\overline{)51}$ **6.** $6\overline{)36}$ $6\overline{)41}$

PRACTICE

Divide.

7. $2\overline{)7}$ **8.** $3\overline{)20}$ **9.** $6\overline{)44}$ **10.** $5\overline{)38}$ **11.** $4\overline{)21}$

12. $2\overline{)17}$ **13.** $7\overline{)43}$ **14.** $8\overline{)10}$ **15.** $6\overline{)33}$ **16.** $5\overline{)34}$

17. $3\overline{)10}$ **18.** $4\overline{)39}$ **19.** $5\overline{)19}$ **20.** $6\overline{)41}$ **21.** $7\overline{)25}$

22. $3\overline{)20}$ **23.** $4\overline{)30}$ **24.** $7\overline{)66}$ **25.** $9\overline{)70}$ **26.** $3\overline{)26}$

27. $3\overline{)29}$ **28.** $8\overline{)69}$ **29.** $6\overline{)58}$ **30.** $7\overline{)38}$ **31.** $2\overline{)15}$

32. $5\overline{)39}$ **33.** $7\overline{)46}$ **34.** $9\overline{)20}$ **35.** $5\overline{)48}$ **36.** $7\overline{)50}$

37. $4\overline{)37}$ **38.** $6\overline{)39}$ **39.** $2\overline{)11}$ **40.** $4\overline{)35}$ **41.** $9\overline{)75}$

MIXED REVIEW

Write the answer.

42. $\begin{array}{r} 326 \\ +\ 125 \\ \hline \end{array}$ **43.** $\begin{array}{r} 145 \\ \times 3 \\ \hline \end{array}$ **44.** $\begin{array}{r} 478 \\ \times 8 \\ \hline \end{array}$ **45.** $\begin{array}{r} 856 \\ -\ 279 \\ \hline \end{array}$

46. $\begin{array}{r} 444 \\ +\ 356 \\ \hline \end{array}$ **47.** $\begin{array}{r} 780 \\ -\ 215 \\ \hline \end{array}$ **48.** $\begin{array}{r} 426 \\ -\ 399 \\ \hline \end{array}$ **49.** $\begin{array}{r} 155 \\ \times 6 \\ \hline \end{array}$

PROBLEM SOLVING APPLICATIONS
Too Little Information

Write the letter of the fact you need. Solve.

50. Six of the cards in a box of greeting cards have flowers. How many cards don't have flowers?

51. Rosie sells flowers. She has 48 roses. How many bunches can she sell?

★ **52.** Clark sells boxes of greeting cards. He gets 4 points for the first 4 boxes he sells and 8 points for each box he sells after that. How many boxes did he sell?

a. There are 6 roses in a bunch.

b. Clark earned 64 points.

c. There are 25 cards in a box.

DIVIDING TENS AND HUNDREDS

Once you know how to divide 6 by 2, you can divide 60 by 2 and 600 by 2.

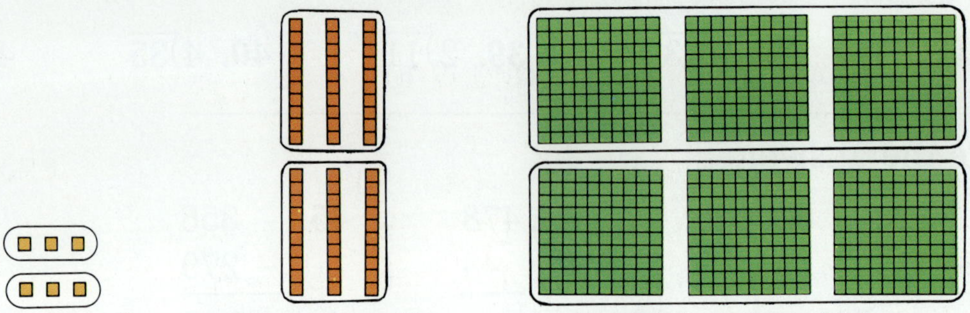

$6 \div 2 = 3$ $\quad$ $60 \div 2 = 30$ $\quad$ $600 \div 2 = 300$

This is how to find $600 \div 2$ on a calculator.

600 [÷] 2 [=] 300

CLASS EXERCISES

What are the quotients? How are the quotients the same? How are they different?

1. $6 \div 3$	**2.** $7 \div 7$	**3.** $8 \div 4$	**4.** $9 \div 3$
$60 \div 3$	$70 \div 7$	$80 \div 4$	$90 \div 3$
$600 \div 3$	$700 \div 7$	$800 \div 4$	$900 \div 3$

What is the quotient?

5. $60 \div 2$	**6.** $80 \div 2$	**7.** $50 \div 5$	**8.** $40 \div 2$
9. $400 \div 4$	**10.** $900 \div 3$	**11.** $600 \div 2$	**12.** $300 \div 1$

PRACTICE

Divide.

13. $7\overline{)700}$	**14.** $1\overline{)60}$	**15.** $1\overline{)90}$	**16.** $5\overline{)500}$	**17.** $4\overline{)40}$
18. $6\overline{)60}$	**19.** $1\overline{)80}$	**20.** $2\overline{)800}$	**21.** $1\overline{)600}$	**22.** $9\overline{)90}$

23. $1\overline{)40}$	**24.** $2\overline{)200}$	**25.** $1\overline{)500}$	**26.** $2\overline{)20}$	**27.** $8\overline{)800}$
28. $8\overline{)80}$	**29.** $1\overline{)70}$	**30.** $1\overline{)50}$	**31.** $2\overline{)400}$	**32.** $6\overline{)600}$
33. $1\overline{)20}$	**34.** $3\overline{)300}$	**35.** $1\overline{)900}$	**36.** $3\overline{)30}$	**37.** $1\overline{)400}$
★ **38.** $1\overline{)2000}$	★ **39.** $9\overline{)9000}$	★ **40.** $2\overline{)8000}$	★ **41.** $2\overline{)6000}$	★ **42.** $3\overline{)9000}$

CALCULATOR

Which division matches the quotient?
Write *a*, *b*, or *c*.

43. 300	**44.** 200	**45.** 40
a. 600 ÷ 3	**a.** 400 ÷ 1	**a.** 80 ÷ 2
b. 900 ÷ 3	**b.** 80 ÷ 4	**b.** 80 ÷ 4
c. 90 ÷ 3	**c.** 600 ÷ 3	**c.** 400 ÷ 4

46. **Think:** For Exercises 43–45, which would be faster, to do the division mentally or with a calculator?

PROBLEM SOLVING APPLICATIONS
Choosing the Operation

Solve.

47. There are 80 students in all. There are the same number of students in each of 4 classrooms. How many students are in each of the 4 classrooms?

48. A teacher puts an equal number of note pads in each of 4 cabinets. If there are 400 note pads, how many does he put in each cabinet?

49. There are 400 sheets of paper in a package. How many sheets of paper are in 2 packages?

50. Each of the 600 students has a pen. There are 3 extra pens. How many pens are there in all?

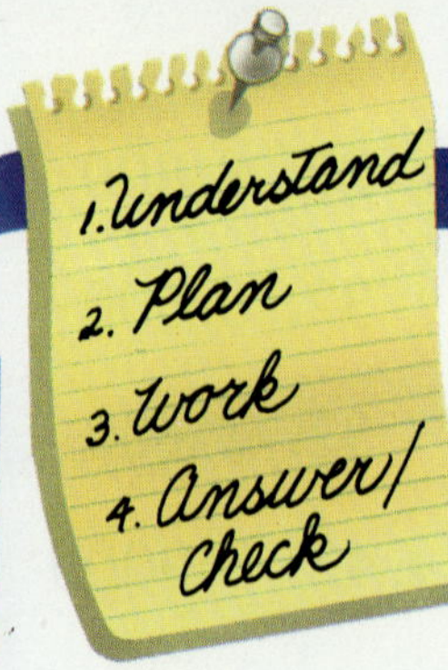

PROBLEM SOLVING

Strategy: Interpreting Answers

The remainders in answers can have different meanings. In some problems you don't use the remainder.

There are 45 tickets for 8 students. Each student gets the same number of tickets. How many tickets does each student get?

$$\begin{array}{r} 5 \text{ R5} \\ 8\overline{)45} \\ -40 \\ \hline 5 \end{array}$$

Each student gets 5 tickets. The remainder is not used.

In other problems the remainder is a clue to add 1 to the quotient.

There are 3 boxes of juice in a package. Each student gets 1 box. How many packages are needed for 23 students?

$$\begin{array}{r} 7 \text{ R2} \\ 3\overline{)23} \\ -21 \\ \hline 2 \end{array}$$

Eight packages are needed. If there were 7 packages, 2 students would not get any juice.

CLASS EXERCISES

Is the remainder needed? Explain why or why not.

1. The students are traveling to the park in cars. Each car can carry 4 students. How many cars are needed for 23 students?

$$\begin{array}{r} 5 \text{ R3} \\ 4\overline{)23} \\ -20 \\ \hline 3 \end{array}$$

2. It takes 3 nickels to buy a ticket. How many tickets can you buy with 28 nickels?

$$\begin{array}{r} 9 \text{ R1} \\ 3\overline{)28} \\ -27 \\ \hline 1 \end{array}$$

PRACTICE

Solve. Decide how to use the remainder.

3. Each car in the long ride holds 9 people. How many cars will be used for 83 people?

4. Four children can sit at a lunch table. How many tables are needed for 34 children?

5. Some of the students brought bread to make sandwiches. Each sandwich takes 2 slices. How many whole sandwiches can they make with 19 slices?

6. Eight students have sliced apples for dessert. There are 75 slices. The students share them evenly. How many slices does each student get?

7. The class made a model of the park when they got back to school. They used 6 sheets of poster board for each building. How many buildings could they build with 34 sheets?

★ 8. Every fifth person through the gate gets a free ticket. How many tickets are given away if 38 people walk through the gate?

CHECKPOINT 1

Write the answer.
(pages 308–313)

1. $3\overline{)16}$ **2.** $5\overline{)21}$

3. $2\overline{)400}$ **4.** $3\overline{)90}$

Solve. *(pages 314–315)*

5. It takes 4 students to carry a table. How many tables can 17 students carry?

Extra practice on page 420

TWO-DIGIT QUOTIENTS

Let's divide 46 by 2.
Think of 4 tens and 6 ones.

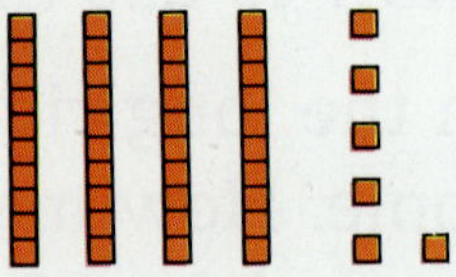

First divide the tens.

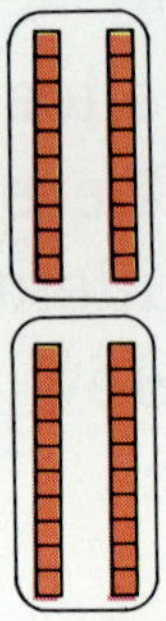

Divide 4 by 2.
Subtract 2 × 2.

$$\begin{array}{r} 2 \\ 2\overline{)46} \\ -4 \\ \hline 0 \end{array}$$

Then divide the ones.

Divide 6 by 2.
Subtract 3 × 2.

$$\begin{array}{r} 23 \\ 2\overline{)46} \\ -4\downarrow \\ \hline 6 \\ -6 \\ \hline 0 \end{array}$$

M To divide 46 by 2 mentally, think of separating 4 tens and 6 ones into 2 piles to get 2 tens and 3 ones or 23.

When you divide 47 by 2, you have a remainder.

First divide the tens.

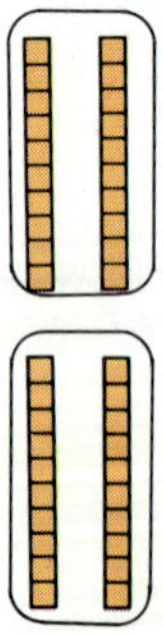

$$\begin{array}{r} 2 \\ 2\overline{)47} \\ -4 \\ \hline 0 \end{array}$$

Next divide the ones.

$$\begin{array}{r} 23 \\ 2\overline{)47} \\ -4\downarrow \\ \hline 7 \\ -6 \\ \hline 1 \end{array}$$

Write the remainder with the quotient.

$$\begin{array}{r} 23\text{ R1} \\ 2\overline{)47} \\ -4\downarrow \\ \hline 7 \\ -6 \\ \hline 1 \end{array}$$

CLASS EXERCISES

Divide.

1. $2\overline{)80}$ $2\overline{)88}$ $2\overline{)89}$ **2.** $3\overline{)60}$ $3\overline{)63}$ $3\overline{)64}$

3. $3\overline{)30}$ $3\overline{)36}$ $3\overline{)38}$ **4.** $5\overline{)50}$ $5\overline{)55}$ $5\overline{)59}$

PRACTICE

Divide.

5. $3\overline{)37}$	**6.** $2\overline{)69}$	**7.** $3\overline{)64}$	**8.** $2\overline{)63}$	**9.** $2\overline{)68}$
10. $8\overline{)87}$	**11.** $3\overline{)95}$	**12.** $3\overline{)93}$	**13.** $7\overline{)74}$	**14.** $3\overline{)67}$
15. $6\overline{)65}$	**16.** $4\overline{)88}$	**17.** $5\overline{)58}$	**18.** $5\overline{)55}$	**19.** $2\overline{)85}$

Divide mentally. Write just the answer.

MENTAL MATH

20. $2\overline{)64}$	**21.** $3\overline{)39}$	**22.** $4\overline{)84}$	**23.** $2\overline{)28}$
24. $2\overline{)82}$	**25.** $4\overline{)44}$	**26.** $2\overline{)42}$	**27.** $4\overline{)48}$

PROBLEM SOLVING APPLICATIONS
Using a Pictograph

Use the information in the pictograph to solve.

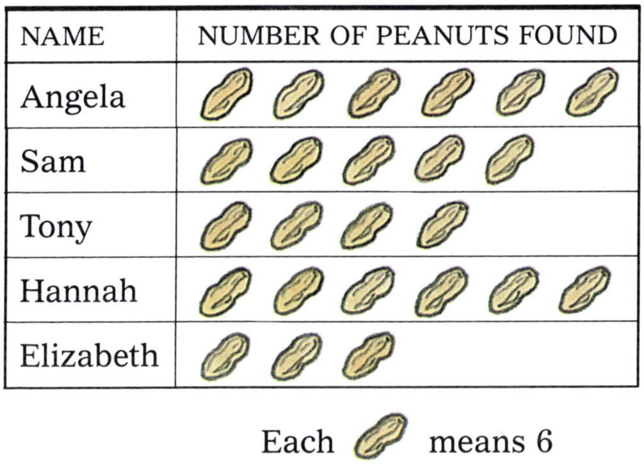

28. How many peanuts did Hannah find?

29. How many more peanuts did Sam find than Elizabeth?

30. How many peanuts did Sam and Tony find altogether?

★ **31.** Angela gives away all of her peanuts. She gives 3 peanuts to each of her friends. How many friends get peanuts?

TWO-DIGIT QUOTIENTS

Here's how to divide 56 by 4.

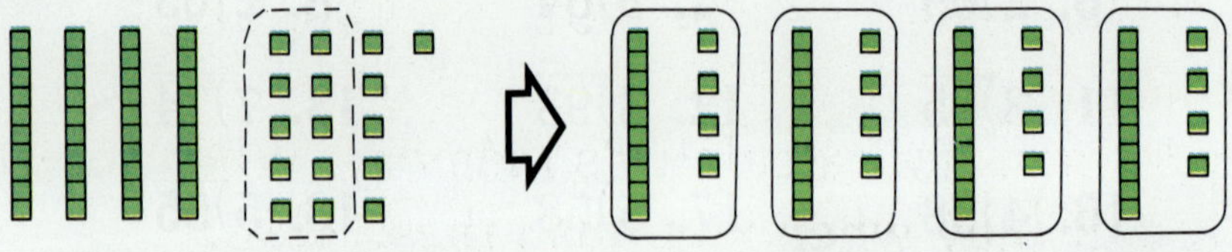

Divide the 5 tens by 4.

$$\begin{array}{r} 1 \\ 4\overline{)56} \\ -\,4 \\ \hline 1 \end{array}$$

Subtract 1 × 4.

Divide the 16 ones by 4.

$$\begin{array}{r} 14 \\ 4\overline{)56} \\ -\,4 \\ \hline 16 \\ -\,16 \\ \hline 0 \end{array}$$

Subtract 4 × 4.

Some calculators have a memory key, [M+]. If you press [5] [6] [M+], the calculator remembers 56. To see 56 again press [MR].

You can use [M+] and [MR] to divide the same number many times.

[5] [6] [M+] [÷] [4] [=] 14 [MR] 56 [÷] 2 [=] 28

CLASS EXERCISES

Divide. Tell how many tens and ones are in the quotient.

1. $3\overline{)7}$ $3\overline{)75}$ **2.** $2\overline{)5}$ $2\overline{)52}$ **3.** $5\overline{)7}$ $5\overline{)75}$

4. $4\overline{)9}$ $4\overline{)96}$ **5.** $6\overline{)8}$ $6\overline{)84}$ **6.** $3\overline{)8}$ $3\overline{)87}$

PRACTICE

Divide.

7. $3\overline{)78}$ **8.** $5\overline{)70}$ **9.** $6\overline{)96}$ **10.** $4\overline{)56}$ **11.** $8\overline{)96}$

12. $6\overline{)72}$ **13.** $4\overline{)92}$ **14.** $6\overline{)78}$ **15.** $2\overline{)58}$ **16.** $5\overline{)65}$

17. $3\overline{)51}$ **18.** $2\overline{)76}$ **19.** $6\overline{)90}$ **20.** $3\overline{)87}$ **21.** $4\overline{)72}$

22. $2\overline{)96}$ **23.** $7\overline{)98}$ **24.** $3\overline{)57}$ **25.** $4\overline{)76}$ **26.** $2\overline{)32}$

27. $4\overline{)64}$ **28.** $5\overline{)90}$ **29.** $7\overline{)91}$ **30.** $2\overline{)92}$ **31.** $6\overline{)84}$

CALCULATOR

The number 60 is in the calculator's memory. What do you see on the display when you push these keys?

32. MR ÷ 2 = **33.** MR ÷ 4 =

34. MR ÷ 3 = **35.** MR ÷ 5 =

PROBLEM SOLVING APPLICATIONS

Using a Table

Students had a magazine drive. Students earned 4 points for each magazine they sold. The table shows the points earned by some students.

POINTS EARNED		
STUDENT	WEEK 1	WEEK 2
Marjory	52	44
Peter	44	36
Miguel	28	68
Kristen	48	24

36. How many points did Marjory earn in all?

37. How many more points did Peter earn in Week 1 than in Week 2?

How many magazines did the student sell during Week 1?

38. Marjory **39.** Peter **40.** Miguel **41.** Kristen

How many magazines did the student sell during Week 2?

42. Marjory **43.** Peter **44.** Miguel **45.** Kristen

How many magazines did the student sell in all?

★ **46.** Marjory ★ **47.** Peter ★ **48.** Miguel ★ **49.** Kristen

TWO-DIGIT QUOTIENTS

The Flower Shop has 85 carnations. The shop sells flowers in bunches of 6. How many bunches are there? How many are left over?

Divide the 8 tens by 6.

$$\begin{array}{r} 1 \\ 6\overline{)85} \\ -\,6 \\ \hline 2 \end{array}$$

Divide the 25 ones by 6.

$$\begin{array}{r} 14 \text{ R1} \\ 6\overline{)85}\phantom{\text{ R1}} \\ -\,6\downarrow\phantom{\text{ R1}} \\ \hline 25\phantom{\text{ R1}} \\ -\,24\phantom{\text{ R1}} \\ \hline 1\phantom{\text{ R1}} \end{array}$$

The quotient is 14. The remainder is 1.

There are 14 bunches with 1 flower left over.

You know that $60 \div 6 = 10$. When you divide 85 by 6, you can estimate that the quotient will be greater than 10.

CLASS EXERCISES

What number goes in the box? What did you do to find the number?

1. $\begin{array}{r} 1 \\ 7\overline{)81} \\ \square \end{array}$

2. $\begin{array}{r} 1 \\ 6\overline{)76} \\ -6\downarrow \\ \hline 1\square \end{array}$

3. $\begin{array}{r} 1\square \\ 3\overline{)59} \\ -3\downarrow \\ \hline 29 \end{array}$

4. $\begin{array}{r} 12 \\ 8\overline{)97} \\ -8\downarrow \\ \hline 17 \\ \square \end{array}$

5. $\begin{array}{r} 14 \text{ R } \square \\ 3\overline{)43} \\ -3\downarrow \\ \hline 13 \\ -12 \\ \hline 1 \end{array}$

PRACTICE

Divide.

6. $5\overline{)79}$	**7.** $3\overline{)43}$	**8.** $3\overline{)73}$	**9.** $6\overline{)83}$	**10.** $4\overline{)67}$
11. $7\overline{)95}$	**12.** $7\overline{)89}$	**13.** $8\overline{)95}$	**14.** $4\overline{)57}$	**15.** $8\overline{)98}$
16. $2\overline{)77}$	**17.** $7\overline{)87}$	**18.** $5\overline{)68}$	**19.** $6\overline{)88}$	**20.** $5\overline{)92}$
21. $5\overline{)69}$	**22.** $3\overline{)74}$	**23.** $4\overline{)71}$	**24.** $6\overline{)85}$	**25.** $7\overline{)83}$

You know that $50 \div 5 = 10$. Will the quotient be greater than 10? Estimate. Write *yes* or *no*.

ESTIMATE

26. $5\overline{)73}$	**27.** $5\overline{)42}$	**28.** $5\overline{)38}$	**29.** $5\overline{)58}$
30. $5\overline{)25}$	**31.** $5\overline{)75}$	**32.** $5\overline{)60}$	★ **33.** $2\overline{)53}$

PROBLEM SOLVING APPLICATIONS
Using Logic

Choose the best answer. Write *a*, *b*, or *c*.

34. The address of The Flower Shop has 3 numbers in it. They are 3, 6, and 8. The first number can be divided equally by 4. The second number isn't 3. What is the number?
a. 368 **b.** 863 **c.** 638

35. Three people work at The Flower Shop. Their names are Adam, Sue, and Mary. One of them is leaving for another job. Her name has four letters. Who is leaving?
a. Adam **b.** Sue **c.** Mary

★ **36.** At the shop, more daisies are sold in a day than roses. More mums are sold than daisies. If 200 mums and 150 roses are sold, how many daisies are sold?
a. 210 **b.** 175 **c.** 125

DIVIDING THREE-DIGIT NUMBERS

A company has 164 calculators to ship. If it puts 6 calculators in each box, how many boxes will be filled? How many calculators are left?

To find out, divide 164 by 6. $6\overline{)164}$

You cannot divide the hundreds by 6. Think of 1 hundred 6 tens as 16 tens.

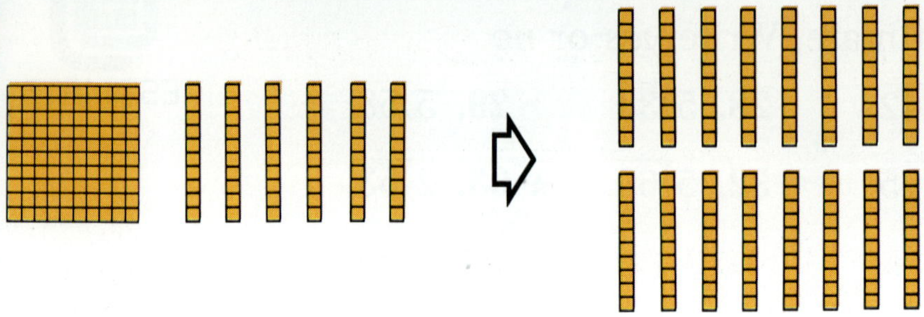

Divide the 16 tens.

Divide 16 by 6. Subtract 2 × 6.

$$\begin{array}{r} 2 \\ 6\overline{)164} \\ -\,12 \\ \hline 4 \end{array}$$

Then divide the 44 ones.

Divide 44 by 6. Subtract 7 × 6.

$$\begin{array}{r} 27 \text{ R2} \\ 6\overline{)164} \\ -\,12 \\ \hline 44 \\ -\,42 \\ \hline 2 \end{array}$$

The company will fill 27 boxes. There will be 2 calculators left over.

CLASS EXERCISES

Divide.

1. $5\overline{)474}$ **2.** $5\overline{)473}$ **3.** $5\overline{)472}$ **4.** $5\overline{)471}$ **5.** $5\overline{)470}$

6. $5\overline{)469}$ **7.** $5\overline{)468}$ **8.** $5\overline{)467}$ **9.** $5\overline{)466}$ **10.** $5\overline{)465}$

PRACTICE

Divide.

11. $7\overline{)654}$	**12.** $8\overline{)753}$	**13.** $6\overline{)373}$	**14.** $5\overline{)426}$	**15.** $4\overline{)375}$
16. $9\overline{)131}$	**17.** $6\overline{)434}$	**18.** $8\overline{)234}$	**19.** $9\overline{)357}$	**20.** $3\overline{)291}$
21. $6\overline{)279}$	**22.** $9\overline{)254}$	**23.** $7\overline{)447}$	**24.** $8\overline{)500}$	**25.** $6\overline{)592}$
26. $2\overline{)155}$	**27.** $7\overline{)537}$	**28.** $4\overline{)253}$	**29.** $3\overline{)137}$	**30.** $6\overline{)135}$

Write +, −, ×, or ÷ to make the sentence true.

★ **31.** $150 \div 5 = 35 \;\square\; 5$ ★ **32.** $72 \;\square\; 4 < 57 \div 3$

Estimate the answer.

MIXED REVIEW

33. $\begin{array}{r} 66 \\ +\,52 \\ \hline \end{array}$	**34.** $\begin{array}{r} 39 \\ \times 4 \\ \hline \end{array}$	**35.** $\begin{array}{r} 87 \\ -\,42 \\ \hline \end{array}$	**36.** $\begin{array}{r} 79 \\ +\,36 \\ \hline \end{array}$
37. $\begin{array}{r} 73 \\ -\,29 \\ \hline \end{array}$	**38.** $\begin{array}{r} 44 \\ +\,58 \\ \hline \end{array}$	**39.** $\begin{array}{r} 61 \\ \times 5 \\ \hline \end{array}$	**40.** $\begin{array}{r} 76 \\ -\,38 \\ \hline \end{array}$

PROBLEM SOLVING APPLICATIONS
Choosing the Operation

Solve.

41. A robot can check 656 calculators in 8 hours. How many can it check in 1 hour?

42. Five stores each order 150 calculators. How many calculators are ordered in all?

43. Kim works 160 hours in 4 weeks. She works the same number of hours each week. How many hours is that in 1 week?

★ **44.** A truck traveled 216 mi in 4 hours. If it traveled the same distance each hour, how far did it travel in 2 hours?

CHECKING DIVISION

Multiplying by 4 is the opposite of dividing by 4.

You can check division with multiplication.

$$\begin{array}{r} 18 \\ 4\overline{)72} \\ -\ 4\downarrow \\ \hline 32 \\ -\ 32 \\ \hline 0 \end{array} \qquad \begin{array}{r} {}^{3} \\ 18 \\ \times 4 \\ \hline 72\checkmark \end{array}$$

The numbers match. The quotient is correct.

To check $4\overline{)73}$ you must use addition and multiplication.

$$\begin{array}{r} 18\text{ R1} \\ 4\overline{)73} \\ -\ 4\downarrow \\ \hline 33 \\ -\ 32 \\ \hline 1 \end{array}$$

Multiply.

$$\begin{array}{r} {}^{3} \\ 18 \\ \times 4 \\ \hline 72 \end{array}$$

Add the remainder.

$$\begin{array}{r} 72 \\ +\ \ 1 \\ \hline 73\checkmark \end{array}$$

CLASS EXERCISES

Is the division correct? How can you tell?

1. $\begin{array}{r} 17 \\ 4\overline{)68} \end{array}$ $\begin{array}{r} {}^{2} \\ 17 \\ \times 4 \\ \hline 68 \end{array}$

2. $\begin{array}{r} 11 \\ 5\overline{)65} \end{array}$ $\begin{array}{r} 11 \\ \times 5 \\ \hline 55 \end{array}$

3. $\begin{array}{r} 16 \\ 6\overline{)92} \end{array}$ $\begin{array}{r} {}^{3} \\ 16 \\ \times 6 \\ \hline 96 \end{array}$

4. $\begin{array}{r} 12\text{ R2} \\ 5\overline{)62} \end{array}$ $\begin{array}{r} {}^{1} \\ 12 \\ \times 5 \\ \hline 60 \end{array}$ $\begin{array}{r} 60 \\ +\ \ 2 \\ \hline 62 \end{array}$

5. $\begin{array}{r} 13\text{ R6} \\ 6\overline{)83} \end{array}$ $\begin{array}{r} {}^{1} \\ 13 \\ \times 6 \\ \hline 78 \end{array}$ $\begin{array}{r} {}^{1} \\ 78 \\ +\ \ 6 \\ \hline 84 \end{array}$

PRACTICE

Divide and check.

6. $6\overline{)84}$	**7.** $6\overline{)72}$	**8.** $5\overline{)65}$	**9.** $3\overline{)48}$	**10.** $8\overline{)96}$
11. $2\overline{)85}$	**12.** $9\overline{)96}$	**13.** $4\overline{)91}$	**14.** $7\overline{)89}$	**15.** $8\overline{)94}$
16. $7\overline{)83}$	**17.** $6\overline{)74}$	**18.** $3\overline{)85}$	**19.** $4\overline{)73}$	**20.** $2\overline{)39}$
21. $5\overline{)328}$	**22.** $7\overline{)572}$	**23.** $7\overline{)597}$	**24.** $7\overline{)648}$	**25.** $6\overline{)459}$

Use the numbers to write a division and a multiplication.

★ **26.** 3, 32, 96 ★ **27.** 2, 41, 82 ★ **28.** 8, 11, 88

MIXED REVIEW

Choose the better estimate. Write *a* or *b*.

29. length of a pencil	**a.** 18 cm	**b.** 18 km
30. water in a pail	**a.** 100 L	**b.** 1 L
31. length of a street	**a.** 1 cm	**b.** 1 km
32. mass of an egg	**a.** 30 g	**b.** 30 kg

PROBLEM SOLVING APPLICATIONS
Choosing a Strategy

Choose the facts you need. Solve.

33. Matthew has 38 new stamps. He had 125 stamps. He puts the same number of new stamps in 2 books. How many stamps does he put in each book?

34. Matthew can buy 5 stamps on sale for 95¢. He must buy them before Saturday. Today is Wednesday. How many days does he have to buy stamps?

35. The price of a stamp album is \$8.50. Matthew buys one on sale for \$7.98. What is his change from \$10.00?

36. Matthew has 164 stamps. He has the same number of stamps in 2 books. How many stamps are in each book?

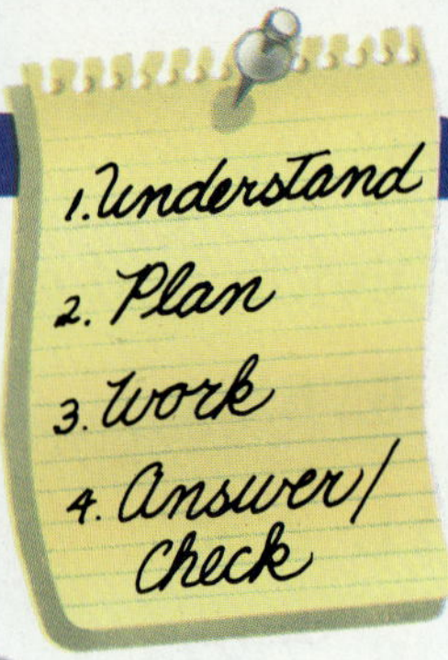

PROBLEM SOLVING

Strategy: Choosing the Operation

Bars of soap are on sale at 3 for 99¢. How much does 1 bar of soap cost?

To find the answer, you can divide 99¢ by 3.

$$
\begin{array}{r}
33 \\
3\overline{)99} \\
-\,9\downarrow \\
\hline
9 \\
-\,9 \\
\hline
0
\end{array}
$$

One bar of soap costs 33¢.

SAVE WITH US	
SOAP	**3 bars** *for* **99¢**
CARROTS	**3 lb** *for* **90¢**
APPLES	**8** *for* **96¢**
SOUP	**2 cans** *for* **44¢**
CEREAL	**$1.34**
ORANGE JUICE	**89¢ can**
FISH STICKS	**$1.28 pack**
BREAD	**2 loaves** *for* **88¢**
PAPER TOWELS	**2 packs** *for* **84¢**
LIGHT BULBS	**2 packs** *for* **98¢**
TOOTHPASTE	**$1.89**

CLASS EXERCISES

Look at the ad above. Tell whether you would add, subtract, multiply, or divide. Then solve.

1. How much do you pay for 1 apple?

2. How much do 2 boxes of cereal cost?

3. How much do you pay for 1 can of orange juice and 8 apples?

4. How much more do you pay for 8 apples than 3 lb of carrots?

PRACTICE

Use the ad to solve.

5. Bill buys 1 pack of light bulbs. What does he spend?

6. Ann buys 1 loaf of bread. What does she spend?

7. You buy 2 packs of light bulbs and 3 lb of carrots. What is your total cost?

8. You buy 3 cans of orange juice. What is your total cost?

9. You buy a pound of carrots. How much does it cost?

10. You buy 2 packs of paper towels and 2 loaves of bread. What is your total cost?

11. You buy a box of cereal and a tube of toothpaste. What is your change from $20.00?

12. You buy a loaf of bread, a pack of fish sticks, and a can of soup. What is your change from $20.00?

★ 13. You buy 4 bars of soap. What is your total cost?

★ 14. You buy 10 apples. What is your total cost?

★ 15. Find the total cost of the items on the list.

4 lb of carrots
1 can of orange juice
cereal
3 packs of paper towels
4 bars of soap

CHECKPOINT 2

Write the answer.
(pages 316–325)

1. $6\overline{)69}$ **2.** $3\overline{)65}$

3. $7\overline{)84}$ **4.** $6\overline{)96}$

5. $4\overline{)67}$ **6.** $5\overline{)78}$

7. $3\overline{)146}$ **8.** $9\overline{)649}$

Solve. *(pages 326–327)*

9. Envelopes are marked 5 for 85¢. How much does one envelope cost?

Extra practice on page 420

CHAPTER 11 TEST

Write the answer. *(pages 308–311)*

1. $8 \div 4$ **2.** $36 \div 9$ **3.** $6\overline{)52}$ **4.** $7\overline{)31}$

Write the answer. *(pages 312–313)*

5. $5\overline{)50}$ **6.** $1\overline{)70}$ **7.** $8\overline{)800}$ **8.** $2\overline{)600}$

Solve. Decide how to use the remainder.
(pages 314–315)

9. It takes 8 dimes to buy a magazine. How many magazines can you buy with 43 dimes?

10. A packing box can hold 3 bikes. How many boxes are needed to pack 22 bikes?

Write the answer. Check. *(pages 316–325)*

11. $4\overline{)84}$ **12.** $3\overline{)97}$ **13.** $5\overline{)75}$ **14.** $6\overline{)96}$

15. $4\overline{)69}$ **16.** $7\overline{)97}$ **17.** $9\overline{)289}$ **18.** $8\overline{)514}$

Use the table to solve. *(pages 326–327)*

FLOWER SUPPLIES

seeds	2 packs for 34¢
small pots	4 for 84¢
potting soil	1 bag for $1.29
tulips	3 for 90¢

19. How much does 1 tulip cost?

20. How much does 1 small pot cost?

21. What is the cost of 1 pack of seeds?

22. You buy 2 packs of seeds and 1 bag of soil. What is your total cost?

23. How much do you spend for 2 tulips?

Extra practice on page 421

MATHEMATICS and HEALTH

The food label shows the number of Calories in one biscuit. To find that number, the baker had to know the number of Calories in each ingredient.

The baker added to find the total number of Calories.

whole wheat flour	400
milk	48
butter	100
baking powder	10
salt	+ 0
	558

The baker divided to find the Calories in each biscuit.

$$\begin{array}{r} 93 \\ 6\overline{)558} \\ -54 \\ \hline 18 \\ -18 \\ \hline 0 \end{array}$$

93 Calories in one biscuit

HOW MANY IN ONE?

How many Calories are in each serving?

1. Vegetable Soup (7 servings)

dried white beans	350
chopped cabbage	10
tomato paste	50
macaroni	156
salt pork	20
onion	20
garlic	3

2. Fruit Punch (8 servings)

pineapple juice	360
orange juice	280
ice	0

3. Avocado Dip (8 servings)

avocado	342
tomato	22
lemon juice	3
seasoning	1

Enrichment

One month after planting bean seeds, Brad measured his 9 plants.

15 cm	18 cm	6 cm
12 cm	21 cm	4 cm
10 cm	9 cm	16 cm

Brad wrote the numbers in order to find the number in the middle, or the *median.*

4 6 9 10 **12** 15 16 18 21

↑

12 is the median.

The median height of his plants is 12 cm.

Which number is the median?

1. 1 2 3 4 5

2. 18 19 20 21 22

3. 2 4 6 8 10

4. 9 13 26 82 91

Write the numbers in order. Draw a line under the median.

5. 3 2 5 4 7

6. 16 13 18 21 14

7. 32 16 18 23 15

MEDIAN

Find the information in the tables below. Solve.

8. How deep is the deepest lake in the United States?

9. What is the name of the world's longest river?

10. Where is the third highest mountain peak in North America?

11. What is the median height of the mountain peaks in the table?

12. Which river in the table has the median length?

13. What is the median depth of the lakes in the table?

DEEPEST LAKES IN THE UNITED STATES

LAKE	DEPTH
Chelan	489m
Crater	589 m
Iliamma	299 m
Pend Oreille	366 m
Superior	406 m
Tahoe	401 m
Walker	305 m

HIGHEST MOUNTAIN PEAKS IN NORTH AMERICA

PEAK	PLACE	HEIGHT
Citlatepetl	Mexico	5700 m
Logan	Canada	5950 m
McKinley	Alaska	6190 m

WORLD'S LONGEST RIVERS

RIVER	LENGTH
Amazon	6570 km
Mississippi	6020 km
Nile	6690 km
Yangtze	5980 km
Yenisey	5870 km

CUMULATIVE REVIEW

Choose the correct answer. Choose *a*, *b*, *c*, or *d*.

Find the matching value.

1. 4 nickels
2 pennies

a. \$.22
b. \$.42
c. \$.17
d. none of these

2. 3 quarters
3 dimes

a. \$.83
b. \$.95
c. \$1.08
d. none of these

3. 3 dollars
1 half dollar

a. \$3.05
b. \$3.50
c. \$350
d. none of these

Find the answer.

4. $\begin{array}{r} \$.47 \\ +\ .37 \\ \hline \end{array}$

a. \$.74
b. \$.84
c. \$.10
d. none of these

5. $\begin{array}{r} \$30.00 \\ -\ 4.81 \\ \hline \end{array}$

a. \$25.19
b. \$26.29
c. \$35.19
d. none of these

6. $\begin{array}{r} \$52.64 \\ +\ 39.35 \\ \hline \end{array}$

a. \$81.99
b. \$91.99
c. \$92.99
d. none of these

Find the matching time.

7. 

a. 6:25
b. 7:35
c. 7:25
d. none of these

8. 

a. 9:12
b. 2:45
c. 9:17
d. none of these

9. 

a. 10:10
b. 2:53
c. 3:53
d. none of these

Choose the best estimate.

10. the length of a broom
 a. 3 cm
 b. 30 m
 c. 100 km
 d. 1 m

11. the length of a crayon
 a. 12 km
 b. 12 m
 c. 12 cm
 d. 2 km

Choose the best estimate.

12. the width of a kitchen table
 a. 27 ft
 b. 27 in.
 c. 27 yd
 d. 27 mi

13. the length of your nose
 a. 1 in.
 b. 1 ft
 c. 1 yd
 d. 1 mi

14. the width of a sidewalk
 a. 1 yd
 b. 1 ft
 c. 2 mi
 d. 2 in.

15. the length of the Ohio River
 a. 1000 in.
 b. 1000 yd
 c. 1000 ft
 d. 1000 mi

LANGUAGE and VOCABULARY REVIEW

Read each sentence. Write *true* or *false*.

1. To check $27 \div 4 = 6$ R3, multiply 6×4, then add the remainder 3.

2. In the example, $72 \div 8 = 9$, 9 is called the remainder.

3. In the example, $7 \times 6 = 42$, 42 is called the difference.

4. Two pints is the same as 1 cup.

5. The distance between cities is measured in pounds.

LET

In BASIC the word **LET** tells the computer to save a place in its memory for a value. LET tells the name of the address and the value.

```
10 LET K = 15 ← The value of K is 15.
20 PRINT K
```

Look at this program. The computer does the arithmetic. Then it shows only the answer.

```
10 LET B = 8 - 1
20 PRINT B
```

Write the output for each program.

1.
```
10 LET B = 7
20 PRINT B
```

2.
```
10 LET T = 146
20 PRINT T
```

3.
```
10 LET X = 5 + 6
20 PRINT X
```

4.
```
10 LET M = 8 * 4
20 PRINT M
```

★ **5.**
```
10 LET W = 72/8
20 PRINT "I KNOW THE"
30 PRINT "ANSWER IS"
40 PRINT W
```

★ **6.**
```
10 LET Y = 54/9
20 PRINT "SECRET"
30 PRINT "NUMBER IS"
40 PRINT Y
```

12

The watermelon has been split into two pieces. If each piece is split again, how many pieces will there be?

FRACTIONS AND DECIMALS

FRACTIONS

The paper is divided into 2 equal parts. One of the two parts is shaded.

The **fraction** $\frac{1}{2}$ shows what part is shaded. *One half* of the paper is shaded.

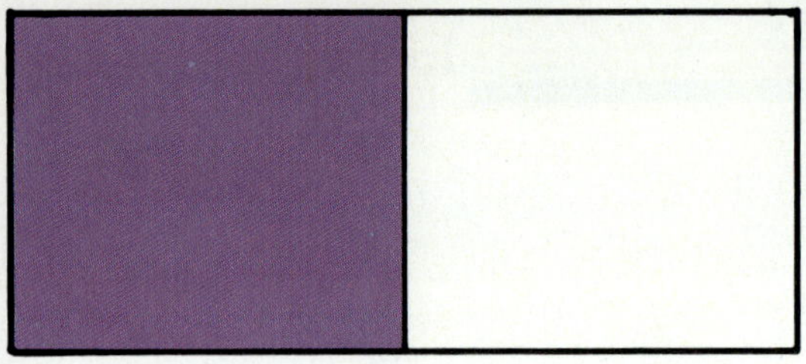

The spinner is divided into 4 equal parts. Three of the four parts are shaded.

The fraction $\frac{3}{4}$ shows what part is shaded. *Three fourths* of the spinner is shaded.

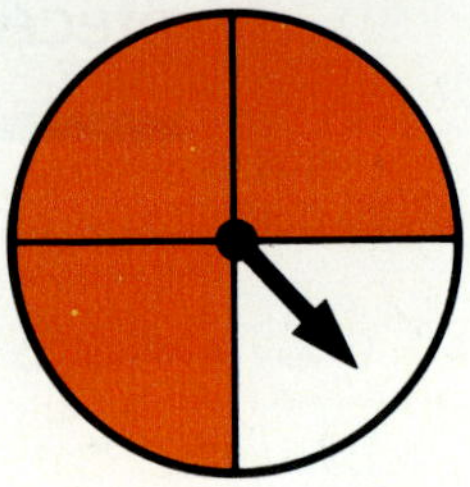

E You can estimate what part of this spinner is blue.

Think of dividing the whole spinner into parts about the same size as the blue part. There would be about 3 parts in all. About $\frac{1}{3}$ of the spinner is blue.

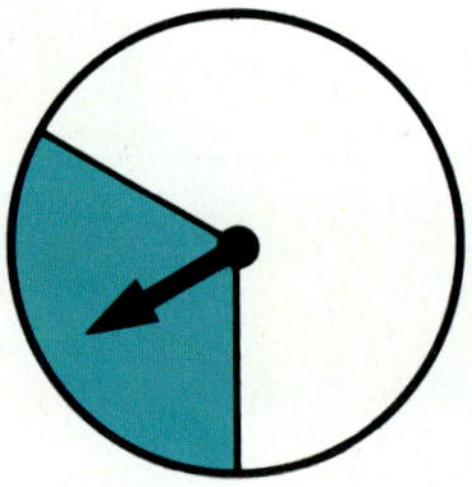

CLASS EXERCISES

Read the fraction.

1. $\frac{1}{4}$ **2.** $\frac{2}{4}$ **3.** $\frac{1}{3}$ **4.** $\frac{3}{10}$ **5.** $\frac{7}{9}$ **6.** $\frac{5}{6}$

Complete.

7.

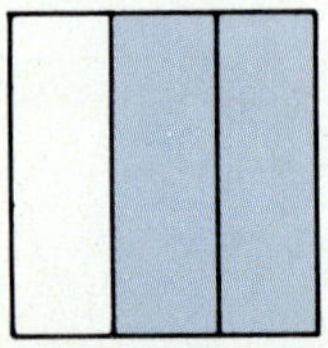

▒ parts shaded
▒ equal parts
$\frac{▒}{3}$ are shaded.

8.

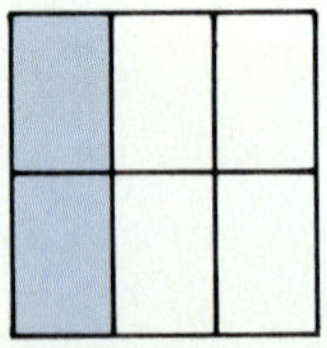

▒ parts shaded
▒ equal parts
$\frac{▒}{6}$ are shaded.

9.

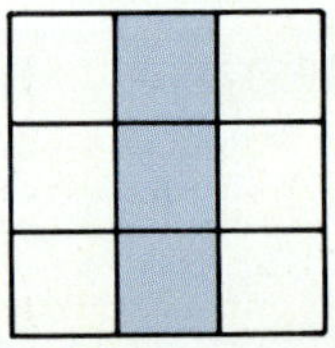

▒ parts shaded
▒ equal parts
$\frac{▒}{9}$ are shaded.

PRACTICE

Write the fraction for the shaded part.

10. 

$\frac{\square}{3}$

11. 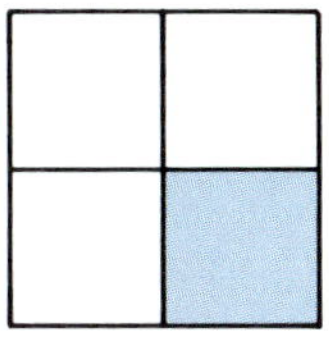

$\frac{\square}{4}$

12. 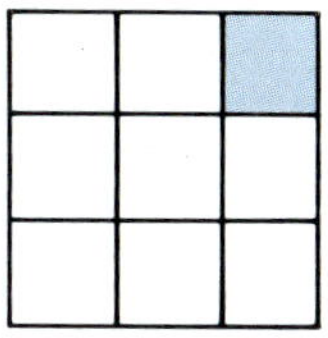

$\frac{\square}{9}$

13. 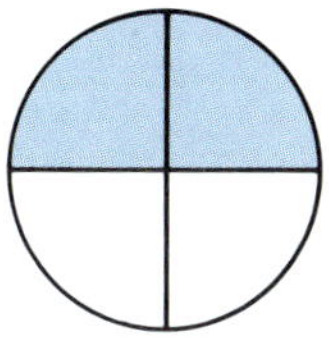

$\frac{\square}{4}$

14. 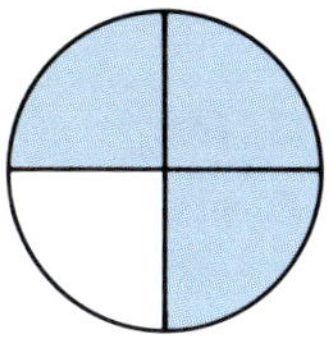

$\frac{\square}{4}$

15. 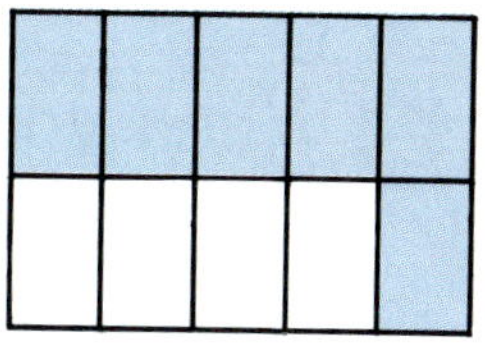

$\frac{\square}{10}$

Estimate the fraction for the shaded part.

ESTIMATE

16. 

17. 

18. 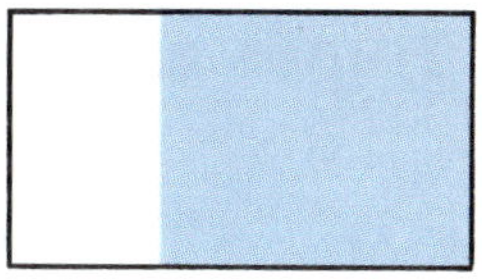

19. 

PROBLEM SOLVING APPLICATIONS
Writing Fractions

Write the fraction for the words.

20. Craig paints *two thirds* of a poster red.

21. Jane makes *five sixths* of a rug.

22. John washes *one fourth* of the chalkboard.

23. Kathy uses *three fifths* of a jar of paste.

★ **24.** One half of the shape is shaded. What fraction would show one half of one half?

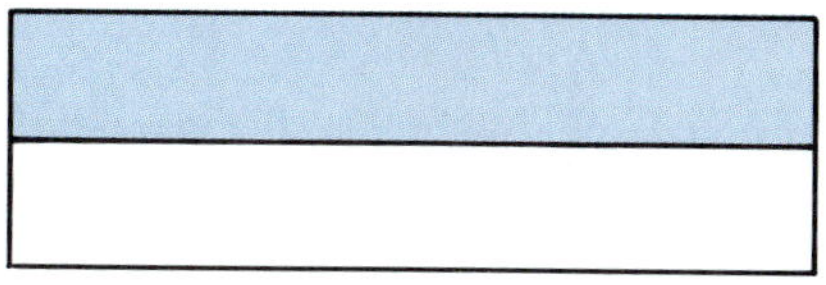

MORE ABOUT FRACTIONS

2 of the 8 cubes are blue.

$\frac{2}{8}$ of the cubes are blue.

$\frac{6}{8}$ of the cubes are red.

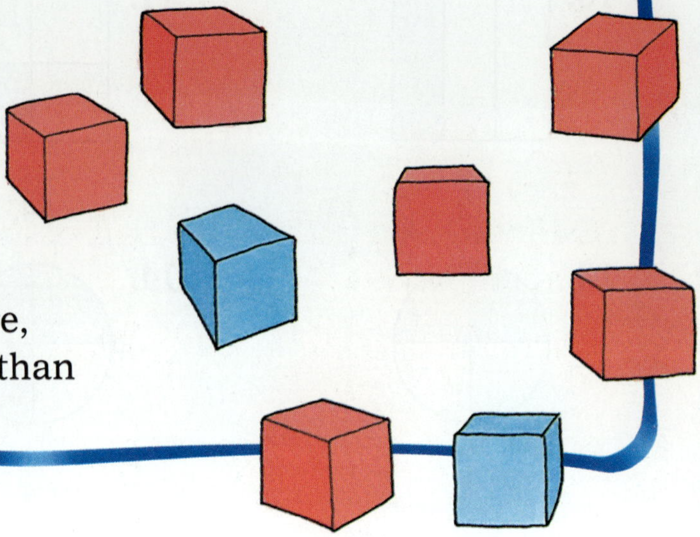

E When you look at the picture, you can estimate that more than half of the cubes are red.

CLASS EXERCISES

Complete the sentence.

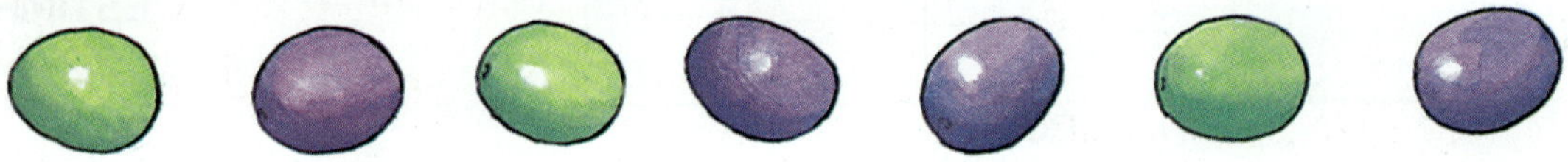

1. ? of the 7 grapes are purple.
   $\frac{\blacksquare}{7}$ are purple.

2. ? of the 7 grapes are green.
   $\frac{\blacksquare}{7}$ are green.

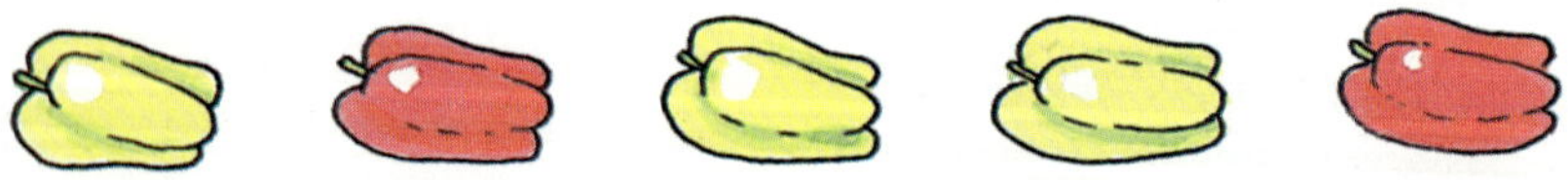

3. $\frac{\blacksquare}{5}$ of the peppers are red.

4. $\frac{\blacksquare}{5}$ of the peppers are yellow.

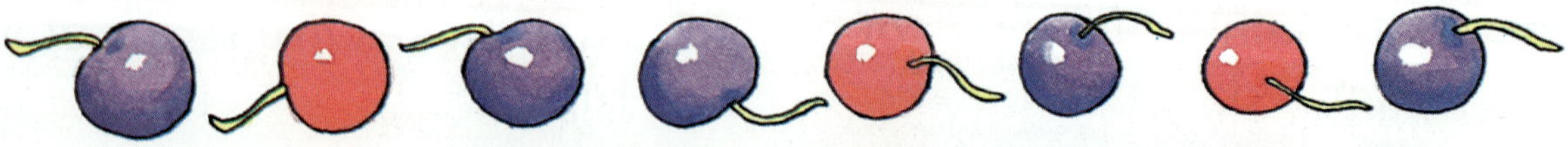

5. $\frac{\blacksquare}{\blacksquare}$ of the cherries are purple.

6. $\frac{\blacksquare}{\blacksquare}$ of the cherries are red.

PRACTICE

Write the fraction for the shaded part of the group.

7. ▲ △ △ △

8. ● ● ● ○ ○ ○ ○

9. ■ ■ ■ ■ □

10. ●●●●
●○○○

11. ■■□□
■■■□□

12. ▲▲▲▲△
△△

13. ■□

14. ▲▲▲△▲▲

15. ○●●

16. ▲▲▲▲
▲▲△

17. ●○○
○○○

18. ■■■■
■□□□

Estimate. Are more than half of the parts shaded? Write *yes* or *no*.

ESTIMATE

19. ■■□□□
□□□□□

20. ■□■■■
□□■■■

21. ■□■■■
□■□■■

22. ■■□□□□
■□□■□■

PROBLEM SOLVING APPLICATIONS
Using Fractions

Solve.

23. Three of Jim's 4 seeds grew. What fraction of Jim's seeds did not grow?

24. Jean has 2 red pots and 3 green pots. What fraction of her pots are green?

25. Jean plants 6 rows of tomatoes with 7 in each row. How many tomatoes does she plant in one row?

26. Jim has 5 plants. Two of his plants have flowers. What fraction of his plants have flowers?

★ **27.** Jean uses $\frac{1}{3}$ of these dimes and $\frac{1}{4}$ of these nickels to buy a tulip. How much money does she spend?

NUMERATORS AND DENOMINATORS

The numbers in a fraction have names.

numerator → 2 → tells how many parts
denominator → 5 → tells how many in all

$\frac{2}{5}$

Two fifths of the children are in the clubhouse.

numerator → 2 → children in the clubhouse
denominator → 5 → children in all

One half of the door is red.

numerator → 1 → part that is red
denominator → 2 → parts in all

CLASS EXERCISES

Name the numerator. Name the denominator.

1. $\frac{2}{8}$ **2.** $\frac{2}{3}$ **3.** $\frac{4}{7}$ **4.** $\frac{6}{8}$ **5.** $\frac{3}{4}$

PRACTICE

Write the fraction.

6. numerator 2
denominator 7

7. numerator 1
denominator 6

8. numerator 7
denominator 8

9. numerator 3
denominator 5

10. numerator 5
denominator 9

11. numerator 3
denominator 7

Write the letter of the picture that matches.

12. numerator 1
denominator 10

13. numerator 3
denominator 5

14. numerator 5
denominator 10

15. numerator 3
denominator 8

16. denominator 8
numerator 2

17. denominator 6
numerator 5

A. 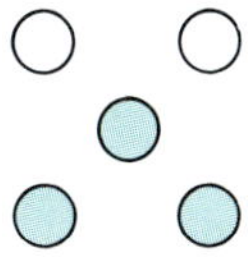

B. 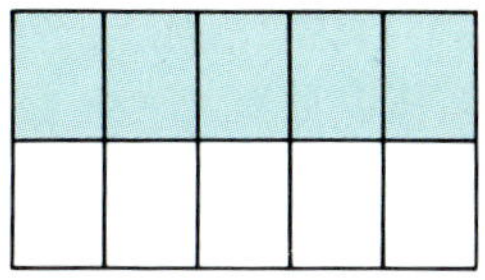

C. 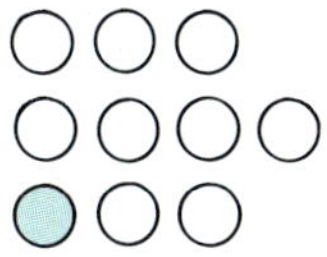

D. 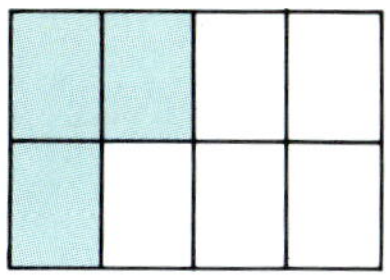

E. 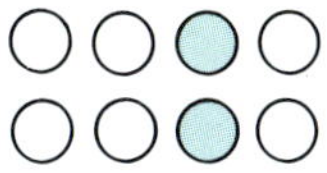

F. 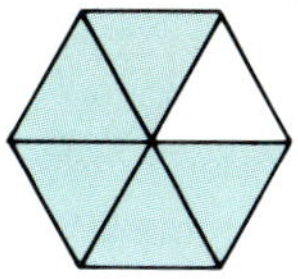

Estimate the answer.

MIXED REVIEW

18. $\begin{array}{r} 28 \\ +\ 52 \\ \hline \end{array}$ **19.** $\begin{array}{r} 59 \\ -\ 23 \\ \hline \end{array}$ **20.** $\begin{array}{r} 82 \\ -\ 51 \\ \hline \end{array}$ **21.** $\begin{array}{r} 79 \\ -\ 47 \\ \hline \end{array}$

22. $\begin{array}{r} 67 \\ -\ 25 \\ \hline \end{array}$ **23.** $\begin{array}{r} 62 \\ +\ 59 \\ \hline \end{array}$ **24.** $\begin{array}{r} 85 \\ -\ 39 \\ \hline \end{array}$ **25.** $\begin{array}{r} 78 \\ -\ 29 \\ \hline \end{array}$

PROBLEM SOLVING APPLICATIONS

Using Fractions

Solve.

26. Anna buys 9 cans of paint. She uses 2 cans to paint the floor. What fraction of the paint is left?

27. The club had a meeting at half past 1. Eddie came 18 minutes late. At what time did Eddie arrive?

★ **28.** The club voted to have a race. Five children said yes. Two said no. What fraction of the club said no?

★ **29.** The box is divided into 4 equal parts. Draw two other ways the box can be divided into four equal parts.

COMPARING FRACTIONS

This corn bread was cut into 6 equal pieces. $\frac{5}{6}$ of the corn bread is left.

This corn bread was cut into 6 equal pieces. Only $\frac{2}{6}$ of the corn bread is left.

Which fraction is greater? When the denominators are the same, compare the numerators.

$\frac{5}{6}$ is greater than $\frac{2}{6}$. $\frac{2}{6}$ is less than $\frac{5}{6}$.

$\frac{5}{6} > \frac{2}{6}$ $\frac{2}{6} < \frac{5}{6}$

CLASS EXERCISES

Which fraction is less?

1. 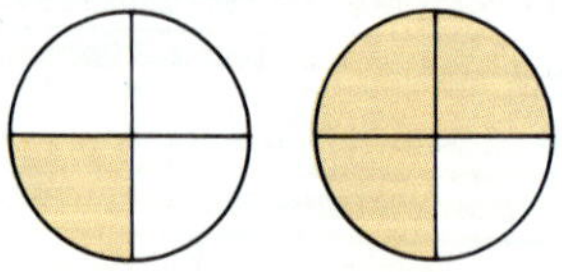

$\frac{1}{4}$ or $\frac{3}{4}$

2. 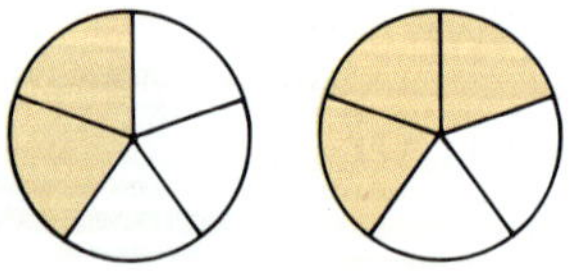

$\frac{2}{5}$ or $\frac{3}{5}$

3. 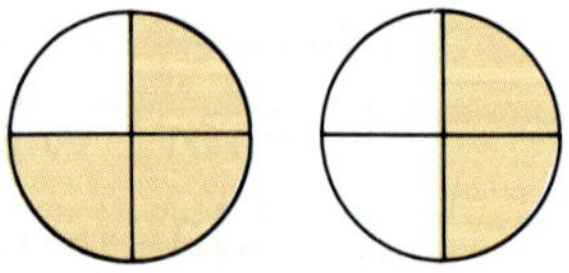

$\frac{3}{4}$ or $\frac{2}{4}$

4. 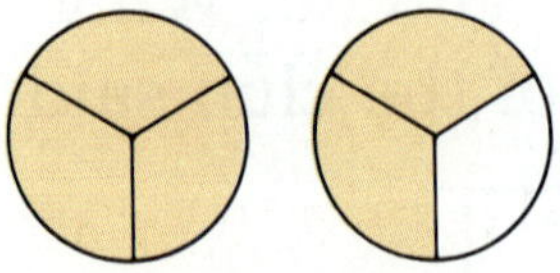

$\frac{3}{3}$ or $\frac{2}{3}$

5. 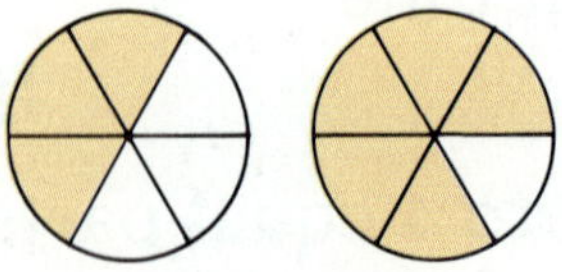

$\frac{3}{6}$ or $\frac{5}{6}$

6. 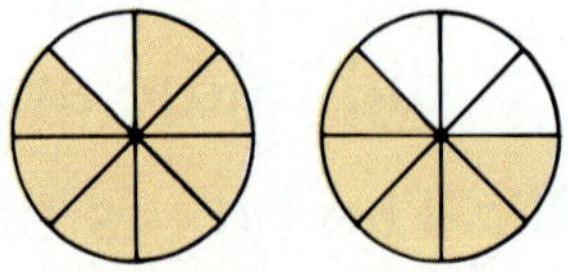

$\frac{7}{8}$ or $\frac{5}{8}$

PRACTICE

Compare. Write < or >.

7. 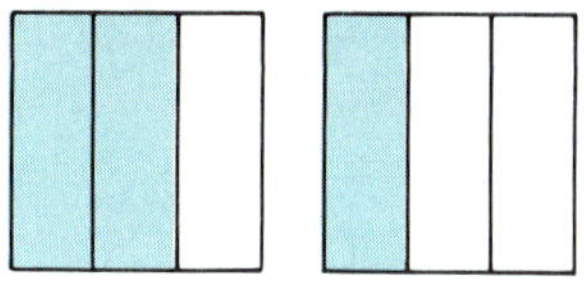

$\frac{2}{3}$ ■ $\frac{1}{3}$

8. 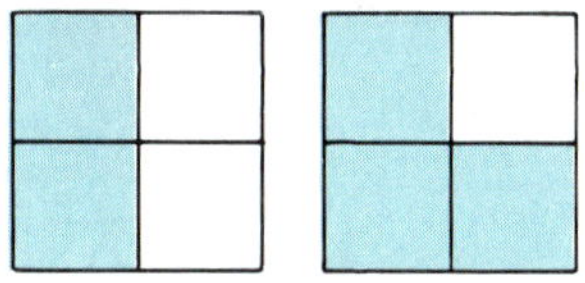

$\frac{2}{4}$ ■ $\frac{3}{4}$

9. 

$\frac{3}{4}$ ■ $\frac{1}{4}$

10. 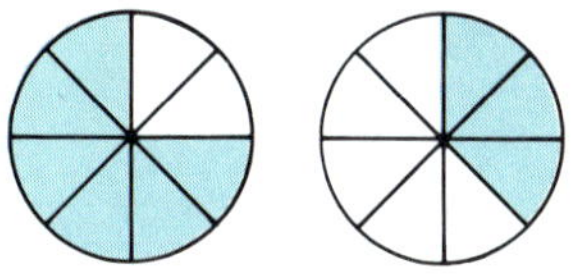

$\frac{6}{8}$ ■ $\frac{3}{8}$

11. 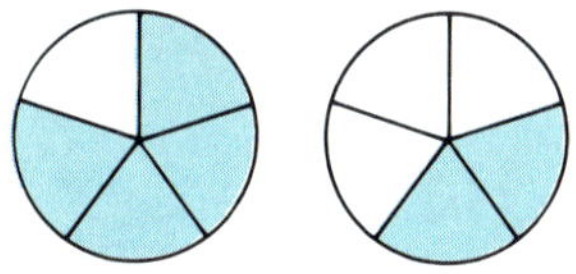

$\frac{4}{5}$ ■ $\frac{2}{5}$

12. 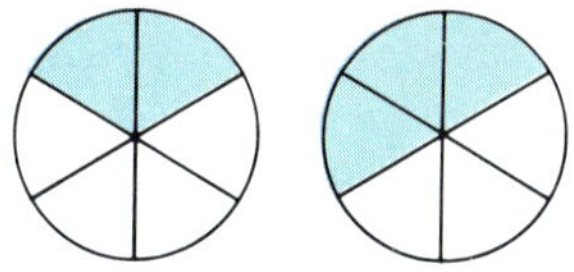

$\frac{2}{6}$ ■ $\frac{3}{6}$

13. $\frac{1}{8}$ ■ $\frac{3}{8}$ **14.** $\frac{4}{6}$ ■ $\frac{2}{6}$ **15.** $\frac{5}{7}$ ■ $\frac{3}{7}$ **16.** $\frac{1}{9}$ ■ $\frac{8}{9}$

17. $\frac{5}{9}$ ■ $\frac{2}{9}$ **18.** $\frac{1}{6}$ ■ $\frac{5}{6}$ **19.** $\frac{4}{5}$ ■ $\frac{3}{5}$ **20.** $\frac{7}{8}$ ■ $\frac{5}{8}$

MIXED REVIEW

Choose the better estimate. Write *a* or *b*.

21. a pen **a.** 6 in. **b.** 6 ft

22. a pair of scissors **a.** 8 oz **b.** 8 lb

23. a bucket of water **a.** 2 c **b.** 2 gal

PROBLEM SOLVING APPLICATIONS
Fractions in Measurement

Solve.

24. A recipe calls for $\frac{2}{3}$ cup of milk and $\frac{1}{3}$ cup of cream. Do you put in more milk, or more cream?

★ **25.** Marty wants to make half as much mashed potatoes as usual. He usually uses 2 cups of milk. Should he use more, or less milk?

ADDING AND SUBTRACTING FRACTIONS

$\frac{1}{4}$ of the paper is red.

$\frac{2}{4}$ of the paper is blue.

$\frac{3}{4}$ of the paper is shaded.

1 fourth + 2 fourths = 3 fourths

$$\frac{1}{4} + \frac{2}{4} = \frac{3}{4}$$
(3 ← parts shaded; 4 ← parts in all)

Pete shaded $\frac{7}{8}$ of a paper. He will erase 4 of the eighths. The x's show where Pete will erase. $\frac{3}{8}$ of the paper will still be shaded.

7 eighths − 4 eighths = 3 eighths

$$\frac{7}{8} - \frac{4}{8} = \frac{3}{8}$$
(3 ← parts shaded; 8 ← parts in all)

You can use a number line to add and subtract fractions.

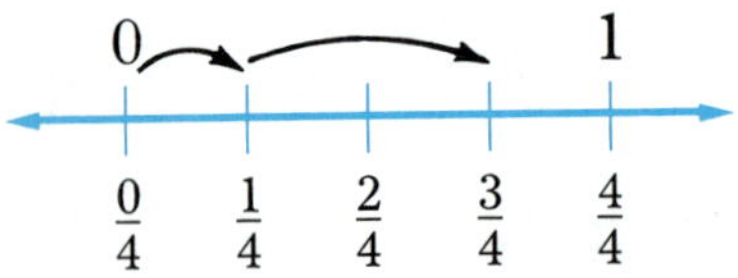

$$\frac{1}{4} + \frac{2}{4} = \frac{3}{4}$$

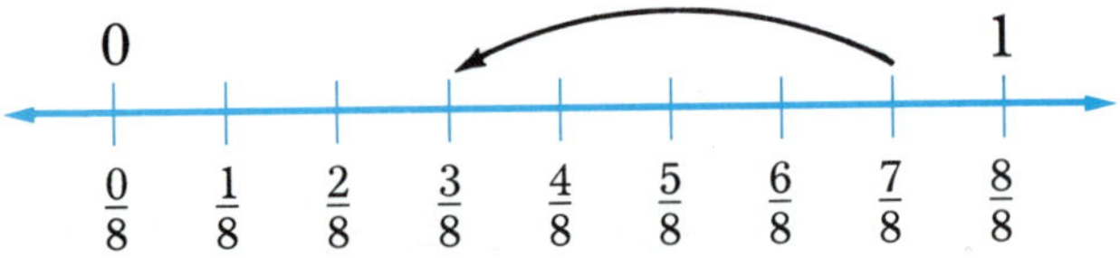

$$\frac{7}{8} - \frac{4}{8} = \frac{3}{8}$$

CLASS EXERCISES

Complete.

1.

1 fifth + 3 fifths = __?__ fifths

2.

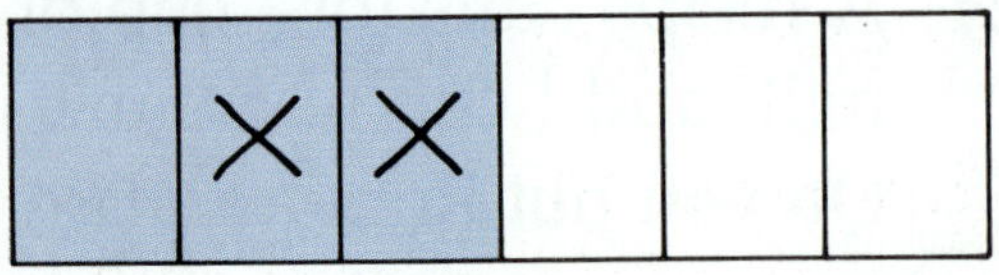

3 sixths − 2 sixths = __?__ sixth

PRACTICE

Add or subtract.

3. 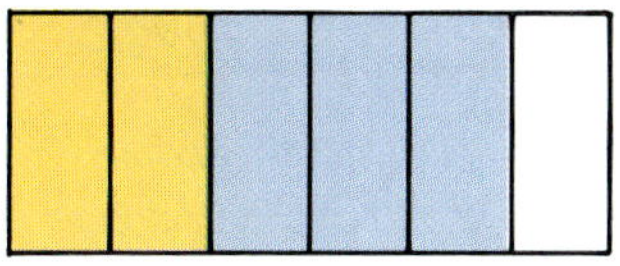

$\frac{2}{6} + \frac{3}{6}$

4. 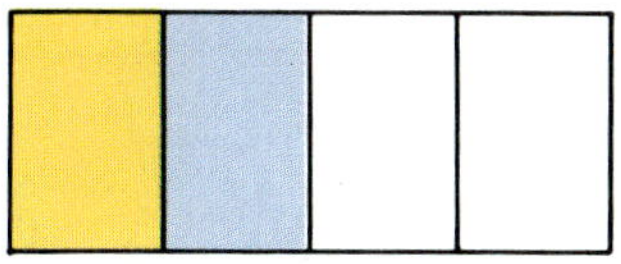

$\frac{1}{4} + \frac{1}{4}$

5. 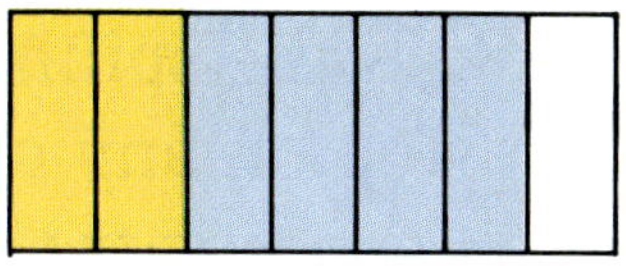

$\frac{2}{7} + \frac{4}{7}$

6. 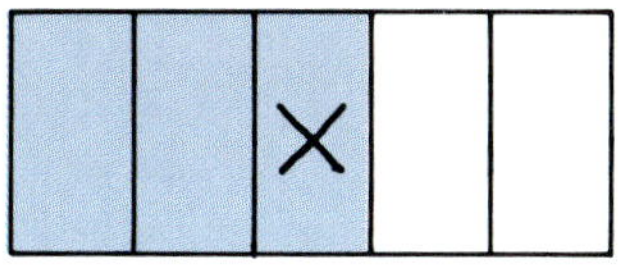

$\frac{3}{5} - \frac{1}{5}$

7. 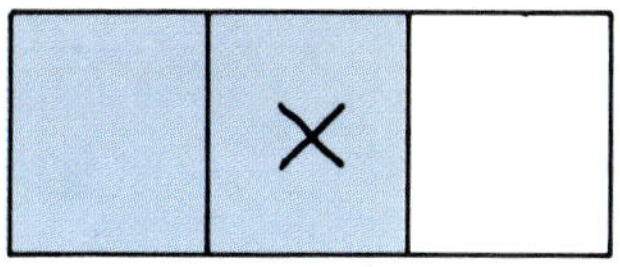

$\frac{2}{3} - \frac{1}{3}$

8. 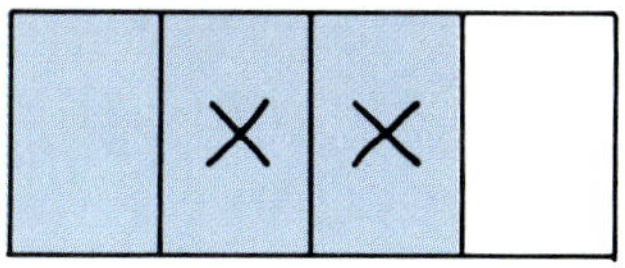

$\frac{3}{4} - \frac{2}{4}$

9. 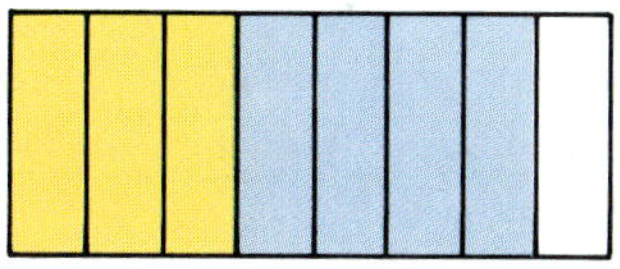

$\frac{3}{8} + \frac{4}{8}$

10. 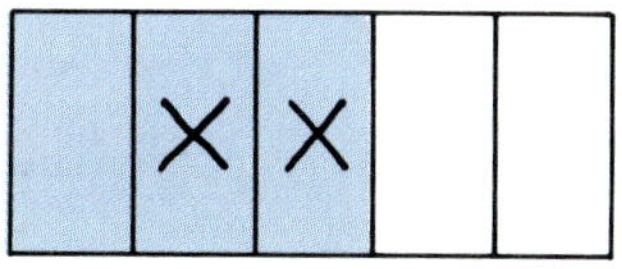

$\frac{3}{5} - \frac{2}{5}$

11. 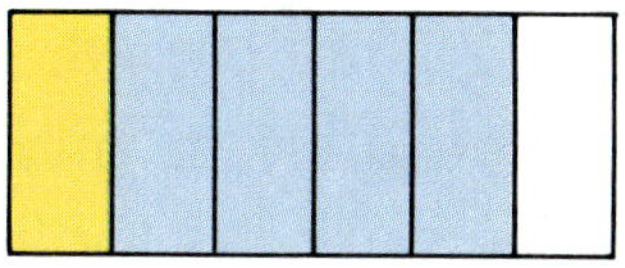

$\frac{1}{6} + \frac{4}{6}$

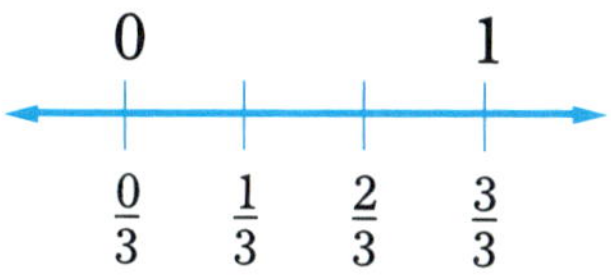

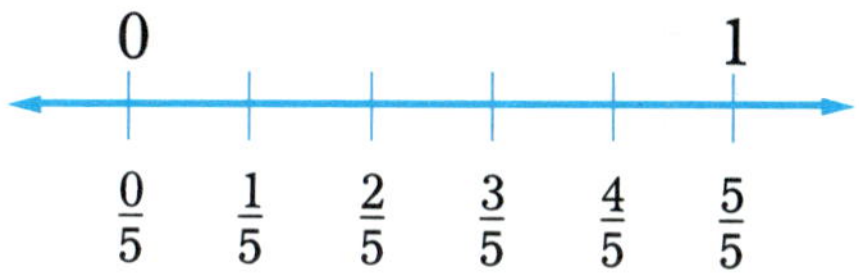

12. $\frac{1}{3} + \frac{1}{3}$ **13.** $\frac{2}{3} - \frac{1}{3}$ **14.** $\frac{2}{5} + \frac{2}{5}$ **15.** $\frac{3}{5} - \frac{2}{5}$

PROBLEM SOLVING APPLICATIONS

Solve.

16. Lena had $\frac{3}{4}$ c of flour. She used $\frac{1}{4}$ c to make a sauce. How much flour did Lena have left?

17. Jose used $\frac{1}{3}$ c of milk to thin a sauce. The sauce was still too thick. Jose added $\frac{1}{3}$ c more. How much milk did Jose use in all?

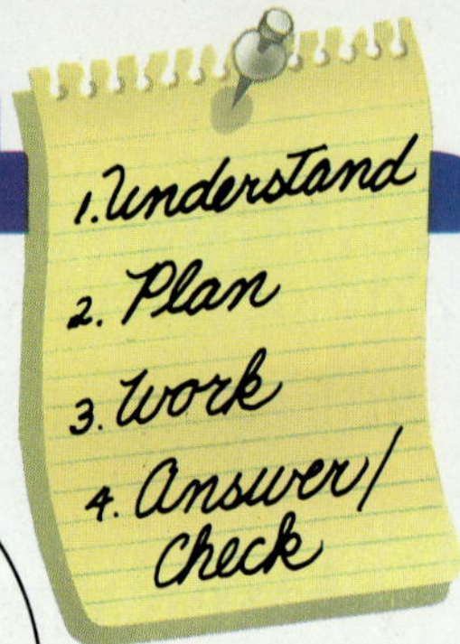

PROBLEM SOLVING

Strategy: Probability and Pictures

Look at the spinner. The spinner can stop on any of the 4 spaces. Each space is the same size. One of the spaces is green. The chance or **probability** of the spinner stopping on green is 1 out of 4. You can write the probability as the fraction $\frac{1}{4}$.

Now look at the 6 cubes. There are 2 blue cubes. The probability of picking a blue cube without looking is 2 out of 6, or $\frac{2}{6}$.

CLASS EXERCISES

What is the probability of getting blue?

1. 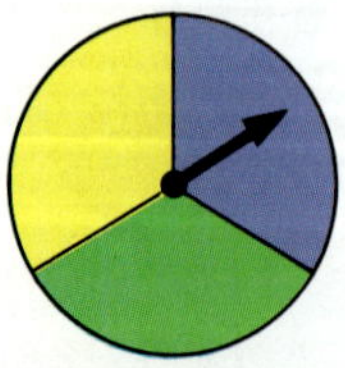 $\frac{\square}{3}$

2. 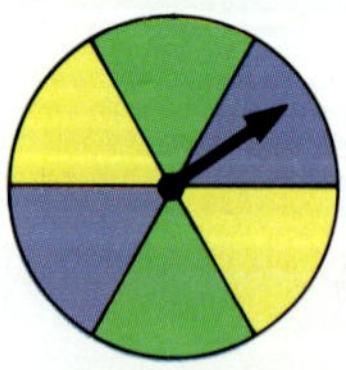 $\frac{\square}{6}$

3. 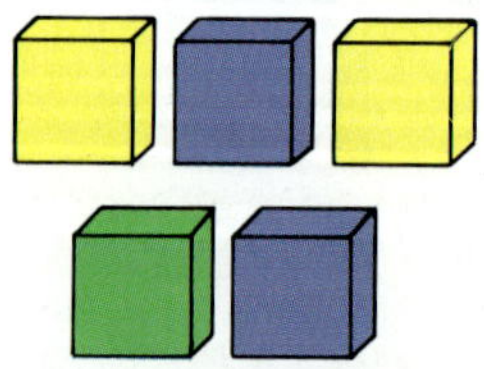 $\frac{2}{\square}$

PRACTICE

Use the spinner to solve.

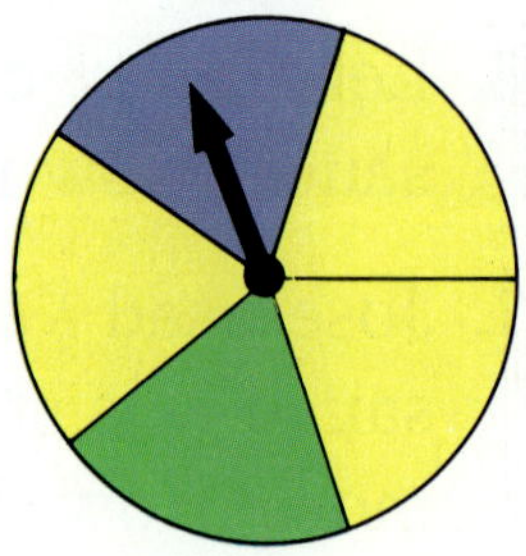

4. What is the probability the spinner will stop on blue?

5. What is the probability the spinner will stop on yellow?

Use the spinner and cubes to solve.

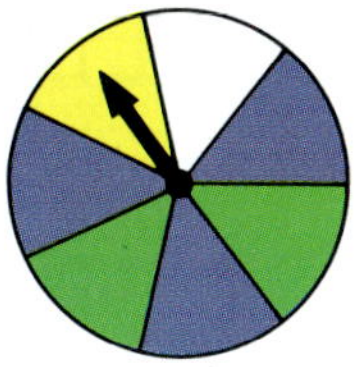

6. Owen spins the spinner. What is the probability the spinner will stop on yellow?

7. Lois spins the spinner. What is the probability the spinner will stop on green?

8. Lois shuts her eyes. What is the probability she'll choose a blue cube?

★ **9.** Lois puts away all of the green cubes. Then she shuts her eyes to choose from the cubes that are left. What is the probability she'll choose a yellow cube?

★ **10.** Owen spins the spinner. It stops on blue. Owen spins again. What is the probability he'll get blue again?

CHECKPOINT 1

Write the fraction for the shaded part. *(pages 336–341)*

1. 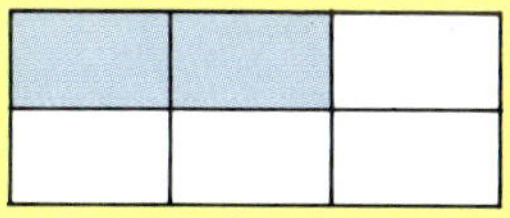

2. 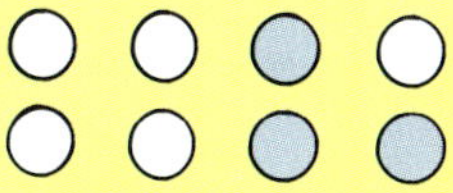

Compare the fractions. Write $<$ or $>$. *(pages 342–343)*

3. $\frac{2}{5}$ ▢ $\frac{4}{5}$ **4.** $\frac{3}{8}$ ▢ $\frac{1}{8}$

Write the answer. *(pages 344–345)*

5. 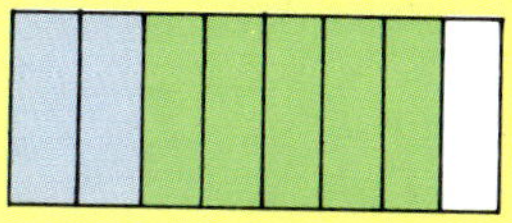 $\frac{2}{8} + \frac{5}{8}$

6. 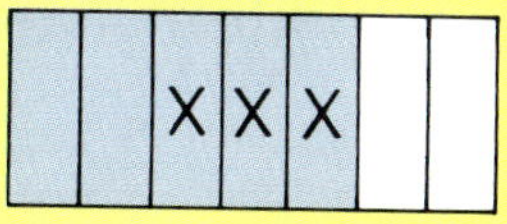 $\frac{5}{7} - \frac{3}{7}$

Write the answer. *(pages 346–347)*

7. What is the probability that the spinner will stop on blue?

Extra practice on page 422

EQUIVALENT FRACTIONS

Some fractions name the same amount.

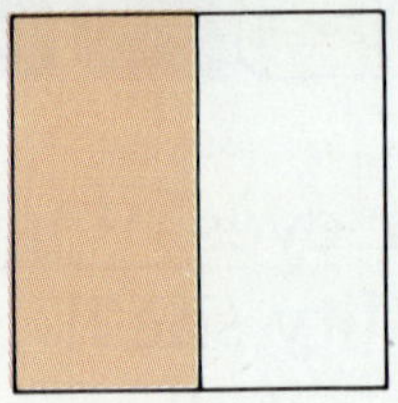

$\frac{1}{2}$ is shaded.

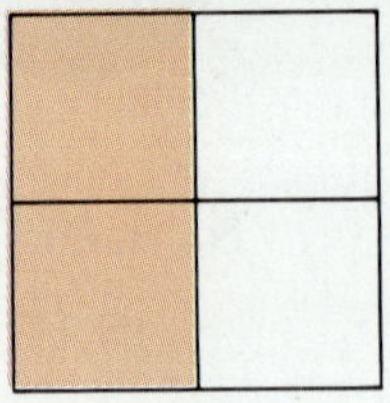

$\frac{2}{4}$ is shaded.

Fractions that name the same amount are called **equivalent fractions**. The fractions $\frac{1}{2}$ and $\frac{2}{4}$ are equivalent fractions.

On the number line $\frac{5}{6}$ is close to 1. You can estimate that $\frac{5}{6}$ is about 1.

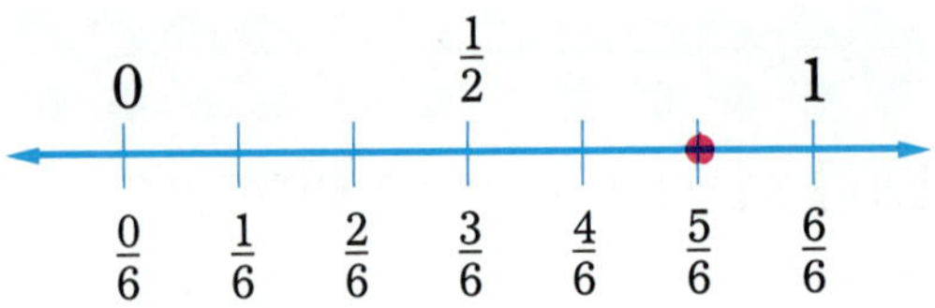

Think: Is $\frac{2}{6}$ about $\frac{1}{2}$ or 0?

CLASS EXERCISES

Complete the equivalent fraction.

1. 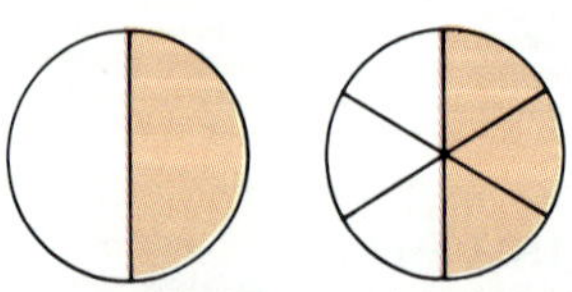

$\frac{1}{2} = \frac{\blacksquare}{6}$

2. 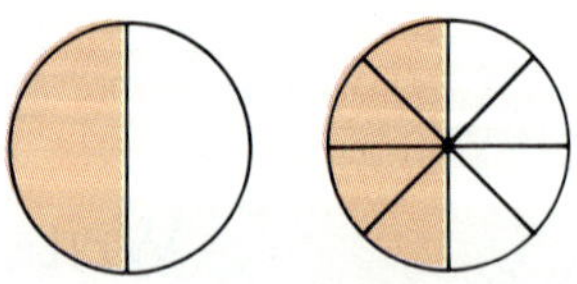

$\frac{1}{2} = \frac{\blacksquare}{8}$

3. 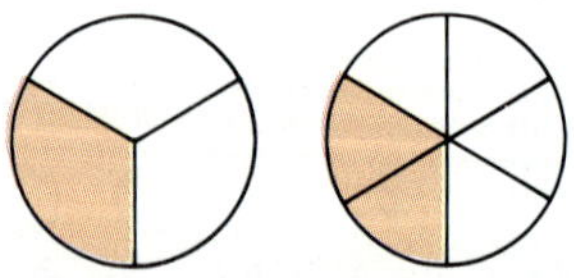

$\frac{1}{3} = \frac{\blacksquare}{6}$

4. 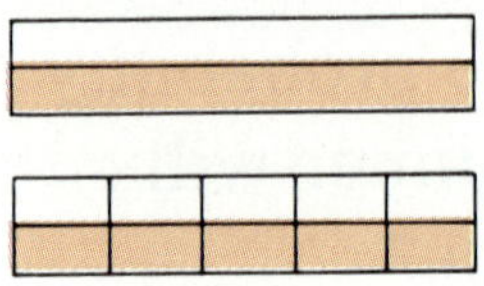

$\frac{1}{2} = \frac{\blacksquare}{10}$

5. 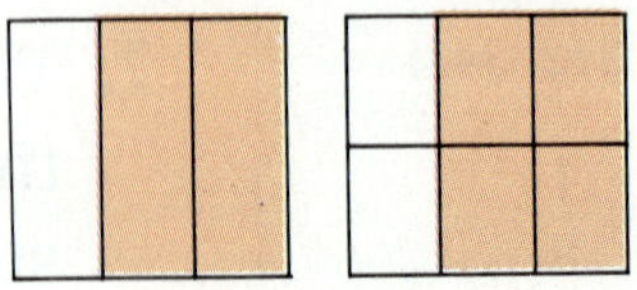

$\frac{2}{3} = \frac{\blacksquare}{6}$

6. 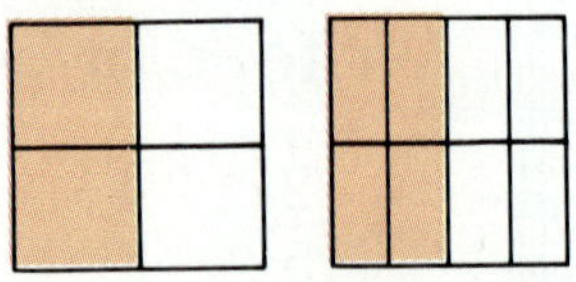

$\frac{2}{4} = \frac{\blacksquare}{8}$

PRACTICE

Write the equivalent fractions.

7. 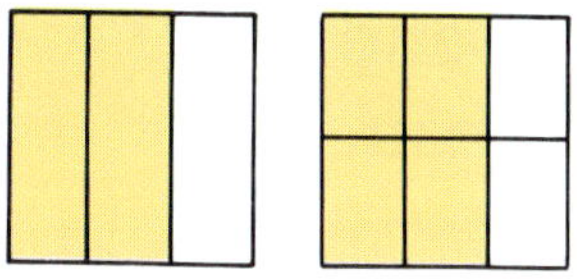

8. 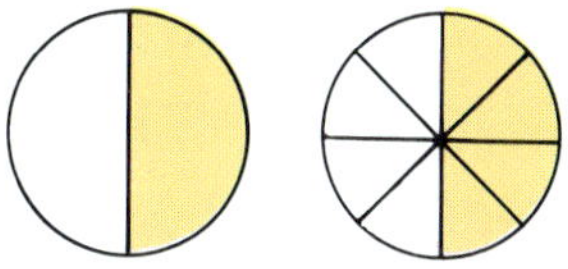

9. 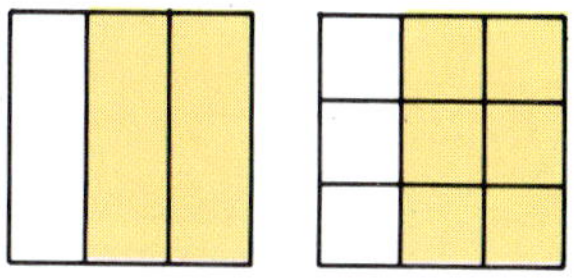

10. 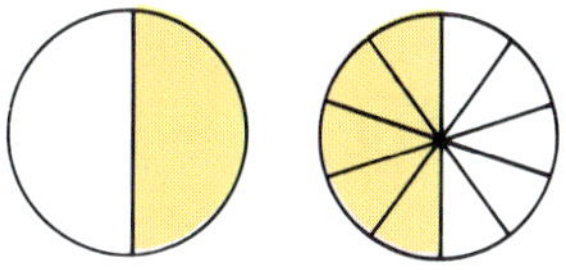

11. 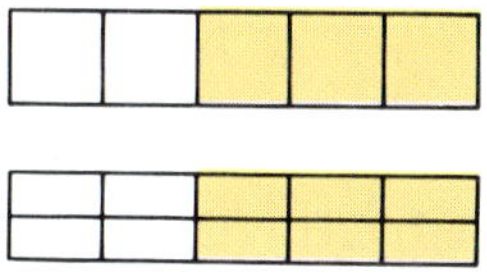

12. 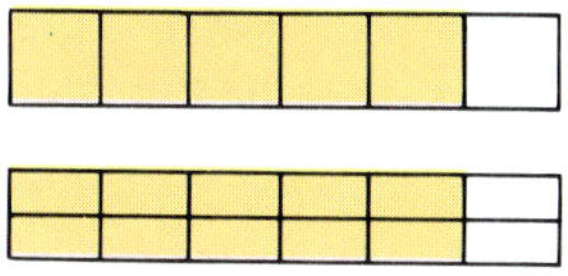

13. 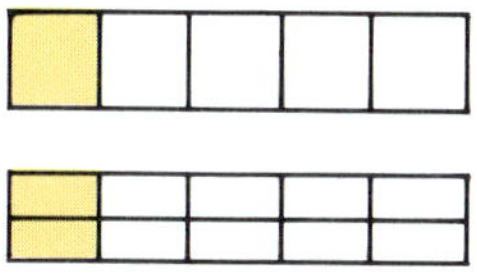

★ 14. 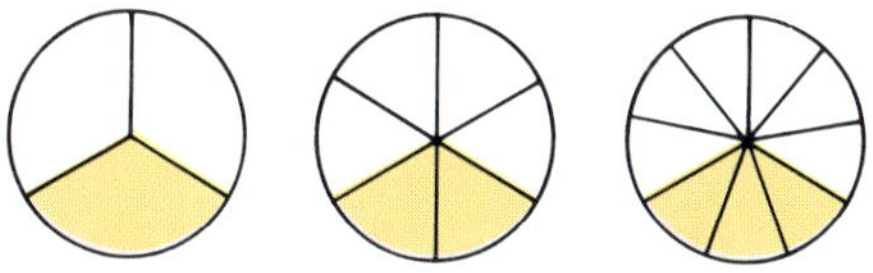

Estimate. Is the fraction closest to 0, $\frac{1}{2}$, or 1?

ESTIMATE

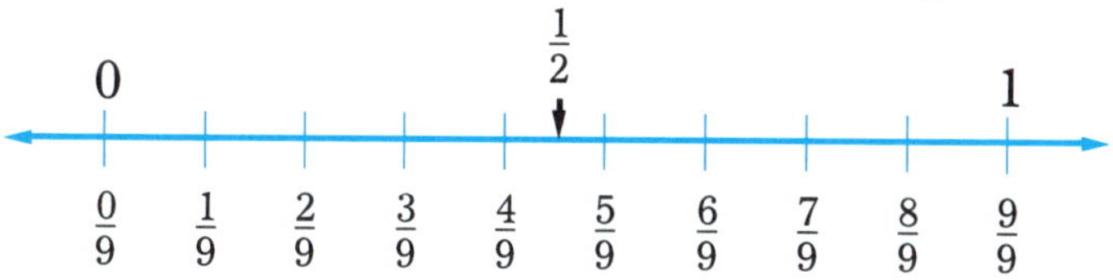

15. $\frac{7}{9}$ 16. $\frac{4}{9}$ 17. $\frac{2}{9}$ 18. $\frac{6}{9}$ 19. $\frac{1}{9}$

PROBLEM SOLVING APPLICATIONS
Comparing Fractions

Are the amounts different or the same? Write *d* or *s*.

20. $\frac{1}{2}$ of a straw, $\frac{3}{8}$ of a straw
21. $\frac{2}{4}$ of a straw, $\frac{1}{2}$ of a straw
22. $\frac{1}{2}$ of a straw, $\frac{3}{4}$ of a straw
23. $\frac{6}{8}$ of a straw, $\frac{3}{4}$ of a straw
24. $\frac{4}{4}$ of a straw, 1 straw

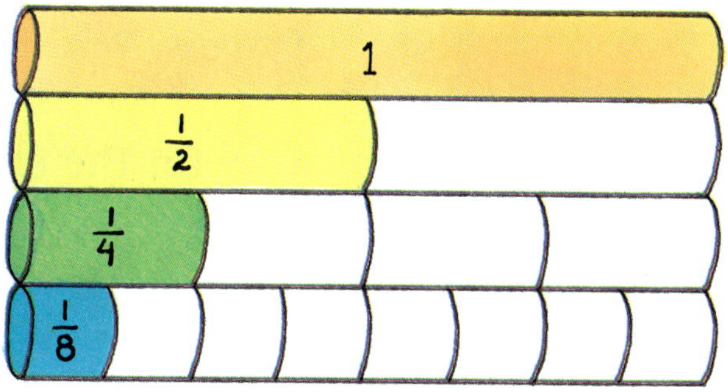

MIXED NUMBERS

You can use **mixed numbers** to name sums of wholes and parts. Three and one half apples are in the bowl.

$$3 + \frac{1}{2} = 3\frac{1}{2}$$

M You can count the oranges mentally by combining halves into wholes.

Think: 3 + 1 + 1 = 5

CLASS EXERCISES

Answer the question.

1. How do you think mixed numbers got their name?

What is the mixed number?

2. 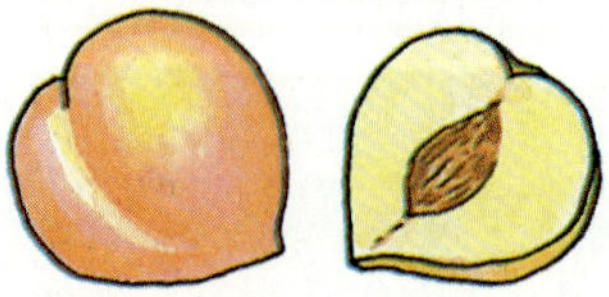

3. 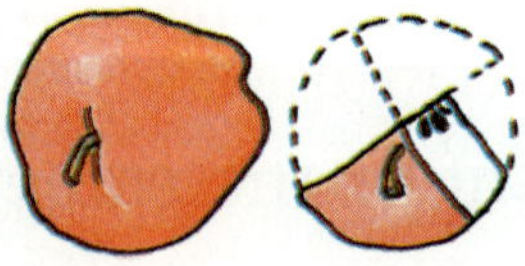

4. 

PRACTICE

Write the mixed number for the shaded parts.

5. 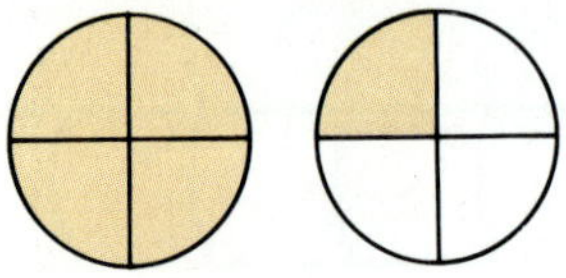

6. 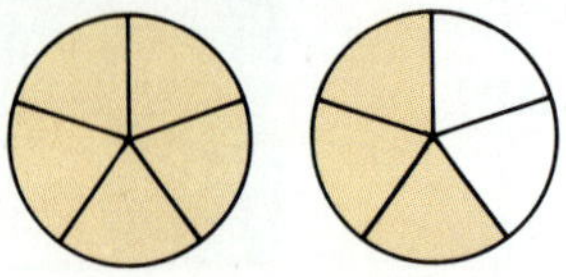

7. 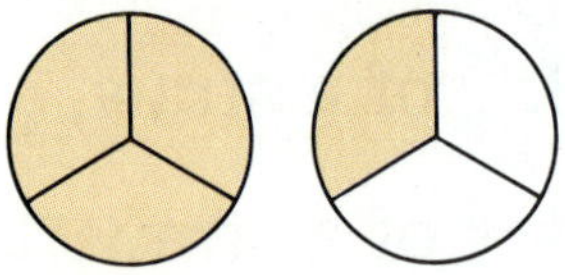

8. 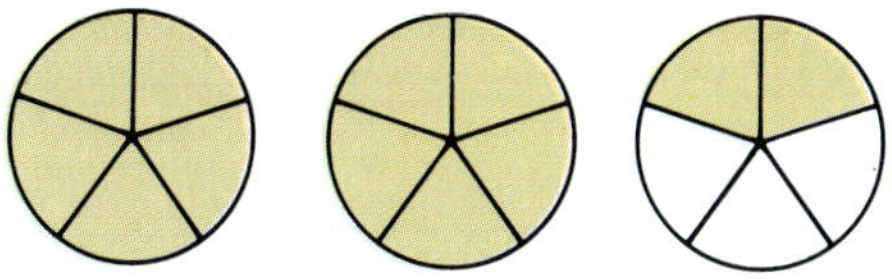

9. 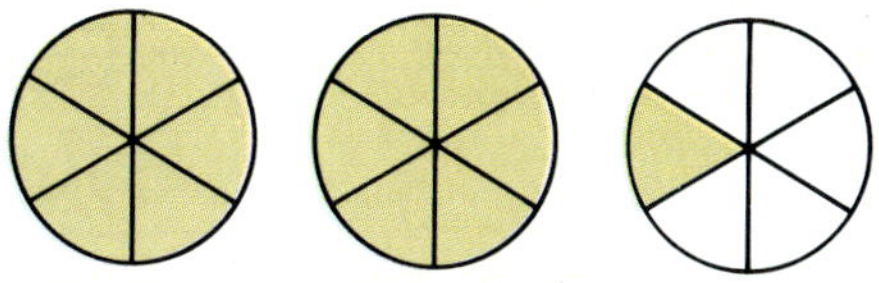

10. 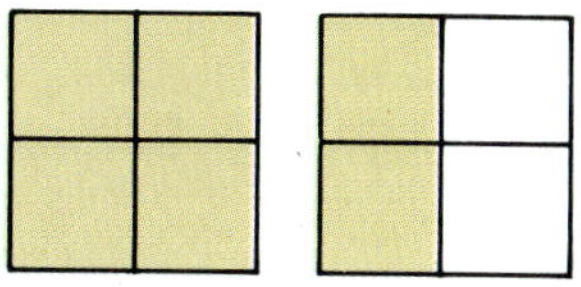

11. 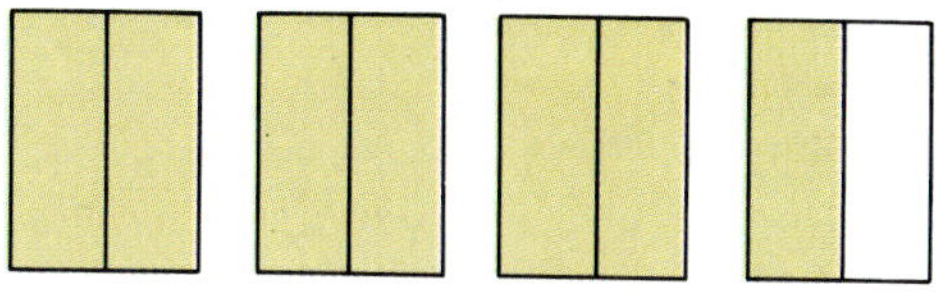

12. 

13. 

Count mentally. Write the number for the shaded parts.

MENTAL MATH

14. 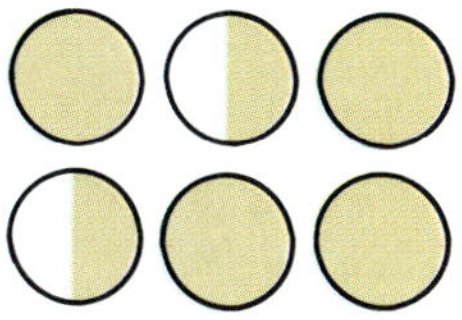

15. 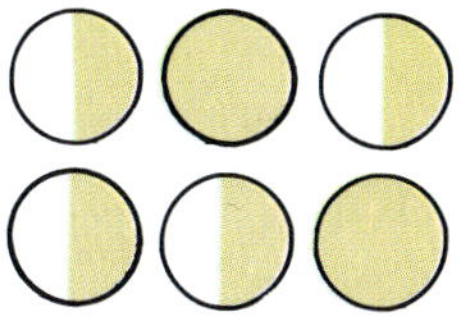

PROBLEM SOLVING APPLICATIONS
Using Measurements

Solve.

16. Bob rode his bike 2 mi before lunch. After lunch he rode $\frac{3}{4}$ mi. How many miles did Bob ride?

17. Bob's bike weighs 22 lb. Ruth's bike weighs $\frac{3}{4}$ lb more. How much does Ruth's bike weigh?

18. Ruth used 2 ft of tape for each end of her handlebar. How much tape did Ruth use in all?

★ 19. Ruth buys 2 cans of oil for her bike. Each can is filled with $6\frac{1}{2}$ oz of oil. How much oil does she have altogether?

TENTHS AND HUNDREDTHS

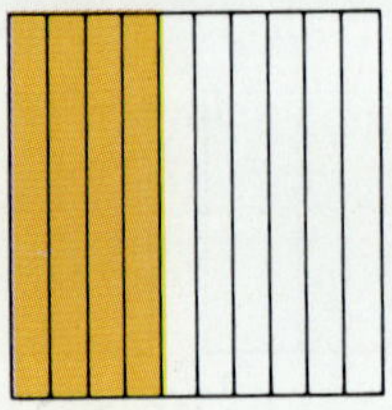

Four of the ten equal parts are shaded. $\frac{4}{10}$ of the shape is shaded. Read $\frac{4}{10}$ as *four tenths*.

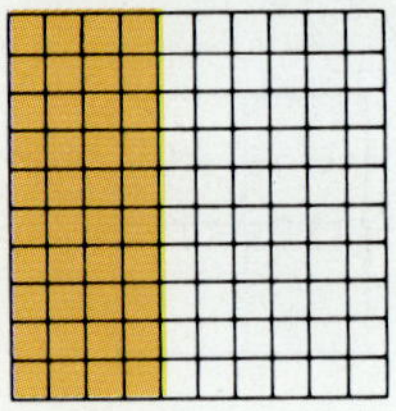

Forty of the hundred equal parts are shaded. $\frac{40}{100}$ of the shape is shaded. Read $\frac{40}{100}$ as *forty hundredths*.

CLASS EXERCISES

Complete. Read the fraction.

1. 

$\frac{\square}{10}$

2. 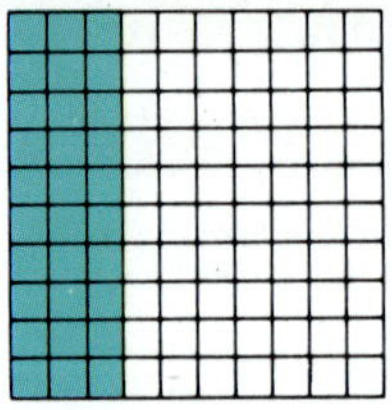

$\frac{\square}{100}$

3. 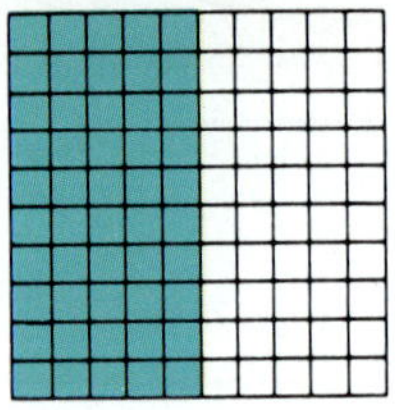

$\frac{\square}{100}$

Write *tenths* or *hundredths* to complete.

4. $\frac{5}{10} = 5$ ___?___

5. $\frac{7}{10} = 7$ ___?___

6. $\frac{21}{100} = 21$ ___?___

PRACTICE

Write the fraction for the shaded part.

7. 

8. 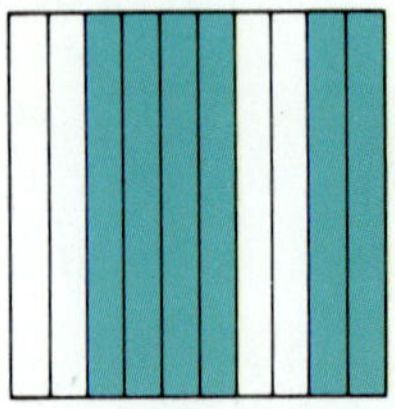

9. 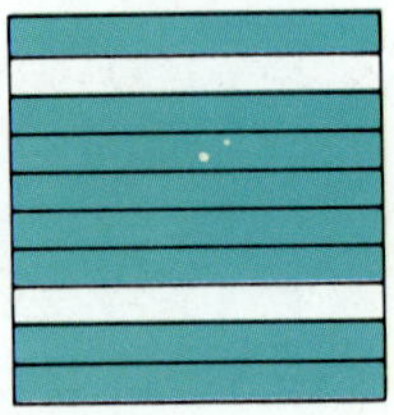

10. 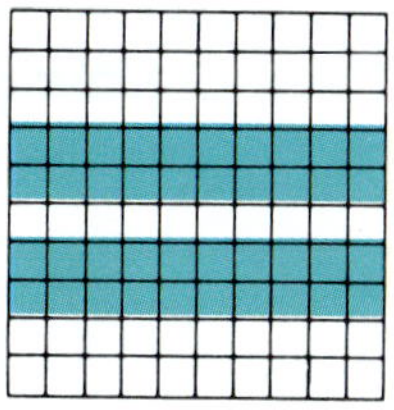

11. 

12. 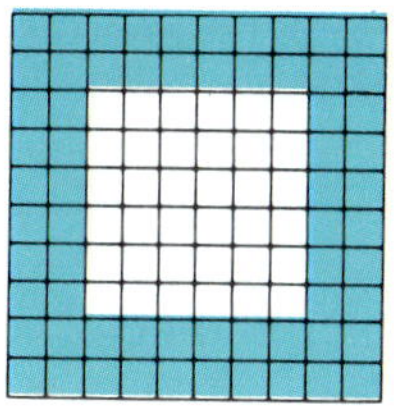

Compare. Write < or >.

13. $\frac{4}{10}$ $\square$ $\frac{8}{10}$

14. $\frac{3}{10}$ $\square$ $\frac{5}{10}$

15. $\frac{9}{10}$ $\square$ $\frac{6}{10}$

16. $\frac{60}{100}$ $\square$ $\frac{65}{100}$

17. $\frac{49}{100}$ $\square$ $\frac{42}{100}$

18. $\frac{60}{100}$ $\square$ $\frac{50}{100}$

MIXED REVIEW

Write the answer.

19. $284 + 48$

20. $94 - 9$

21. $796 - 254$

22. $86 + 29$

23. $708 - 439$

24. $48 + 97$

25. $536 + 221$

26. $90 - 7$

PROBLEM SOLVING APPLICATIONS
Fractions and Money

Solve.

27. Bill had 20¢ in his pocket and 50¢ in his piggy bank. What fraction of a dollar did Bill have in all?

28. Ming had 92¢. She spent 48¢ on a pen. What fraction of a dollar did Ming have left?

Complete.

29. $\square$ dimes make a dollar. A dime is $\frac{1}{\square}$ of a dollar.

30. $\square$ pennies make a dollar. A penny is $\frac{1}{\square}$ of a dollar.

★ 31. A coin worth \$.50 is $\frac{1}{\square}$ of a dollar.

★ 32. A coin worth \$.25 is $\frac{1}{\square}$ of a dollar.

TENTHS AS DECIMALS

There are 10 pigs. You can see that $\frac{3}{10}$ of the pigs are behind the fence. The fraction $\frac{3}{10}$ can be written as the **decimal** 0.3. The point is called a **decimal point.** You read 0.3 as *three tenths*.

CLASS EXERCISES

Tell how to write the decimal.

1. 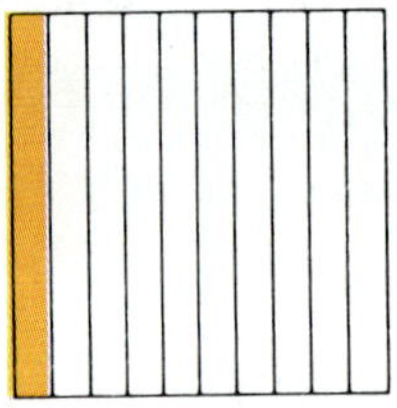

$\frac{1}{10}$ = 0.■

2. 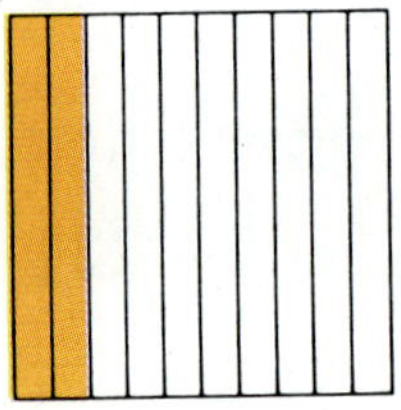

$\frac{2}{10}$ = 0.■

3. 

$\frac{5}{10}$ = 0.■

4. 

0.■

5. 

0.■

6. 

0.■

PRACTICE

Complete.

7. two tenths → 0.■

8. one tenth → 0.■

9. four tenths → 0.■

10. six tenths → 0.■

11. seven tenths → ■.7

12. five tenths → ■.■

Write the decimal.

13. $\frac{3}{10}$ 14. $\frac{5}{10}$ 15. $\frac{2}{10}$ 16. $\frac{9}{10}$

17. $\frac{6}{10}$ 18. $\frac{8}{10}$ 19. $\frac{1}{10}$ 20. $\frac{7}{10}$

Write the decimals in order.

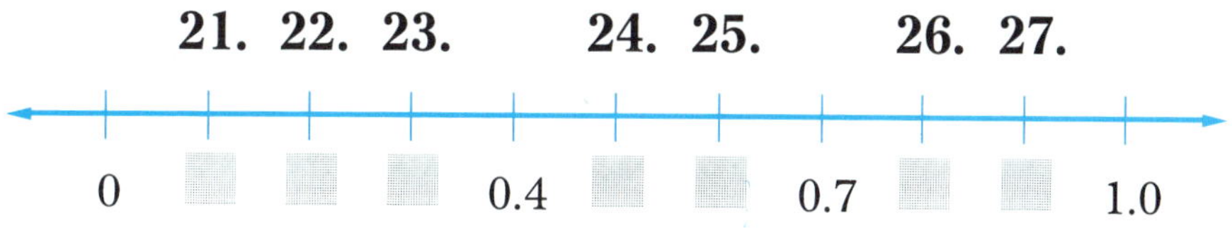

Compare. Write < or >.

28. 0.6 ☐ 0.4 **29.** 0.3 ☐ 0.8 **30.** 0.5 ☐ 0.4

31. 0.7 ☐ 0.9 **32.** 0.1 ☐ 0.3 **33.** 0.9 ☐ 0.8

PROBLEM SOLVING APPLICATIONS
Using Pictures

Use the picture to solve.

34. Write a decimal to show what part of the group are dogs.

35. Write a decimal to show what part of the group are birds.

36. Write a decimal to show what part of the group are birds and cats.

37. Are more than 0.2 of the group dogs?

38. Write a decimal to show what part of the group are not cats.

39. Write a fraction and a decimal to show what part of the group are cats.

DECIMALS GREATER THAN ONE

Two and six tenths are shaded. You can write the mixed number, $2\frac{6}{10}$. You can also write $2\frac{6}{10}$ as a decimal.

ones		tenths
2	.	6

⇨ 2.6

The decimal 2.6 means 2 ones 6 tenths. You read 2.6 as *two and six tenths.*

You can use some calculators to count by tenths. To count from 2, enter 2 [+] 0.1. Then push the equals sign. Watch the calculator count by tenths.

2 [+] 0.1 [=] 2.1
[=] 2.2
[=] 2.3

To count backwards use the [−] key instead of the [+] key.

2 [−] 0.1 [=] 1.9
[=] 1.8
[=] 1.7

CLASS EXERCISES

Say and write the decimal.

1.

ones		tenths
2	.	8

2.

ones		tenths
5	.	3

3.

ones		tenths
13	.	4

Complete.

4. 4.8 = 4 and ▒ tenths

5. 25.4 = ▒ and ▒ tenths

6. $4\frac{3}{10}$ = ▒.▒

7. $2\frac{5}{10}$ = ▒.▒

8. $5\frac{2}{10}$ = ▒.▒

PRACTICE

Write a decimal.

9. $7\frac{1}{10}$ **10.** $1\frac{3}{10}$ **11.** $9\frac{7}{10}$ **12.** $15\frac{4}{10}$ **13.** $3\frac{1}{10}$

14. $30\frac{8}{10}$ **15.** $98\frac{0}{10}$ **16.** $75\frac{6}{10}$ **17.** $0\frac{7}{10}$ **18.** $9\frac{2}{10}$

19. $100\frac{4}{10}$ **20.** $23\frac{5}{10}$ **21.** $36\frac{4}{10}$ **22.** $95\frac{2}{10}$ **23.** $60\frac{0}{10}$

24. 7 and 3 tenths **25.** 17 and 8 tenths **26.** 5 and 6 tenths

27. 29 and 9 tenths **28.** 12 and 0 tenths **29.** 61 and 4 tenths

A calculator was used to count by tenths. Complete the missing numbers.

CALCULATOR

30. **31.** **32.** **33.**

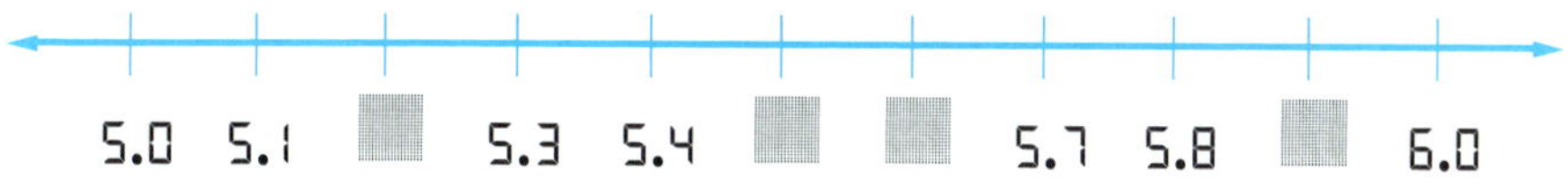

34. **35.** **36.** **37.** **38.**

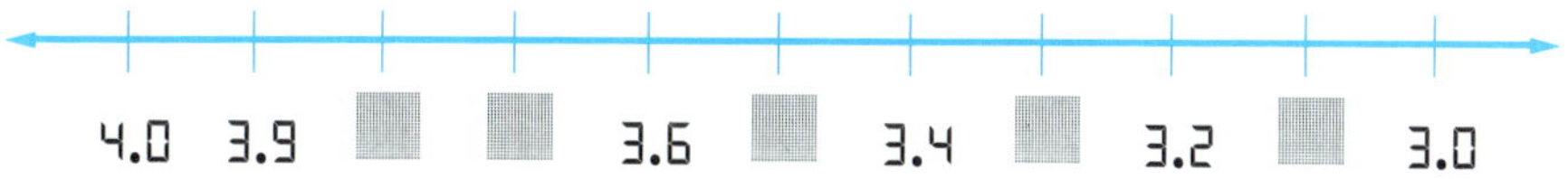

PROBLEM SOLVING APPLICATIONS
Using a Table

Use the table to solve.

39. Which animal has the highest body temperature?

40. Which animal has the lowest body temperature?

★ **41.** Which animal has a temperature closest to the goldfish?

★ **42.** Which animal has a temperature closest to a person's (98.6°F)?

BODY TEMPERATURES

ANIMAL	TEMPERATURE
Catfish	68.9°F
Crocodile	78.1°F
Goldfish	74.3°F
Polar Bear	99.1°F

ADDING AND SUBTRACTING DECIMALS

You can add 24.4 and 23.9 like other numbers. Just line up the decimal points, then write the decimal point in your answer.

Add the tenths.	Add the ones.	Add the tens.
$\begin{array}{r} {}^{1}\ \ \\ 24.4 \\ +\ 23.9 \\ \hline 3 \end{array}$	$\begin{array}{r} {}^{1}\ \ \\ 24.4 \\ +\ 23.9 \\ \hline 8.3 \end{array}$	$\begin{array}{r} {}^{1}\ \ \ \ \\ 24.4 \\ +\ 23.9 \\ \hline 48.3 \end{array}$

Remember to write the decimal point in the answer.

Here's how you subtract 23.9 from 56.4.

Subtract the tenths.	Subtract the ones.	Subtract the tens.
$\begin{array}{r} {}^{5\ 14} \\ 5\ \not{6}.\not{4} \\ -\ 2\ 3.9 \\ \hline 5 \end{array}$	$\begin{array}{r} {}^{5\ 14} \\ 5\ \not{6}.\not{4} \\ -\ 2\ 3.9 \\ \hline 2.5 \end{array}$	$\begin{array}{r} {}^{5\ 14} \\ 5\ \not{6}.\not{4} \\ -\ 2\ 3.9 \\ \hline 3\ 2.5 \end{array}$

CLASS EXERCISES

What is the sum or difference?

1. $\begin{array}{r} 6 \\ +\ 2 \\ \hline \end{array}$ $\begin{array}{r} 0.6 \\ +\ 0.2 \\ \hline \end{array}$ **2.** $\begin{array}{r} 29 \\ +\ 16 \\ \hline \end{array}$ $\begin{array}{r} 2.9 \\ +\ 1.6 \\ \hline \end{array}$ **3.** $\begin{array}{r} 34 \\ -\ 27 \\ \hline \end{array}$ $\begin{array}{r} 3.4 \\ -\ 2.7 \\ \hline \end{array}$

PRACTICE

Add or subtract.

4. $5.6 + 7.2$ **5.** $9.4 - 7.1$ **6.** $15.9 + 25.4$ **7.** $12.5 + 7.6$ **8.** $18.6 - 9.3$

9. $54.3 - 43.4$ **10.** $10.3 + 9.2$ **11.** $49.8 - 48.9$ **12.** $42.7 + 17.3$ **13.** $20.5 - 11.7$

14. $54.3 + 25.4$ **15.** $40.6 - 13.9$ **16.** $58.7 - 23.5$ **17.** $50.2 - 41.6$ **18.** $58.6 + 32.8$

19. $36.5 - 2.7$ **20.** $52.0 + 19.5$ **21.** $83.4 + 26.8$ **22.** $49.0 - 5.6$ **23.** $23.8 + 38.1$

24. $8.7 + 9.2$ **25.** $10.3 - 9.2$ **26.** $40.6 + 53.4$

27. $41.7 - 30.9$ **28.** $25.3 - 24.9$ ★ **29.** $56.5 + 6.7 + 23.4$

PROBLEM SOLVING APPLICATIONS

The table shows which cities in the United States get the least amount of rain in a year. Use the table to solve.

CITY	AMOUNT OF RAIN
Bakersfield, CA	14.5 cm
Las Vegas, NV	9.6 cm
Palm Springs, CA	13.5 cm
Phoenix, AZ	17.9 cm

30. Which city gets the least amount of rain?

31. Which of these cities gets the most rain?

32. How much more rain does Phoenix get than Bakersfield?

33. How much more rain does Palm Springs get than Las Vegas?

PROBLEM SOLVING
Strategy: Drawing a Picture

Suppose you want to cut this piece of paper into fifths. How many cuts do you make?

To answer the question, you can draw a picture. Then you can count the number of cuts.

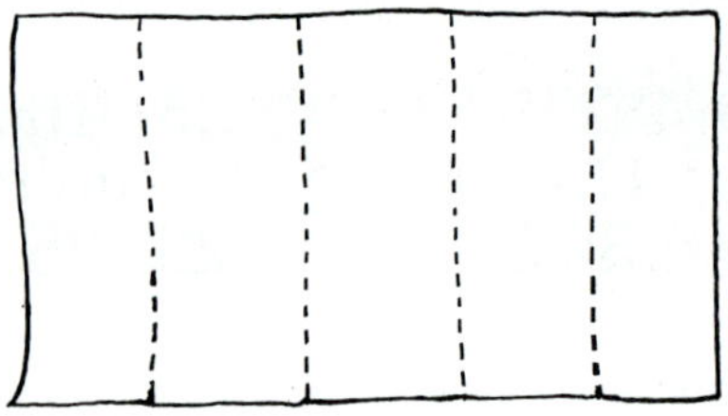

You would make 4 cuts.

CLASS EXERCISES

Use the picture to answer the question.

1. Anna paints $\frac{3}{6}$ of a paper red. She paints $\frac{2}{6}$ of the paper blue. What fraction of the paper does she paint?

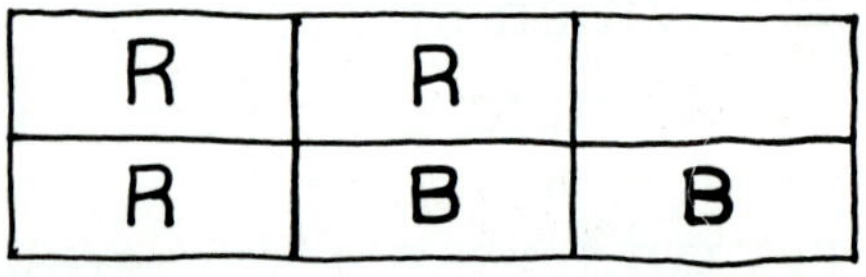

2. Pearl has 8 oranges. She gives $\frac{1}{4}$ of the oranges to her brother. How many oranges does she give to her brother?

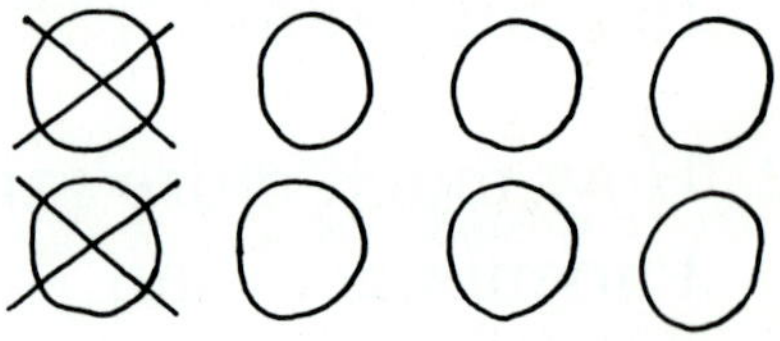

3. Carl makes 3 cuts across a loaf of bread. Then he cuts each piece in half. How many pieces of bread does Carl have?

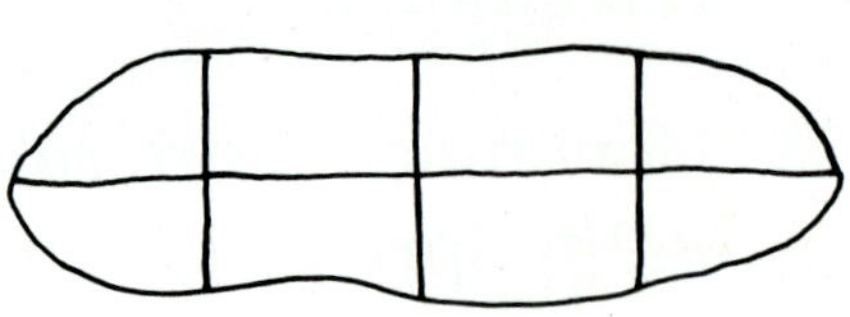

PRACTICE

Draw a picture to help you solve.

4. Six birds sit on a branch. One third of the birds fly away. How many fly away?

5. Carol paints $\frac{3}{8}$ of a poster blue. What fraction of the poster is not painted?

6. Rosa cuts bread into 10 equal pieces. She uses 6 of the pieces for sandwiches. What fraction of the bread is left?

7. Bill made 10 masks. He took $\frac{1}{2}$ of the masks to school. What decimal shows the fraction of masks he took to school?

★ 8. One third of Jim's 12 marbles are blue. One half of his blue marbles are clear. How many of Jim's marbles are clear blue?

★ 9. What is the least number of straight slices you can make to cut a wheel of cheese into 8 equal pieces?

CHECKPOINT 2

Write the equivalent fractions. *(pages 348–349)*

1. 

Write the mixed number. *(pages 350–351)*

2. 

Write a decimal. *(pages 352–357)*

3. $\frac{6}{10}$ 4. $2\frac{5}{10}$ 5. $43\frac{3}{10}$

Write the answer. *(pages 358–359)*

6. $\begin{array}{r} 32.7 \\ +\ 25.6 \\ \hline \end{array}$ 7. $\begin{array}{r} 58.2 \\ -\ 16.8 \\ \hline \end{array}$

Solve. Draw a picture to help. *(pages 360–361)*

8. How many cuts would you have to make to divide a string into 6 equal parts?

Extra practice on page 422

CHAPTER 12 TEST

Compare the fractions. Write > or <. *(pages 342–343)*

1. $\frac{3}{4} \square \frac{1}{4}$ **2.** $\frac{2}{5} \square \frac{3}{5}$ **3.** $\frac{3}{8} \square \frac{5}{8}$ **4.** $\frac{6}{7} \square \frac{4}{7}$

Write the answer. *(pages 344–345)*

5. 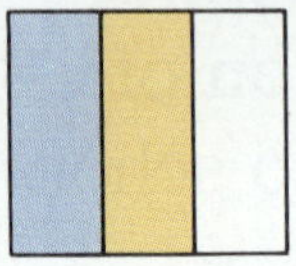

$\frac{1}{3} + \frac{1}{3}$

6. 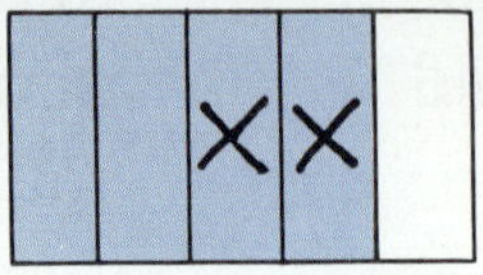

$\frac{4}{5} - \frac{2}{5}$

7. 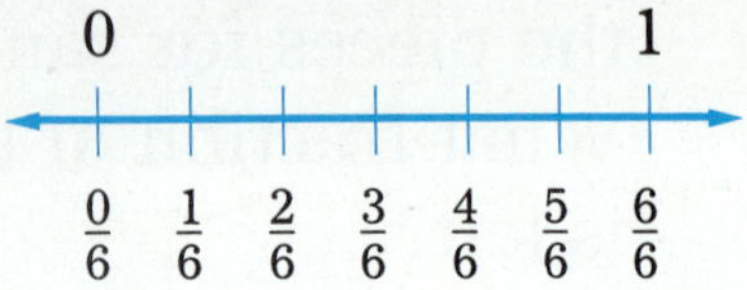

$\frac{1}{6} + \frac{3}{6}$

Write the answer.
(pages 346–347)

8. What is the probability that the spinner will stop on purple?

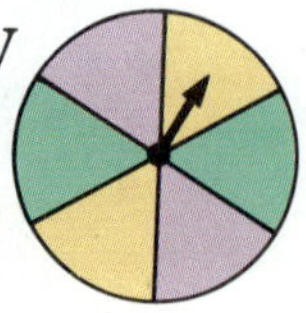

Write the equivalent fraction.
(pages 336–341, 348–349)

9. 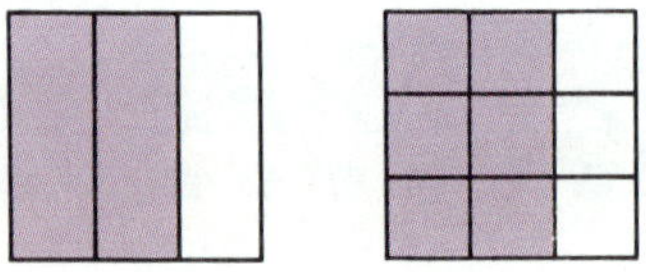

Write the mixed number for the shaded parts. *(pages 350–351)*

10. 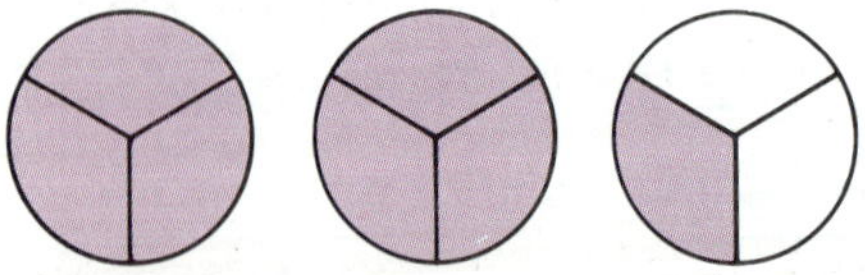

Write the decimal.
(pages 354–357)

11. $\frac{4}{10}$ **12.** $13\frac{1}{10}$

Write the answer. *(pages 358–359)*

13. $\begin{array}{r} 21.8 \\ +\ 16.3 \\ \hline \end{array}$ **14.** $\begin{array}{r} 46.2 \\ -\ 33.7 \\ \hline \end{array}$ **15.** $\begin{array}{r} 27.8 \\ +\ 3.2 \\ \hline \end{array}$ **16.** $\begin{array}{r} 46.8 \\ +\ 12.9 \\ \hline \end{array}$ **17.** $\begin{array}{r} 58.7 \\ -\ 4.8 \\ \hline \end{array}$

Draw a picture to help solve. *(pages 360–361)*

18. How many cuts would you have to make to saw a log into 8 equal parts?

Extra practice on page 423

MATHEMATICS and ART

In art class students made modeling dough. They each used this recipe.

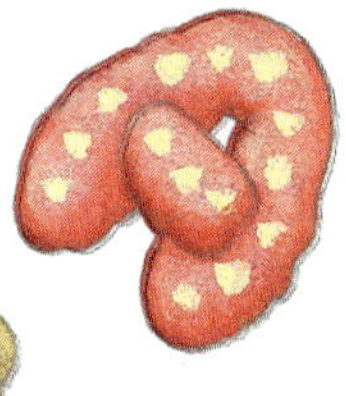

FLOUR AND SALT DOUGH

1 cup water
1 cup flour
½ cup salt
2 tablespoons cream of tartar
food coloring

Cook over medium heat a few minutes.

WHAT'S COOKING?

Solve.

1. Tracy is getting water for everyone. Her pitcher holds 1 quart. That's enough for __?__ batches of dough.

2. Something is missing from Robert's dough. He has mixed water, flour, cream of tartar, and food coloring. What is missing?

3. The students decide to make more dough. They double the recipe. How much of each ingredient do they use?

4. The students each stored their dough in plastic jars. There are 7 jars of red, 9 jars of green, 2 jars of yellow, and 6 jars of blue. How many jars do the students have?

5. The 3 students at Eric's table made an elephant, a monkey, and a giraffe. Melanie didn't make the monkey. Philip made the giraffe. What did Eric make?

Enrichment

Fifty of the hundred parts are shaded. You can write the fraction, $\frac{50}{100}$, to show the shaded parts.

You can also write $\frac{50}{100}$ as the decimal, 0.50.

You read 0.50 as *fifty hundredths*.

There is still another way to show parts of a hundred. **Percent** means hundredths. You can say fifty percent of the boxes are shaded. You write the percent like this: 50%.

Notice that $\frac{1}{2}$ of the box is shaded. 50% of the box is the same as $\frac{1}{2}$ of the box. 70% is more than $\frac{1}{2}$. 40% is less than $\frac{1}{2}$.

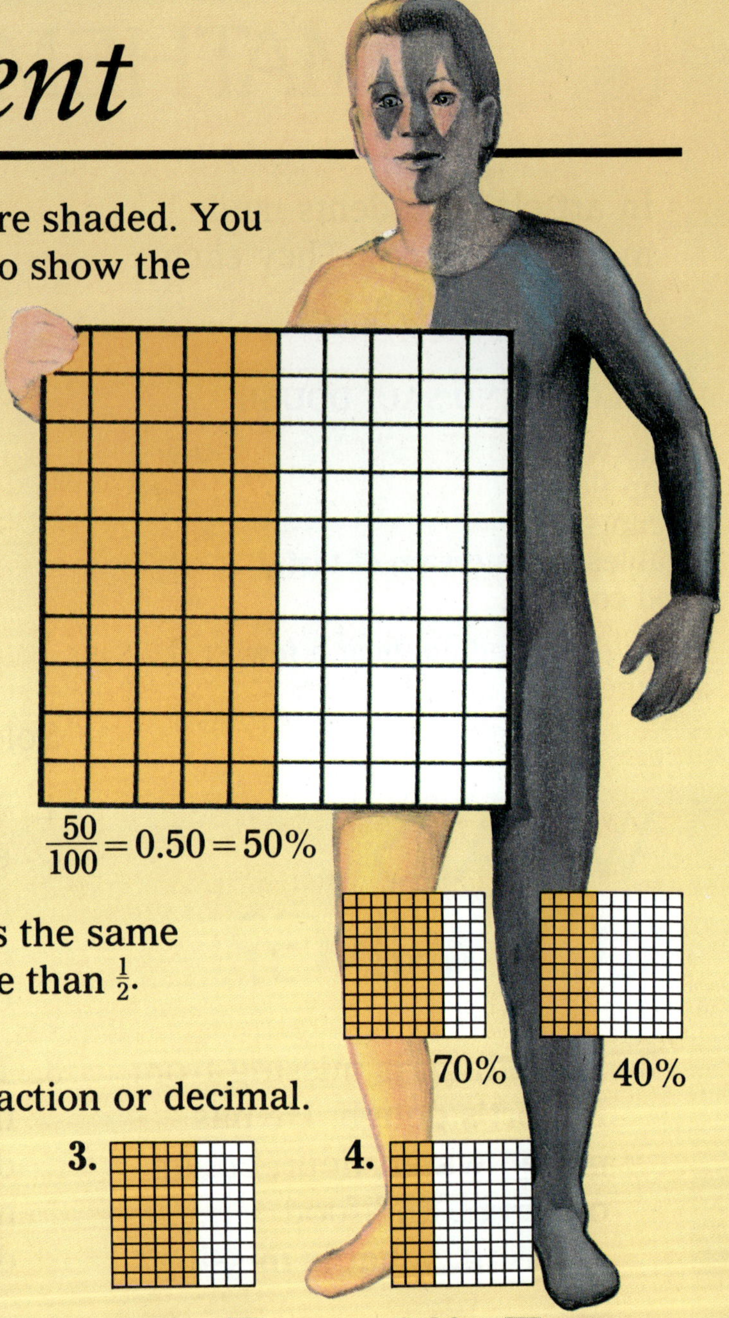

$\frac{50}{100} = 0.50 = 50\%$

70%   40%

Write the percent for the fraction or decimal.

1. 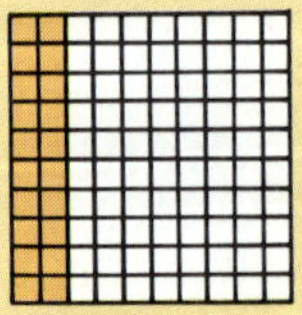

$\frac{20}{100} =$ ▒

2. 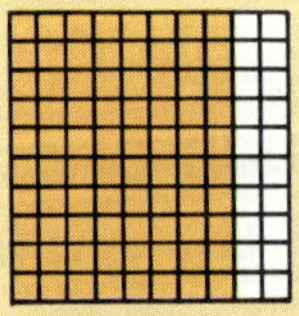

$\frac{80}{100} =$ ▒

3.

$0.60 =$ ▒

4.

$0.30 =$ ▒

PERCENTS AND CIRCLE GRAPHS

Compare the percents. Write < or >.

5. 20% ▒ 60%

6. 30% ▒ 10%

7. 40% ▒ 50%

The pie-shaped graph is called a **circle graph.**

At camp 100 children signed up for morning activities. The circle graph shows the percent of the children who signed up for each activity. 30% of the children signed up for swimming.

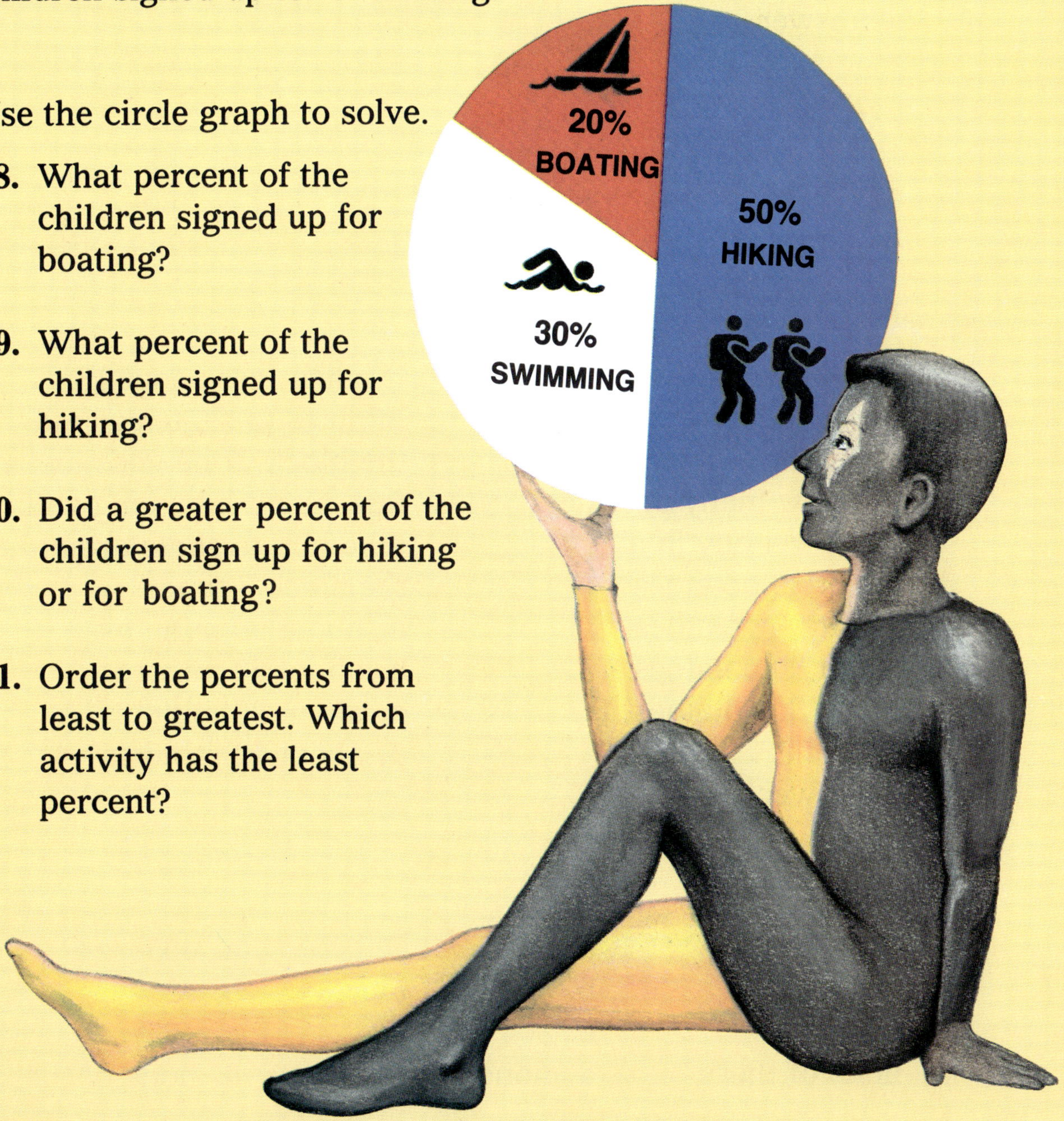

Use the circle graph to solve.

8. What percent of the children signed up for boating?

9. What percent of the children signed up for hiking?

10. Did a greater percent of the children sign up for hiking or for boating?

11. Order the percents from least to greatest. Which activity has the least percent?

CUMULATIVE REVIEW

Choose the correct answer. Choose *a*, *b*, *c* or *d*.

Estimate the product.

1. 4×31
a. 100 **b.** 120
c. 200 **d.** 12

2. 7×78
a. 800 **b.** 420
c. 560 **d.** 400

3. 6×544
a. 3000 **b.** 4000
c. 5000 **d.** 6000

Find the answer.

4. 4×82
a. 328
b. 325
c. 128
d. none of these

5. 3×76
a. 218
b. 228
c. 208
d. none of these

6. 8×35
a. 240
b. 243
c. 280
d. none of these

Estimate to solve.

7. Min-wei bought 4 bags of potatoes. There were 12 potatoes in each bag. About how many potatoes did Min-wei buy in all?
a. about 80 potatoes
b. about 40 potatoes
c. about 60 potatoes
d. about 30 potatoes

8. It takes Jess about 18 minutes to skate around the block. If he goes just as fast, about how long will it take him to skate around the block 3 times?
a. about 90 minutes
b. about 60 minutes
c. about 20 minutes
d. about 10 minutes

Find the answer.

9. 194×3
a. 472
b. 582
c. 382
d. none of these

10. 206×4
a. 824
b. 624
c. 804
d. none of these

11. 651×7
a. 4558
b. 4257
c. 4557
d. none of these

Find the answer.

12. 8 × \$.72
a. \$5.66
b. \$5.76
c. \$5.60
d. none of these

13. 5 × \$2.18
a. \$10.50
b. \$11.90
c. \$10.90
d. none of these

14. 6 × \$.69
a. \$4.14
b. \$3.15
c. \$4.04
d. none of these

15. $9\overline{)0}$
a. 9
b. 1
c. 0
d. none of these

16. $6\overline{)19}$
a. 3
b. 3 R1
c. 3 R2
d. none of these

17. $5\overline{)43}$
a. 9
b. 8 R3
c. 8 R4
d. none of these

18. $7\overline{)79}$
a. 10 R9
b. 11
c. 11 R2
d. none of these

19. $3\overline{)85}$
a. 26 R1
b. 28 R1
c. 28
d. none of these

20. $8\overline{)371}$
a. 46 R3
b. 45 R3
c. 46 R7
d. none of these

Solve.

21. Party hats are marked 5 for 90¢. How much does one hat cost?
a. 25¢ **b.** 20¢ **c.** 18¢ **d.** none of these

LANGUAGE and VOCABULARY REVIEW

Use the words to complete the sentences.

numerator denominator probability difference decimal

1. The likelihood that something will happen is called the __?__.

2. The top number in a fraction is called the __?__.

3. The answer in subtraction is the __?__.

4. 0.7 is an example of a __?__.

LET AND PRINT

Here are more ways to use LET and PRINT in a program.

```
10 LET A = 12
20 LET B = 4
30 PRINT A/B
```

Output

```
3
```

PRINT tells the computer to divide 12 by 4 and show the output.

```
10 LET A = 12
20 LET C = 1 + 1
30 PRINT A - C
```

Output

```
10
```

PRINT tells the computer to subtract 2 from 12 and show the output.

The BASIC word **END** tells the computer that the program is finished.

The BASIC word **RUN** tells the computer to process the program.

```
10 LET A = 3
20 LET B = 4
30 PRINT "3 PLUS 4 IS"
40 PRINT A + B
50 END

RUN

3 PLUS 4 IS
7
```

Write the output for each program.

1.
```
10 LET T = 8
20 LET Q = 9
30 PRINT T * Q
40 END
```

2.
```
10 LET M = 5 + 1
20 LET P = 4
30 PRINT M + P
40 END
```

3.
```
10 LET A = 49
20 LET G = 7
30 PRINT "SEVEN"
40 PRINT A/G
50 END
```

13

Look at the house. Where do you see a 3-sided shape? Where do you see some 4-sided shapes?

GEOMETRY

CIRCLE, TRIANGLE, SQUARE, RECTANGLE

Figures like those below are flat. The square and the rectangle each have four sides. Each of the sides of the square is the same length. A square is a special kind of rectangle.

circle **triangle** **square** **rectangle**

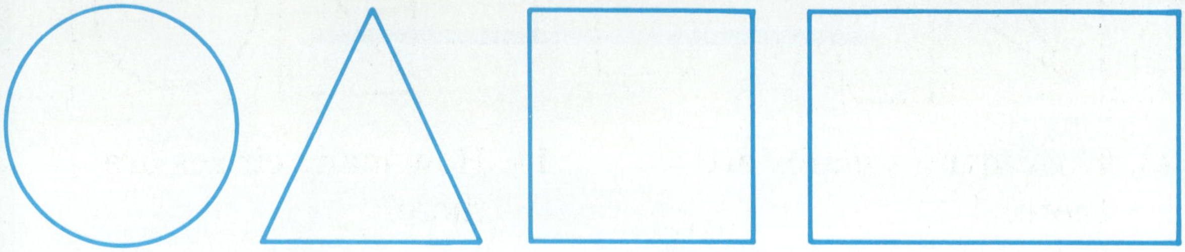

CLASS EXERCISES

Match. Write the letter.

1. circle
2. triangle
3. rectangle
4. square

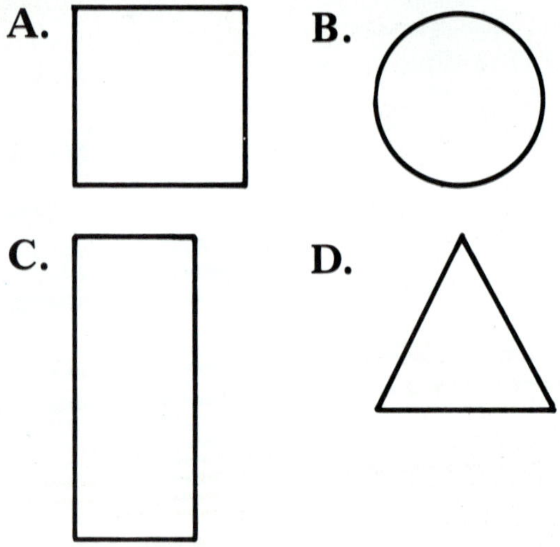

PRACTICE

Name the figure.

5.

6.

7.

8.

9. 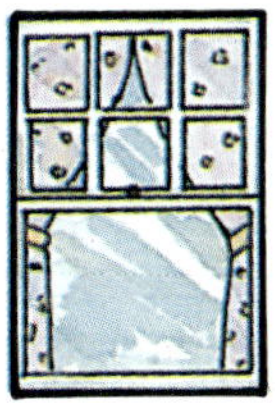 **10.**  **11.** 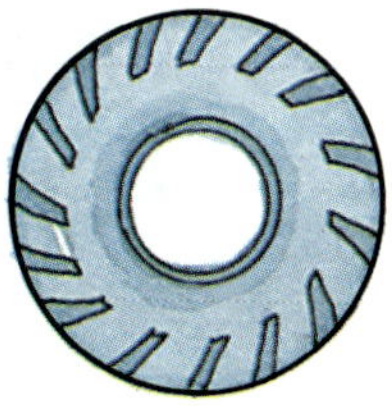 **12.** 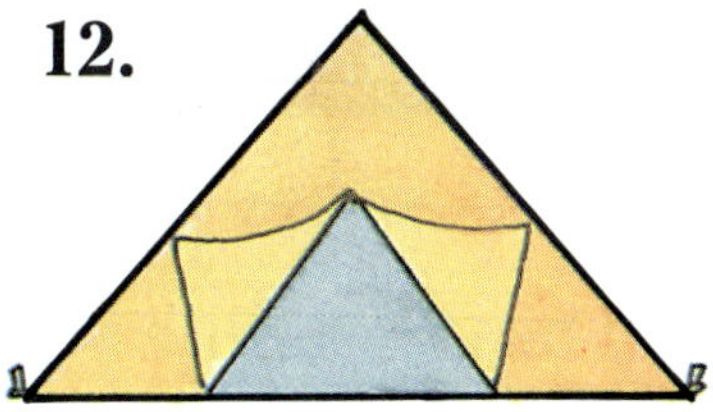

Tell how many.

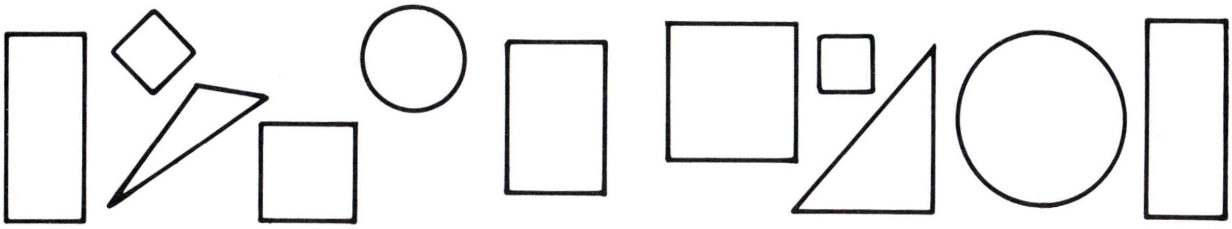

13. How many squares are there?

14. How many circles are there?

15. How many rectangles that are not squares are there?

16. How many triangles are there?

Compare. Write $<$ or $>$.

MIXED REVIEW

17. 362 ▢ 485 **18.** 996 ▢ 862 **19.** 4537 ▢ 5263

20. $\frac{1}{8}$ ▢ $\frac{3}{8}$ **21.** $\frac{5}{7}$ ▢ $\frac{3}{7}$ **22.** $\frac{4}{5}$ ▢ $\frac{3}{5}$

23. 0.6 ▢ 0.4 **24.** 0.1 ▢ 0.3 **25.** 0.9 ▢ 0.4

PROBLEM SOLVING APPLICATIONS
Using Measurement

The picture shows some parts of a circle. Use a centimeter ruler to measure.

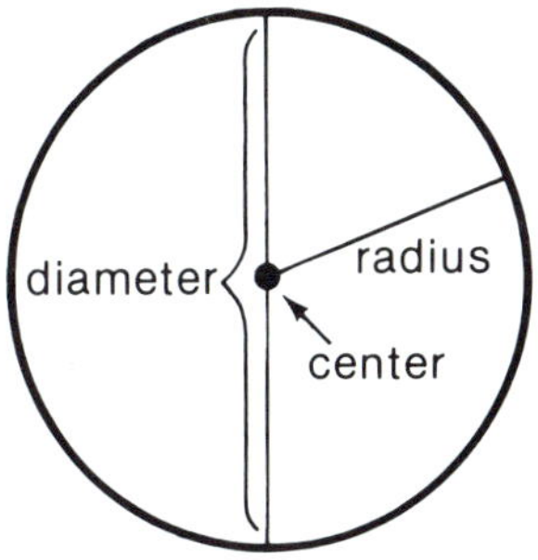

26. How long is the radius?

27. How long is the diameter?

★ **28.** A circle has a radius of 3 cm. What is the length of its diameter?

SEGMENTS AND POLYGONS

These are line **segments**. These are not line segments.

Segments can be used to make figures. A figure formed by joining three or more segments is called a **polygon.** The segments are **sides** of the polygon.

CLASS EXERCISES

Is the figure a polygon? Tell why or why not.

1. 

2. 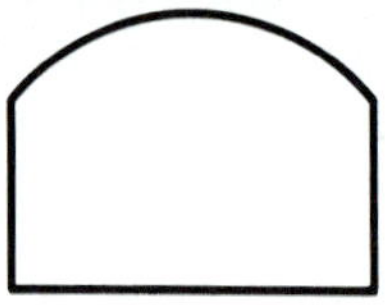

3. 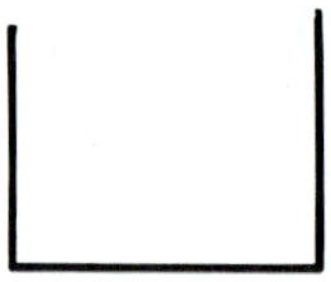

4. 

PRACTICE

Is the figure a polygon? Write *yes* or *no.*

5. 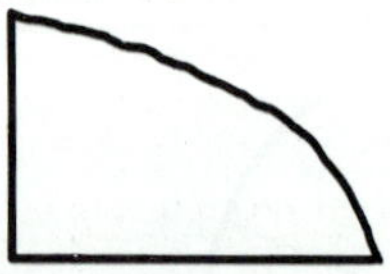

6. 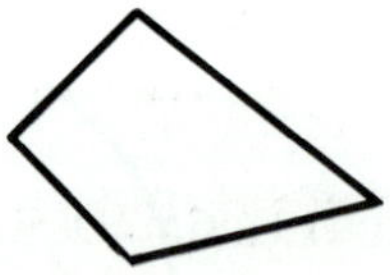

7. 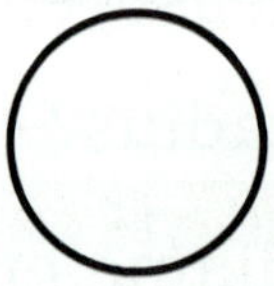

8. 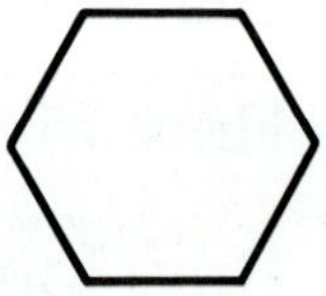

9. 

10. 

11. 

12. 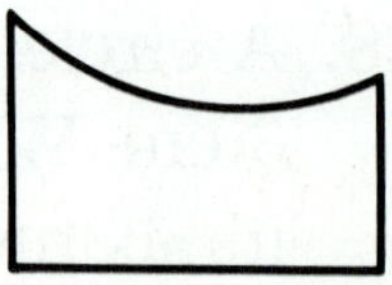

13. 

14. 

15. 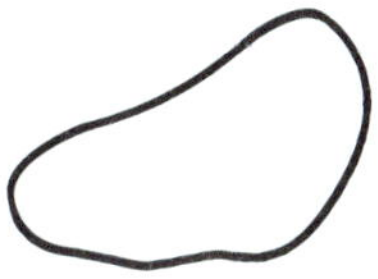

16. 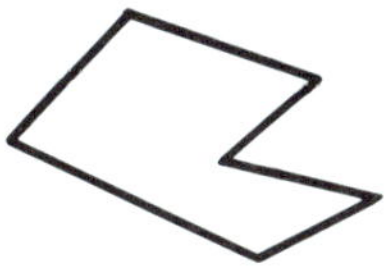

How many segments are in each figure?

17. 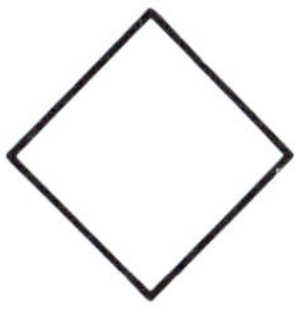

18. 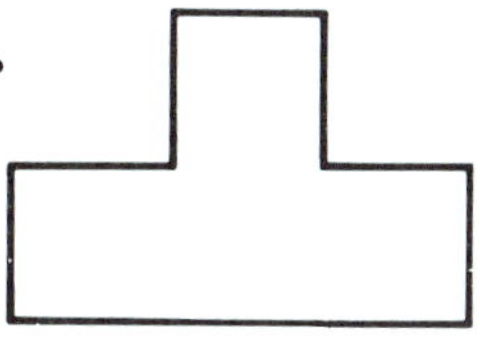

19. 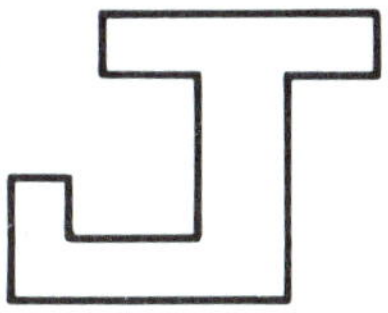

20. 

21. 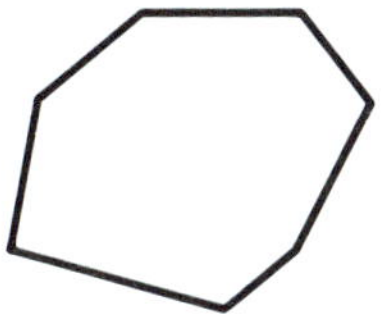

22. 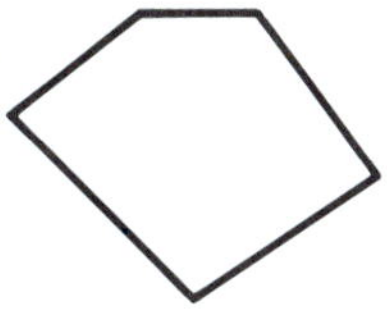

23. 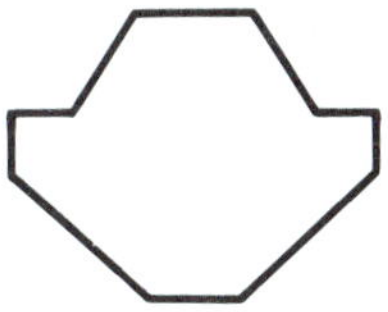

24. 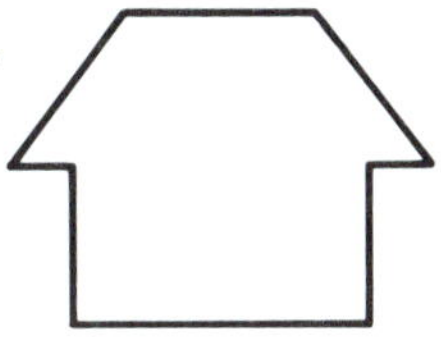

★ **25.** **Think:** Do all squares have the same number of segments?

★ **26.** **Think:** Do all rectangles have the same number of segments?

★ **27.** **Think:** Do all polygons have the same number of segments?

PROBLEM SOLVING APPLICATIONS
Choosing the Operation

Solve.

28. Bob buys 3 boxes of straws. Each box holds 326 straws. How many straws does Bob have?

29. Bob cuts the straws into different lengths. He has 90 straws and he cuts 37. How many straws are not cut?

30. Bob wants to make 6 polygons with 6 sides each. He uses 1 straw for each side. How many straws does he use?

★ **31.** Bob is building polygons with straws. He can build 5 polygons in 15 minutes. How long would it take him to build 15 polygons?

PERIMETER

The distance around a figure is its **perimeter.** To find a perimeter, you add the lengths of the sides.

10 cm
5 cm
10 cm
+ 5 cm
30 cm

The perimeter of the rectangle is 30 cm.

CLASS EXERCISES

Complete to find the perimeter.

1.

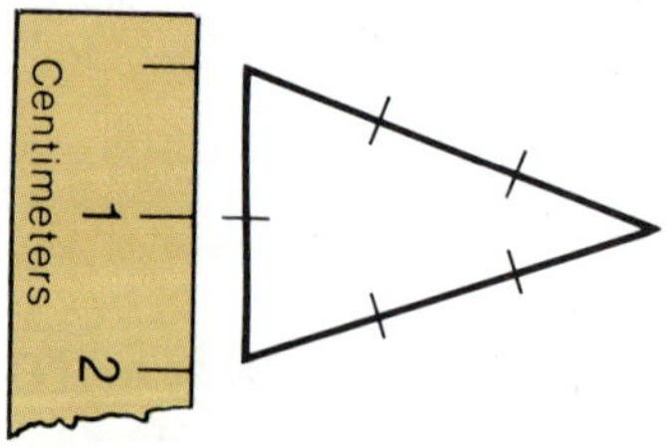

2 cm
3 cm
+ 3 cm
▢ cm

2.

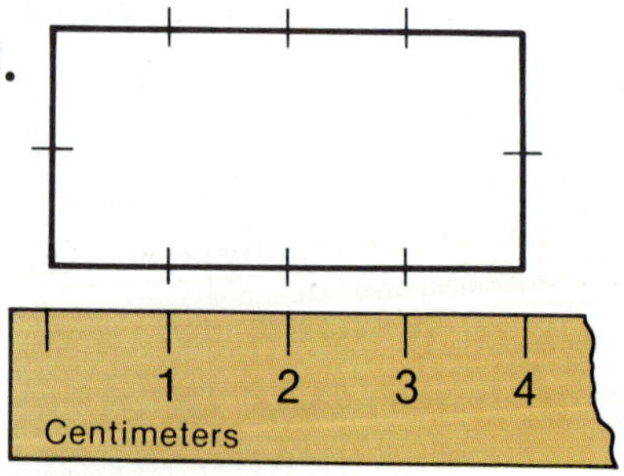

4 cm
2 cm
4 cm
+ 2 cm
▢ cm

PRACTICE

Find the perimeter. Use a centimeter ruler.

3.

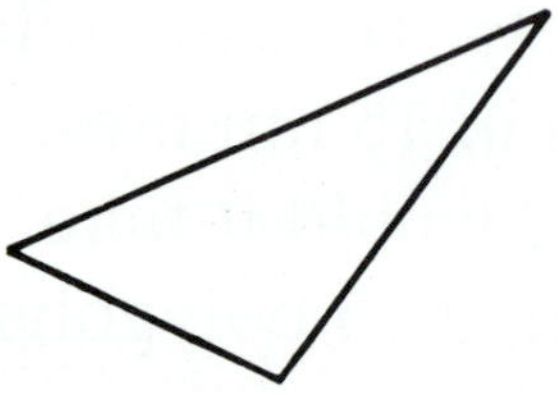

4.

5.

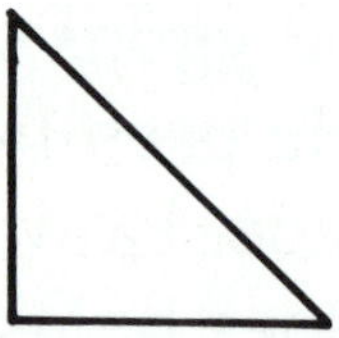

Find the perimeter of a figure with these measurements.

6. 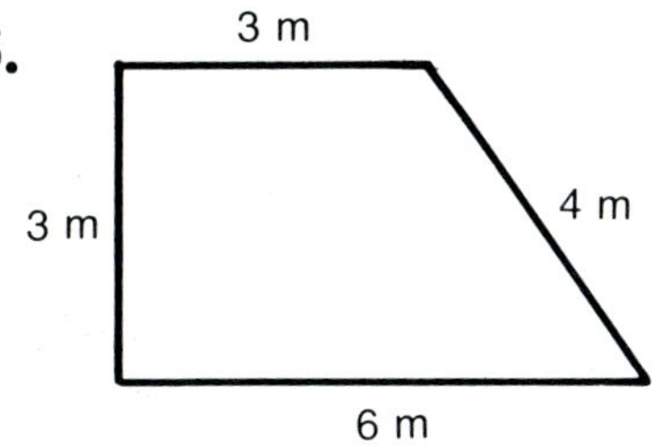

7. 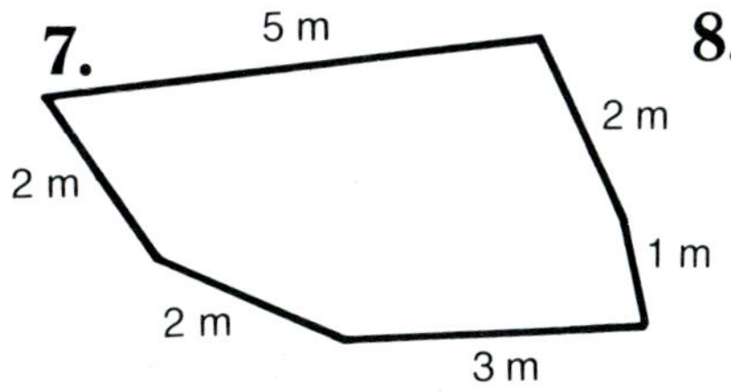

8. 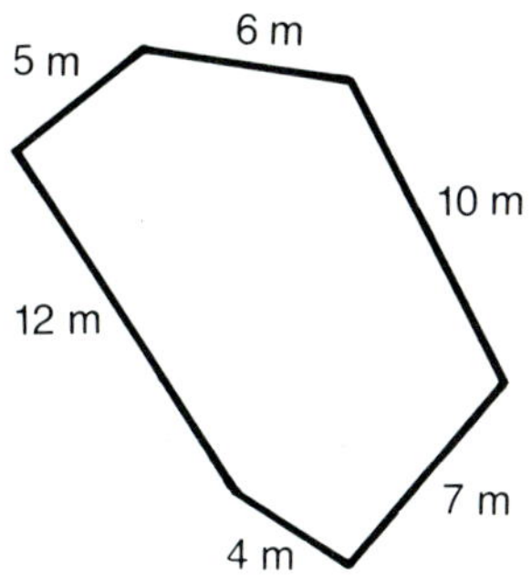

9. 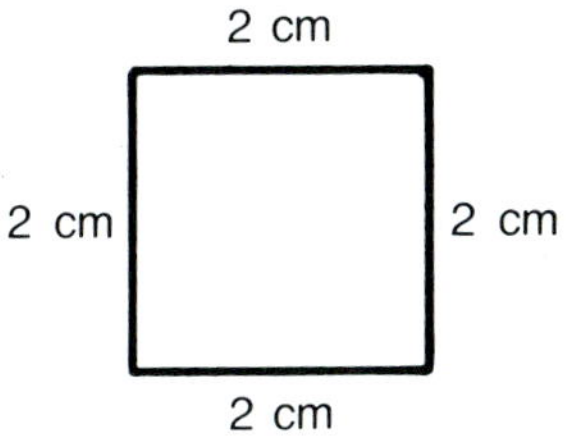

10. 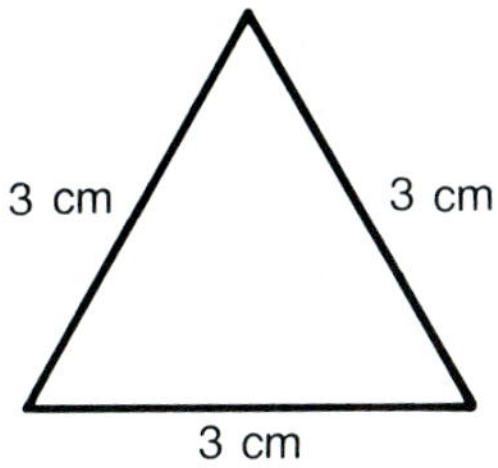

11. 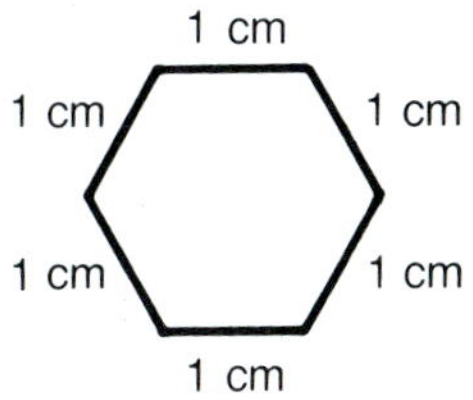

PROBLEM SOLVING APPLICATIONS
Using Pictures

Use the picture to help solve the problem.

12. A tennis court is the shape of a rectangle. Two sides are each 24 m long. Two sides are each 11 m long. What is the perimeter?

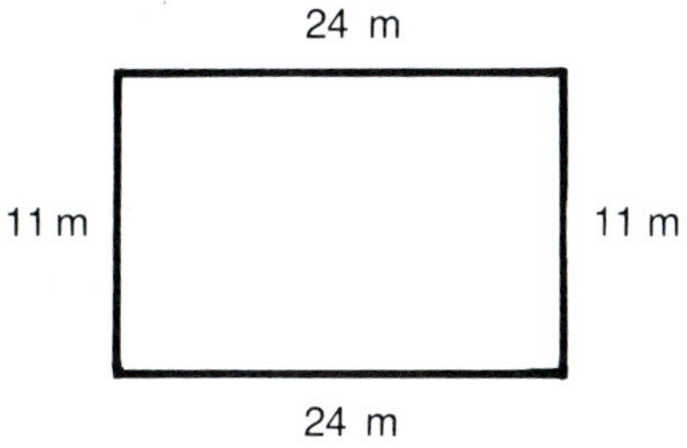

13. The class baseball team decided to make their baseball diamond 27 m on each side. What is the perimeter of the baseball diamond?

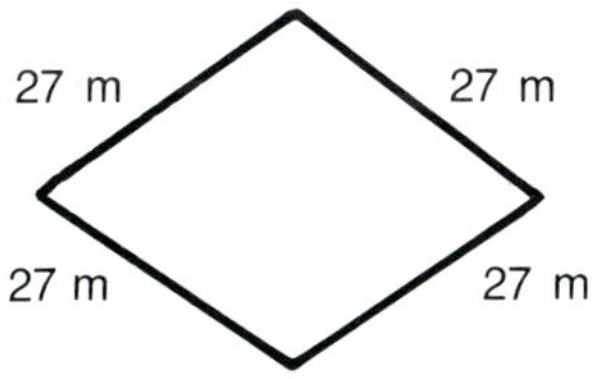

Draw a picture to help you solve.

★ 14. The perimeter of a rectangle is 100 m. One side is 20 m long. How long are the other sides?

AREA

Area is measured in **square units.** The area of the rectangle is the number of square units that fit inside the rectangle.

1 square unit

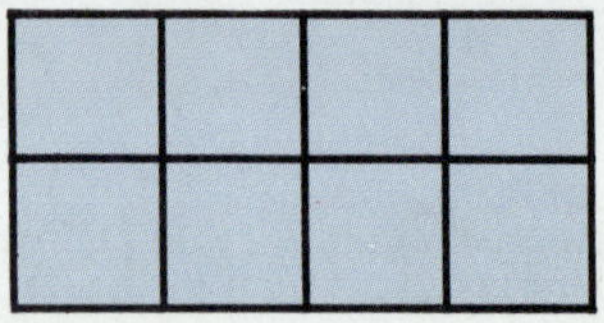

The rectangle has 2 rows of 4 square units. The area of the rectangle is 8 square units.

You can estimate that the area of this figure is less than 8 square units. There are 2 rows, but one row has fewer than 4 square units.

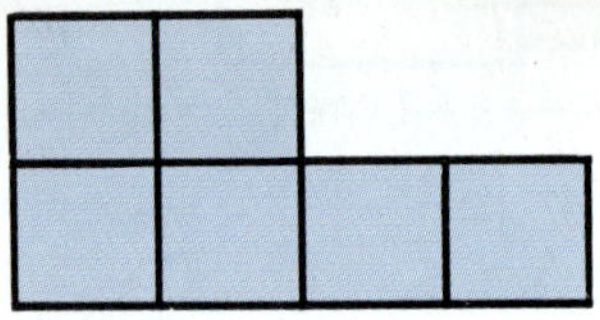

CLASS EXERCISES

How many square units are there?

1. 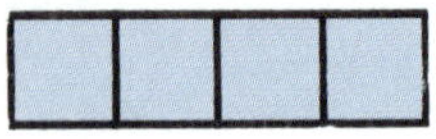

2. 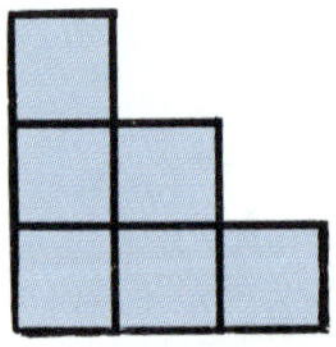

3. 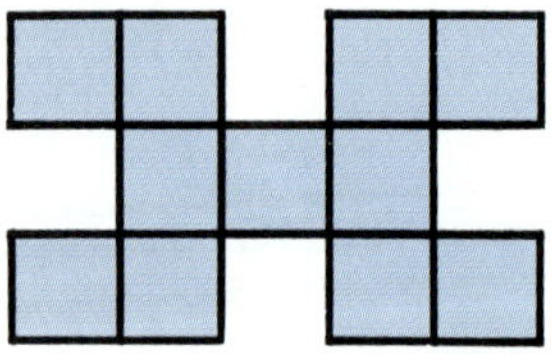

PRACTICE

What is the area?

4. 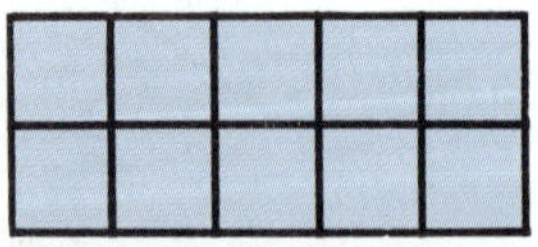

5. 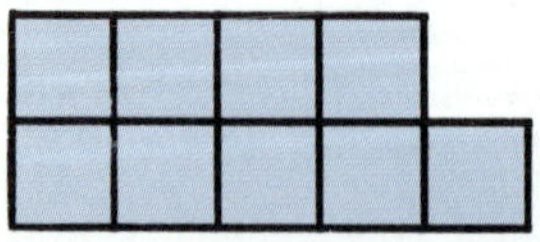

6. 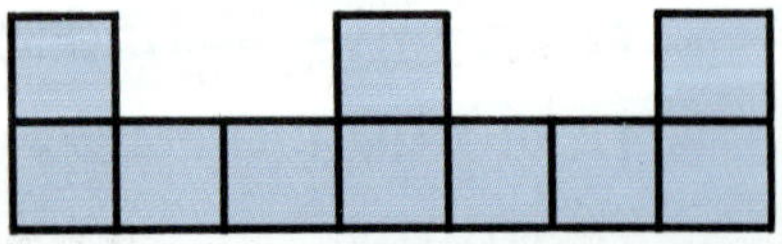

7. 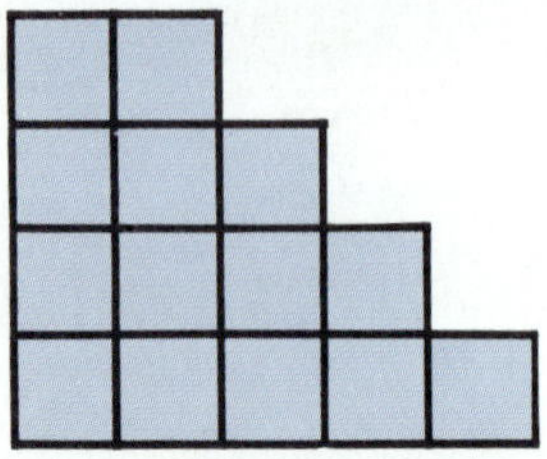

8. 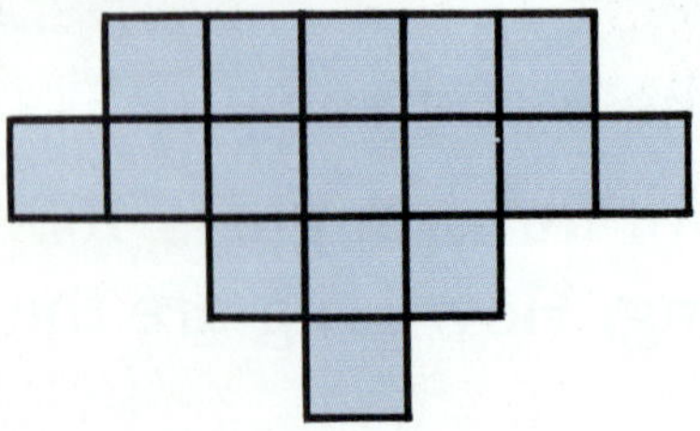

9. 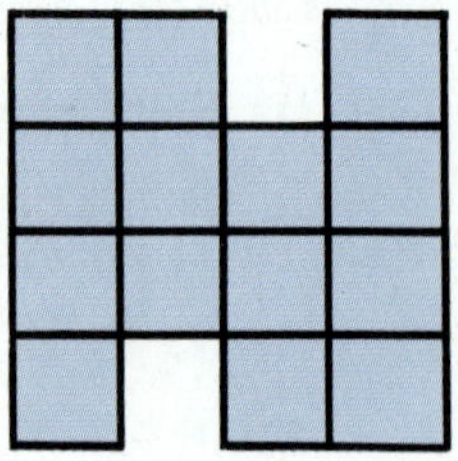

10.

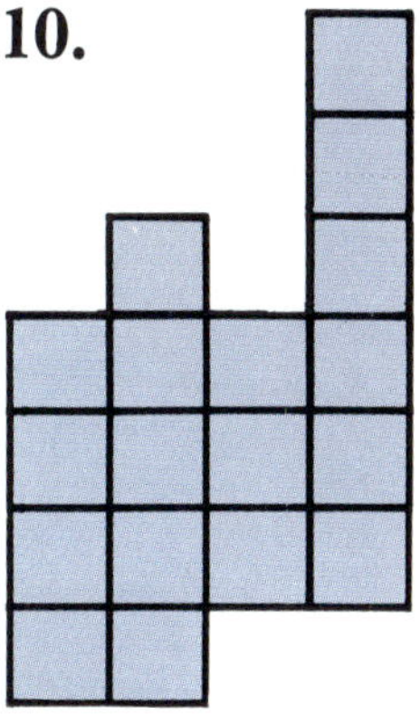

11.

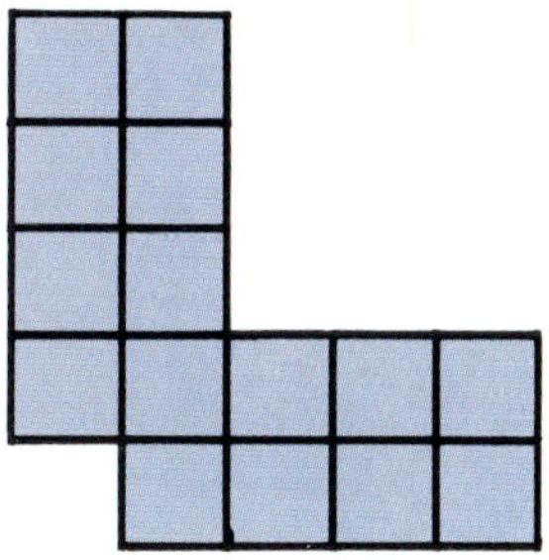

12.

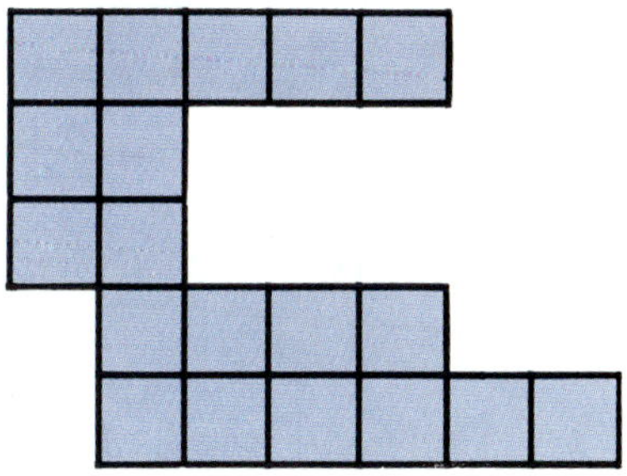

Estimate which has the greater area. Write *a* or *b*. Then count to check your answer.

ESTIMATE

13. a.

b.

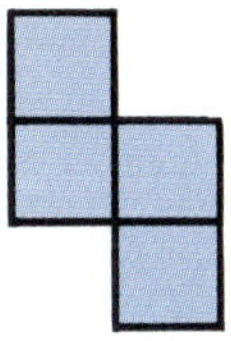

14. a.

b.

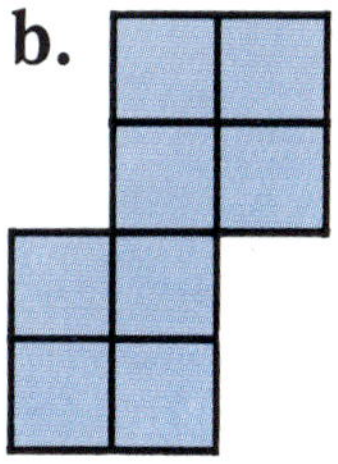

15. a.

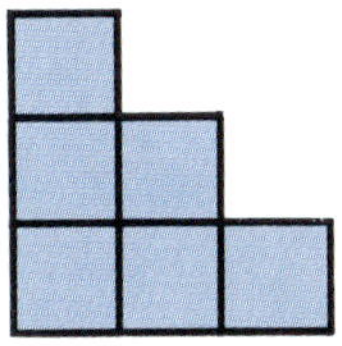

b.

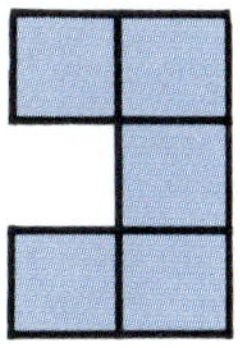

PROBLEM SOLVING APPLICATIONS

Solve.

16. Molly is making a quilt. It has 6 rows of 8 squares. How many squares are in the quilt?

17. It takes Molly 1 hour to sew a hem. She starts sewing at 7:00 P.M. What time does Molly finish?

★ **18.** When Molly has one half of a 48-square quilt made, how many squares will she have in the quilt?

★ **19.** Bill sews 4 small squares together to make a large square. How many sides of each small square does he sew?

PROBLEM SOLVING

Strategy: Sorting and Classifying

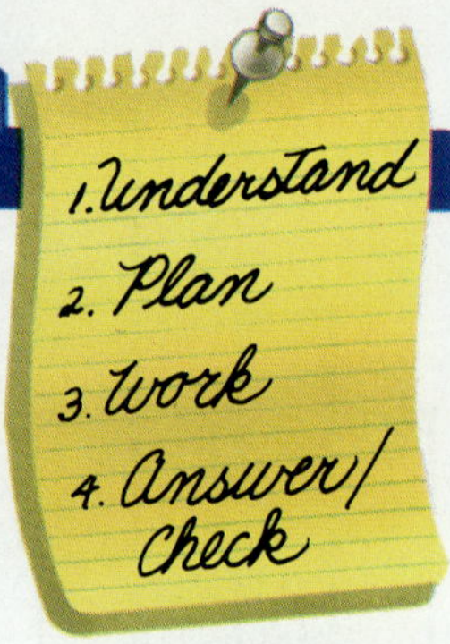

Have you ever grouped objects that are the same?

The objects in this circle are the same shape.

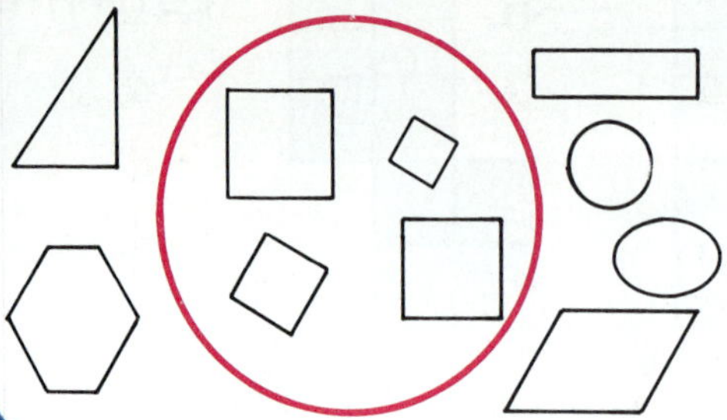

The objects in this circle are not polygons.

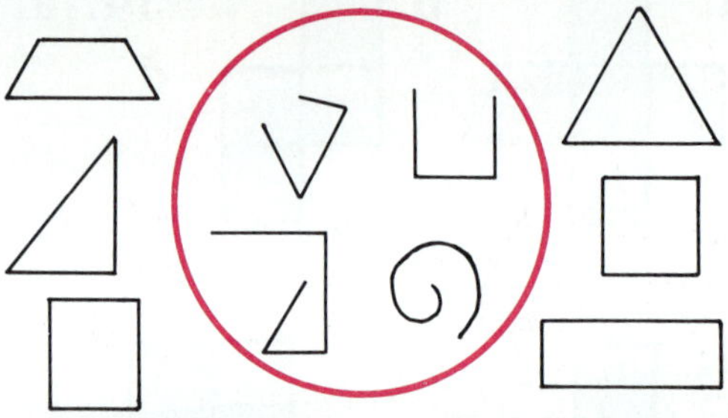

CLASS EXERCISES

How are the objects in the circle alike?

1.

2.

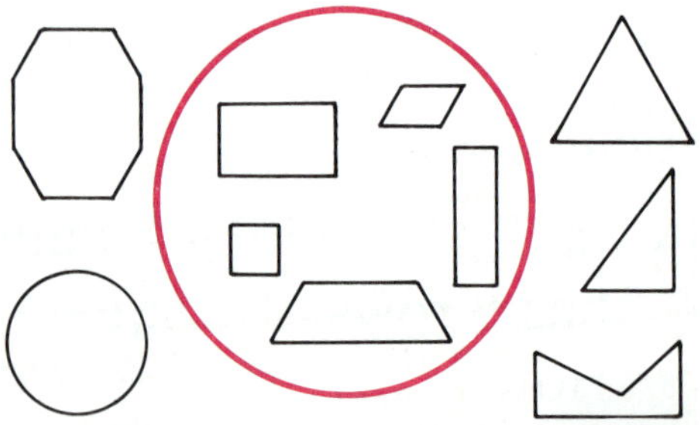

3.

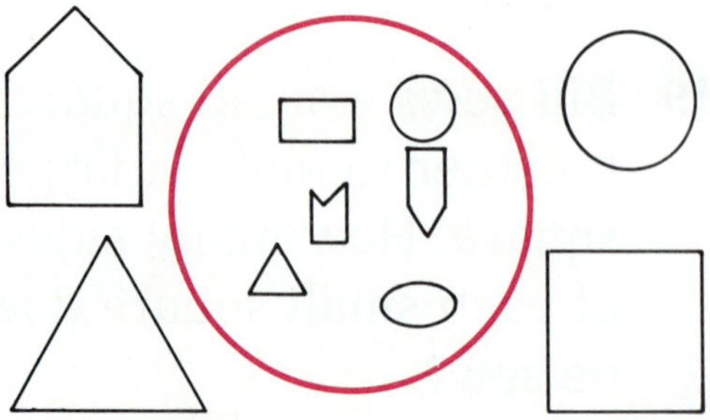

4.

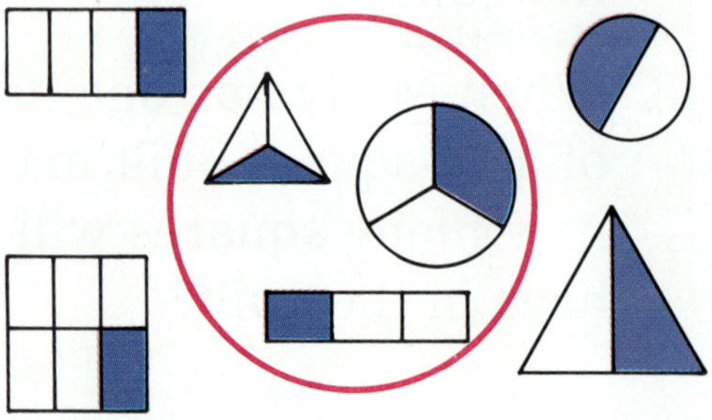

PRACTICE

Write the letter of the figure that does not belong.

5. 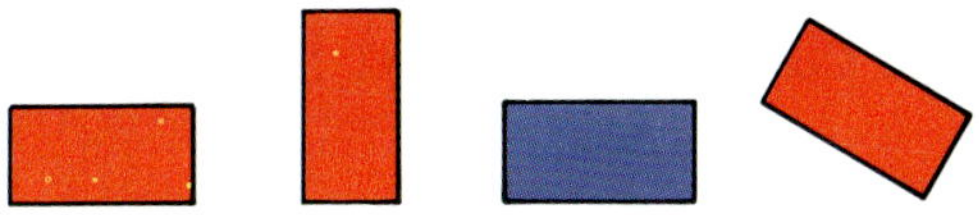

a. b. c. d.

6. 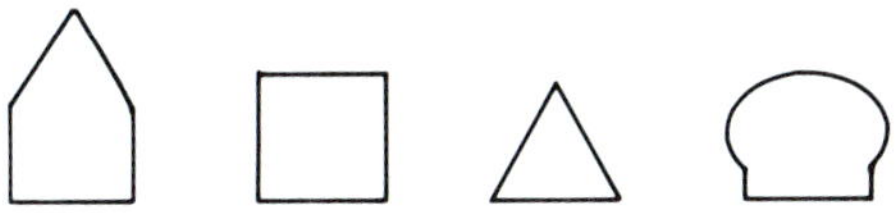

a. b. c. d.

7. 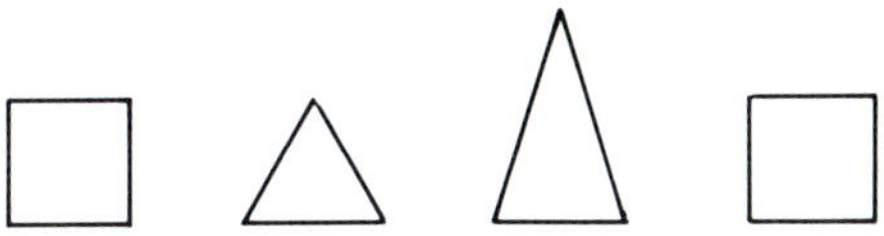

a. b. c. d.

8. 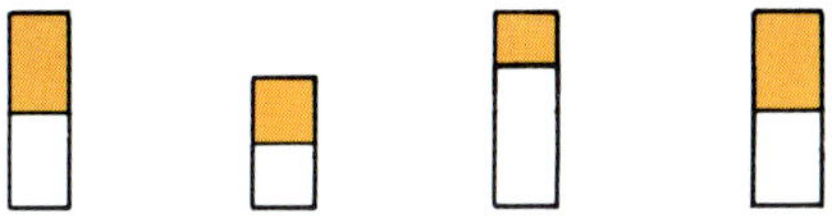

a. b. c. d.

9. 

a. b. c. d.

10. 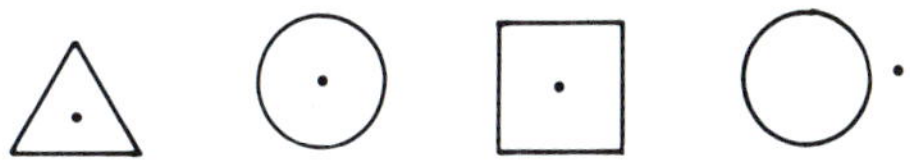

a. b. c. d.

11. 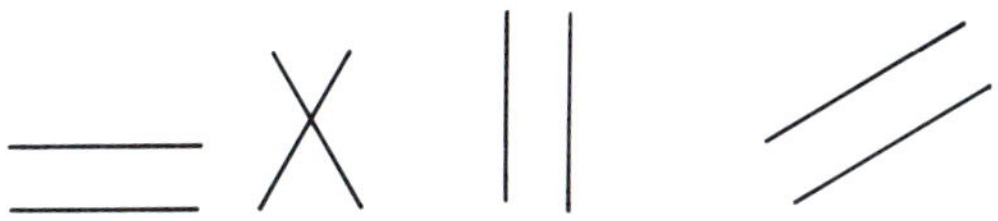

a. b. c. d.

12. 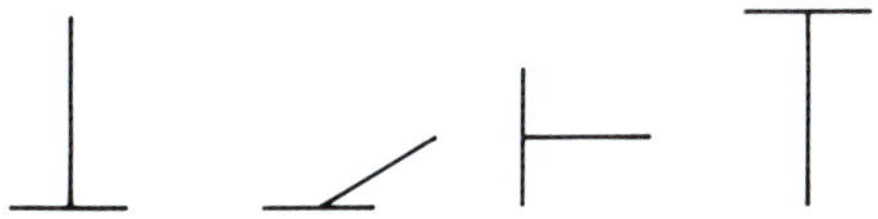

a. b. c. d.

CHECKPOINT 1

Name the polygon. *(pages 370–373)*

1. 

2. 

Find the perimeter. *(pages 374–375)*

3. 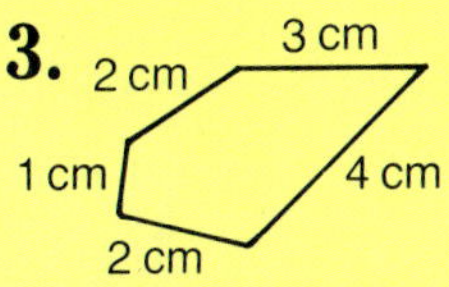

4. 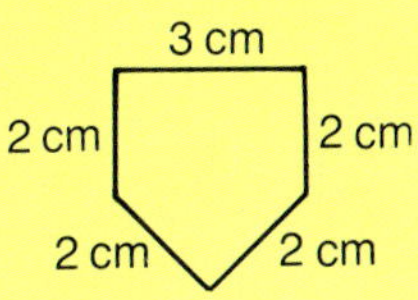

Find the area. *(pages 376–377)*

5. 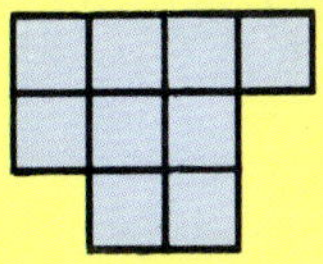

6. Write the letter of the shape that does not belong. *(pages 378–379)*

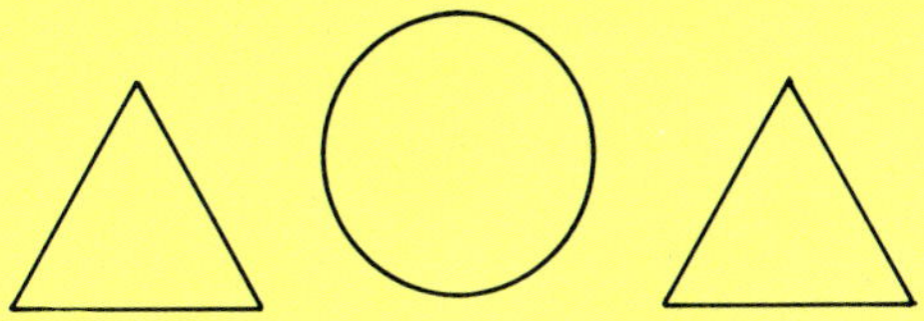

a. b. c.

Extra practice on page 424

SYMMETRY

You can fold these figures on the dotted line so that the two parts match. You call the dotted line a **line of symmetry.**

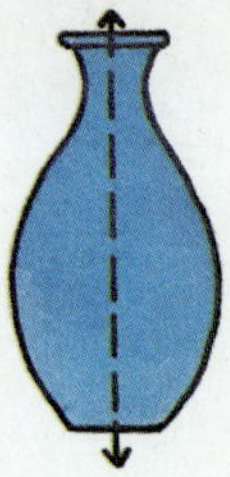
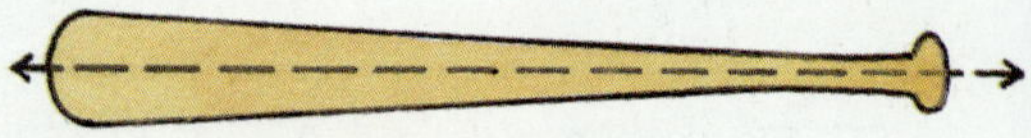

You can fold this figure two ways. Each way the two parts match. This figure has two lines of symmetry.

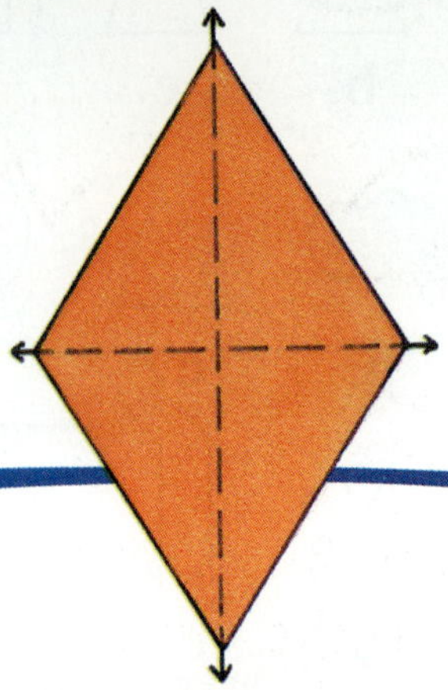

CLASS EXERCISES

Do the parts match when you fold them on the dotted line? Tell why or why not.

1. 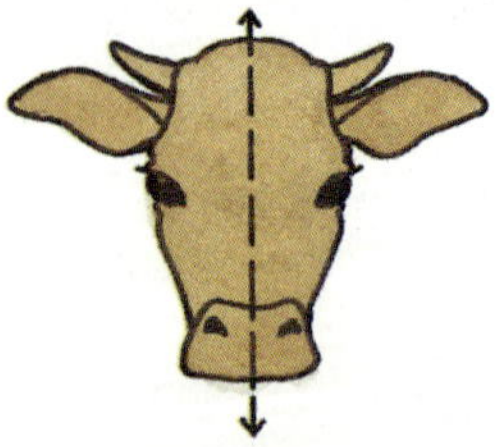

2. 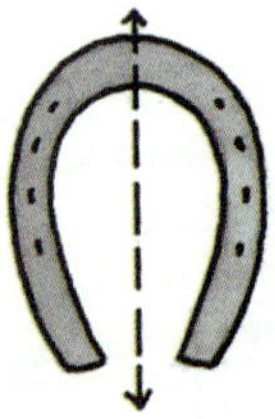

3. 

PRACTICE

Are the dotted lines on the figure lines of symmetry? Write *yes* or *no*.

4. 

5. 

6. 

7. 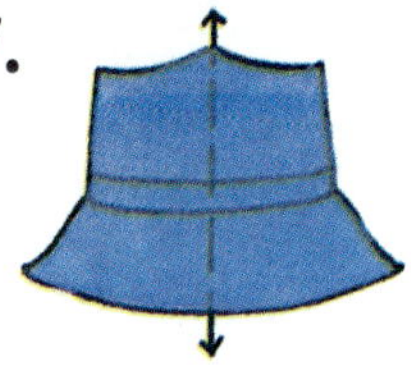 **8.** 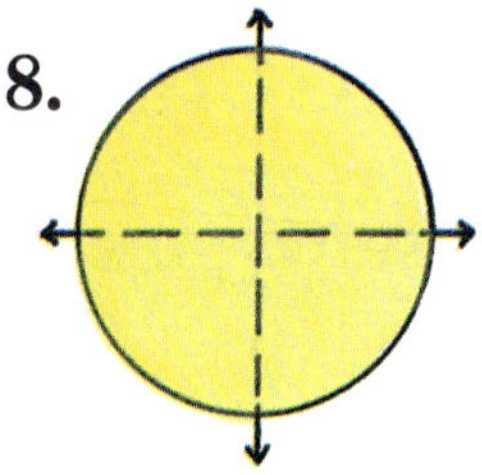 **9.**  **10.** 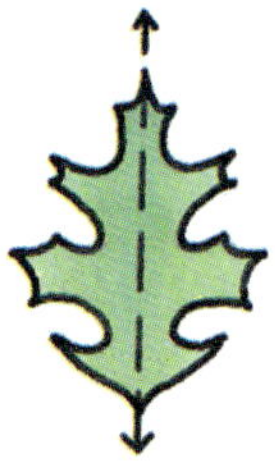

11. 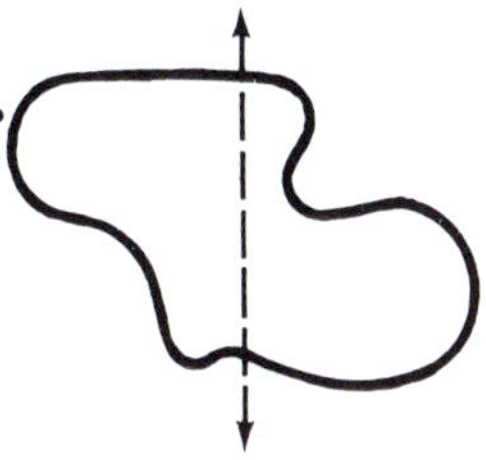 **12.** 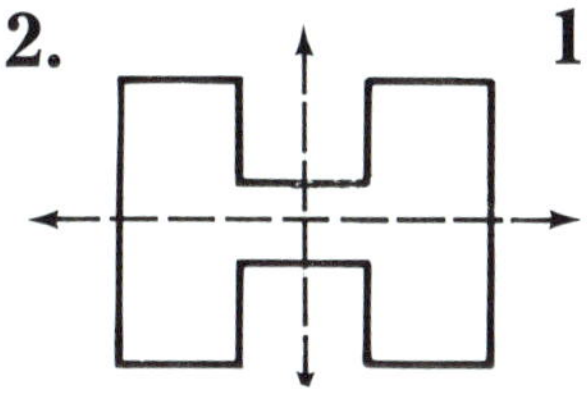 **13.** 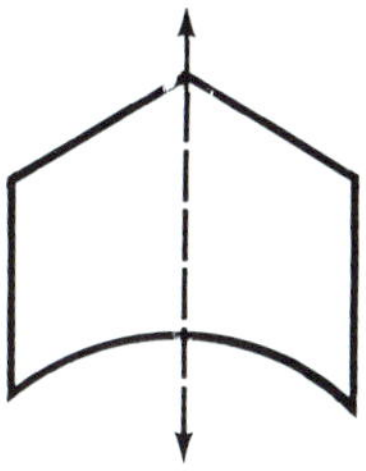 **14.** 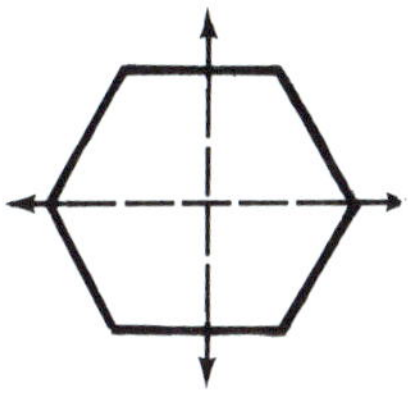

15. 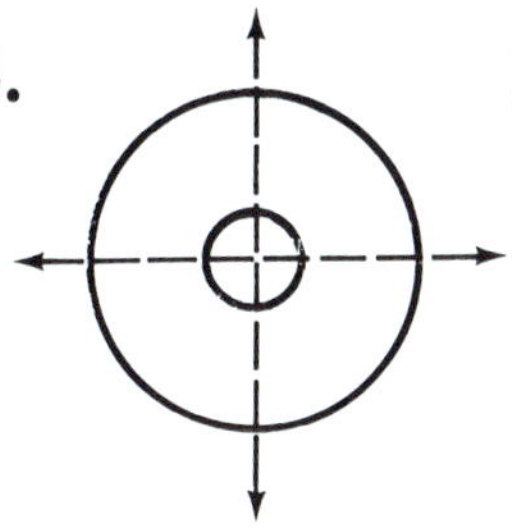 **16.** 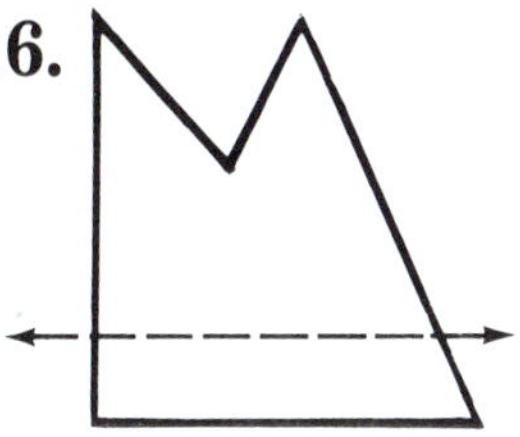 **17.** 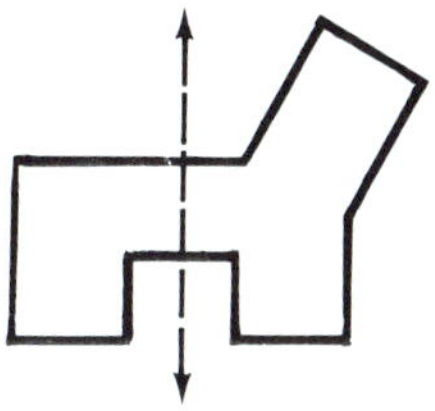 **18.** 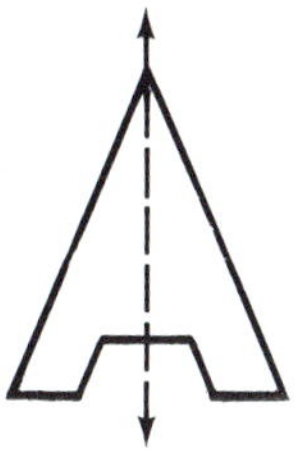

Write 0, 1, or 2 for the number of lines of symmetry in the picture.

19.  **20.** 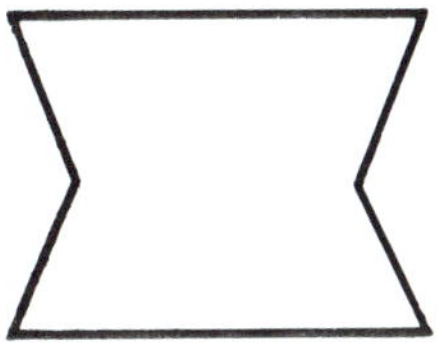 **21.** 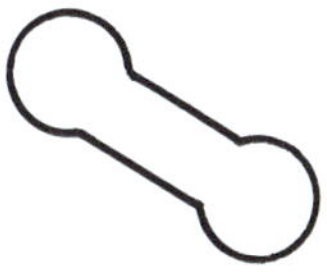 **22.** 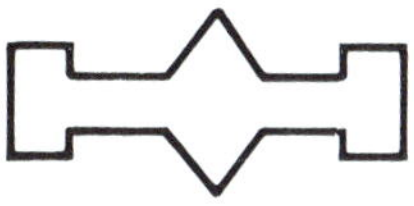

23.  **24.** 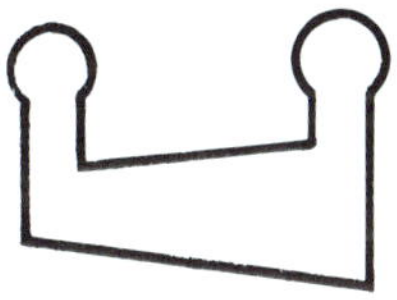 **25.**  **26.** 

PROBLEM SOLVING APPLICATIONS
Letters and Numbers

Solve.

27. Write the letters that have lines of symmetry.

G, M, D, O, T, B

28. Write the digits that have lines of symmetry.

0, 2, 8, 5, 3, 7

★ **29.** Write the digits that could have two lines of symmetry.

CONGRUENT FIGURES

Figures that are exactly the same size and shape are **congruent**.

These two figures are congruent.

These two figures are not congruent.

When two figures are congruent, you can match them in one of these ways.

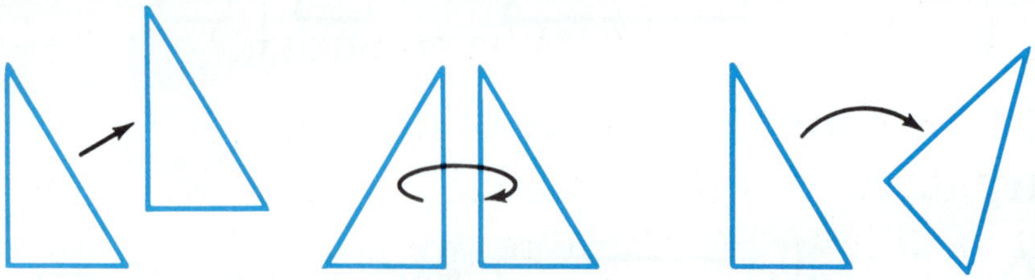

slide flip turn

You can picture a slide, flip, or turn in your mind to decide if two figures are congruent.

CLASS EXERCISES

Do the figures look congruent? Think of a slide, flip, or turn.

1. 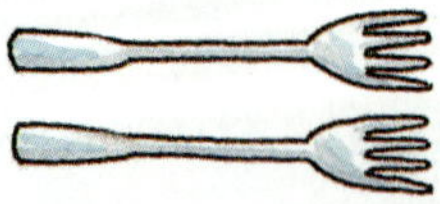
2. 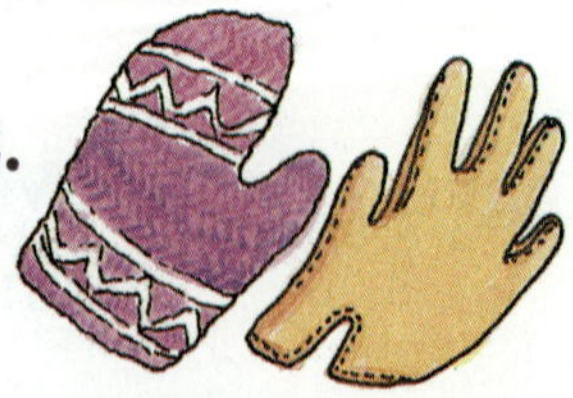
3. 
4. 
5. 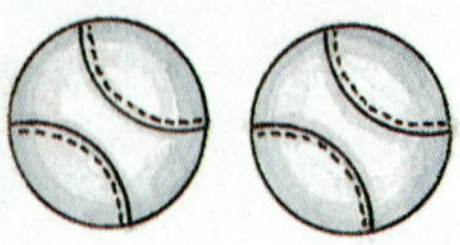
6. 

PRACTICE

Do these figures look congruent? Write *yes* or *no*.

7. 

8. 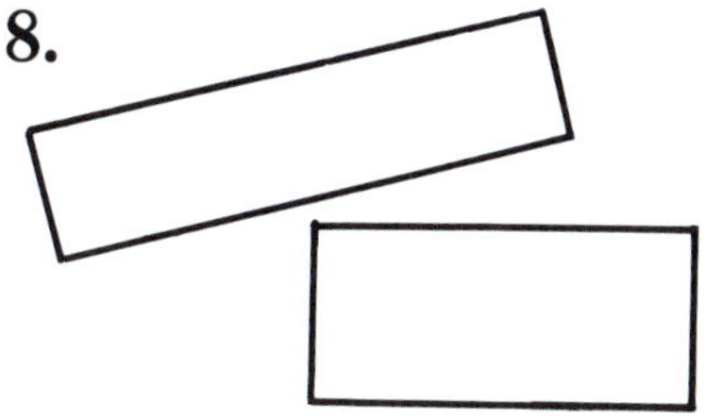

9. 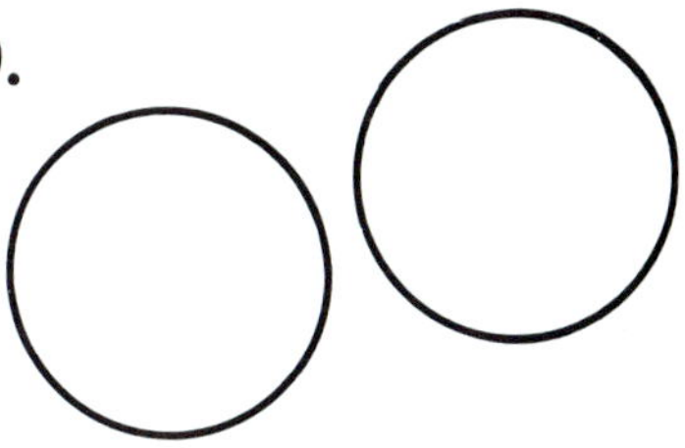

10. 

11. 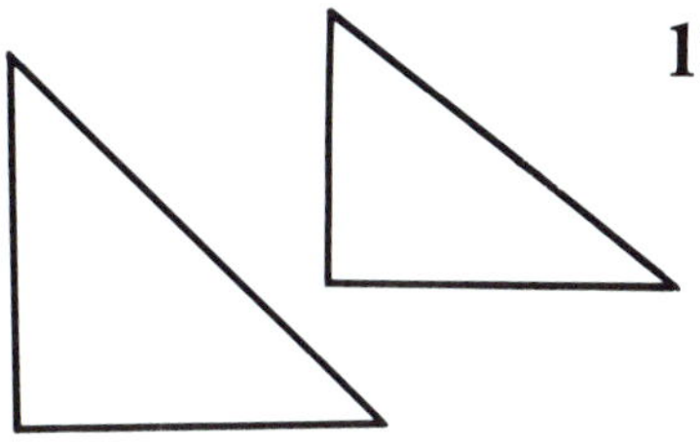

12. 

Think: Will the figure *always* be congruent? Write *yes* or *no*.

★ **13.** two figures that each have 5 sides

★ **14.** two figures that are both round

★ **15.** two squares that each have sides measuring 4 in.

PROBLEM SOLVING APPLICATIONS
Nonroutine Problems

Match. Write the letter.

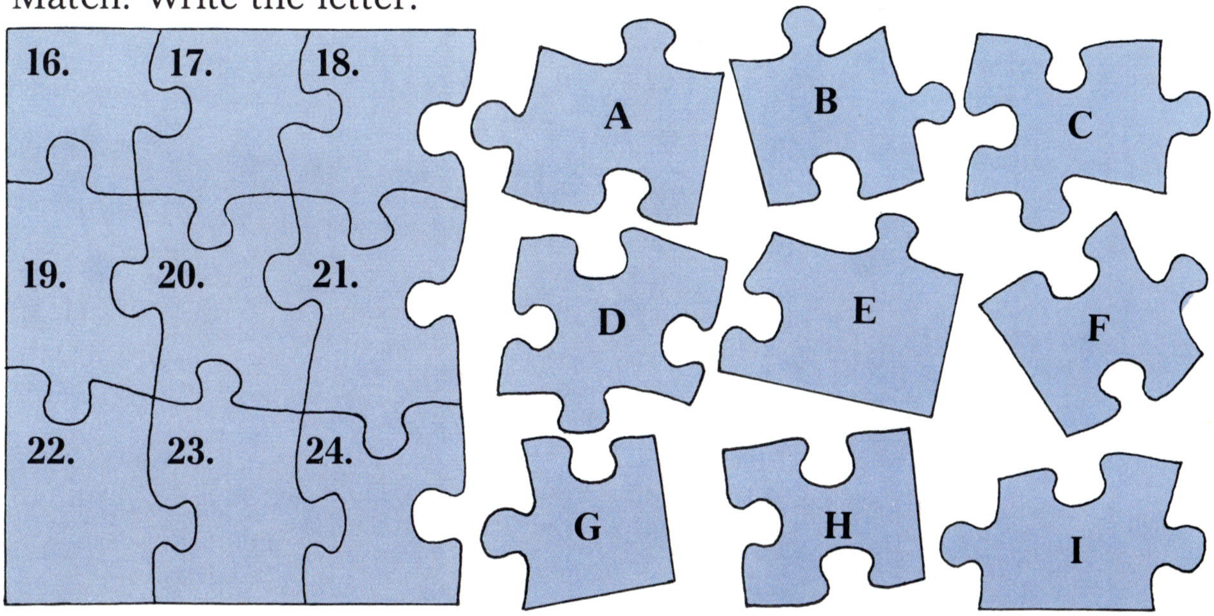

SIMILAR FIGURES

Figures that are the same shape but not necessarily the same size are **similar**.

These two shapes are similar.

These two shapes are not similar.

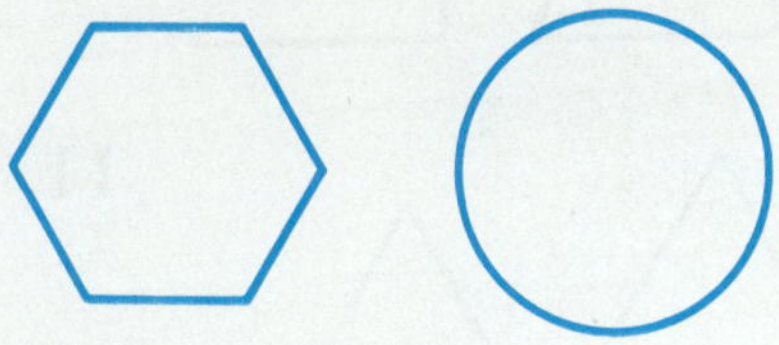

CLASS EXERCISES

Are the figures similar? Why or why not?

1. 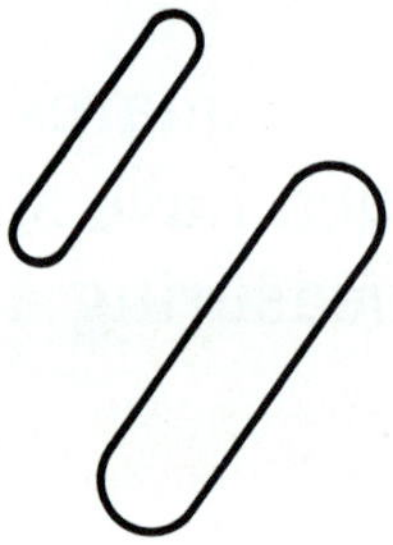

2. 

3. 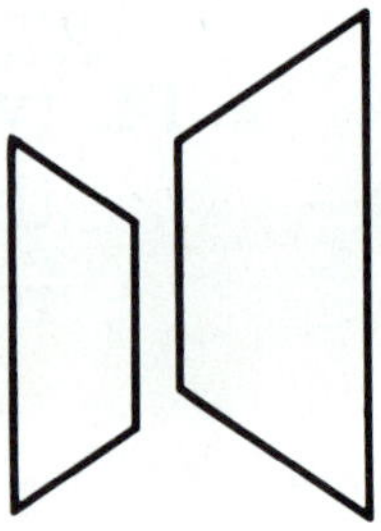

4. 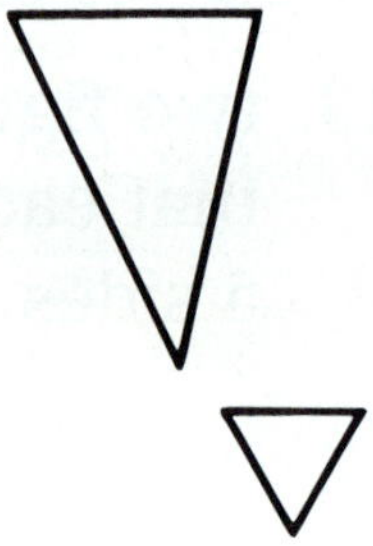

PRACTICE

Are the figures similar? Write *yes* or *no*.

5. 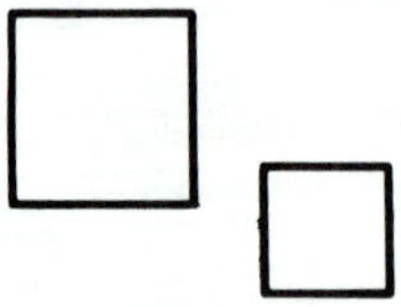

6. 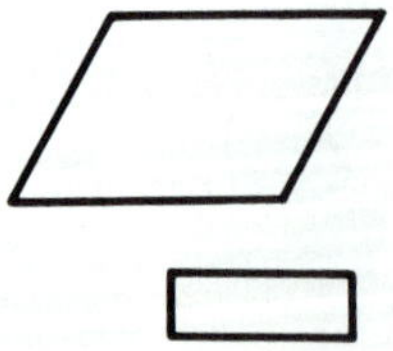

7. 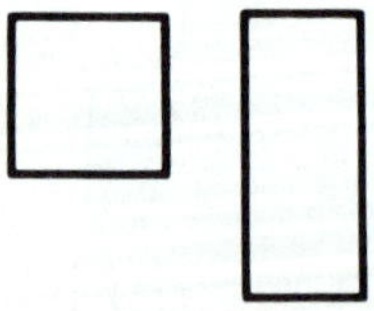

8. 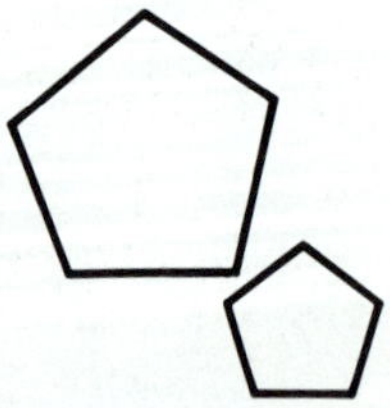

9. 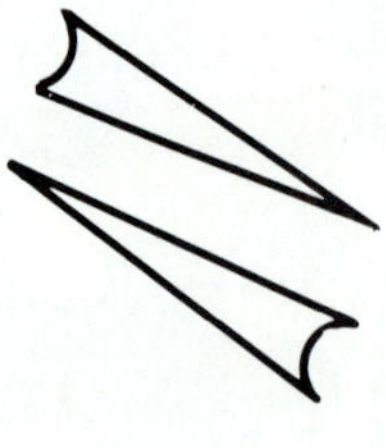

10. 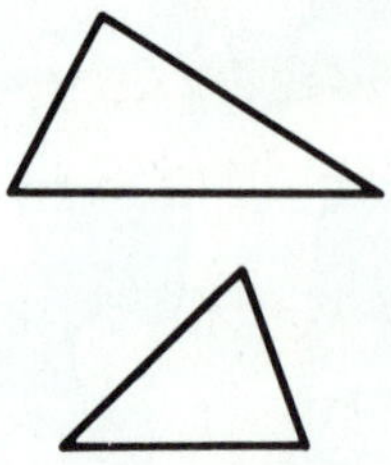

11. 

12. 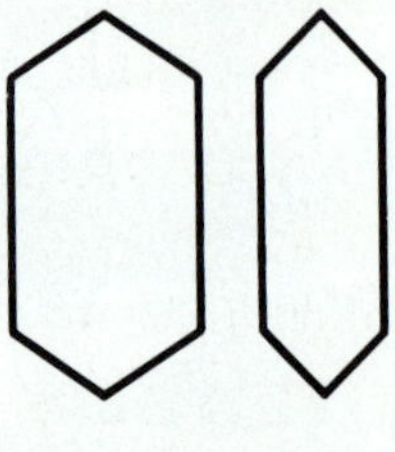

13. 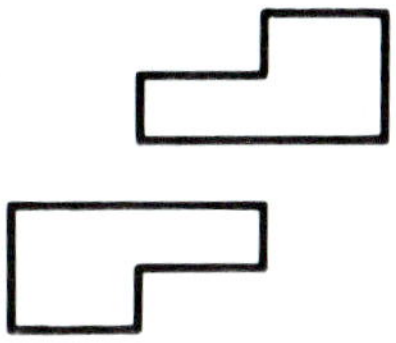

14. 

15. 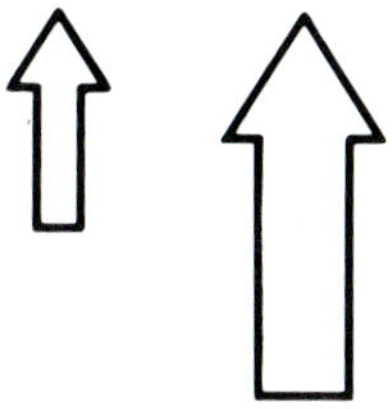

16. 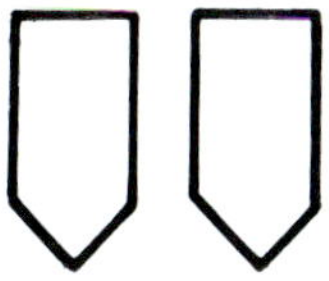

17. 

18. 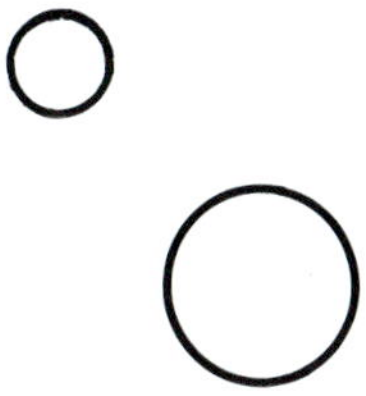

19. 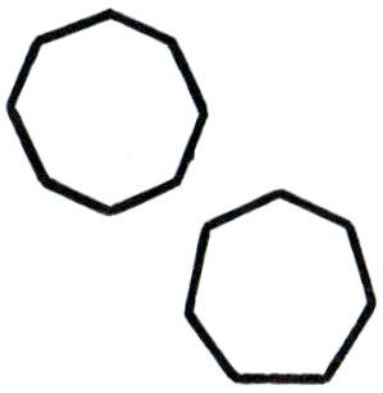

20. 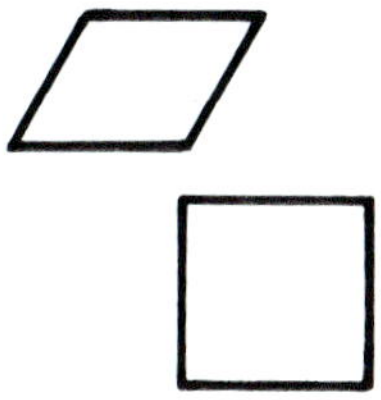

Write the answer.

MIXED REVIEW

21. $\begin{array}{r} 0.6 \\ +\ 0.2 \\ \hline \end{array}$ **22.** $\begin{array}{r} 3.4 \\ -\ 2.7 \\ \hline \end{array}$ **23.** $\begin{array}{r} 5.6 \\ +\ 7.2 \\ \hline \end{array}$ **24.** $\begin{array}{r} 20.5 \\ -\ 11.7 \\ \hline \end{array}$

25. $\begin{array}{r} 29 \\ \times 2 \\ \hline \end{array}$ **26.** $\begin{array}{r} 435 \\ \times 3 \\ \hline \end{array}$ **27.** $3\overline{)78}$ **28.** $4\overline{)248}$

PROBLEM SOLVING APPLICATIONS
Choosing a Strategy

Solve.

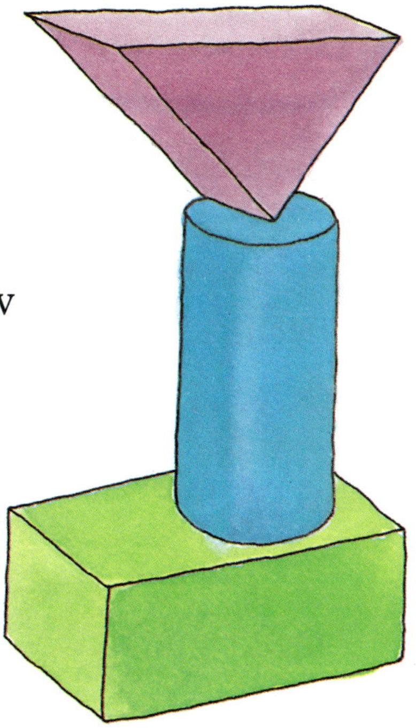

29. Diana is making a dress. She cuts out two sleeves to match. Are the sleeves similar?

30. Mary is doing a puzzle. There are 296 pieces. She fits 132 of the pieces. About how many more pieces does she still have to fit?

31. Antoine bought 28 toy shapes. He has an equal number of rectangles, squares, and triangles. How many circles does he have?

★ **32.** Diana has 320 blocks. Florence has 5 more blocks than Diana and 7 fewer blocks than Mary. How many blocks does Mary have?

SOLID SHAPES

You have probably seen objects that have these shapes.

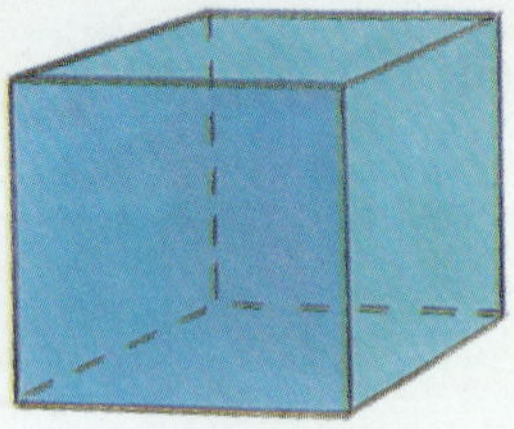

cube

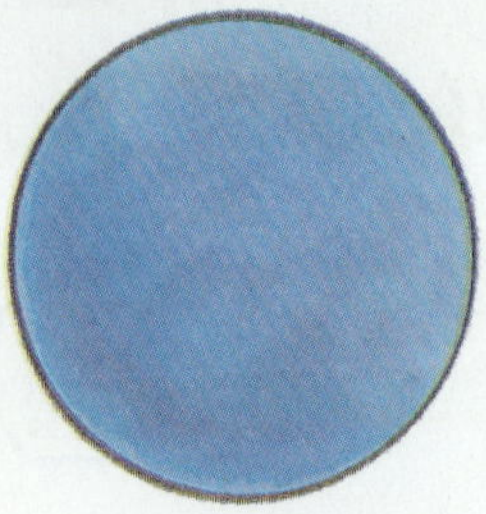

sphere

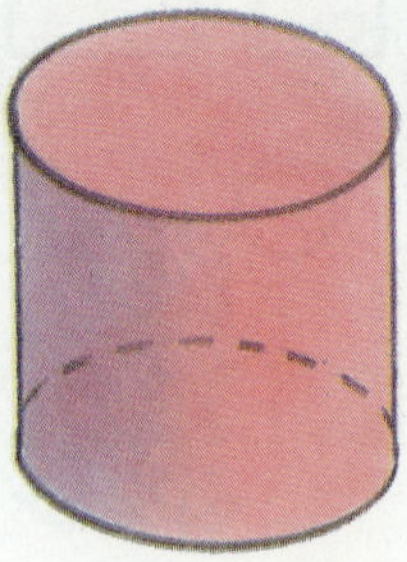

cylinder

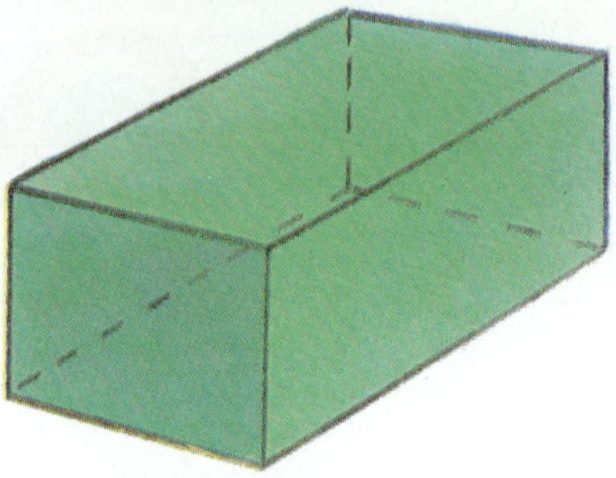

rectangular prism

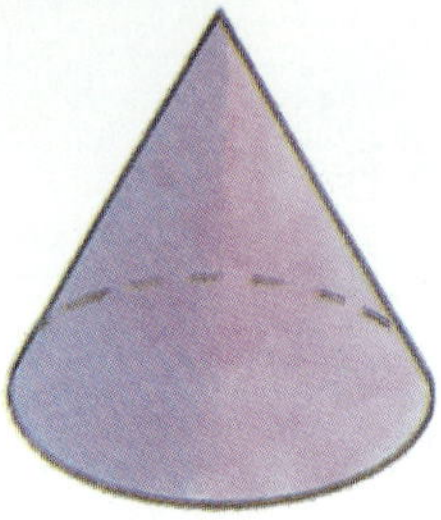

cone

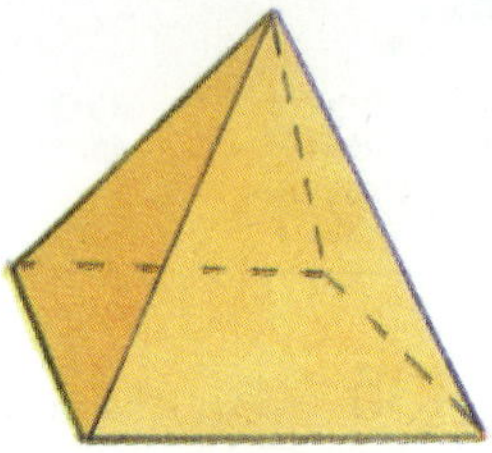

pyramid

M You can think of real objects that have these shapes. For example, a tennis ball is a sphere.

Think: What object has the shape of a cylinder?

CLASS EXERCISES

Match. Write the letter.

1. cube
2. sphere
3. cylinder
4. cone
5. pyramid
6. rectangular prism

A. 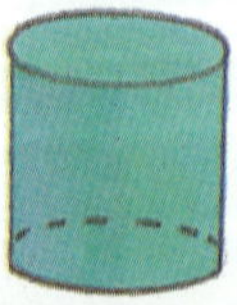

B. 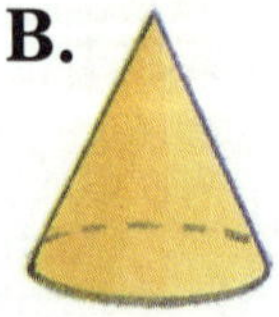

C. 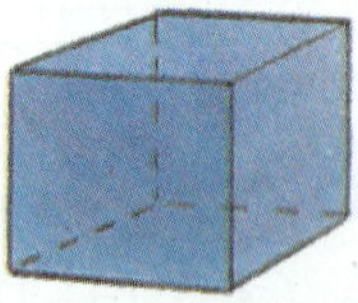

D. 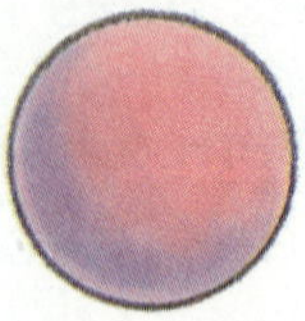

E. 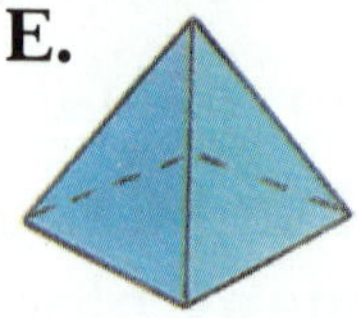

F. 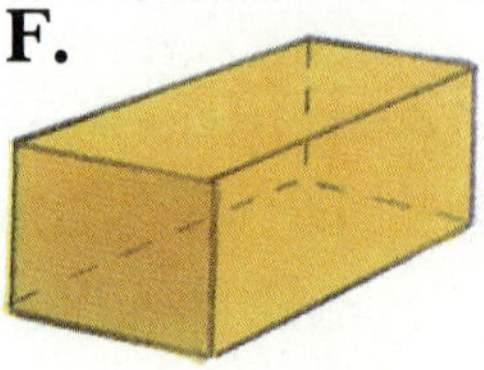

PRACTICE

Name the shape. Write *cube, cone, sphere, cylinder, pyramid,* or *rectangular prism.*

7. 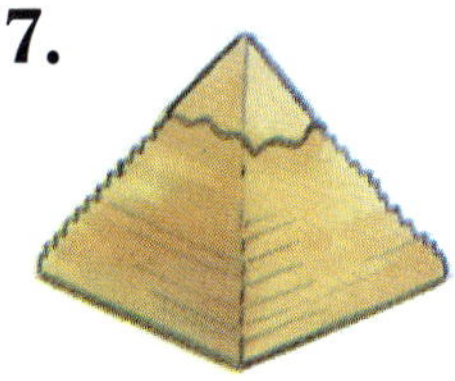

8. 

9. 

10. 

11. 

12. 

13. 

14. 

15. 

16. 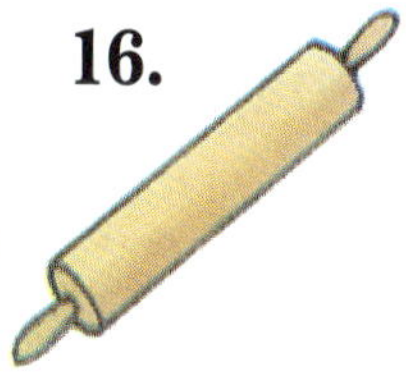

Think of the most likely shape.

MENTAL MATH

17. Is a shoe box shaped like a cube or a rectangular prism?

18. Is a globe shaped like a sphere or a pyramid?

19. Is a funnel shaped like a cone or a cylinder?

PROBLEM SOLVING APPLICATIONS
Sorting and Classifying Shapes

Write the name for the shape or shapes.

20. Which shapes can roll?

21. Which shapes cannot roll?

22. Which shapes have no curved parts?

23. Which shape has a flat part at only one end?

24. Which shape has no flat parts?

25. Which shape has one circle at each end?

★ **26.** How many corners does a cube have?

★ **27.** How many flat parts does a rectangular prism have?

VOLUME

This is a **cubic unit.** The **volume** of a figure is the number of cubic units it contains. You count cubic units to find the volume of a shape.

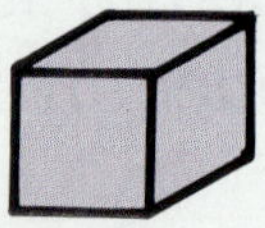

The volume of this shape is 8 cubic units. You can see all of them and count them easily.

You cannot always see all the cubic units of a shape. This shape has 4 cubic units in each layer. The volume is 8 cubic units.

M Different figures can have the same volume.

Think: What is another way to picture a figure with a volume of 8 cubic units?

CLASS EXERCISES

Complete.

1.

___?___ cubic units

2.

___?___ cubic units

3.

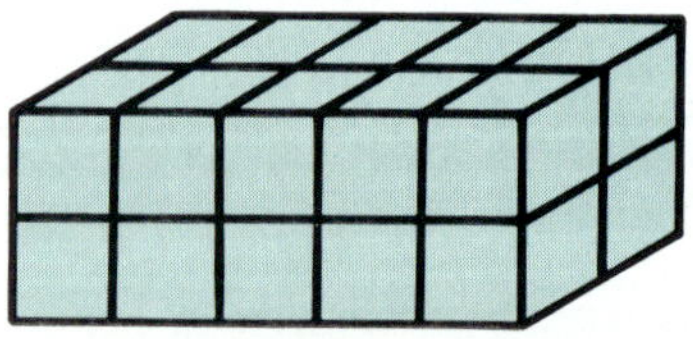

___?___ cubic units

PRACTICE

Write the volume in cubic units.

4.

5.

6.

7. 

8. 

9. 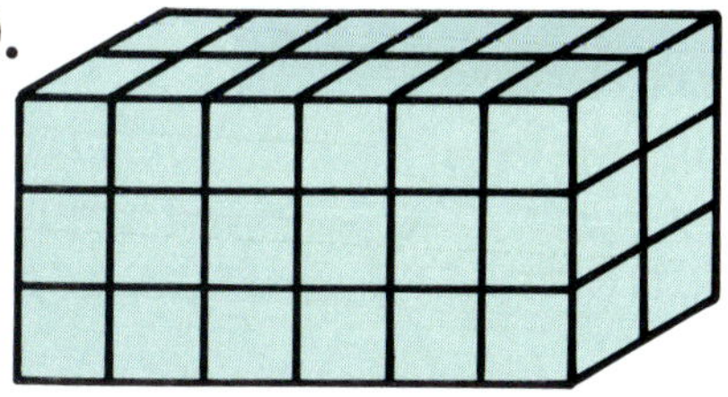

Which has the greater volume, *a* or *b*?

10. a. 

b. 

11. a. 

b. 

Picture the figure in your mind. Then match.
Write the letter.

MENTAL MATH

12. Four cubic units in a row

13. A rectangular prism missing a cubic unit

14. Four cubic units forming a T

15. A cube with 4 cubic units on each side

A. 

B. 

C. 

D. 

PROBLEM SOLVING APPLICATIONS
Drawing a picture

Use 1 block as 1 cubic unit. Solve.
Draw a picture to help you.

16. Sam is building with blocks. He puts 3 blocks in each row and makes 4 rows. What is the volume of his shape?

★ **17.** Janet fills a box with blocks. Each layer has 3 rows of 5 blocks. She makes 3 layers. What is the volume of the box?

PROBLEM SOLVING

Strategy: Patterns and Logic

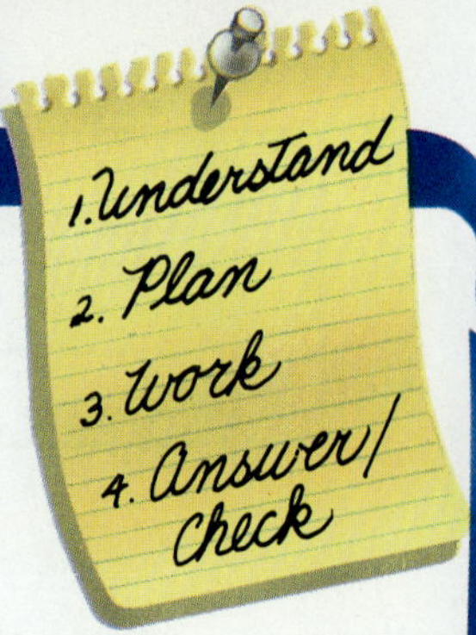

Patterns are everywhere.

The key flipped to make this pattern.

The key turned to make this pattern.

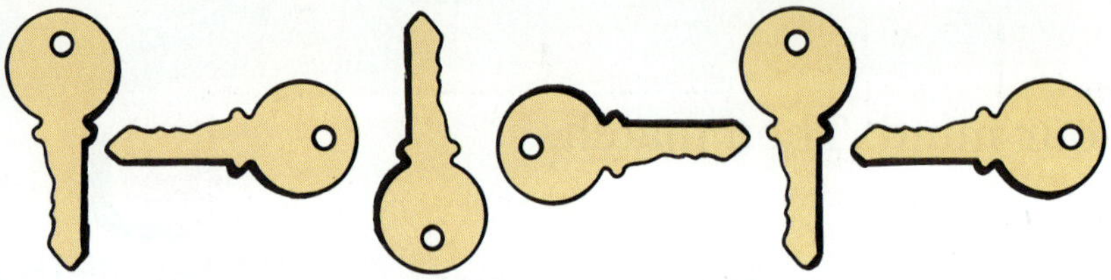

CLASS EXERCISES

Do you flip or turn the figure to make the pattern?

1. 

2. 

3. 

4. 

PRACTICE

Draw the shape that comes next in the pattern.

5. 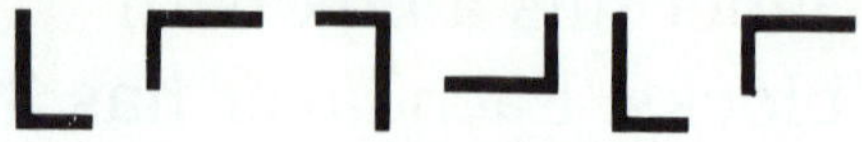

6. 

7. 

8. 

9. 

10. 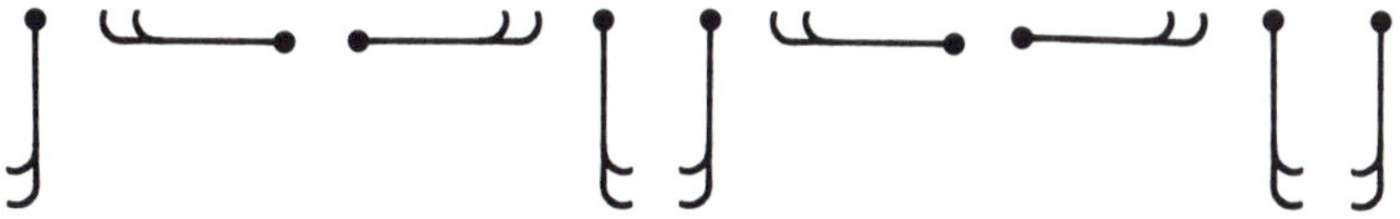

11. 

12. 

★ 13. 

CHECKPOINT 2

Is there a line of symmetry? Write *yes* or *no*. *(pages 380–381)*

1. 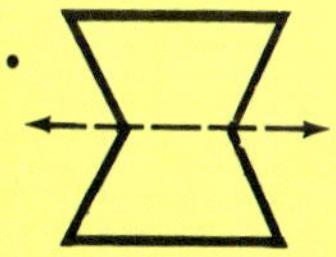

2. 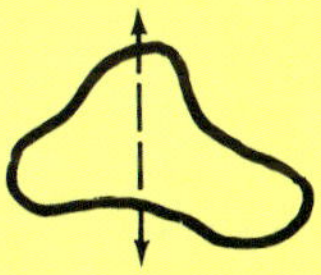

Write *C* if the figures look congruent. Write *S* if the figures look similar. *(pages 382–385)*

3. 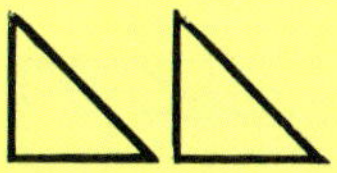

4. 

Write the volume in cubic units. *(pages 388–389)*

5. 

Draw the shape that comes next. *(pages 390–391)*

6. 

Extra practice on page 424

CHAPTER 13 TEST

Write the number. *(pages 370–373)*

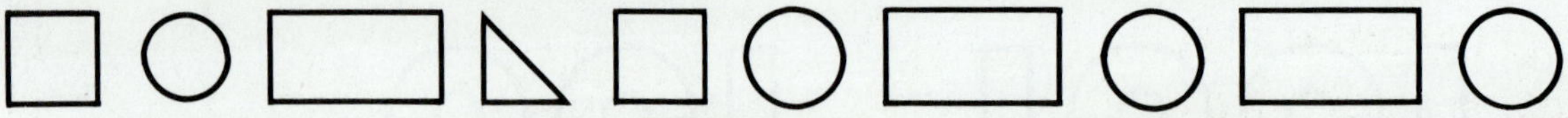

1. squares **2.** line segments **3.** triangles **4.** circles

5. polygons **6.** rectangles that are not squares

Find the perimeter. *(pages 374–375)*

7.

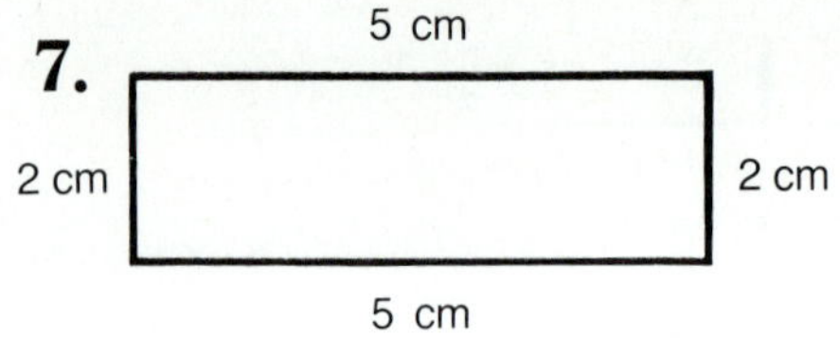

Find the area. *(pages 376–377)*

8.

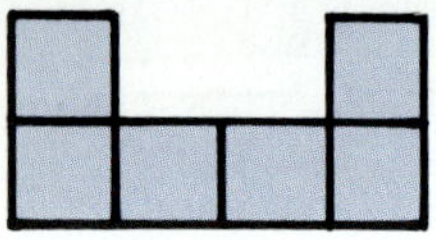

Write the letter of the figure that does not belong.

(pages 378–379)

9. **a.** **b.** **c.** **d.**

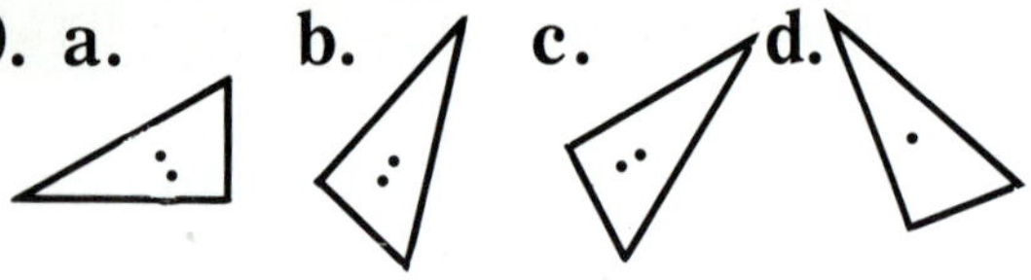

Draw the shape that comes next in the pattern.

(pages 390–391)

10.

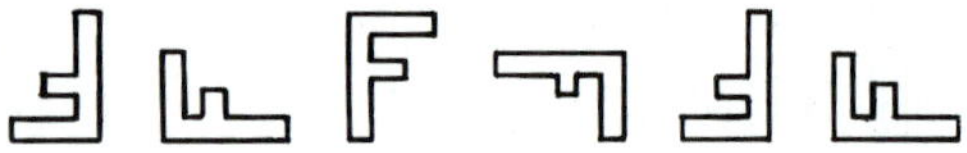

Write *0, 1,* or *2* for the number of lines of symmetry. *(pages 380–381)*

11.

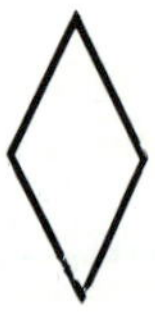

12.

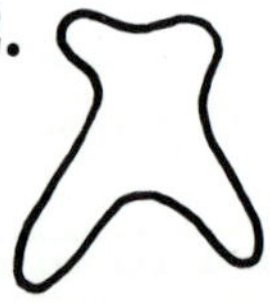

13.

14.

Write C if the figures look congruent. Write *S* if the figures look similar. *(pages 382–385)*

15.

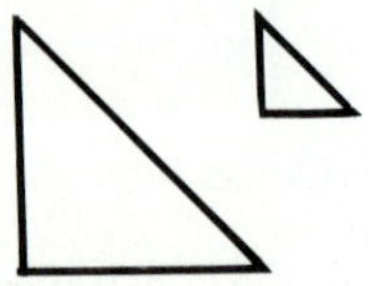

16.

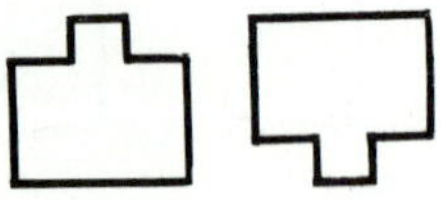

Write the volume in cubic units. *(pages 388–389)*

17.

Extra practice on page 425

Here's a puzzle for you. Your job is to make copies of these figures and then arrange them to form a square.

This problem is a very old puzzle and is solved by arranging the pieces as shown here.

Ready for more puzzles like it? Then try these.

9. Make copies of these four figures. Arrange them to make a triangle.

10. Make copies of these five figures. Arrange them to make a square.

11. Make copies of these six figures. Arrange them to make a pentagon.

12. Make copies of these five figures. Arrange them to make a hexagon.

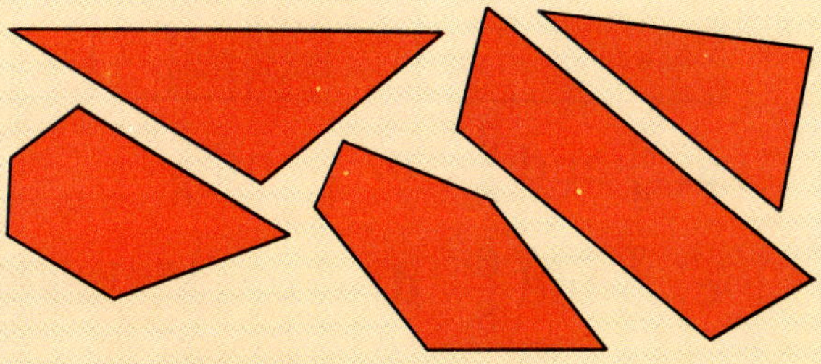

CUMULATIVE REVIEW

Choose the correct answer. Choose *a, b, c,* or *d.*

Find the fraction that matches the shaded part.

1. 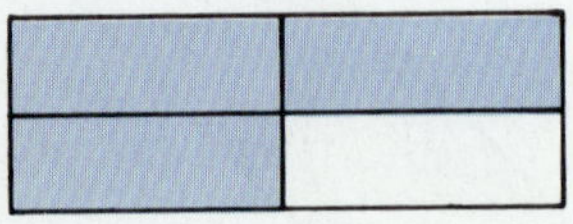

a. $\frac{1}{2}$ **b.** $\frac{1}{3}$ **c.** $\frac{1}{4}$
d. none of these

2. 

a. $\frac{5}{8}$ **b.** $\frac{5}{7}$ **c.** $\frac{5}{5}$
d. none of these

3. 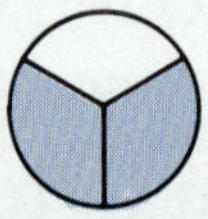

a. $\frac{1}{3}$ **b.** $\frac{2}{3}$ **c.** $\frac{1}{4}$
d. none of these

Compare the fractions.

4. $\frac{5}{6}$ ▢ $\frac{3}{6}$

a. $>$ **b.** $<$ **c.** $=$
d. none of these

5. $\frac{3}{8}$ ▢ $\frac{7}{8}$

a. $>$ **b.** $<$ **c.** $=$
d. none of these

6. $\frac{3}{4}$ ▢ $\frac{4}{4}$

a. $>$ **b.** $<$ **c.** $=$
d. none of these

Find the answer.

7. 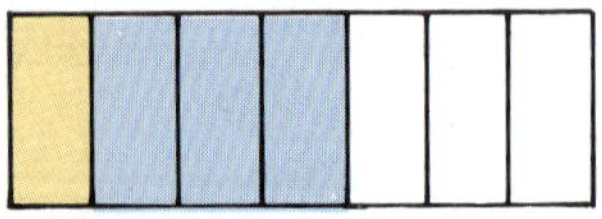

$\frac{1}{7} + \frac{3}{7}$

a. $\frac{2}{7}$ **b.** $\frac{4}{7}$ **c.** $\frac{3}{7}$
d. none of these

8. 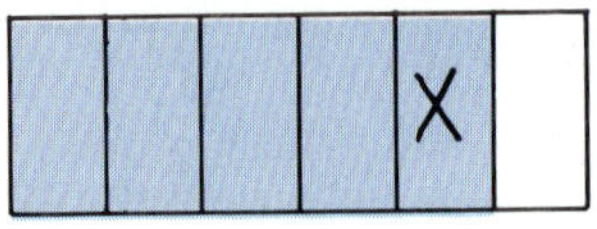

$\frac{5}{6} - \frac{1}{6}$

a. $\frac{4}{6}$ **b.** $\frac{6}{4}$ **c.** $\frac{6}{6}$
d. none of these

9. 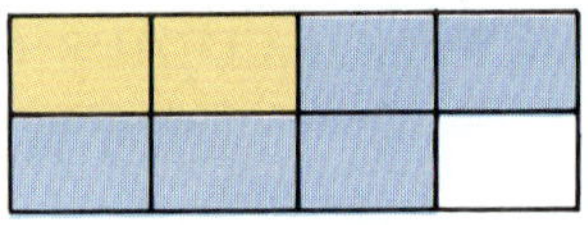

$\frac{2}{8} + \frac{5}{8}$

a. $\frac{6}{8}$ **b.** $\frac{7}{8}$ **c.** $\frac{8}{8}$
d. none of these

Find the equivalent fractions.

10. 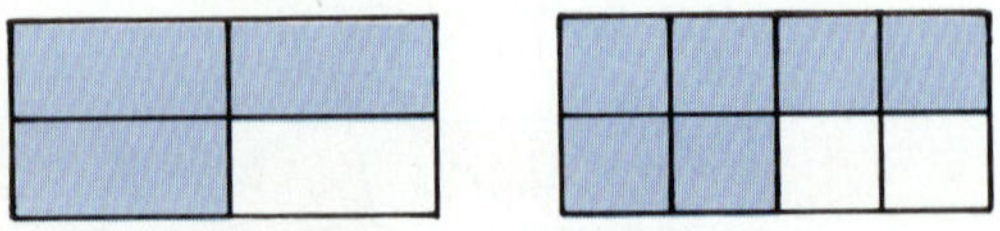

a. $\frac{3}{4}$ and $\frac{3}{8}$ **b.** $\frac{3}{4}$ and $\frac{5}{8}$
c. $\frac{3}{4}$ and $\frac{6}{8}$ **d.** none of these

Find the mixed number.

11. 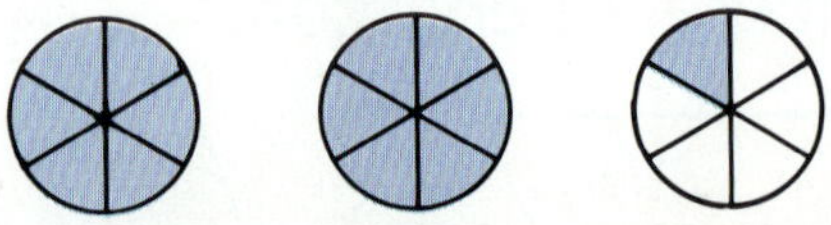

a. $1\frac{1}{6}$ **b.** $2\frac{1}{6}$ **c.** $2\frac{2}{6}$
d. none of these

Find the matching decimal.

12. $\frac{3}{10}$

a. 3.10
b. 0.3
c. 0.03
d. none of these

13. $1\frac{5}{10}$

a. 15.0
b. 5.10
c. 1.05
d. none of these

14. $27\frac{7}{10}$

a. 27.7
b. 2.77
c. 27.07
d. none of these

Find the answer.

15. $5.3 + 4.6$

a. 0.7
b. 10.9
c. 9.9
d. none of these

16. $30.4 - 12.7$

a. 17.7
b. 43.1
c. 18.1
d. none of these

17. $58.7 - 56.8$

a. 2.9
b. 1.9
c. 0.9
d. none of these

Solve. Draw a picture to help solve the problem.

18. Bruce bought 18 fish for his fish tanks. If he keeps 6 fish in each tank, how many fish tanks does Bruce have?

a. 3 **b.** 6 **c.** 9
d. none of these

19. At the pet store Bruce looked at 8 fish. Of those, $\frac{1}{4}$ were guppies. How many were guppies?

a. 4 **b.** 5 **c.** 2
d. none of these

LANGUAGE and VOCABULARY REVIEW

Match the meaning to the word. Write the letter.

1. perimeter
2. congruent
3. polygon
4. mixed number
5. similar

a. a figure with three or more segments
b. a whole number plus a fraction
c. exactly the same size and shape
d. the distance around a figure
e. the same shape but not necessarily the same size

GRAPHICS

Many computers can draw pictures.

Imagine that the screen is divided into many tiny boxes.

You can draw shapes by putting an X in some squares and leaving others empty.

This program tells the computer to draw a rectangle.

The computer reads line numbers from least to greatest.

```
10 PRINT "XXXX"
20 PRINT "X  X"
30 PRINT "X  X"
40 PRINT "XXXX"
50 END
```

Leave 2 spaces.

```
RUN

XXXX
X  X
X  X
XXXX
```

Use graph paper. Put the program lines in order and draw the design.

1.

```
20 PRINT "   X X   "
40 PRINT " X     X "
30 PRINT "  X   X  "
10 PRINT "    X    "
60 END
50 PRINT "XXXXXXXXX"
```

2.

```
80 PRINT "XXXXXXX"
30 PRINT "X X X X"
10 PRINT "XXXXXXX"
50 PRINT "X     X"
40 PRINT "X  X  X"
20 PRINT "X     X"
70 PRINT "X     X"
60 PRINT "X XXX X"
90 END
```

TABLE OF MEASURES

Time

60 seconds(s) = 1 minute (min)
60 minutes = 1 hour (h)
24 hours = 1 day (d)
7 days = 1 week

365 days, 52 weeks, 12 months = 1 year (y)
10 years = 1 decade
100 years = 1 century

Metric

LENGTH

10 millimeters (mm) = 1 centimeter (cm)
100 centimeters = 1 meter (m)
1000 meters = 1 kilometer (km)

MASS

1000 milligrams (mg) = 1 gram (g)
1000 grams = 1 kilogram (kg)

CAPACITY

1000 milliliters (mL) = 1 liter (L)

United States Customary

LENGTH

12 inches (in.) = 1 foot (ft)
3 feet, 36 inches = 1 yard (yd)
5280 feet, 1760 yards = 1 mile (mi)

WEIGHT

16 ounces (oz) = 1 pound (lb)
2000 pounds = 1 ton (t)

CAPACITY

8 fluid ounces (fl oz) = 1 cup (c)
2 cups = 1 pint (pt)
2 pints = 1 quart (qt)
4 quarts = 1 gallon (gal)

CHAPTER 1 EXTRA PRACTICE

FOR USE AFTER CHECKPOINT 1

Add. *(pages 2–7, 8–9)*

1. 3 + 4	**2.** 4 + 5	**3.** 6 + 2	**4.** 9 + 1	**5.** 2 + 8	**6.** 7 + 3	**7.** 8 + 6
8. 4 + 9	**9.** 5 + 7	**10.** 6 + 6	**11.** 9 + 5	**12.** 3 + 9	**13.** 9 + 7	**14.** 8 + 8
15. 3 + 6 + 7	**16.** 4 + 5 + 8	**17.** 2 + 6 + 9	**18.** 5 + 3 + 7	**19.** 4 + 4 + 7	**20.** 6 + 3 + 9	**21.** 5 + 2 + 8
22. 6 + 1 + 5	**23.** 4 + 3 + 8	**24.** 1 + 5 + 5	**25.** 7 + 1 + 3	**26.** 5 + 4 + 7	**27.** 3 + 7 + 3	**28.** 4 + 4 + 3

Write the letter of each fact you need. Solve. *(pages 10–11)*

29. Are there more yellow cars or red cars?
- **a.** 8 red cars are in the lot.
- **b.** 3 blue cars are in the lot.
- **c.** 7 yellow cars are in the lot.

30. How many bowls are there?
- **a.** There are 6 bowls of salad.
- **b.** 4 plates of spaghetti are eaten.
- **c.** There are 4 bowls of soup.

FOR USE AFTER CHECKPOINT 2

Subtract. *(pages 12–19)*

1. 10 − 5	**2.** 9 − 3	**3.** 10 − 3	**4.** 8 − 4	**5.** 9 − 2	**6.** 9 − 5	**7.** 12 − 9
8. 14 − 7	**9.** 13 − 9	**10.** 14 − 8	**11.** 18 − 9	**12.** 11 − 2	**13.** 13 − 5	**14.** 15 − 6
15. 17 − 9	**16.** 13 − 7	**17.** 15 − 9	**18.** 17 − 8	**19.** 16 − 9	**20.** 14 − 7	**21.** 15 − 8

Write *add* or *subtract*, then solve. *(pages 20–21)*

22. There are 8 tigers in the ring. 3 tigers leave. How many tigers are left in the ring?

23. There are 9 big dogs and 6 little dogs. How many dogs are there in all?

EXTRA PRACTICE — CHAPTER 1

FOR USE AFTER THE CHAPTER TEST

Add. *(pages 2–9, 8–9)*

1. 6 + 3 **2.** 7 + 9 **3.** 5 + 8 **4.** 7 + 7 **5.** 4 + 9 **6.** 3 + 7 **7.** 6 + 5

8. 7 + 6 **9.** 9 + 9 **10.** 8 + 9 **11.** 8 + 3 **12.** 4 + 8 **13.** 9 + 3 **14.** 5 + 6

15. 3 + 2 + 8 **16.** 5 + 4 + 9 **17.** 1 + 5 + 6 **18.** 2 + 6 + 5 **19.** 4 + 3 + 7 **20.** 2 + 1 + 9 **21.** 5 + 0 + 3

22. 1 + 2 + 4 **23.** 5 + 2 + 2 **24.** 4 + 1 + 2 **25.** 1 + 6 + 1 **26.** 2 + 2 + 5 **27.** 3 + 5 + 1 **28.** 6 + 1 + 3

Write the letter of each fact you need, then solve. *(pages 10–11)*

29. How many flowers in all?

a. 8 pumpkins are in the garden.
b. 6 blue flowers bloomed.
c. 7 yellow flowers were planted.

30. How many more children are on wagons than scooters?

a. 6 children are on bikes.
b. 8 children are on wagons.
c. 3 children are on scooters.

Subtract. *(pages 12–19)*

31. 12 − 7 **32.** 16 − 8 **33.** 17 − 9 **34.** 13 − 8 **35.** 11 − 8 **36.** 14 − 6 **37.** 14 − 8

38. 13 − 7 **39.** 13 − 9 **40.** 18 − 9 **41.** 17 − 8 **42.** 15 − 7 **43.** 15 − 9 **44.** 15 − 6

45. 16 − 7 **46.** 14 − 7 **47.** 15 − 8 **48.** 16 − 9 **49.** 14 − 9 **50.** 13 − 5 **51.** 12 − 8

Write *add* or *subtract*, then solve. *(pages 20–21)*

52. There are 9 big monkeys and 8 little monkeys. How many monkeys are there in all?

53. There are 11 elephants with red blankets and 7 elephants with blue blankets. How many more elephants have red blankets?

CHAPTER 2 EXTRA PRACTICE

FOR USE AFTER CHECKPOINT 1

Write the standard form. *(pages 30–31, 34–35)*

1. 8 tens **2.** fifty-four **3.** 3 hundreds **4.** 6 hundreds 8 tens 4 ones

Write < or >. *(pages 32–33, 38–39)*

5. 18 ■ 22 **6.** 39 ■ 40 **7.** 462 ■ 429 **8.** 698 ■ 940

Use $ and . to write the value. *(pages 36–37)*

9. 824¢ **10.** 798¢ **11.** 3 dollars 7 dimes 2 pennies

Round to the nearest ten or hundred. *(pages 40–41)*

12. 42 **13.** 78 **14.** 19 **15.** 428 **16.** 361 **17.** 550 **18.** 819

Estimate to solve. *(pages 42–43)*

19. 57 children are on the bus. About how many children are on the bus?

20. 42 children brought their lunch. About how many children brought their lunch?

FOR USE AFTER CHECKPOINT 2

Write the standard form. *(pages 44–45, 48–49)*

1. 1 thousand 8 hundreds 1 ten 5 ones **2.** 8 thousands 5 hundreds 7 tens

3. 352 thousand 905 **4.** 603 thousand 42 **5.** 248 thousand 124

6. one hundred fifty-one thousand **7.** fifteen thousand six hundred two

Write < or >. *(pages 46–47)*

8. 3642 ■ 3898 **9.** 4613 ■ 6342 **10.** 1500 ■ 1900 **11.** 3892 ■ 5200

12. 6431 ■ 8752 **13.** 7805 ■ 7294 **14.** 5069 ■ 5864 **15.** 3951 ■ 4100

16. 2000 ■ 5000 **17.** 2109 ■ 3120 **18.** 4700 ■ 4500 **19.** 9207 ■ 8700

Use the table. Solve. *(pages 50–51)*

20. Who spent more than $6.00?

21. Who spent more than $4.00 but less than $5.00?

CHILD	SPENT
Ron	$6.85
Nancy	$3.62
Bonny	$4.89

EXTRA PRACTICE — CHAPTER 2

FOR USE AFTER THE CHAPTER TEST

Write the standard form. *(pages 30–31, 34–35)*

1. 6 tens 4 ones **2.** 8 tens 2 ones **3.** seventy-five

4. 3 hundreds **5.** 1 hundred 5 tens 2 ones **6.** six hundred forty-eight

Write < or >. *(pages 32–33, 38–39)*

7. 78 ☐ 56 **8.** 22 ☐ 25 **9.** 42 ☐ 37 **10.** 68 ☐ 81

11. 123 ☐ 476 **12.** 345 ☐ 302 **13.** 916 ☐ 972 **14.** 614 ☐ 592

Use $ and . to write the value. *(pages 36–37)*

15. 876¢ **16.** 321¢ **17.** one dollar and thirty-five cents

Round to the nearest ten or hundred. *(pages 40–41)*

18. 49 **19.** 27 **20.** 85 **21.** 481 **22.** 219 **23.** 750 **24.** 382

Estimate to solve. *(pages 42–43)*

25. 28 books are on the shelf. About how many books are on the shelf?

26. 36 children are in the library. About how many children are in the library?

Write the standard form. *(pages 44–45, 48–49)*

27. 2 thousand 386 **28.** four thousand eighty-six

29. 982 thousand 638 **30.** two hundred thousand

Write < or >. *(pages 46–47)*

31. 6428 ☐ 3990 **32.** 5867 ☐ 2418 **33.** 9611 ☐ 9087 **34.** 4825 ☐ 5038

Use the table. Solve. *(pages 50–51)*

35. Who collected more than 200 stamps?

36. Who collected more than 160 stamps but less than 190 stamps?

CHILD	STAMPS COLLECTED
Julio	158
Eric	237
Margo	186

CHAPTER 3 EXTRA PRACTICE

FOR USE AFTER CHECKPOINT 1

Add. *(pages 60–65, 68–71)*

1. $19 + 8$
2. $29 + 7$
3. $46 + 2$
4. $61 + 8$
5. $23 + 17$
6. $48 + 22$
7. $48 + 79$
8. $85 + 28$
9. $38 + 64$
10. $98 + 89$
11. $83 + 74$
12. $43 + 92$

Round to the nearest ten.
Estimate the sum. *(pages 66–67)*

13. $29 + 36$
14. $72 + 21$
15. $46 + 38$
16. $38 + 17$
17. $55 + 26$
18. $49 + 39$

Solve. *(pages 72–73)*

19. How many marbles are there?

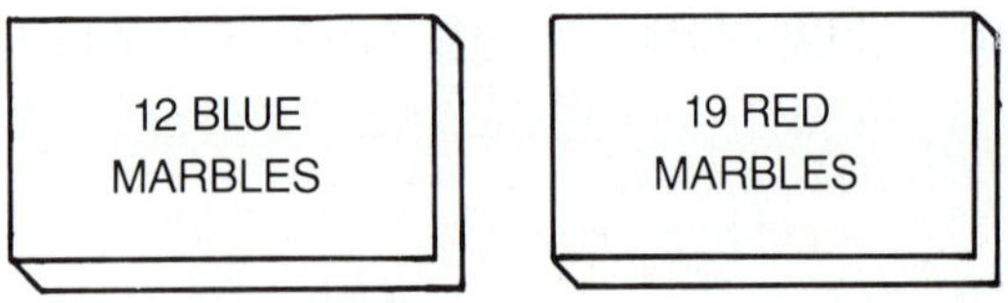

20. How many hats are there?

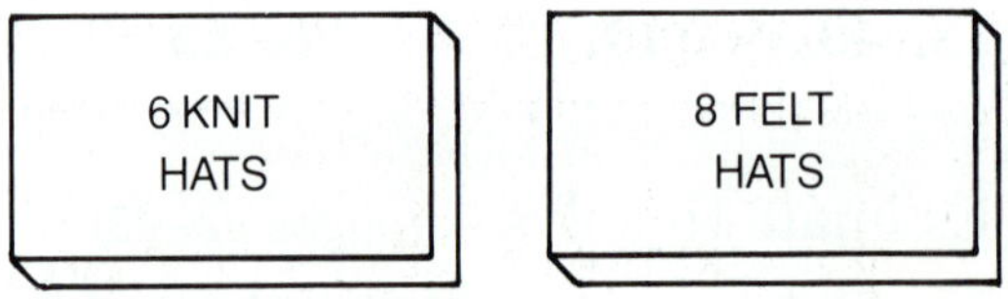

FOR USE AFTER CHECKPOINT 2

Add. *(pages 74–77, 78–85)*

1. $6 + 5 + 4$
2. $9 + 6 + 2$
3. $3 + 7 + 6$
4. $38 + 23 + 15$
5. $29 + 13 + 28$
6. $17 + 35 + 14$
7. $731 + 239$
8. $248 + 119$
9. $585 + 274$
10. $342 + 295$
11. $545 + 276$
12. $133 + 387$
13. $3162 + 4236$
14. $4765 + 2139$
15. $6243 + 1936$
16. $5843 + 2817$
17. $7635 + 1766$
18. $3621 + 4021$

Solve. *(pages 86–87)*

19. How many glasses of milk did Kim sell?

20. How many more glasses did Meg sell than Athana?

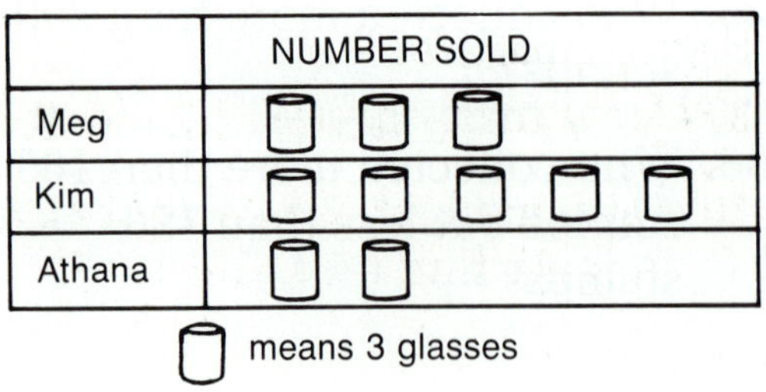

EXTRA PRACTICE — CHAPTER 3

FOR USE AFTER THE CHAPTER TEST

Add. *(pages 60–65, 68–71)*

1. 46 + 3
2. 38 + 2
3. 68 + 5
4. 41 + 29
5. 65 + 25
6. 58 + 32
7. 45 + 27
8. 38 + 56
9. 74 + 68
10. 55 + 94
11. 45 + 53
12. 91 + 47

Round to the nearest ten.
Estimate the sum. *(pages 66–67)*

13. 29 + 31
14. 47 + 65
15. 22 + 34
16. 67 + 15
17. 31 + 47
18. 92 + 74

Solve. *(pages 72–73)*

19. How many balls are there?

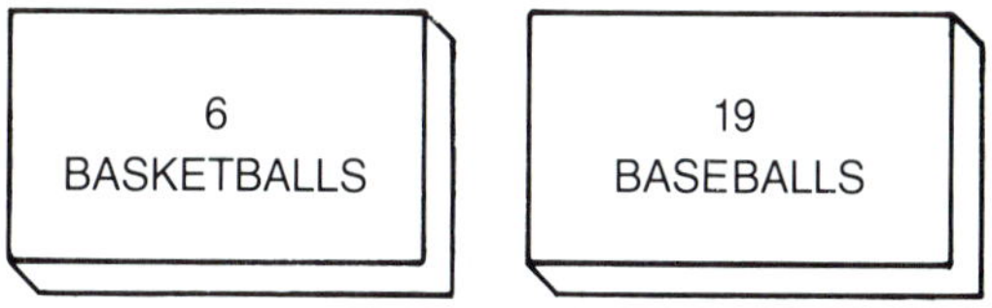

20. How many flowers are there?

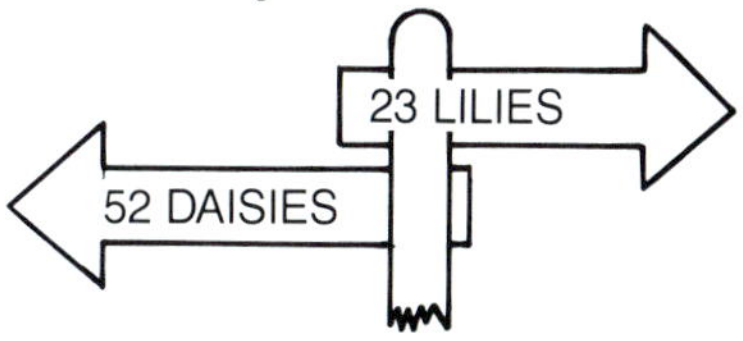

Add. *(pages 74–77, 78–85)*

21. 9 + 7 + 9
22. 3 + 2 + 8
23. 7 + 6 + 4
24. 31 + 15 + 19
25. 12 + 26 + 87
26. 62 + 20 + 38
27. 786 + 198
28. 455 + 266
29. 762 + 234
30. 673 + 495
31. 219 + 976
32. 461 + 273
33. 3425 + 3766
34. 2345 + 1434
35. 3565 + 2908
36. 6840 + 1997
37. 2614 + 4739
38. 5482 + 2517

Solve. *(pages 86–87)*

39. How many butterflies did Tony find?
40. How many more butterflies did Angela find than Clifford?

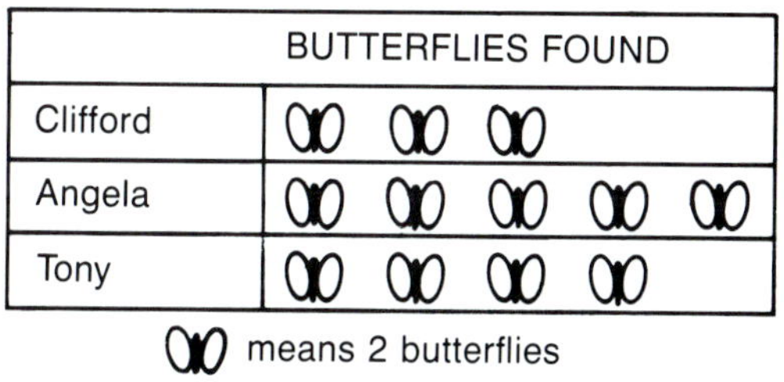

CHAPTER 4 EXTRA PRACTICE

FOR USE AFTER CHECKPOINT 1

Subtract. *(pages 96–101, 104–105)*

1. 60 − 3	**2.** 40 − 5	**3.** 70 − 8	**4.** 30 − 13	**5.** 86 − 41	**6.** 60 − 21
7. 74 − 56	**8.** 61 − 25	**9.** 45 − 13	**10.** 94 − 66	**11.** 83 − 44	**12.** 79 − 28

Round each number to the nearest ten.
Estimate the difference. *(pages 102–103)*

13. 48 − 12	**14.** 79 − 56	**15.** 45 − 23	**16.** 61 − 25	**17.** 89 − 23	**18.** 48 − 15

Solve. *(pages 106–107)*

19. The camp had 48 lb of hamburger. It used 24 lb for dinner and 18 lb for lunch. How many pounds were left?

FOR USE AFTER CHECKPOINT 2

Subtract. *(pages 108–117)*

1. 471 − 132	**2.** 385 − 167	**3.** 864 − 252	**4.** 462 − 191	**5.** 569 − 278	**6.** 772 − 481
7. 861 − 475	**8.** 925 − 546	**9.** 698 − 213	**10.** 800 − 276	**11.** 900 − 670	**12.** 700 − 421
13. 7248 − 1326	**14.** 3849 − 2135	**15.** 8962 − 3794	**16.** 5234 − 1863	**17.** 6432 − 2759	**18.** 8421 − 2930

If the answer is reasonable, write R. If not, give the correct answer. *(pages 118–119)*

19. The costume shop had 184 clown hats and 245 magician hats. How many hats were there in all?
Answer: 61 hats

EXTRA PRACTICE

FOR USE AFTER THE CHAPTER TEST

Subtract. *(pages 96–101, 104–105)*

1.	2.	3.	4.	5.	6.
80 − 5	90 − 7	60 − 2	60 − 23	40 − 15	80 − 60

7.	8.	9.	10.	11.	12.
72 − 37	46 − 28	75 − 19	82 − 56	51 − 29	63 − 29

Round each number to the nearest ten.
Estimate the difference. *(pages 102–103)*

13.	14.	15.	16.	17.	18.
49 − 21	38 − 16	92 − 43	47 − 25	81 − 52	82 − 35

Solve. *(pages 106–107)*

19. 18 children went hiking and 26 children went horseback riding. Of all the children, 35 wore sweaters. How many did not wear sweaters?

Subtract. *(pages 108–117)*

20.	21.	22.	23.	24.	25.
476 − 329	465 − 218	697 − 283	538 − 186	875 − 192	596 − 241

26.	27.	28.	29.	30.	31.
623 − 285	515 − 276	422 − 287	800 − 255	500 − 161	600 − 387

32.	33.	34.	35.	36.	37.
2795 − 1289	3684 − 1946	9420 − 6532	7513 − 2671	4280 − 1393	3263 − 1637

If the answer is reasonable, write R. If not, give the correct answer. *(pages 118–119)*

38. The costume shop had 364 magic wands. They sold 189 wands. How many magic wands do they have now?
Answer: 553 magic wands

CHAPTER 5 EXTRA PRACTICE

FOR USE AFTER CHECKPOINT 1

Use $ and . to write the value. *(pages 128–133)*

1. 8 dimes **2.** 3 dimes 4 pennies **3.** 9 dimes 3 pennies **4.** 6 dimes

Write the answer. *(pages 134–135)*

5. $.40 + .08

6. $.72 + .24

7. $.83 − .37

8. $.90 − .65

9. $.19 + .78

10. $.72 − .28

11. $8.70 − 3.95

12. $24.86 + 12.98

13. $89.95 − 8.68

14. $5.00 − 2.63

15. $57.84 + 32.98

16. $19.85 − 6.98

Estimate to solve. *(pages 136–137)*

17. A club bought ribbon for $4.85 and badges for $3.96. About how much did the club pay in all?

18. Students paid for a $14.95 prize with a $20 bill. About how much change did they get back?

FOR USE AFTER CHECKPOINT 2

Write the time. *(pages 138–143)*

1.

? : ?

2.

? : ?

3.

? : ?

4.

? minutes before ?

5.

? : ?

6.

? : ?

7.

? : ?

8.

? minutes after ?

Solve. *(pages 144–149)*

9. School starts at 8:25. It takes Jake 15 minutes to walk there. What time should he leave home?

10. What day comes just after Tuesday?

11. What month is 2 months after July?

EXTRA PRACTICE CHAPTER 5

FOR USE AFTER THE CHAPTER TEST

Use $ and . to write the value. *(pages 128–133)*

1. 3 dimes 2 pennies **2.** 4 dimes **3.** 9 dimes **4.** 8 dimes 5 pennies

Write the answer. *(pages 134–135)*

5.	**6.**	**7.**	**8.**	**9.**	**10.**
\$.46	\$.38	\$.41	\$.68	\$.65	\$.45
− .23	+ .22	+ .29	− .15	− .27	+ .35

11.	**12.**	**13.**	**14.**	**15.**	**16.**
\$9.58	\$18.45	\$23.38	\$65.74	\$38.55	\$99.85
+ .36	− .27	+ 2.56	− 27.68	+ 46.49	− 67.98

Estimate to solve. *(pages 136–137)*

17. Tom bought a book for \$5.98 and a pen for \$1.27. About how much did he spend in all?

18. Eloise has saved \$35.27. She wants to spend \$8.98. About how much will she have left?

Write the time. *(pages 138–143)*

19. 

? : ?

20. 

? : ?

21. 

? : ?

22. 

? minutes after ?

23. 

? : ?

24. 

? : ?

25. 

? : ?

26. 

? minutes before ?

Solve. *(pages 144–149)*

27. The soccer game started at 9:30 and lasted 47 minutes. What time did it end?

28. The Perrys went on vacation on Friday. They were gone 10 days. What day did they get back?

CHAPTER 6 EXTRA PRACTICE

FOR USE AFTER CHECKPOINT 1

Add or multiply. *(pages 158–159, 162–163)*

1. $2 + 2 + 2$
3×2

2. $2 + 2 + 2 + 2 + 2 + 2$
6×2

3. $3 + 3 + 3$
3×3

4. $3 + 3 + 3 + 3 + 3$
5×3

Multiply. *(pages 158–167)*

5. 4×2 **6.** 8×2 **7.** 5×2 **8.** 9×2 **9.** 7×2

10. 2×3 **11.** 8×3 **12.** 3×3 **13.** 7×3 **14.** 6×3

15. 6×3, 3×6 **16.** 6×2, 2×6 **17.** 9×3, 3×9 **18.** 7×2, 2×7 **19.** 9×2, 2×9

20. 3×6 **21.** 2×8 **22.** 3×9 **23.** 2×9 **24.** 3×8 **25.** 3×7 **26.** 2×6

27. 3×5 **28.** 3×4 **29.** 3×9 **30.** 3×7 **31.** 3×6 **32.** 3×8 **33.** 3×2

FOR USE AFTER CHECKPOINT 2

Which fact is missing? Write the letter. Solve the problem. *(pages 168–169)*

1. Alicia is 24 years older than her nephew. How old is Alicia?

2. Alicia's birthday is in four days. What is the date of her birthday?

A. Today is December 20.

B. Alicia's nephew is 6.

Multiply. *(pages 170–173)*

3. 4×8 **4.** 4×7 **5.** 4×2 **6.** 4×5 **7.** 4×9 **8.** 4×3 **9.** 4×4

10. 1×7 **11.** 0×5 **12.** 0×9 **13.** 1×9 **14.** 0×6 **15.** 1×5 **16.** 1×8

Solve. *(pages 174–175)*

17. Mary adds three odd numbers. Is the sum even or odd?

EXTRA PRACTICE CHAPTER 6

FOR USE AFTER THE CHAPTER TEST

Multiply. *(pages 158–167)*

1. 5×2 **2.** 8×2 **3.** 7×2 **4.** 9×2 **5.** 3×2

6. 6×3 **7.** 3×3 **8.** 8×3 **9.** 7×3 **10.** 2×3

11. 2×2 **12.** 4×3 **13.** 9×3 **14.** 4×2 **15.** 5×3

16. $\begin{array}{r} 3 \\ \times 5 \\ \hline \end{array}$ **17.** $\begin{array}{r} 8 \\ \times 2 \\ \hline \end{array}$ **18.** $\begin{array}{r} 7 \\ \times 3 \\ \hline \end{array}$ **19.** $\begin{array}{r} 9 \\ \times 2 \\ \hline \end{array}$ **20.** $\begin{array}{r} 4 \\ \times 3 \\ \hline \end{array}$ **21.** $\begin{array}{r} 7 \\ \times 2 \\ \hline \end{array}$ **22.** $\begin{array}{r} 2 \\ \times 2 \\ \hline \end{array}$

23. $\begin{array}{r} 2 \\ \times 6 \\ \hline \end{array}$ **24.** $\begin{array}{r} 3 \\ \times 2 \\ \hline \end{array}$ **25.** $\begin{array}{r} 4 \\ \times 2 \\ \hline \end{array}$ **26.** $\begin{array}{r} 9 \\ \times 3 \\ \hline \end{array}$ **27.** $\begin{array}{r} 5 \\ \times 2 \\ \hline \end{array}$ **28.** $\begin{array}{r} 8 \\ \times 3 \\ \hline \end{array}$ **29.** $\begin{array}{r} 6 \\ \times 3 \\ \hline \end{array}$

Which fact is missing? Write the letter.
Solve the problem. *(pages 168–169)*

30. The children in Earl's group each have 2 books. How many books do they have in all?

31. Anna swam 3 laps each day. How many laps did she swim in one week?

A. There are 7 days in a week.

B. There are 8 children in Earl's group.

Multiply. *(pages 170–173)*

32. $\begin{array}{r} 4 \\ \times 4 \\ \hline \end{array}$ **33.** $\begin{array}{r} 4 \\ \times 7 \\ \hline \end{array}$ **34.** $\begin{array}{r} 4 \\ \times 9 \\ \hline \end{array}$ **35.** $\begin{array}{r} 4 \\ \times 5 \\ \hline \end{array}$ **36.** $\begin{array}{r} 4 \\ \times 6 \\ \hline \end{array}$ **37.** $\begin{array}{r} 8 \\ \times 4 \\ \hline \end{array}$ **38.** $\begin{array}{r} 5 \\ \times 4 \\ \hline \end{array}$

39. $\begin{array}{r} 0 \\ \times 5 \\ \hline \end{array}$ **40.** $\begin{array}{r} 1 \\ \times 2 \\ \hline \end{array}$ **41.** $\begin{array}{r} 3 \\ \times 1 \\ \hline \end{array}$ **42.** $\begin{array}{r} 0 \\ \times 4 \\ \hline \end{array}$ **43.** $\begin{array}{r} 5 \\ \times 1 \\ \hline \end{array}$ **44.** $\begin{array}{r} 2 \\ \times 0 \\ \hline \end{array}$ **45.** $\begin{array}{r} 0 \\ \times 9 \\ \hline \end{array}$

Solve. *(pages 174–175)*

46. Syd adds two even numbers. Is the sum even or odd?

47. Maria multiplies two even numbers. Is the product even or odd?

CHAPTER 7 EXTRA PRACTICE

FOR USE AFTER CHECKPOINT 1

Multiply. *(pages 184–189)*

1. $\begin{array}{r}5\\ \times 7\\ \hline\end{array}$	**2.** $\begin{array}{r}8\\ \times 5\\ \hline\end{array}$	**3.** $\begin{array}{r}6\\ \times 5\\ \hline\end{array}$	**4.** $\begin{array}{r}5\\ \times 7\\ \hline\end{array}$	**5.** $\begin{array}{r}5\\ \times 5\\ \hline\end{array}$	**6.** $\begin{array}{r}5\\ \times 4\\ \hline\end{array}$	**7.** $\begin{array}{r}5\\ \times 3\\ \hline\end{array}$
8. $\begin{array}{r}2\\ \times 6\\ \hline\end{array}$	**9.** $\begin{array}{r}7\\ \times 5\\ \hline\end{array}$	**10.** $\begin{array}{r}3\\ \times 5\\ \hline\end{array}$	**11.** $\begin{array}{r}5\\ \times 8\\ \hline\end{array}$	**12.** $\begin{array}{r}7\\ \times 6\\ \hline\end{array}$	**13.** $\begin{array}{r}4\\ \times 6\\ \hline\end{array}$	**14.** $\begin{array}{r}9\\ \times 6\\ \hline\end{array}$

Solve. Check to make sure your answer is reasonable. *(pages 190–191)*

15. Bob, Rita, and Chris each won 2 ribbons at the fair. How many ribbons did they win in all?

16. Larz plants 6 rows of carrots. There are 8 carrots in each row. How many carrots does Larz plant?

FOR USE AFTER CHECKPOINT 2

Multiply. *(pages 192–199)*

1. $\begin{array}{r}2\\ \times 7\\ \hline\end{array}$	**2.** $\begin{array}{r}7\\ \times 7\\ \hline\end{array}$	**3.** $\begin{array}{r}9\\ \times 7\\ \hline\end{array}$	**4.** $\begin{array}{r}5\\ \times 7\\ \hline\end{array}$	**5.** $\begin{array}{r}7\\ \times 8\\ \hline\end{array}$	**6.** $\begin{array}{r}7\\ \times 6\\ \hline\end{array}$	**7.** $\begin{array}{r}3\\ \times 7\\ \hline\end{array}$
8. $\begin{array}{r}8\\ \times 8\\ \hline\end{array}$	**9.** $\begin{array}{r}5\\ \times 8\\ \hline\end{array}$	**10.** $\begin{array}{r}8\\ \times 9\\ \hline\end{array}$	**11.** $\begin{array}{r}8\\ \times 4\\ \hline\end{array}$	**12.** $\begin{array}{r}6\\ \times 8\\ \hline\end{array}$	**13.** $\begin{array}{r}8\\ \times 7\\ \hline\end{array}$	**14.** $\begin{array}{r}2\\ \times 8\\ \hline\end{array}$
15. $\begin{array}{r}5\\ \times 9\\ \hline\end{array}$	**16.** $\begin{array}{r}9\\ \times 8\\ \hline\end{array}$	**17.** $\begin{array}{r}3\\ \times 9\\ \hline\end{array}$	**18.** $\begin{array}{r}9\\ \times 9\\ \hline\end{array}$	**19.** $\begin{array}{r}9\\ \times 4\\ \hline\end{array}$	**20.** $\begin{array}{r}9\\ \times 5\\ \hline\end{array}$	**21.** $\begin{array}{r}6\\ \times 9\\ \hline\end{array}$
22. $\begin{array}{r}4\\ \times 0\\ \hline\end{array}$	**23.** $\begin{array}{r}5\\ \times 5\\ \hline\end{array}$	**24.** $\begin{array}{r}3\\ \times 6\\ \hline\end{array}$	**25.** $\begin{array}{r}8\\ \times 5\\ \hline\end{array}$	**26.** $\begin{array}{r}6\\ \times 9\\ \hline\end{array}$	**27.** $\begin{array}{r}4\\ \times 9\\ \hline\end{array}$	**28.** $\begin{array}{r}6\\ \times 0\\ \hline\end{array}$
29. $\begin{array}{r}4\\ \times 8\\ \hline\end{array}$	**30.** $\begin{array}{r}7\\ \times 5\\ \hline\end{array}$	**31.** $\begin{array}{r}7\\ \times 0\\ \hline\end{array}$	**32.** $\begin{array}{r}9\\ \times 8\\ \hline\end{array}$	**33.** $\begin{array}{r}8\\ \times 3\\ \hline\end{array}$	**34.** $\begin{array}{r}8\\ \times 1\\ \hline\end{array}$	**35.** $\begin{array}{r}7\\ \times 9\\ \hline\end{array}$

Use the bar graph to solve the problem. *(pages 200–201)*

36. In 4 weeks, how many days does Sue work?

37. How many days does Bob work in 9 weeks?

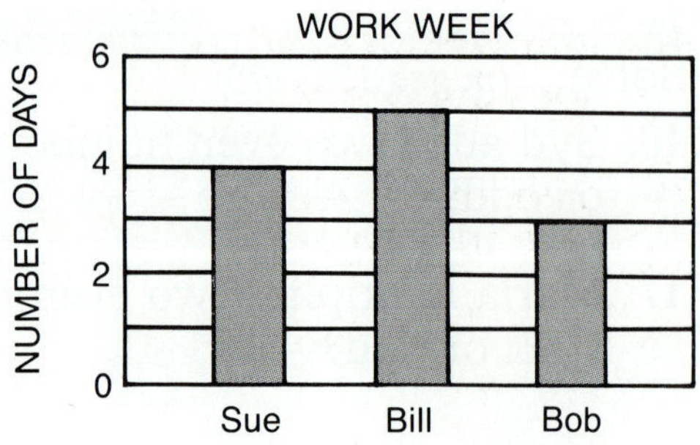

EXTRA PRACTICE

FOR USE AFTER THE CHAPTER TEST

Multiply. *(pages 184–189)*

1. 5×4 **2.** 6×7 **3.** 9×6 **4.** 5×6 **5.** 8×5 **6.** 6×6 **7.** 5×2

8. 7×5 **9.** 8×6 **10.** 5×8 **11.** 6×3 **12.** 6×5 **13.** 6×4 **14.** 9×5

Solve. Check to make sure your answer is reasonable.
(pages 190–191)

15. Josh has 3 trains. Each train has 6 cars. How many cars are there in all?

16. Annie bought 6 packages of tomatoes. Each package had 4 tomatoes. How many tomatoes were there in all?

Multiply. *(pages 192–199)*

17. 5×6 **18.** 4×9 **19.** 8×7 **20.** 7×5 **21.** 7×4 **22.** 8×1 **23.** 5×0

24. 7×9 **25.** 6×9 **26.** 9×8 **27.** 7×6 **28.** 9×3 **29.** 1×9 **30.** 5×8

31. 6×6 **32.** 8×5 **33.** 8×6 **34.** 7×7 **35.** 3×8 **36.** 9×6 **37.** 8×9

38. 8×8 **39.** 4×6 **40.** 9×9 **41.** 9×5 **42.** 7×3 **43.** 6×4 **44.** 7×0

Use the bar graph to solve the problem.
(pages 200–201)

45. In 3 weeks how much money does Julio save?

46. How much money does Alicia save in 6 weeks?

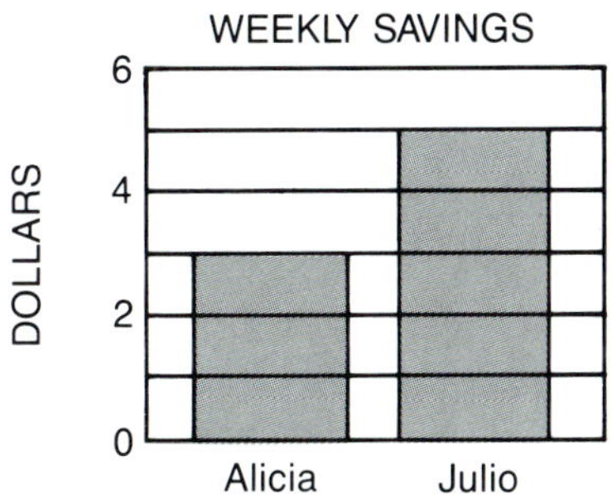

CHAPTER 8 EXTRA PRACTICE

FOR USE AFTER CHECKPOINT 1

Write the answer. *(pages 210–215)*

1. __?__ twos are in 16
$16 \div 2 =$ __?__

2. __?__ twos are in 10
$10 \div 2 =$ __?__

3. __?__ threes are in 24
$24 \div 3 =$ __?__

4. $8 \div 2$ **5.** $12 \div 2$ **6.** $18 \div 2$ **7.** $6 \div 2$ **8.** $10 \div 2$

9. $15 \div 3$ **10.** $21 \div 3$ **11.** $12 \div 3$ **12.** $18 \div 3$ **13.** $9 \div 3$

Write the answer. *(pages 216–221)*

14. $16 \div 4$ **15.** $24 \div 4$ **16.** $12 \div 4$ **17.** $28 \div 4$ **18.** $36 \div 4$

19. $20 \div 5$ **20.** $30 \div 5$ **21.** $15 \div 5$ **22.** $45 \div 5$ **23.** $40 \div 5$

24. $5\overline{)25}$ **25.** $4\overline{)20}$ **26.** $3\overline{)18}$ **27.** $4\overline{)32}$ **28.** $3\overline{)27}$ **29.** $2\overline{)16}$

Write the answer. *(pages 222–223)*

30. Each juggler has the same amount of time to perform. There are 5 jugglers and the show lasts 40 minutes. How much time does each juggler have?

FOR USE AFTER CHECKPOINT 2

Write the answer. *(pages 224–227)*

1. $36 \div 6$ **2.** $49 \div 7$ **3.** $21 \div 7$ **4.** $54 \div 6$ **5.** $42 \div 6$

6. $7\overline{)56}$ **7.** $7\overline{)63}$ **8.** $6\overline{)48}$ **9.** $6\overline{)30}$ **10.** $7\overline{)42}$ **11.** $7\overline{)28}$

Write the answer. *(pages 228–233)*

12. $8\overline{)24}$ **13.** $9\overline{)81}$ **14.** $8\overline{)72}$ **15.** $8\overline{)64}$ **16.** $9\overline{)63}$ **17.** $8\overline{)56}$

18. $8\overline{)48}$ **19.** $9\overline{)27}$ **20.** $9\overline{)45}$ **21.** $9\overline{)72}$ **22.** $8\overline{)32}$ **23.** $9\overline{)54}$

Write the answer. *(pages 234–235)*

24. Each seal does 5 tricks and each dolphin does 3 tricks. There are 6 seals and 5 dolphins. How many tricks are performed?

EXTRA PRACTICE

CHAPTER 8

FOR USE AFTER THE CHAPTER TEST

Write the answer. *(pages 210–215)*

1. $8 \div 2$ **2.** $12 \div 2$ **3.** $16 \div 2$ **4.** $4 \div 2$ **5.** $14 \div 2$

6. $9 \div 3$ **7.** $15 \div 3$ **8.** $6 \div 3$ **9.** $21 \div 3$ **10.** $24 \div 3$

11. $4 \div 2$ **12.** $10 \div 2$ **13.** $12 \div 3$ **14.** $18 \div 3$ **15.** $18 \div 2$

Write the answer. *(pages 216–221)*

16. $40 \div 5$ **17.** $20 \div 5$ **18.** $30 \div 5$ **19.** $32 \div 4$ **20.** $16 \div 4$

21. $4\overline{)12}$ **22.** $5\overline{)35}$ **23.** $4\overline{)36}$ **24.** $4\overline{)28}$ **25.** $4\overline{)16}$ **26.** $5\overline{)40}$

27. $4\overline{)24}$ **28.** $5\overline{)15}$ **29.** $4\overline{)20}$ **30.** $5\overline{)45}$ **31.** $4\overline{)28}$ **32.** $4\overline{)36}$

Write the answer. *(pages 224–227)*

33. $6\overline{)36}$ **34.** $6\overline{)54}$ **35.** $6\overline{)42}$ **36.** $6\overline{)48}$ **37.** $6\overline{)30}$ **38.** $6\overline{)24}$

39. $7\overline{)49}$ **40.** $7\overline{)21}$ **41.** $7\overline{)56}$ **42.** $7\overline{)63}$ **43.** $7\overline{)42}$ **44.** $7\overline{)28}$

45. $7\overline{)14}$ **46.** $7\overline{)35}$ **47.** $6\overline{)6}$ **48.** $6\overline{)18}$ **49.** $6\overline{)12}$ **50.** $7\overline{)7}$

Write the answer. *(pages 228–233)*

51. $8\overline{)24}$ **52.** $9\overline{)81}$ **53.** $8\overline{)72}$ **54.** $8\overline{)64}$ **55.** $9\overline{)63}$ **56.** $9\overline{)45}$

57. $9\overline{)27}$ **58.** $8\overline{)32}$ **59.** $8\overline{)40}$ **60.** $9\overline{)54}$ **61.** $9\overline{)72}$ **62.** $8\overline{)48}$

63. $9\overline{)36}$ **64.** $8\overline{)8}$ **65.** $9\overline{)18}$ **66.** $8\overline{)16}$ **67.** $9\overline{)9}$ **68.** $8\overline{)56}$

Write the answer. *(pages 222–223, 234–235)*

69. There are 6 students in the cooking class. They each make 3 loaves of bread. How many loaves are there in all?

70. The class bakes 9 muffins in each pan. There are 6 full pans and a pan with 3 muffins. How many muffins do they bake in all?

CHAPTER 9 EXTRA PRACTICE

FOR USE AFTER CHECKPOINT 1

Choose the better estimate. Write *a* or *b*. *(pages 244–249)*

1. The height of a drinking glass
   a. 11 m **b.** 11 cm
2. the distance between the state park and home
   a. 70 km **b.** 70 m

Choose the better estimate. Write *a* or *b*. *(pages 250–255)*

3. a pitcher **a.** 3 L **b.** 30 L
4. a plant pot **a.** 2 g **b.** 2 kg
5. a warm day **a.** 10°C **b.** 40°C
6. a feather **a.** 2 g **b.** 2 kg

Use the map to find the distance. *(pages 256–257)*

7. It is __?__ km from Clarksville to Nashville to Franklin.

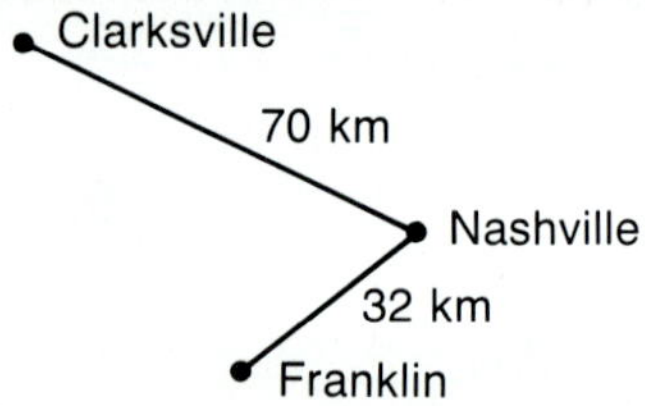

FOR USE AFTER CHECKPOINT 2

Choose the better estimate. Write *a* or *b*. *(pages 260–261)*

1. the height of a candle
   a. 10 in. **b.** 10 ft
2. distance from home to school
   a. 3 mi **b.** 3 in.

Choose the better estimate. Write *a* or *b*. *(pages 262–267)*

3. a package of cheese
   a. 10 oz **b.** 10 lb
4. slice of cheese
   a. 1 lb **b.** 1 oz
5. a full kitchen sink
   a. 4 pt **b.** 4 gal
6. very cold day
   a. 10°F **b.** 70°F

Solve. Check the label. *(pages 268–269)*

7. Each picnic jug holds 2 gal of water. There are 6 jugs. How much water is that?
8. The temperature at 12:00 P.M. was 70°F. By 7:30 P.M. it had fallen 21°. What was the temperature at 7:30?

EXTRA PRACTICE

FOR USE AFTER THE CHAPTER TEST

Choose the better estimate. Write *a* or *b*.
(pages 244–249)

1. length of a pen
a. 14 km **b.** 14 cm

2. height of a door
a. 2 m **b.** 2 km

Choose the better estimate. Write *a* or *b*.
(pages 250–255)

3. a table **a.** 50 g **b.** 20 kg

4. a pitcher of juice **a.** 2 L **b.** 20 L

5. a television **a.** 20 kg **b.** 20 g

6. a hot drink **a.** 70°C **b.** 10°C

Use the map to find the distance. *(pages 256–257)*

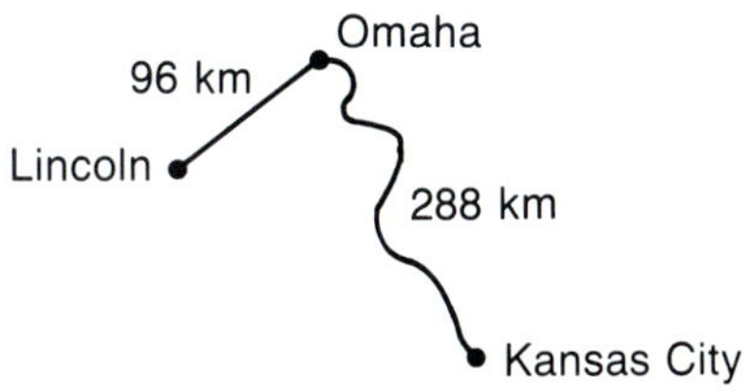

7. It is ___?___ km from Lincoln to Omaha to Kansas City.

8. How much farther is it from Omaha to Kansas City than from Lincoln to Omaha?

Choose the better estimate. Write *a* or *b*. *(pages 258–261)*

9. length of the school yard
a. 300 ft **b.** 300 mi

10. length of a pencil
a. 7 in. **b.** 7 ft

Choose the better estimate. Write *a* or *b*.
(pages 262–267)

11. a bag of onions **a.** 1 oz **b.** 1 lb

12. water in a vase **a.** 1 qt **b.** 10 gal

13. a cold day **a.** 30°F **b.** 80°F

14. water in a bathtub **a.** 3 qt **b.** 30 gal

Solve. Check the label. *(pages 268–269)*

15. Each tent sleeps 4 people. There are 6 tents. How many people can sleep in the tents?

16. Eric bought six 12 oz cans of insect spray. Each can costs \$3. How much did Eric spend?

CHAPTER 10 EXTRA PRACTICE

FOR USE AFTER CHECKPOINT 1

Round to the nearest ten.
Estimate the product. *(pages 280–281)*

1. 89 ×3	**2.** 29 ×6	**3.** 62 ×5	**4.** 35 ×7	**5.** 25 ×3	**6.** 87 ×5

Multiply. *(pages 278–279, 282–289)*

7. 10 ×3	**8.** 20 ×4	**9.** 400 ×2	**10.** 21 ×4	**11.** 13 ×2	**12.** 32 ×2
13. 13 ×4	**14.** 19 ×2	**15.** 12 ×7	**16.** 24 ×3	**17.** 26 ×3	**18.** 25 ×2
19. 19 ×6	**20.** 32 ×2	**21.** 27 ×4	**22.** 46 ×3	**23.** 52 ×7	**24.** 34 ×5

Estimate. Write *more than* or *less than* with your answer. *(pages 290–291)*

25. Jason bought 5 bags of carrots. There were 18 carrots in each bag. About how many carrots did he buy?

26. The store has 4 cases of juice. There are 24 cans of juice in a case. About how many cans of juice are there?

FOR USE AFTER CHECKPOINT 2

Multiply. *(pages 292–295)*

1. 123 ×4	**2.** 248 ×2	**3.** 317 ×3	**4.** 119 ×5	**5.** 489 ×3	**6.** 129 ×6
7. 131 ×5	**8.** 251 ×6	**9.** 362 ×3	**10.** 453 ×2	**11.** 799 ×5	**12.** 305 ×7

Multiply. *(pages 296–297)*

13. \$1.21 ×5	**14.** \$2.42 ×3	**15.** \$.89 ×7	**16.** \$1.80 ×7	**17.** \$2.15 ×3	**18.** \$6.87 ×5

Write two possible answers for the problem. *(pages 298–299)*

19. A blue card is worth 10 points. A red card is worth 5 points. Carl has 15 points. What cards does he have?

FOR USE AFTER THE CHAPTER TEST

Write the answer. *(pages 308–311)*

1. $6\overline{)48}$ **2.** $6\overline{)50}$ **3.** $8\overline{)64}$ **4.** $8\overline{)67}$ **5.** $3\overline{)19}$ **6.** $5\overline{)27}$

7. $9\overline{)24}$ **8.** $5\overline{)38}$ **9.** $7\overline{)54}$ **10.** $4\overline{)30}$ **11.** $8\overline{)73}$ **12.** $2\overline{)11}$

13. $5\overline{)37}$ **14.** $6\overline{)38}$ **15.** $7\overline{)50}$ **16.** $9\overline{)82}$ **17.** $4\overline{)18}$ **18.** $7\overline{)37}$

Write the answer. *(pages 312–313)*

19. $7\overline{)70}$ **20.** $4\overline{)80}$ **21.** $3\overline{)90}$ **22.** $2\overline{)60}$ **23.** $3\overline{)60}$ **24.** $4\overline{)40}$

Solve. *(pages 314–315)*

25. Oranges are packed 8 in a box. How many boxes are needed for 55 oranges?

26. 6 students share 32 cherries evenly. How many cherries will each student get?

Write the answer. *(pages 316–325)*

27. $4\overline{)84}$ **28.** $3\overline{)93}$ **29.** $7\overline{)79}$ **30.** $5\overline{)55}$ **31.** $4\overline{)46}$ **32.** $6\overline{)68}$

33. $6\overline{)90}$ **34.** $4\overline{)76}$ **35.** $3\overline{)54}$ **36.** $4\overline{)64}$ **37.** $5\overline{)75}$ **38.** $6\overline{)75}$

39. $8\overline{)98}$ **40.** $2\overline{)75}$ **41.** $6\overline{)86}$ **42.** $2\overline{)31}$ **43.** $7\overline{)92}$ **44.** $3\overline{)76}$

45. $5\overline{)243}$ **46.** $2\overline{)144}$ **47.** $6\overline{)351}$ **48.** $7\overline{)251}$ **49.** $3\overline{)219}$ **50.** $4\overline{)153}$

51. $2\overline{)176}$ **52.** $9\overline{)173}$ **53.** $6\overline{)85}$ **54.** $2\overline{)37}$ **55.** $4\overline{)98}$ **56.** $5\overline{)268}$

Solve. *(pages 326–327)*

57. Oranges are 4 for 84¢. How much does one orange cost?

58. Watermelon sells for 19¢ a lb. What is the cost of a watermelon that weighs 3 lb?

CHAPTER 12 EXTRA PRACTICE

FOR USE AFTER CHECKPOINT 1

Compare. Write < or >. *(pages 336–343)*

1. $\frac{1}{7}$ ■ $\frac{2}{7}$ **2.** $\frac{3}{9}$ ■ $\frac{2}{9}$ **3.** $\frac{4}{5}$ ■ $\frac{2}{5}$ **4.** $\frac{3}{8}$ ■ $\frac{1}{8}$ **5.** $\frac{1}{3}$ ■ $\frac{2}{3}$

Write the answer. *(pages 344–345)*

6.

$\frac{2}{5} + \frac{1}{5}$

7.

$\frac{3}{4} - \frac{2}{4}$

8.
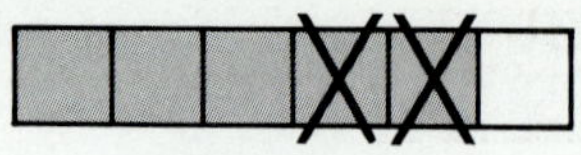
$\frac{5}{6} - \frac{2}{6}$

Write the answer. *(pages 346–347)*

9. What is the probability that the spinner will stop on yellow?

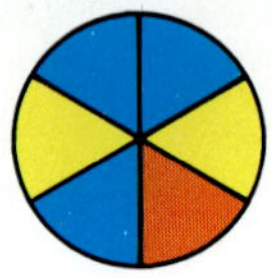

FOR USE AFTER CHECKPOINT 2

Write the equivalent fractions. *(pages 348–349)*

1.
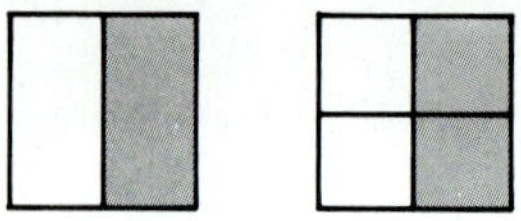

2.
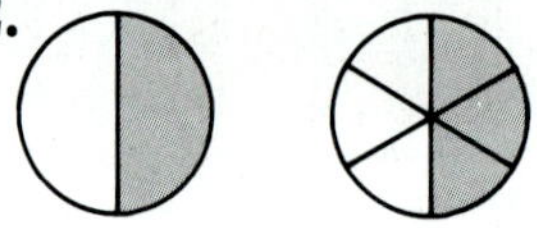

3.
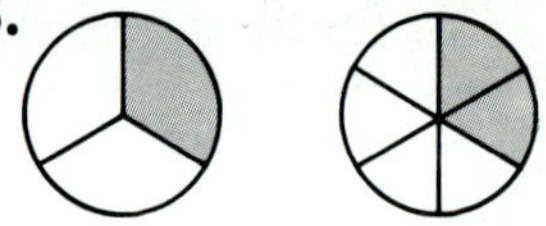

Write the mixed number. *(pages 350–351)*

4.
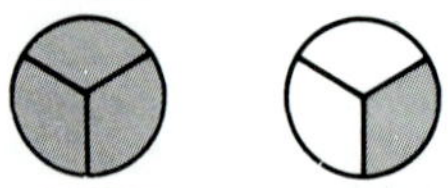

5.
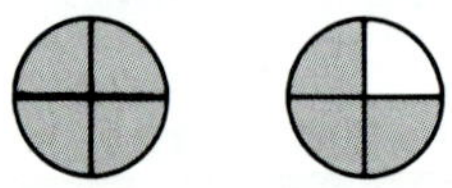

6.
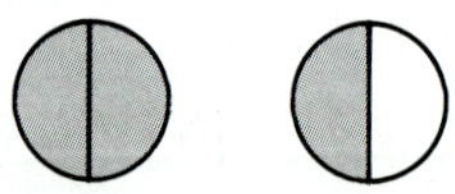

Write the decimal. *(pages 352–357)*

7. $\frac{3}{10}$ **8.** $\frac{7}{10}$ **9.** $\frac{1}{10}$ **10.** $1\frac{5}{10}$ **11.** $2\frac{2}{10}$ **12.** $7\frac{4}{10}$

Add or subtract. *(pages 358–359)*

13. $4.2 + 3.1$ **14.** $7.8 + 3.9$ **15.** $3.4 - 2.2$ **16.** $7.4 - 1.8$ **17.** $6.5 - 2.3$

Draw a picture to help solve. *(pages 360–361)*

18. Diana has 4 books. She read $\frac{1}{4}$ of the books. What fraction of the books didn't she read?

EXTRA PRACTICE

FOR USE AFTER THE CHAPTER TEST

Compare. Write < or >. *(pages 336–343)*

1. $\frac{3}{6} \square \frac{5}{6}$ **2.** $\frac{7}{8} \square \frac{2}{8}$ **3.** $\frac{3}{5} \square \frac{1}{5}$ **4.** $\frac{3}{7} \square \frac{5}{7}$ **5.** $\frac{7}{9} \square \frac{2}{9}$

Write the answer. *(pages 344–345)*

6. 

$\frac{2}{4} + \frac{1}{4}$

7. 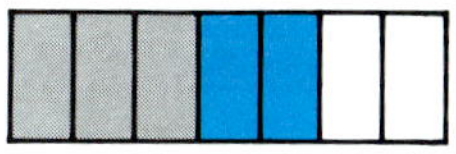

$\frac{3}{7} + \frac{2}{7}$

8. 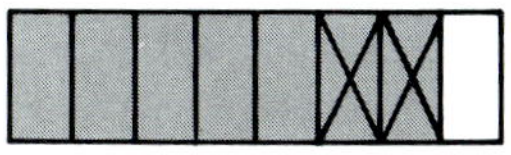

$\frac{7}{8} - \frac{2}{8}$

Write the equivalent fractions. *(pages 348–349)*

9. 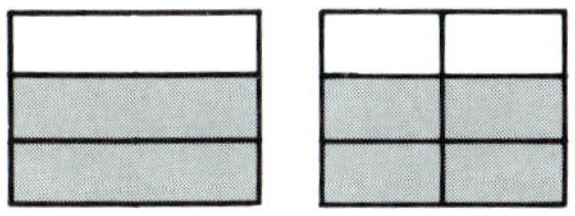

10. 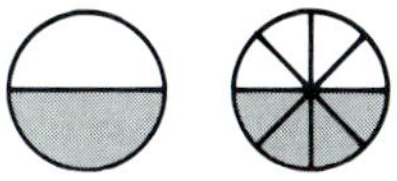

11. 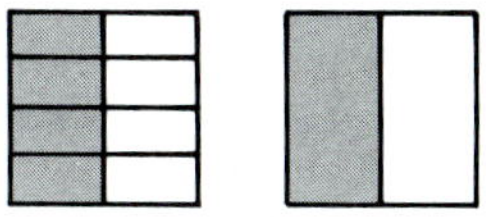

Write the mixed number. *(pages 350–351)*

12. 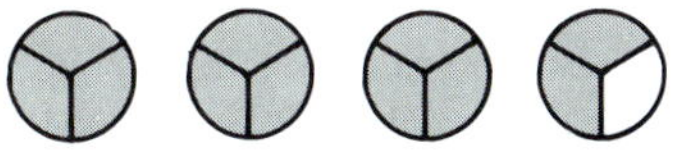

13. 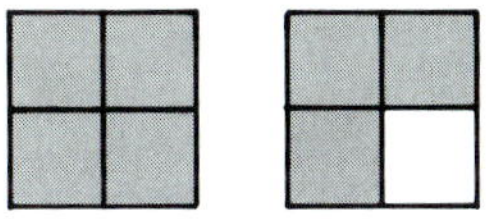

14. 

Write the decimal. *(pages 352–357)*

15. $\frac{8}{10}$ **16.** $\frac{4}{10}$ **17.** $\frac{1}{10}$ **18.** $\frac{9}{10}$ **19.** $\frac{2}{10}$ **20.** $\frac{7}{10}$

Add or subtract. *(pages 358–359)*

21. $2.5 + 1.3$ **22.** $3.1 + 4.9$ **23.** $6.7 + 3.8$ **24.** $8.9 - 2.4$ **25.** $2.7 - 1.8$ **26.** $7.6 - 3.2$

Write the answer. *(pages 346–347)*

27. What is the probability that the spinner will stop on red?

Draw a picture to help you solve. *(pages 360–361)*

28. Bill has 8 tomatoes. He uses 4 in a salad. What fraction of the tomatoes are left?

CHAPTER 13 EXTRA PRACTICE

FOR USE AFTER CHECKPOINT 1

Name the figure. *(pages 370–373)*

1. 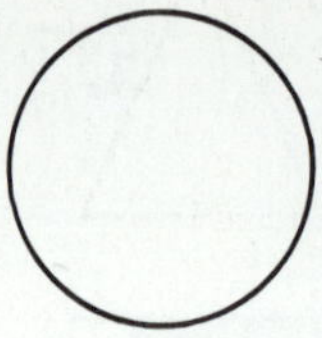

2. 

3. 

Find the perimeter. *(pages 374–375)*

4. 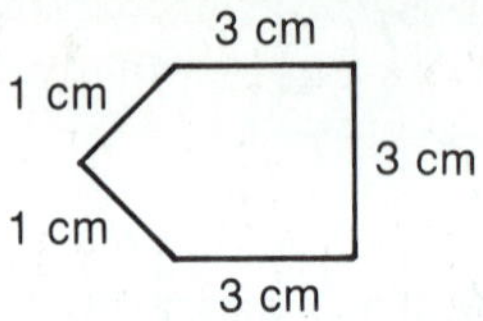

5. 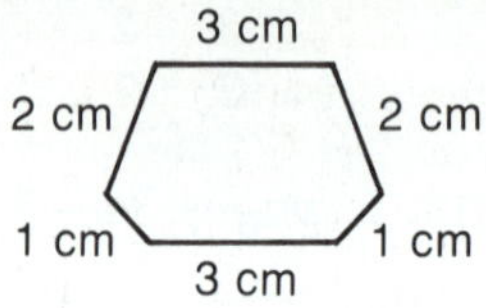

6. 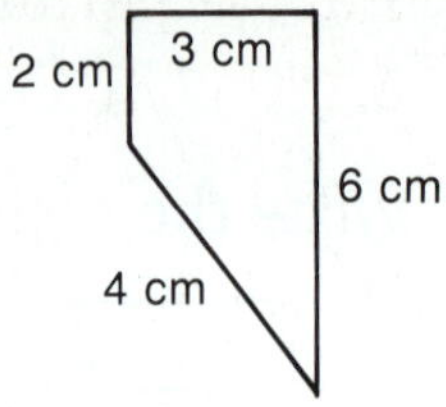

Find the area. *(pages 376–377)*

7. 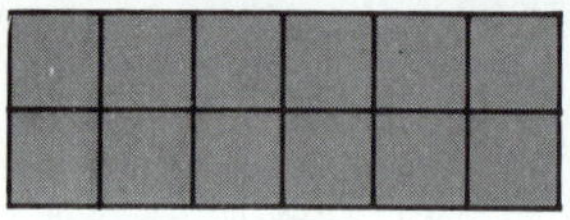

8. 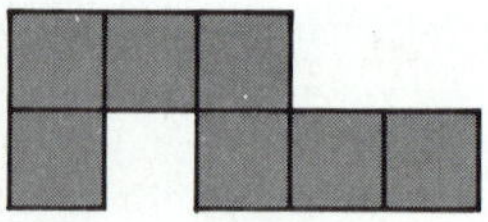

Write the letter of the figure that does not belong. *(pages 378–379)*

9. **a.**  **b.** 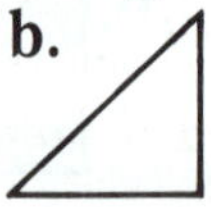 **c.**  **d.** 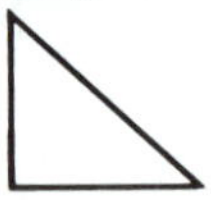

FOR USE AFTER CHECKPOINT 2

Tell if the figures are congruent or similar. *(pages 380–385)*

1. 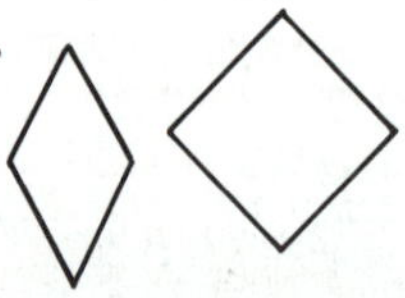

2. 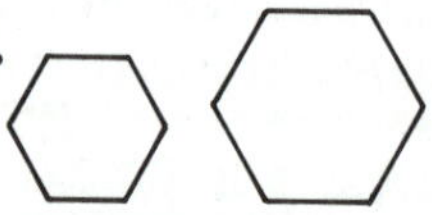

3. 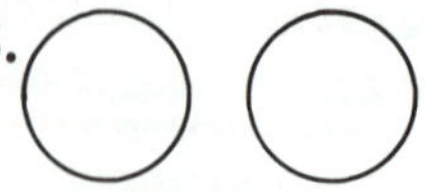

4. 

Tell the volume in cubic units. *(pages 386–389)*

5. 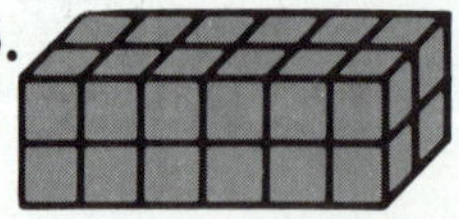

6. 

7. 

8. 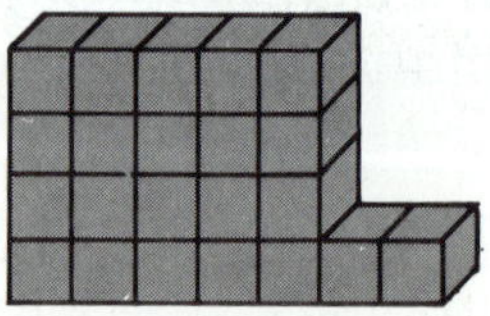

Draw the shape that comes next. *(pages 390–391)*

9.

EXTRA PRACTICE CHAPTER 13

FOR USE AFTER THE CHAPTER TEST

Name the figure. *(pages 370–373)*

1. 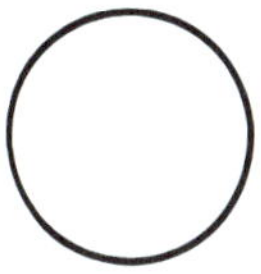
2. 
3. 
4. 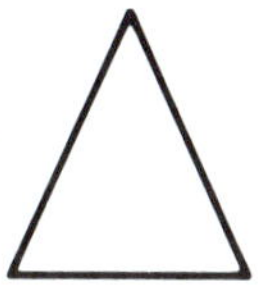

Find the perimeter. *(pages 374–375)*

5. 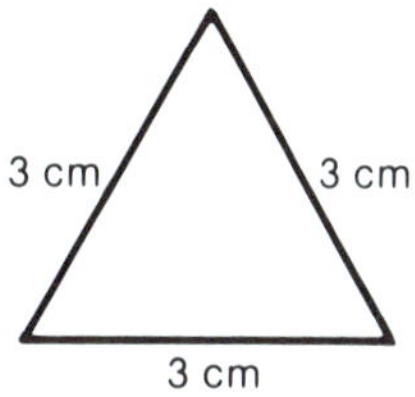

6. 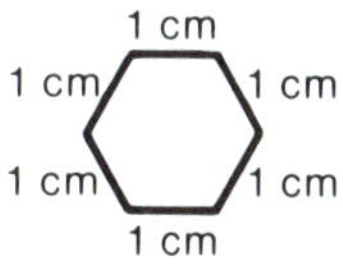

7. 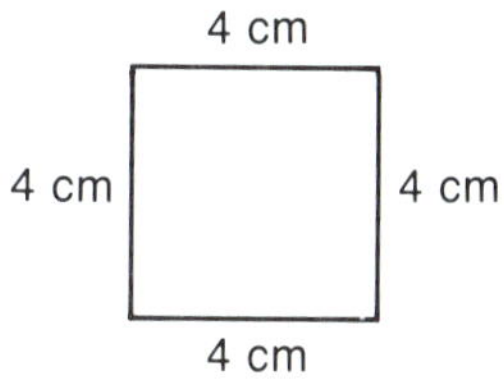

Find the area. *(pages 376–377)*

8. 
9. 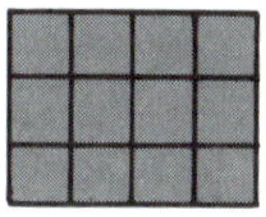
10. 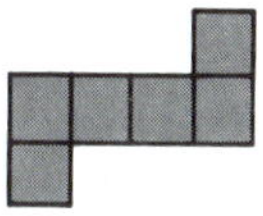

Tell if the figures are congruent or similar. *(pages 382–385)*

11. 
12. 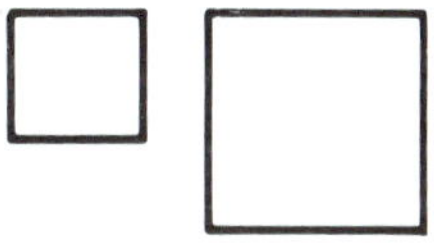
13. 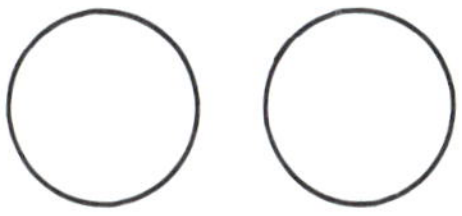
14. 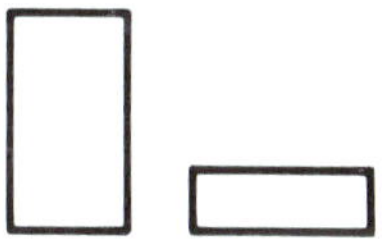

Tell the volume in cubic units. *(pages 388–389)*

15. 
16. 
17. 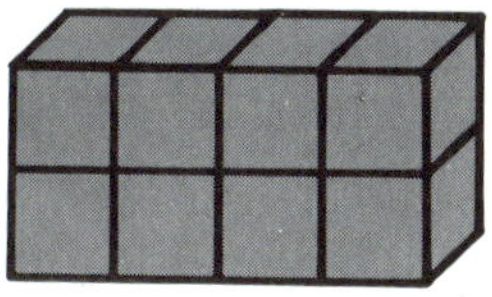
18. 

Write the letter of the figure that does not belong. *(pages 378–379)*

19. a.  b.  c. 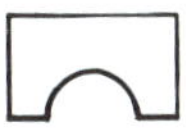 d. 

Draw the shape that comes next. *(pages 390–391)*

20. 

USING MENTAL MATH STRATEGIES

Sometimes you can use mental mathematics to solve problems. You may be doubling a recipe in cooking, building a birdhouse, or counting change in a store. You use mental math to find an exact answer without using pencil and paper or a calculator. In this book strategies for mental math are used that will help you improve your skills. Here are some examples.

Counting On and Back

The change from a dollar bill for 79¢ is counted on as:

1 penny	1 dime	1 dime
80¢	90¢	$1.00

Using Facts

If you forget $6 + 7$, you may remember that $6 + 6 = 12$, so $6 + 7 = 13$.

Comparing and Ordering

To compare the numbers 234 and 287, mentally compare the hundreds. If they are the same, compare the tens. 8 tens > 3 tens, so $287 > 234$.

Using Properties

To add $8 + 0$, you can think: The sum of zero and any other number is that number. $8 + 0 = 8$.

Using Patterns

$8 + 7 = 15$
so $18 + 7 = 25$
and $28 + 7 = 35$

Using Visual Images

You can think of $1\frac{1}{2}$ as one pizza and a half pizza.

Changing Numbers and Operations

To add $23 + 25$, you can think: $23 + 5 = 28$
and $28 + 20 = 48$.

To divide 72 by 8, you can think: $9 \times 8 = 72$,
so $72 \div 8 = 9$.

When you add 78 and 19, you can think of 19 as $20 - 1$. Then $78 + 20 = 98$ and $98 - 1 = 97$. The sum is 97.

USING ESTIMATION STRATEGIES

Sometimes you may not need an exact answer, and an estimate will do. You will find your own favorite ways to estimate when you're shopping, figuring the time needed to complete a job, or walking to a friend's house. In this book, strategies for estimation are used that should help you use math in everyday life. Here are some examples.

Rounding The school records show that 832 children attended a musical event. In the school paper 832 was rounded to the nearest hundred as 800.

The examples at the right show the exact difference and an estimated difference between 87 and 26. An estimate shows you whether your answer is reasonable.

$$\begin{array}{r} 87 \\ -\ 26 \\ \hline 61 \end{array} \qquad \begin{array}{r} 90 \\ -\ 30 \\ \hline 60 \end{array}$$

Comparing 7 × 9 is less than 70, because 7 × 10 is 70 and 9 is less than 10.

To estimate 19 × 3, you can round 19 to 20. 20 × 3 is greater than 19 × 3, because you rounded up.

Using Measurement

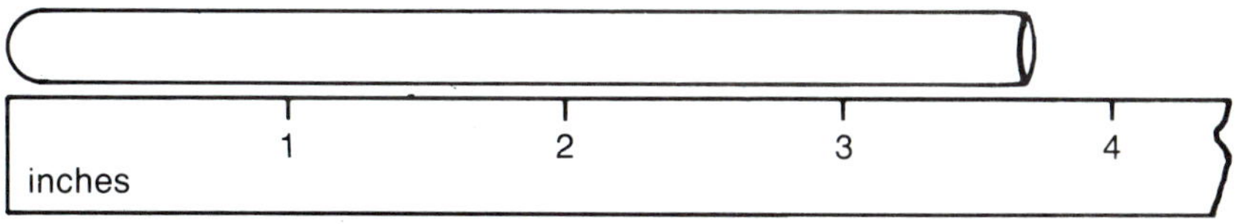

The piece of chalk measures 4 in. to the nearest inch.

The best estimate from the following choices for the amount of milk that you would share with a friend at lunch is 1 pint.

1 pint   1 quart   1 gallon

You can estimate the part of this cheese that is missing. Think of dividing the whole cheese into parts of about the same size. There would be 4 parts in all. About $\frac{1}{4}$ of the cheese is missing.

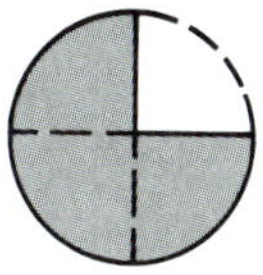

USING A CALCULATOR

Every calculator is different. You should read the instructions for your calculator to learn how to use it. Most calculators have the keys (buttons) pictured below, but the keys may be in different places.

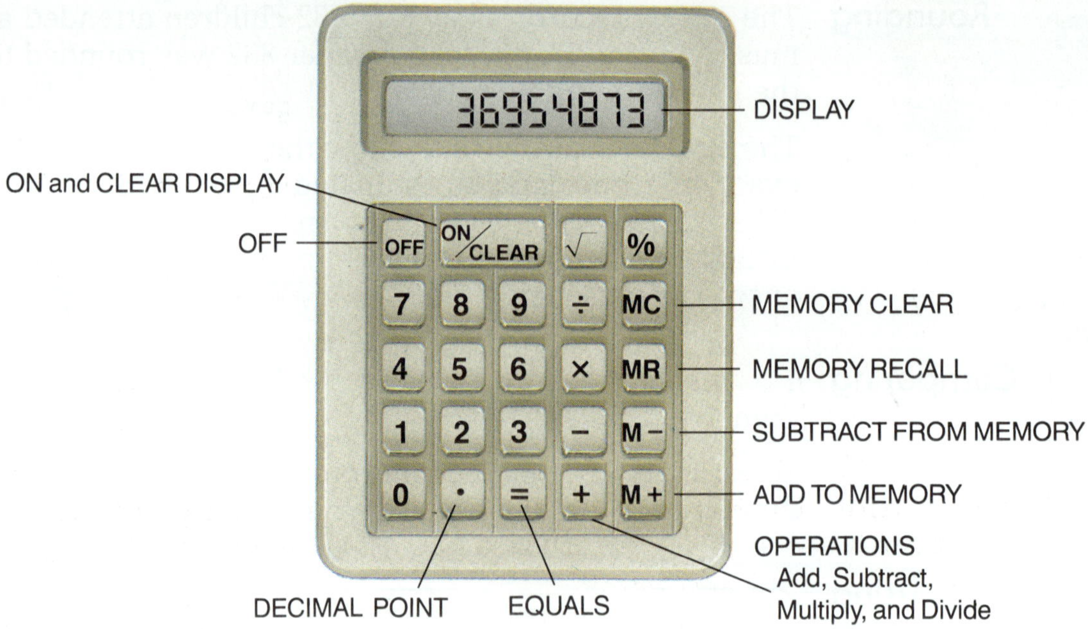

The Display A calculator display usually does not show commas. Usually 8 digits are the most the display will show. A display never shows a dollar sign. You must press the decimal point key to show a decimal number. You press the clear key to remove the display.

The Memory Feature You can add the same number to several other numbers by using the memory keys.

Add 36 to each of these numbers: 9, 29, 58.

Press	*Display*
3 6	36
M+	36 M
9 +	9 M
MR	36 M
=	45 M
2 9 +	29 M
MR	36 M
=	65 M
5 8 +	58 M
MR	36 M
=	94 M

So, $9 + 36 = 45$, $29 + 36 = 65$, $58 + 36 = 94$

The Constant Feature On many calculators the equals key can also be used to repeat an operation with the same number over and over again.

For example, you can count by twos on the calculator.

Press	*Display*
2	2
+	2
=	4
=	6
=	8
=	10

The calculator is adding 2 each time you press the equals key.

For each problem, choose the method you think is best: calculator, mental math, or estimation. Write *C*, *M*, or *E*. Then solve the problem using that method.

Chapter 1

1. Is the sum $2 + 5 + 8 + 0$ more than 20?
2. Add or subtract from left to right. Write the answer.
   $7 + 6 - 8 + 4 + 6 - 9 = \square$
3. Zack walked 5 miles, Angelo walked 2 miles and Pepe walked 6 miles. Did they walk more than 10 miles altogether?
4. Martha has 15 cents. She gives her brother 7 cents. Who has more money, Martha or her brother?

Chapter 2

1. Is the sum of 22 and 34 between 50 and 60, or 60 and 70?
2. What number is 3000 more than 6000?
3. Mary's container had 123 marbles, Joe's container had 112, Cisco's had 121, and Maria's had 132. Order these numbers from least to greatest.
4. About 70 children said they liked to play on a water slide. What is the least number of children who could have liked playing on a water slide?

Chapter 3

1. Which is greater, $27 + 33$ or $12 + 25$?
2. What is the sum of 30, 76, and 20?
3. During a treasure hunt, 2685 gold coins were found and 5298 silver coins were found. How many coins were found?
4. A mama elephant ate 768 Brazil nuts. The baby elephant ate 342 Brazil nuts. Were more than 1000 Brazil nuts eaten?

Chapter 4

1. How much more is 83 than 52?
2. How many 125's make 625?
3. If 6525 people attend a basketball game and there are 9273 seats, how many seats are empty?
4. Jane's milk truck has 886 quarts of milk. Today she delivers 713 quarts of milk. About how many quarts of milk are left on the truck?

Chapter 5

1. Complete: \$67.72 − \$28.84 = ▒.
2. Today is December 11. What will the date be 14 days from now?
3. You want to buy 2 toys. One costs \$7.32 and the other costs \$13.12. If you have a twenty-dollar bill, do you have enough money to pay for them?
4. Bernice buys two cans of tennis balls for \$3.98 each. How much change does she get from \$10.00?

Chapter 6

1. Is 4×8 greater than or less than 4×7?
2. Complete: $8 \times 12 \times 0 =$ ▒.
3. A bicycle has two wheels. If 8 bicycles are lined up in a row, how many wheels are there?
4. Joe buys 4 hammers at a cost of \$4.79 each. If he pays for the hammers with one bill, what is the smallest bill he can use?

Chapter 7

1. If $8 \times 7 = 56$, then $9 \times 7 =$ ▒.
2. Which is greater, 6×9 or 5×8?
3. Each box has 5 pairs of mittens. If there are 4 boxes, how many mittens are there?
4. Rosa is planting 6 plants in each row of a garden. If she has 50 plants, does she have enough plants for 8 rows?

For each problem, choose the method you think is best: calculator, mental math, or estimation. Write *C*, *M*, or *E*. Then solve the problem using that method.

Chapter 8

1. Complete: If $8 \div 8 = 1$, then $8 \div 1 = \square$.
2. Complete: If $30 \div 5 = 6$, then $30 \div 6 = \square$.
3. There are 30 students in Jill's class. There are 5 people on a basketball team. How many teams can be formed from Jill's class?
4. Pearl took two vacations this summer. The first vacation was 14 days. The second vacation was 35 days. Were both vacations together more than 5 weeks?

Chapter 9

1. Complete: 8 m = $\square$ cm.
2. Which is greater, 10,000 feet or 2 miles?
3. On a trip Justin traveled 253 km the first day, 327 km the second, and 462 km the third day. How far did he travel?
4. Lee is 182 cm tall. Robby is 98 cm tall, and Tammy is 89 cm tall. If Robby's height and Tammy's height are added together, would the sum be greater than Lee's height?

Chapter 10

1. When 888 is rounded to the nearest hundred, $888 \times 6 = \square$.
2. Complete: $9 \times 8 + 9 = \square$.
3. Eva ran 3 km in 20 minutes. Tomorrow she plans to run 12 km. How many minutes should she plan to run tomorrow?
4. Mary went to the store and bought 8 cans of orange juice. It cost \$.48 for each can. How much did Mary pay for the juice?

Chapter 11

1. Complete: $800 \div 8 = \square$.
2. Which is greater, $47 \div 2$ or $98 \div 3$?
3. An address of a shop has 3 digits. The first digit is twice the second digit. The second digit is twice the third digit. What is the address?
4. If 6 is the greatest remainder you can have when you divide by 7, what is the greatest remainder you can have when you divide by 8? What is the greatest remainder you can have when you divide by 15?

Chapter 12

1. Complete: $\frac{5}{8} - \frac{3}{8} = \square$
2. Which is greater, $\frac{5}{7}$, $\frac{2}{7}$, or $\frac{3}{7}$?
3. One farm is 67.3 m wide. A second farm is 85.6 m wide and a third farm is 98.5 m wide. How wide are all of the farms together?
4. Pancho ran the 100 m dash in 12.7 seconds. Alex ran the same distance in 11.7 seconds. How much faster was Alex in the 100 m dash?

Chapter 13

1. Find the perimeter.

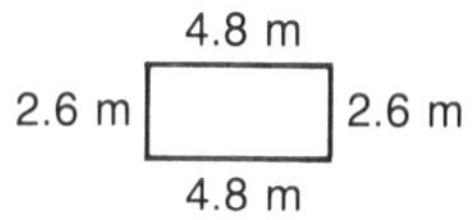

2. The Earth is shaped like a __?__.
3. The length of one side of a square is 8 cm. What is the perimeter of the square?
4. The length of one side of a square is 9 cm. Is the perimeter greater than, less than, or equal to 40 cm?

TABLE OF NUMBERS

	A	B	C	D	E	F	G	H
1	6	6	8	15	62	58	8¢	7¢
2	6	7	18	23	162	98	75¢	60¢
3	7	7	28	35	262	87	89¢	54¢
4	7	8	38	29	362	326	19¢	28¢
5	8	8	48	54	462	246	42¢	39¢
6	8	9	58	38	562	792	$2.00	$1.75
7	2	17	68	76	662	854	$6.00	$2.50
8	5	1	78	52	762	267	$8.00	$3.25
9	2	75	88	74	862	332	$1.25	$1.75
10	6	46	98	70	962	726	$4.50	$3.50
11	4	25	108	230	400	321	$7.80	$1.20
12	9	72	118	109	300	545	$.75	$4.20
13	8	46	128	276	200	185	$8.88	$.12
14	1	28	138	158	100	23	$5.19	$.31

Ideas for using this table for mental math, estimation, and calculator activities are found under *Computation Strategies* on the Cumulative Review pages at the end of each chapter of the Teacher's Edition.

PROBLEM SOLVING ACTIVITIES

CHAPTER 1

Once each month, your class is going to celebrate the birthdays of everyone who was born during that particular month.

Work in a small group to come up with a plan for these parties.

- Find the total number of birthdays for each month.
- Decide how to celebrate birthdays that occur during the summer months.
- Make a "Birthday Reminder" chart for the school year. How will you do it?

CHAPTER 2

Have you ever heard of a *palindrome*? You may think it's some kind of an animal, but it's not! A palindrome is a number, a word, a phrase, or a sentence that reads the same forwards and backwards.

See how many number palindromes you can find during the next two days. What are some places you might find some? Make a list of each of your palindromes and where you saw it.

Work with a partner to think of some word or sentence palindromes. Compare your palindromes with another group's.

CHAPTER 3

Your class is putting on a play. Students from the first, second, and third grades in your school will see the play one afternoon. In the evening, each student in your class can invite 3 guests.

You are ordering the programs. Work with a partner. Find how many programs will be needed altogether.

CHAPTER 4

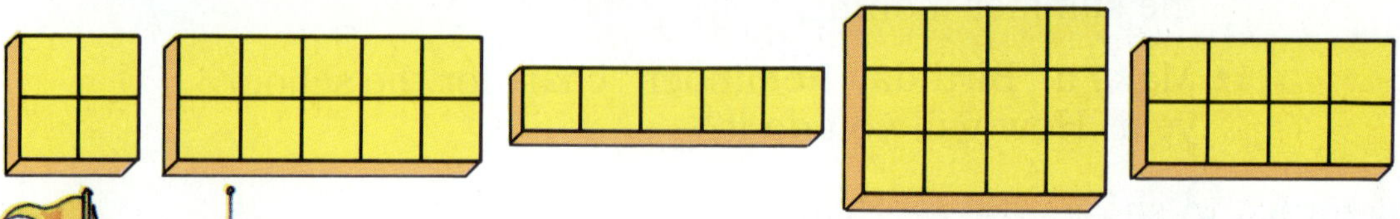

You need to pack 88 toys in boxes. The boxes you can use have small sections that hold one toy each. You can use as many of each kind of box as you need but every section of a box must be filled.

- Draw a picture to show all the boxes you would use.
- Compare your work with another group's. Did they pack the toys in the same boxes? Is one way better than another? Why?

CHAPTER 5

You want to surprise your family by cooking breakfast. Follow these steps to help you plan.

- Write the menu.
  What foods does your family like?
  What do you know how to cook?
- Shop for the food you need.
  Make a shopping list.
  Go to the supermarket or look at supermarket ads to find the prices of the foods you need.
- Find the cost.
  You have $15.00 to spend. Will you have enough?
  Change the menu if you need to. Make a chart to show the cost of the different foods.

CHAPTER 6

FUNLAND	
RIDE	TICKETS NEEDED FOR EACH RIDE
Roller Coaster	4
Merry-Go-Round	2
Ferris Wheel	3
Rocket Ships	3
Bumper Cars	4

Tomorrow you are going to Funland. You have a book of 20 tickets for the rides.

Make a list to show how you will use your tickets. You might want to take more than one ride on some of your favorites.

Now work with a partner. Compare your lists. How are the lists alike? How are they different? Did you both use all tickets?

CHAPTER 7

Play this game with a partner. Make a chart like this:

Math Words Beginning With:				
a-e	f-j	k-o	p-t	u-z
	fraction		sum	

- Decide how long you will play.
- Take turns thinking of math words that begin with different letters. Write them in the correct columns.
- Figure your score at the end of the game. Use this point system.

a–e words	5 points each
f–j words	6 points each
k–o words	7 points each
p–t words	8 points each
u–z words	9 points each

CHAPTER 8

You will need an old calendar page for this activity.

Cut the boxes apart so that you have many squares with a number on each.

- Use the squares to make division facts. Keep a list of the facts you make.
- Try to make as many facts as you can. Work with a partner to compare your facts.
- Use your squares to make up a math game. (You can use other operations besides division.) Try it with your partner.

MARCH						
S	M	T	W	T	F	S
		1	2	3	4	5
6	7	8	9	10	11	12
13	14	15	16	17	18	19
20	21	22	23	24	25	26
27	28	29	30	31		

$12 \div 4 = 3$

CHAPTER 9

Make a box. You will need a sheet of construction paper, scissors, a ruler, a pencil, and tape. Follow these steps: Use the picture to help you.

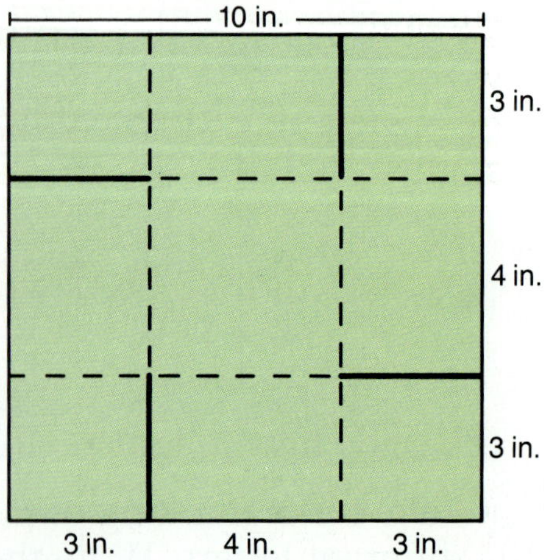

- Use the ruler to draw a square that is 10 inches on each side. Cut out the square.
- Put your ruler along each side of the square. Make marks to show lengths of 3 in., 4 in., and 3 in., on each side.
- Draw lines to connect the marks. Then fold along these lines.
- Cut along the 4 heavy black lines as shown on the diagram.
- Bend the sides up and glue them together to make a box.

Is the box large enough to hold a pint of berries? A quart? How could you find out?

CHAPTER 10

You have $5.00 to spend on rubber stamps. Decide what stamps you will buy. Make an order form like the one below. Fill it out to show the stamps you would like to buy.

Dinosaurs
$1.25 each

Zoo Animals
$.45 each

Faces
$.88 each

ORDER FORM

Item	How Many	Cost for One	Total Cost

Do you have any money left over? Can you buy more stamps?

CHAPTER 11

You are the art teacher! Your class will work at tables. Groups of students can work at each table.

Work with a partner. Decide how many students will work at each table. Make a list to show how you can divide these art items equally among the tables of students. (There may be some of each item left over.)

ART ITEM	NUMBER EACH TABLE RECEIVES
100 sheets of shiny paper	?
200 pipe cleaners	?
75 plastic straws	?
50 felt pieces	?
125 stars	?

Work with your partner and create a project for the groups to do with their art materials. Write about your project or draw a picture to show it.

CHAPTER 12

Precipitation is rain or snow.
Make a weather chart to show the amount of precipitation where you live.

Look in the newspaper each day for two weeks to find the precipitation. Work with a partner to make a weather chart.

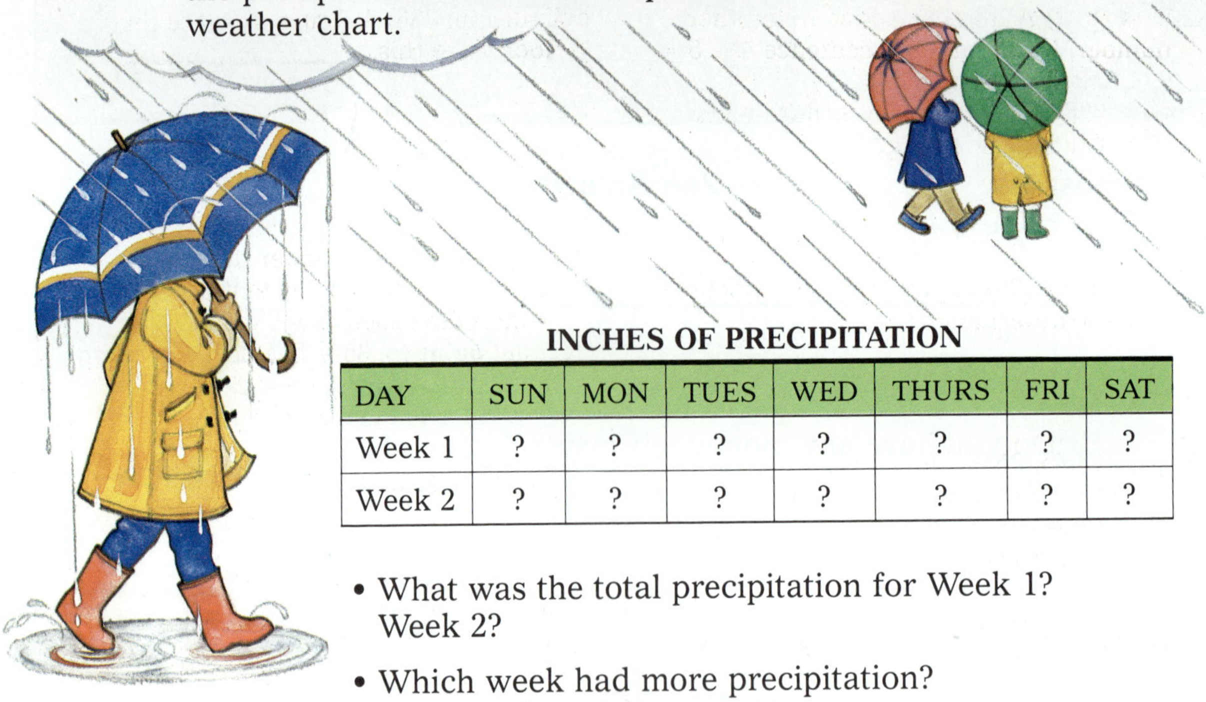

INCHES OF PRECIPITATION

DAY	SUN	MON	TUES	WED	THURS	FRI	SAT
Week 1	?	?	?	?	?	?	?
Week 2	?	?	?	?	?	?	?

- What was the total precipitation for Week 1? Week 2?
- Which week had more precipitation? How much more?

CHAPTER 13

Work with a group. You are decorating your classroom. You want to outline each bulletin board with crepe paper. How much crepe paper will you need in all?

- Describe how you will find the amount of crepe paper you need for each bulletin board.
- Find the total amount of crepe paper that you will need.

Suppose you could use two different colors of crepe paper to trim the boards.

- Draw a picture to show what you would do.
- How much of each color paper would you need in all?

GLOSSARY

A

addend (p. 2) A number added to another number. In the number sentence $4 + 5 = 9$, 4 and 5 are addends.

area (p. 376) The number of square units that will fit inside a figure.

B

bar graph (p. 200) A picture that uses bars to show information.

C

Celsius (C) (p. 254) The metric temperature scale that measures the freezing point as 0° and the boiling point as 100°.

centimeter (cm) (p. 246) A standard metric unit for measuring length.

circle (p. 370) A round figure like this.

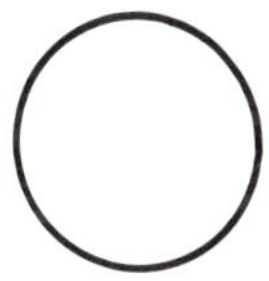

circle graph (p. 365) A circle divided into parts to show numbers.

cone (p. 386) A figure in space like this.

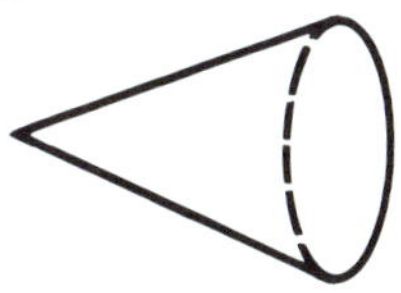

congruent (p. 382) Having exactly the same size and shape.

cube (p. 386) A figure in space with six sides, all squares, of the same size.

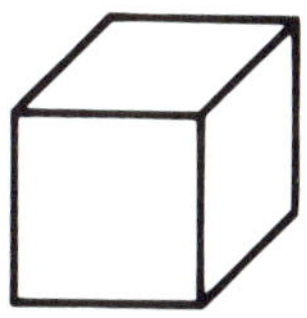

cubic unit (p. 388) A unit used for measuring volume.

cup (c) (p. 264) A United States Customary unit of capacity. 2 c = 1 pt

cylinder (p. 386) A figure in space that looks like this.

D

decimal (p. 354) A number that uses a decimal point to show tenths and hundredths such as 0.5 or 0.05.

decimal point (p. 354) The dot in a decimal number. In 2.5 the dot between the 2 and the 5 is the decimal point.

degrees (°) (p. 254) A standard unit for measuring temperature.

denominator (p. 340) In the fraction $\frac{5}{8}$, 8 is the denominator.

difference (p. 12) The answer in subtraction.

digit (p. 30) The symbol 0, 1, 2, 3, 4, 5, 6, 7, 8, or 9.

E

equivalent fractions (p. 348) Fractions that have the same value. $\frac{1}{2}$ and $\frac{2}{4}$ are equivalent fractions.

estimate (p. 42) An answer that is not exact.

even number (p. 174) A number that has 0, 2, 4, 6, or 8 in the ones' place.

F

fact family (p. 18) A group of facts with the same numbers.

$5 + 3 = 8 \qquad 8 - 3 = 5$

$3 + 5 = 8 \qquad 8 - 5 = 3$

factor (p. 160) A number to be multiplied by another number. In the number sentence $3 \times 5 = 15$, 3 and 5 are both factors.

Fahrenheit (F) (p. 266) The United States Customary temperature scale that measures the freezing point as 32° and the boiling point as 212°.

foot (ft) (p. 260) A United States Customary unit for measuring length. 1 ft = 12 in.

fraction (p. 336) A number such as $\frac{1}{2}$, $\frac{2}{3}$, or $\frac{8}{10}$.

G

gallon (gal) (p. 264) A United States Customary unit for measuring capacity. 1 gal = 4 qt

gram (g) (p. 252) A standard metric unit used to measure the mass of light objects. 1000 g = 1 kg

Grouping Property of Addition (p. 74) Changing the grouping of the addends does not change the sum.

H

hour (p. 138) A unit of time equal to 60 minutes.

I

inch (in.) (p. 258) A United States Customary unit for measuring length 12 in. = 1 ft

K

kilogram (kg) (p. 252) A standard metric unit for measuring mass. 1 kg = 1000 g

kilometer (km) (p. 248) A standard metric unit for measuring length. 1 km = 1000 m

L

line graph (p. 272) A picture that uses line segments to show changes in data.

line of symmetry (p. 380) A line dividing a figure into two matching parts.

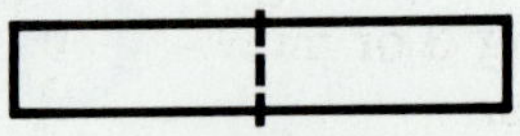

liter (L) (p. 250) A standard metric unit for measuring capacity.

M

meter (m) (p. 248) A standard metric unit for measuring length. 1 m = 100 cm

mile (mi) (p. 260) A United States Customary unit for measuring long distances. 1 mi = 1760 yd

minute (p. 138) A unit of time. There are 60 minutes in 1 hour.

mixed number (p. 350) A whole number plus a fraction. $1\frac{2}{3}$ is a mixed number.

N

number line (p. 32) The line along which numbers can be pictured.

number pair (p. 90) Two numbers whose order shows a location on a grid. (2, 5) is a number pair.

number sentence (p. 2) A sentence that shows how numbers are related. 6 + 2 = 8 is a number sentence.

numerator (p. 340) In the fraction $\frac{5}{8}$, 5 is the numerator.

O

odd number (p. 174) A number that has 1, 3, 5, 7, or 9 in the ones' place.

Order Property (p. 4, 164) Changing the order of addends or factors does not change the sum or product.

ounce (oz) (p. 262) A United States Customary unit for measuring weight. 16 oz = 1 lb

P

percent (p. 364) Hundredths written with a % sign. Example: 50% = $\frac{50}{100}$ = 0.50

perimeter (p. 374) The distance around a figure.

pictograph (p. 86) A graph in which pictures stand for objects.

pint (pt) (p. 264) A United States Customary unit of capacity. 1 pt = 2 c

polygon (p. 372) A figure formed by joining 3 or more segments.

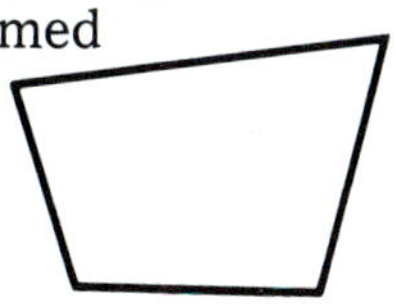

pound (lb) (p. 262) A United States Customary unit measuring weight. 1 lb = 16 oz

probability (p. 346) The chance that something will happen.

product (p. 160) The answer in multiplication. In the number sentence $3 \times 5 = 15$, 15 is the product.

pyramid (p. 386) A figure in space like this.

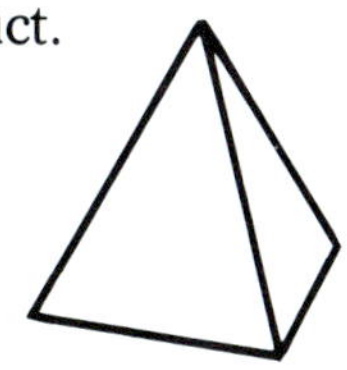

Q

quart (qt) (p. 264) A United States Customary unit for measuring capacity. 1 qt = 2 pt

quotient (p. 212) The answer in division. In the number sentence $8 \div 2 = 4$, 4 is the quotient.

R

rectangle (p. 370) A figure with four sides like this.

rectangular prism (p. 386) A figure in space with six sides, all rectangles, and whose opposite sides are congruent.

remainder (p. 310) The number left over when a division is complete.

Roman numerals (p. 55) Symbols such as I, V, X, and L that the Romans used for numbers many years ago.

round (p. 40) To write a number to the nearest ten or hundred. 52 rounded to the nearest ten is 50.

S

segment (p. 372) Part of a line with a starting point and an end.

sides (p. 372) The segments that make a polygon.

similar (p. 384) Figures that have the same shape, but are not necessarily the same size.

sphere (p. 386) A round figure in space like this.

square (p. 370) A figure with four sides the same length like this.

square unit (p. 376) A unit used for measuring area.

standard form (p. 30) The usual, short form of a number. 573 is the standard form for 5 hundreds 7 tens 3 ones.

sum (p. 2) The answer in addition. In $3 + 2 = 5$, 5 is the sum.

T

temperature (p. 254) Tells how hot or cold something is. Temperature is measured in degrees (°).

tree diagram (p. 153) A picture used to count the ways things can be combined.

triangle (p. 370) A figure with three sides like this.

V

value (p. 34) The amount something such as a number is worth.

variable (p. 239) A letter that takes the place of a number.

volume (p. 388) The number of cubic units that a figure in space contains.

Y

yard (yd) (p. 260) A U.S. Customary unit for measuring length. 1 yd = 3 ft

Z

Zero Property of Addition (p. 2) The sum of zero and any other number is that number.

Zero Property of Subtraction (p. 12) The difference of any number and zero is that number. The difference of any number and itself is zero.

INDEX

N

O

Q

R

S

T

U

CREDITS

Cover concept and photography by Lehman Millet Incorporated.
Title page photography by Lehman Millet Incorporated.
Common Art Elements by Linda Phinney.

ILLUSTRATION

Anthony Accardo 301
Robert Brooks 364, 365
Ruth Brunner-Strosser 90, 91
Bradley Clark 121
Dan Collins 89, 152, 153
Bob Eggleton 54, 55, 151
Simon Galkin 4, 18, 32, 33, 34, 35, 37, 47, 51, 67, 83, 96, 158, 159, 178, 179, 204, 205, 218, 313, 319, 329, 435, 438
Bonnie Gee 203
Lisa Gilman 7, 271
Bob Giuliani 237
Judith Ann Griffith 2, 3, 6, 20, 21, 24, 25, 64, 65, 71, 72, 73, 104, 105, 112, 113, 164, 165, 169, 174, 184, 185, 186, 187, 210, 211, 220, 254, 266, 279, 288, 289, 292, 296, 302, 303, 326, 330, 331, 354, 355, 363, 380, 381, 388, 436, 439, 440
Meryl Henderson 102, 106, 132, 136, 162, 192, 214, 215, 234, 280, 281, 286, 287, 316, 317, 340, 341, 386, 387
Marilyn Janovitz 69, 86, 87, 98, 99, 100, 101, 134, 144, 155, 198, 199, 216, 222, 224, 250, 251, 252, 262, 308, 309, 324, 342, 345, 373
Meg Kelleher 116, 139, 194, 208, 264, 256, 314, 322, 360, 437
John Kilgrew 238, 239, 393
Ron Lehew 12, 13, 60, 61, 84, 85, 109, 118, 160, 161, 170, 171, 172, 173, 190, 195, 232, 233, 356, 357
Terry Presnall 394, 395
Margaret Sanfilippo 23, 177
Collette Slade 8, 9, 14, 15
Ann Sargent Walker 16, 17, 50, 76, 77, 78, 79, 81, 103, 114, 115, 122, 123, 137, 146, 148, 163, 166, 196, 212, 213, 226, 230, 246, 247, 248, 284, 294, 295, 298, 310, 311, 338, 339, 348, 349, 350, 351, 370, 371, 378, 382, 385
Jean Zallinger 272, 273

PHOTOGRAPHY

ANIMALS, ANIMALS J. L. Kooyman 95
J. Ballard 38
BERG AND ASSOCIATES Arnold J. Kaplan 282; Tom Padgitt 374
ED BISHOP PHOTOGRAPHY 36, 58, 62, 63, 128, 130, 131, 132, 133, 184, 244, 245, 258, 320, 321, 339, 353, 376
BRUCE COLEMAN, INC. Pat Lanzafield 358
COMSTOCK 228
FOCUS ON SPORTS 1, 225
FOCUS WEST Peter Read Miller 260 (right)
GRANT HEILMAN PHOTOGRAPHY 29, 231, 253; Holt Confer 260 (left); Linda DuFurrena 227
Michal Heron 40, 48, 70, 74, 144, 168, 219, 242, 290, 368, 382
FRAN HEYL ASSOC. © 1985 Joe Sohm 398
IMAGE BANK Tom Bieber 369; Nicholas Foster 24; Paul Slaughter 307; Santi Visalli 335
Susan Lapides 82
MONKMEYER PRESS Paul Conklin 53

Peabody Museum, Harvard University, © President and Fellows of Harvard College, Hillel Berger 117

PHOTO FAIR 229

PHOTO RESEARCHERS Robert Perron 255

PICTURE CUBE Jeff Albertson 243; Christian Delbert 183; Terry McKoy 283; Eric Roth 277; Frank J. Staub 59

TOM STACK ASSOC. Brian Parker 46; Rod Planck 293

STOCK BOSTON Frederick D. Bodin 66, 157; © 1985 Bill Gallery 267; Raoul Hackel 127; Edith G. Haun 28 (left); © Ellis Herwig 221; R. A. Kirchenbaum 5; Jean Claude Lejeune 30; © Gregg Mancuso 28 (right), 359; Peter Menzel 209

TAURUS Charles E. Schmidt 268

Hilary Wallace © 42, 247

TABLE OF NUMBERS

	A	B	C	D	E	F	G	H
1	6	6	8	15	62	58	8¢	7¢
2	6	7	18	23	162	98	75¢	60¢
3	7	7	28	35	262	87	89¢	54¢
4	7	8	38	29	362	326	19¢	28¢
5	8	8	48	54	462	246	42¢	39¢
6	8	9	58	38	562	792	$2.00	$1.75
7	2	17	68	76	662	854	$6.00	$2.50
8	5	1	78	52	762	267	$8.00	$3.25
9	2	75	88	74	862	332	$1.25	$1.75
10	6	46	98	70	962	726	$4.50	$3.50
11	4	25	108	230	400	321	$7.80	$1.20
12	9	72	118	109	300	545	$.75	$4.20
13	8	46	128	276	200	185	$8.88	$.12
14	1	28	138	158	100	23	$5.19	$.31

Ideas for using this table for mental math, estimation, and calculator activities are found under *Computation Strategies* on the Cumulative Review pages at the end of each chapter of the Teacher's Edition.